HARDPRESS.NET
HOME OF HARD-TO-FIND BOOKS

History of the Discipline of the Methodist Episcopal Church
by Robert Emory

Address:
HardPress
8345 NW 66TH ST #2561
MIAMI FL 33166-2626
USA
Email: info@hardpress.net

ANNEX

(Emon
ZT

HISTORY

OF

THE DISCIPLINE

OF THE

METHODIST EPISCOPAL CHURCH.

BY ROBERT EMORY.

NEW-YORK:

PUBLISHED BY G. LANE & C. B TIPPETT,

FOR THE METHODIST EPISCOPAL CHURCH, AT THE CONFERENCE OFFICE,
200 MULBERRY-STREET.

—

J. Collord, Printer.

1845.

PREFACE.

WHEN a young Methodist preacher enters, in accordance with the direction of his church, upon the study of its Discipline, he is curious to know when and by whom that Discipline was framed. He learns, indeed, from the book itself, that the General Conference has "full powers to make rules and regulations," under certain "limitations and restrictions." But who imposed those "limitations and restrictions," and to what extent has the General Conference used its powers? There is internal evidence that the present Discipline was not all composed at one time. At what periods then were its several parts introduced, and what modifications have they undergone? These are points not only of curious inquiry, but essential often to right interpretation. But they are points on which students generally can obtain no satisfactory information. In our civil governments, the statutes are scattered through the several volumes of laws, which have been published from time to time, and therefore these are all preserved. But, in the Methodist Episcopal Church, the Discipline, as revised at each General Conference, being in itself complete, supplants all that had gone before it, and the previous editions are cast aside as of no further use. Thus it has continued, until now nearly sixty years have elapsed since the organization of the church, and the Discipline has undergone about twenty distinct revisions. Where then shall the student go to find these successive editions? If he resort to the

libraries of the oldest preachers, they are not there:—
to the library of the Book Concern, they are not there:
—to the archives of the General Conference, still they
are not to be found. Despairing of success in this
pursuit, he may perhaps examine the journals of the
General Conference, (though, from the nature of the
case, this is a privilege which few can enjoy.) But
here he will find that all prior to 1800 are missing;
and that those subsequent to that date convey no accurate information as to the changes in the Discipline ;
because, in the alterations, references are made to
chapter, section, question, page, &c., which cannot be
understood without having a copy of the then Discipline in hand : and because, moreover, at each General
Conference the subsequent publication of the Discipline is intrusted to a committee, invested with powers,
(often largely discretionary,) as to the selection, arrangement, and wording of the several parts : and no report
of their proceedings is entered upon the journal:

The embarrassment which is here supposed in the
mind of a student of the Discipline, is precisely such
as the author himself experienced. In such a dilemma,
he endeavoured to collect for himself a set of the different Disciplines. Having his lot cast amid the earliest
seats of Methodism in this country, he had the good
fortune of rescuing one old Discipline after another
from its obscure resting place, until at length, with one
exception,* the series was completed, and the rich grati-
fication was enjoyed of tracing in the original documents
themselves the progress of the Discipline, from the
first simple series of questions and answers, to its present more elaborate structure of parts, chapters, and

* See pages 81, 83.

sections. The collection thus made could not be ren
dered universally accessible. The author has thought
therefore, that he would be doing a service to student
of the Discipline generally, and especially to hi
brethren in the ministry, by publishing the results of
his investigations in a condensed form. Such was the
origin of the present work. In the preparation of it, the
author has aimed at nothing more than the most perfec
accuracy in the statement of facts, and the most lucic
arrangement which the nature of the case admitted
To secure these he has bestowed a degree of labour
and attention which few would suppose, that have no
made a similar attempt. Having no model for such a
work in all the range of civil and ecclesiastical law books
as much time was spent, perhaps, in trying various
plans of presenting the subject, as was necessary to com
plete the undertaking, after the plan was decided on. Tha
which has been adopted combines, it is believed, more
than any other, brevity with accuracy. The changes in
the form and arrangement of the Discipline are noticed
in the first book ; and in the second, the changes in its
contents. That these last might be stated as precisely
as possible, the very words of the Discipline are quoted
This necessarily leads to some repetition, and deprives
the work of a part of the interest which it might have
possessed if the narrative style had been adopted. But
it is believed that this mode will be preferred by the
most of those who will wish to consult the work
There is added, in an Appendix, the greater part of the
Notes on the Discipline, by Dr. Coke and Bishop Asbury, many of which are still intrinsically valuable ;
and all of which are interesting, as presenting the
views of the founders of the Methodist Episcopal

Church. For convenience of reference, there is appended to the whole a copious index.

Some might expect, in such a work, a discussion of the reasons for certain rules, and the interpretation to be put upon them. There can be no doubt that a knowledge of both these will be promoted by the information which is here communicated, as to the time when, and the connection in which the rules were introduced, and the changes they have undergone. But to set forth his own opinion on points of discipline was no part of the author's plan ; nor would it have become either his age in the ministry, or his station in the Church. His object will be accomplished, if he shall promote, in any degree, an understanding of the Discipline of the Church, and an attachment to those great principles of its economy, which, amid all the changes of form, have remained the same from the beginning, and which have proved so signally successful in " spreading Scriptural holiness over these lands."

ROBERT EMORY.

Frederick City, Md., November, 1843.

CONTENTS.

BOOK I.

History of the different editions of the Discipline .... Page 9

Rules and regulations prior to the organization of the Methodist
    Episcopal Church... 9–25
First Discipline of the Methodist Episcopal Church, compared
    with Large Minutes.. 26–79
Subsequent editions.. 80–86

BOOK II.

History of the several sections of the Discipline................... 87

The title 87
The Bishops' Address.. 88
Part 1. Chap. 1. Sec. 1. Of the origin of the M. E. Church......... 92
Sec. 2. Articles of Religion.. 95
Sec. 3. Of the General and Annual Conferences..................... 110
Sec. 4. Of the election and consecration of bishops, and their duty 119
Sec. 5. Of the presiding elders, and their duty...................... 124
Sec. 6. Of the election and ordination of travelling elders, and
    their duty.. 129
Sec. 7. Of the election and ordination of travelling deacons, and
    their duty.. 129
Sec. 8. Of the reception of preachers from the Wesleyan con-
    nection, and from other denominations............................. 131
Sec. 9. Of the method of receiving travelling preachers, and their
    duty... 132
Sec. 10. Of the duties of those who have the charge of circuits.. 137
Sec. 11. Of the trial of those who think they are moved by the
    Holy Ghost to preach 145
Sec. 12. Of the matter and manner of preaching, and other pub-
    lic exercises.. 145
Sec. 13. Of the duty of preachers to God, themselves, and one
    another 146
Sec. 14. Rules by which we should continue or desist from
    preaching at any place... 146
Sec. 15. Of visiting from house to house, guarding against those
    things which are so common to professors, and enforcing prac-
    tical religion... 146
Sec. 16. Of the instruction of children.................................... 147
Sec. 17. Of employing our time profitably when we are not
    travelling, &c.. 157

8 CONTENTS.

Sec. 18. Of the necessity of union among ourselves.................. 156
Sec. 19. Of the method by which immoral travelling ministers or
    preachers shall be brought to trial, &c. 156
Sec. 20. How to provide for the circuits in time of conference,
    and to preserve and increase the work of God.................... 164
Sec. 21. Of local preachers.. 164
Sec. 22. Of baptism 174
Sec. 23. Of the Lord's supper 175
Sec. 24. Of public worship... 175
Sec. 25. Of the spirit and truth of singing........................ 176

Chap. II. Sec. 1. The nature, design, and general rules of our
    united societies... 177
Sec. 2. Of class meetings 181
Sec. 3. Of the band societies...................................... 183
Sec. 4. Of the privileges granted to serious persons who are not
    of our church.. 187
Sec. 5. Of marriage.. 187
Sec. 6. Of dress 189
Sec. 7. Of bringing to trial, finding guilty, and reproving, suspend-
    ing, or excluding disorderly persons from society, &c........... 189

Chap. III. Sacramental Services, &c.
Sec. 1. The order for the administration of the Lord's supper... 193
Sec. 2. The ministration of baptism to infants.................... 200
    The ministration of baptism to such as are of riper years. 202
Sec. 3. Form of solemnization of matrimony......................... 205
Sec. 4. Order of the burial of the dead............................ 207

Chap. IV. Form and manner of making and ordaining bishops,
    elders, and deacons.
Sec. 1. Form and manner of making deacons.......................... 208
Sec. 2. Form and manner of ordaining elders 209
Sec. 3. Form of ordaining a bishop................................. 209
Part II. Sec. 1. Of the boundaries of the annual conferences, &c. 211
Sec. 2. Of building churches, and the order to be observed therein 228
Sec. 3. Of the qualifications, appointment, and duty of the stew-
    ards of circuits.. 235
Sec. 4. Of the allowance to the ministers and preachers, and to
    their wives, widows, and children............................. 236
Sec. 5. Of raising annual supplies for the propagation of the gos-
    pel, for making up the allowance of the preachers, &c......... 240
Sec. 6. Support of missions.. 247
Sec. 7. Of the chartered fund...................................... 251
Sec. 8. Of the printing and circulating of books, and of the profits
    arising therefrom... 254
Sec. 9. Local preachers to have an allowance in given cases.... 273
Sec. 10. Of slavery.. 274

APPENDIX.   Notes on the Discipline........................... 281

HISTORY OF THE DISCIPLINE.

BOOK I.

HISTORY OF THE DIFFERENT EDITIONS.

THE Methodist Societies were originally governed by the General Rules, drawn up by the Wesleys, in 1743, and by the regulations adopted in the conferences, which were held yearly from 1744. These regulations were first published in the Minutes from year to year. They were afterward collected together and printed, with some slight alterations, in a tract entitled "The Large Minutes." The same rules and regulations, so far as applicable to their condition, governed the Methodist Societies in America, from the time of their first formation in 1766. At the first conference, in 1773, the preachers formally recognized "the doctrine and discipline of the Methodists," as contained in the English Minutes, to be "the sole rule of their conduct." They adopted, however, at successive conferences, some additional regulations, rendered necessary by their peculiar circumstances. These were inserted, from year to year, in the Annual Minutes, until 1784, when the Methodists in America ceased to constitute mere societies, and were duly organized into a church. To learn, then, what was the Discipline of the Methodist Societies in America, prior to 1784, the Large Minutes must be compared with the Annual

1*

Minutes of the American conferences. The Large Minutes will be found below, in connection with the Discipline of 1784. Those portions of the Annual Minutes which relate to discipline are as follows :—

1773. At the first conference, held in Philadelphia, June, 1773, "the following queries were proposed to every preacher :—

" *Quest.* 1. Ought not the authority of Mr. Wesley and that conference to extend to the preachers and people in America, as well as in Great Britain and Ireland ?

" *Ans.* Yes.

" *Quest.* 2. Ought not the doctrine and discipline of the Methodists, as contained in the Minutes, to be the sole rule of our conduct, who labour in the connection with Mr. Wesley in America ?

" *Ans.* Yes.

" *Quest.* 3. If so, does it not follow, that if any preachers deviate from the Minutes, we can have no fellowship with them till they change their conduct ?

" *Ans.* Yes.

" The following rules were agreed to by all the preachers present :—

" 1. Every preacher, who acts in connection with Mr. Wesley and the brethren who labour in America, is strictly to avoid administering the ordinances of baptism and the Lord's supper.

" 2. All the people among whom we labour, to be earnestly exhorted to attend the Church, and to receive the ordinances there ; but in a particular manner, to press the people in Maryland and Virginia to the observance of this minute.

" 3. No person or persons to be admitted into our love-feasts oftener than twice or thrice, unless they become members ; and none to be admitted to the society meetings more than thrice.

" 4. None of the preachers in America to reprint any of Mr. Wesley's books, without his authority (when it can be gotten) and the consent of their brethren.

" 5. Robert Williams to sell the books he has already printed, but to print no more, unless under the above restrictions.

" 6. Every preacher who acts as an assistant, to send an account of the work once in six months to the general assistant."

1774. In 1774 the following regulations were adopted :—

" All the preachers to change at the end of six months.

" This conference agreed to the following particulars

" 1. Every preacher who is received into full connection is to have the use and property of his horse, which any of the circuits may furnish him with.

" 2. Every preacher to be allowed six pounds, Pennsylvania currency, per quarter, and his travelling charges besides.

" 3. For every assistant to make a general collection at Easter in the circuits where they labour, to be applied to the sinking of the debts on the houses, and relieving the preachers in want.

" 4. Wherever Thomas Rankin* spends his time, he is to be assisted by those circuits."

1775. In 1775 the following directions are added

" Thomas Rankin* is to travel till the month of December, and then take a quarter in New-York.

" The preachers in New-Jersey to change in one quarter.

" Webster and Cooper to change with Gatch and Watters at the end of six months.

" The preachers in Brunswick and Hanover to change as the assistant thinks proper.

" Thomas Rankin's deficiencies to be paid out of the yearly collection.

" The preachers' expenses from conference to their circuits to be paid out of the yearly collection.

* The general assistant.

" A general fast for the prosperity of the work, and for the peace of America, on Tuesday the 18th of July."

1777.   In 1777 we find the following :—
" *Quest.* 7. As the present distress is such, are the preachers resolved to take no step to detach themselves from the work of God for the ensuing year ?
" *Ans.* We purpose, by the grace of God, not to take any step that may separate us from the brethren, or from the blessed work in which we are engaged.
" *Quest.* 8. Has not the preaching of funeral sermons been carried so far as to prostitute that venerable custom, and in some sort to render it contemptible ?
" *Ans.* Yes.   Therefore let all the preachers inform every society, that we will not preach any but for those who, we have reason to think, died in the fear and favour of God."

1778.   In 1778 the following :—
" *Quest.* 8. What shall the preachers be allowed for quarterage ?
" *Ans.* Eight pounds, Virginia currency."

1779.   In 1779, at the conference in Delaware, the following :—
" No helper to make any alteration in the circuit, or appoint preaching in any new place, without consulting the assistant.
" Every exhorter and local preacher to go by the directions of the assistants where, and only where, they shall appoint.
" *Quest.* 8. Why was the Delaware Conference held ?
" *Ans.* For the convenience of the preachers in the northern stations, that we all might have an opportunity of meeting in conference ; it being unadvisable for brother Asbury and brother Ruff, with some others, to attend in Virginia ; it is considered also as preparatory to the conference in Virginia.   Our sentiments to be given in by brother Watters.

" *Quest.* 9. Ought not every travelling preacher to meet the class wherever he preaches ?

" *Ans.* Yes ; if possible.

" *Quest.* 10. Shall we guard against a separation from the Church, directly or indirectly ?

" *Ans.* By all means.

" *Quest.* 11. What shall be done with the children

" *Ans.* Meet them once a fortnight, and examine the parents with regard to their conduct toward them.

" *Quest.* 12. Ought not brother Asbury to act as general assistant in America ?

" *Ans.* He ought : 1st, on account of his age ; 2d because originally appointed by Mr. Wesley ; 3d, being joined with Messrs. Rankin and Shadford, by express order from Mr. Wesley.

" *Quest.* 13. How far shall his power extend ?

" *Ans.* On hearing every preacher for and against what is in debate, the right of determination shall rest with him, according to the Minutes."

In the same year, at the conference in Virginia, the following :—

" *Quest.* 6. What shall be done with the preacher who were upon trial last year ?

" *Ans.* To be continued till next conference.

" *Quest.* 7. Shall any preacher receive quarterage who is able to travel, and does not ?

" *Ans.* No.

" *Quest.* 8. In what light shall we view those preachers who receive money by subscription ?

" *Ans.* As excluded from the Methodist connection."

1780. In 1780 the following :—

" *Quest.* 7. Ought not all the assistants to see to the settling of all the preaching houses by trustees, and order the said trustees to meet once in half a year, and keep a register of their proceedings ; if there are any vacancies, choose new trustees for the better security of the houses, and let all the deeds be drawn in substance after that in the printed Minutes ?

" *Ans.* Yes.

" *Quest.* 8. Shall all the travelling preachers take a license from every conference, importing that they are assistants or helpers in connection with us?

" *Ans.* Yes.

" *Quest.* 9. Shall brother Asbury sign them in behalf of the conference?

" *Ans.* Yes.

" *Quest.* 10. Ought it to be strictly enjoined on all our local preachers and exhorters that no one presume to speak in public without taking a note every quarter, (if required,) and be examined by the assistant with respect to his life, his qualification, and reception?

" *Ans.* Yes.

" *Quest.* 11. Ought not all our preachers to make conscience of rising at four, and if not, yet at five? (is it not a shame for a preacher to be in bed till six in the morning?)

" *Ans.* Undoubtedly they ought.

" *Quest.* 12. Shall we continue in close connection with the Church, and press our people to a closer communion with her?

" *Ans.* Yes.

" *Quest.* 13. Will this conference grant the privilege to all the friendly clergy of the Church of England, at the request or desire of the people, to preach or administer the ordinances in our preaching houses or chapels?

" *Ans.* Yes.

" *Quest.* 14. What provision shall we make for the wives of married preachers?

" *Ans.* They shall receive an equivalent with their husbands in quarterage, if they stand in need.

" *Quest.* 15. Ought not our preachers, if possible, to speak to every person, one by one, in the families where they lodge, before prayer, if time will permit, or give a family exhortation after reading a chapter?

" *Ans.* They ought.

" *Quest.* 16. Ought not this conference to require

those travelling preachers who hold slaves to give promises to set them free ?

" *Ans.* Yes.

" *Quest.* 17. Does this conference acknowledge that
slavery is contrary to the laws of God, man, and nature, and hurtful to society ; contrary to the dictates of
conscience and pure religion, and doing that which we
would not others should do to us and ours ? Do we
pass our disapprobation on all our friends who keep
slaves, and advise their freedom ?

" *Ans.* Yes.

" *Quest.* 18. Shall we recommend our quarterly
meetings to be held on Saturdays and Sundays when
convenient ?*

" *Ans.* Agreed.

" *Quest.* 19. Shall not the Friday following every
quarter day be appointed as a day of fasting ?

" *Ans.* Yes.

" *Quest.* 20. Does this whole conference disapprove
the step our brethren have taken in Virginia ?

" *Ans.* Yes.

" *Quest.* 21. Do we look upon them no longer as
Methodists in connection with Mr. Wesley and us till
they come back ?†

" *Ans.* Agreed.

" *Quest.* 22. Shall brother Asbury, Garrettson, and
Watters attend the Virginia Conference, and inform
them of our proceedings in this, and receive their answer?

" *Ans.* Yes.

" *Quest.* 23. Do we disapprove of the practice of
distilling grain into liquor ? Shall we disown our friends
who will not renounce the practice ?

" *Ans.* Yes.

" *Quest.* 24. What shall the conference do in case
of brother Asbury's death or absence ?

---

* At first, held on Tuesday.
† " This refers to a partial separation which took place in Virginia
on account of the ordinances."

" *Ans.* Meet once a year, and act according to the Minutes.

" *Quest.* 25. Ought not the assistant to meet the co-oured people himself, and appoint as helpers in his absence proper white persons, and not suffer them to stay late, and meet by themselves ?

" *Ans.* Yes.

" *Quest.* 26. What must be the conditions of our union with our Virginia brethren ?

" *Ans.* To suspend all their administrations for one year, and all meet together in Baltimore."

1781. In 1781 the following :—

" *Quest.* 1. What preachers are now determined, after mature consideration, close observation, and earnest prayer, to preach the old Methodist doctrine, and strictly enforce the Discipline, as contained in the Notes, Sermons, and Minutes published by Mr. Wesley, so far as they respect both preachers and people, according to the knowledge we have of them, and the ability God shall give ; and firmly resolved to discountenance a separation among either preachers or people ?

" *Ans.*" [Here follow the names of thirty-nine preachers.]

" *Quest.* 2. Why was conference begun at Chop-tank ?

" *Ans.* To examine those who could not go to Baltimore, and to provide supplies for the circuits where the Lord is more immediately pouring out his Spirit.

" *Quest.* 3. Is there any precedent for this in the economy of Methodism ?

" *Ans.* Yes : Mr. Wesley generally holds a confer-ence in Ireland for the same purposes.

" *Quest.* 4. Should we take the preachers into full connection after one year's trial ; or would it not be better, after considering how young they are in age, grace, and gifts, to try them two years, unless it be one

of double testimony, of whom there is a general appro
bation ?

"*Ans.* Yes.

"*Quest.* 5. Shall any assistant take a local preache:
to travel in the circuit, in the vacancy of conference
without consulting brother Asbury, or the assistant
near him, by word or letter ?

"*Ans.* No.

"*Quest.* 6. If any former assistant has had jus
cause for removing preaching from any house, shoulc
his successor return to it without consulting brothe:
Asbury, or the assistants in the circuits near him ; anc
if it remains doubtful, leave it till next conference ?

"*Ans.* Agreed.

"*Quest.* 7. Ought not the preachers to examine
every person admitted upon trial for three months
first, whether they have been turned out ; and if so, le
them not be received without they have evidenced re
pentance, and can be generally recommended ?

"*Ans.* Yes.

"*Quest.* 8. Ought not the preachers often to reac
the Rules of the Societies, the Character of a Method
ist, and the Plain Account of Christian Perfection, if
they have got them ?

"*Ans.* Yes."

"*Quest.* 14. Ought not every assistant to give a cir
cumstantial account of the circuit, in writing, both of
societies and local preachers, with a plan, to his suc
cessor ?

"*Ans.* Yes.

"*Quest.* 15. Ought not each assistant to inform al
our societies in his circuit of the sum that is to be madc
up for the preachers' quarterage, exclusive of travellin;
expenses, and urge them to give according to their se
veral abilities ?

"*Ans.* Yes."

"*Quest.* 17. What proper method should be taken
supposing any difference should arise in dealing be
tween our brethren ?

" *Ans.* Let the assistant preacher at quarterly meeting consult with the steward, in appointing proper persons to examine into the circumstances, and if there be any suspicion of injustice or inability in the referees, to appoint men of more skill and probity, and the parties to abide by their decision, or be excluded the society.

" *Quest.* 18. How many general fasts shall we have this year ?

" *Ans.* Four, as follows :—the first Thursday in June, September, January, and April."

1782. In 1782 the following :—

" *Quest.* 11. What shall be done to revive the work ?

" *Ans.* Hold evening meetings, and preach in the mornings in places convenient. ˙

" *Quest.* 12. What shall be done to get a regular and impartial supply for the maintenance of the preachers ?

" *Ans.* Let every thing they receive, either in money or clothing, be valued by the preachers and stewards at quarterly meeting, and an account of the deficiency given in to the conference, that they may be supplied by the profits arising from the books and the conference collections.

" *Quest.* 13. How shall we more effectually guard against disorderly travelling preachers ?

" *Ans.* Write at the bottom of every certificate : ' The authority this conveys is limited to next conference.'

" *Quest.* 14. How must we do if a preacher will not desist after being found guilty ?

" *Ans.* Let the nearest assistant stop him immediately. In brother Asbury's absence, let the preachers inform the people of these rules.

" *Quest.* 15. How shall we more effectually guard against disorderly local preachers ?

" *Ans.* Write at the bottom of the certificate : ' This conveys authority no longer than you walk uprightly, and submit to the direction of the assistant preacher.'

" *Quest.* 16. By what rule shall we conduct our-

selves toward the preachers and people that separat
from us?

" *Ans.* Disown them.

" *Quest.* 17. How shall we more effectually guar
against impostors?

" *Ans.* Let no person remove from north to soutl
without a certificate from the assistant preacher; an
let no one be received into society without."

" *Quest.* 19. Do the brethren in conference unani
mously choose brother Asbury to act according to Mr
Wesley's original appointment, and preside over th
American conferences and the whole work?

" *Ans.* Yes."

" Every assistant preacher must so order his circuit
that either himself or one of his helpers may travel witl
Mr. Asbury through his circuit."

1783.   In 1783 the following:—

" *Quest.* 9. How is this sum [for the support of th
preachers' wives] to be raised?

" *Ans.* Let the preachers make a small collection ir
all the circuits.

" *Quest.* 10. What shall be done with our loca
preachers who hold slaves contrary to the laws whicl
authorize their freedom in any of the United States?

" *Ans.* We will try them another year. In the mear
time let every assistant deal faithfully and plainly witl
every one, and report to the next conference. It maj
then be necessary to suspend them.

" *Quest.* 11. Should our friends be permitted t
make spirituous liquors, sell, and drink them ir
drams?

" *Ans.* By no means: we think it wrong in its na
ture and consequences; and desire all our preachers t
teach the people by precept and example to put awaj
this evil.

" *Quest.* 12. How shall we conduct ourselves to
ward any European Methodists, should they come t
this continent?

" *Ans.* We will not receive them without a letter of recommendation, which we have no reason to doubt the truth of.

" *Quest.* 13. What can be done to supply the circuits with preaching in time of conference ?

" *Ans.* Let the assistants engage as many local preachers as can be depended upon, and such among them as are needy be allowed for their labour in proportion with the travelling preachers.

" *Quest.* 14. How many days of thanksgiving shall we have for our public peace, temporal and spiritual prosperity, and for the glorious work of God ?

" *Ans.* Two : the first Thursday in July and October.

" *Quest.* 15. How many fast days shall we have ?

" *Ans.* Two : the first Friday in January and April."

" *Quest.* 17. How is this money [for the preachers' wives] to be raised ?

" *Ans.*" [The amount is then apportioned to the several circuits.]

1784. In 1784 the following :—

" *Quest.* 8. How shall we keep good order among the preachers, and provide for contingencies in the vacancy of conference, and absence of the general assistant ?

" *Ans.* Let any three assistants do what may be thought most eligible, call to an account, change, suspend, or receive a preacher till conference.

" *Quest.* 9. What can be done with those places we have long tried, and appear to grow worse every year ?

" *Ans.* If you are obliged to make use of such places to get to more valuable ones, appoint no public preaching, but only meet society in the evening, or speak to the black people.

" *Quest.* 10. What can be done toward erecting new chapels, and discharging the debts on those already built?

" *Ans.* Let the assistant preacher put a yearly subscription through the circuits, and insist upon every member that is not supported by charity to give some thing. Let them subscribe the first quarter, and pay the second; and the money to be applied by two general stewards.

" *Quest.* 11. How shall we prevent superfluity in dress among our people ?

" *Ans.* Let the preachers carefully avoid every thing of this kind in themselves, and speak frequently and faithfully against it in all our societies.

" *Quest.* 12. What shall we do with our friends that will buy and sell slaves ?

" *Ans.* If they buy with no other design than to hold them as slaves, and have been previously warned, they shall be expelled, and permitted to sell on no consideration.

" *Quest.* 13. What shall we do with our local preachers who will not emancipate their slaves in the states where the laws admit it ?

" *Ans.* Try those in Virginia another year, and suspend the preachers in Maryland, Delaware, Pennsylvania, and New-Jersey.

" *Quest.* 14. How shall we reform our singing ?

" *Ans.* Let all our preachers who have any knowledge in the notes improve it by learning to sing true themselves, and keeping close to Mr. Wesley's tunes and hymns.

" *Quest.* 15. How shall we enlarge the conference collection to supply the wants of the preachers ?

" *Ans.* Let there be a public collection in all the principal places in the circuits, and brought to conference."

" Let every assistant preacher see that [the money for the preachers' wives] is collected and paid quarterly.

" *Quest.* 18. What shall be allowed the general assistant yearly ?

" *Ans.* Twenty-four pounds, with his expenses for horses and travelling, brought to, and paid at, confer ence."

" *Quest.* 21. How shall we conduct ourselves to ward European preachers ?

" *Ans.* If they are recommended by Mr. Wesley, will be subject to the American conference, preach the doctrine taught in the four volumes of Sermons, and Notes on the New Testament, keep the circuits they are appointed to, follow the directions of the London and American Minutes, and be subject to Francis Asbury as general assistant, whilst he stands approved by Mr. Wesley and the conference, we will receive them ; but if they walk contrary to the above directions, no ancient right or appointment shall prevent their being excluded from our connection.

" *Quest.* 22. What shall be done with our travelling preachers that now are, or hereafter shall be, possessed of slaves, and refuse to manumit them where the law permits ?

" *Ans.* Employ them no more.

" *Quest.* 23. How shall we more effectually appoint and keep days of fasting ?

" *Ans.* By writing it upon every class paper, ' To be the first Friday after every quarterly meeting.' "

The close of the year 1784 constituted a new and most important epoch in American Methodism. The independence of the United States having been con-firmed by the peace of 1783, the authority of England over them, both civil and ecclesiastical, came to an end. The connection with the Church of England being thus providentially *dissolved*, Mr. Wesley, who had always resisted a *separation* from it, took mea-sures, on the application of the American societies, to organize them into a church. In explanation of his views and wishes, he addressed to the brethren in America the following letter :—

"Bristol, Sept. 10, 1784.

" *To Dr. Coke, Mr. Asbury, and our Brethren in North America :—*

"1. By a very uncommon train of providences, many of the provinces of North America are totally disjoined from the British empire, and erected into independent states. The English government has no authority over them, either civil or ecclesiastical, any more than over the states of Holland. A civil authority is exercised over them, partly by the congress, partly by the state assemblies. But no one either exercises or claims any ecclesiastical authority at all. In this peculiar situation some thousands of the inhabitants of these states desire my advice; and in compliance with their desire I have drawn up a little sketch.

"2. Lord King's account of the primitive church convinced me, many years ago, that bishops and presbyters are the same order, and, consequently, have the same right to ordain. For many years I have been importuned, from time to time, to exercise this right, by ordaining part of our travelling preachers; but I have still refused, not only for peace' sake, but because I was determined as little as possible to violate the established order of the national church to which I belonged.

"3. But the case is widely different between England and North America. Here there are bishops who have a legal jurisdiction. In America there are none, and but few parish ministers; so that for some hundred miles together there is none either to baptize or to administer the Lord's supper. Here, therefore, my scruples are at an end; and I conceive myself at full liberty, as I violate no order, and invade no man's right, by appointing and sending labourers into the harvest.

"4. I have, accordingly, appointed Dr. Coke and Mr. Francis Asbury to be joint *superintendents* over our brethren in North America; as also RICHARD WHATCOAT and THOMAS VASEY to act as *elders* among them, by baptizing and administering the Lord's supper.

"5. If any one will point out a more rational and Scriptural way of feeding and guiding those poor sheep in the wilderness, 1 will gladly embrace it.   At present I cannot see any better method than that I have taken.

"6. It has indeed been proposed to desire the English bishops to ordain part of our preachers for America.   But to this I object, (1.) I desired the bishop of London to ordain one only, but could not prevail.   (2.) If they consented, we know the slowness of their proceedings, but the matter admits of no delay.   (3.) If they would ordain them *now*, they would likewise expect to govern them.   And how grievously would this entangle us !   (4.) As our American brethren are now totally disentangled both from the state and from the English hierarchy, we dare not entangle them again either with the one or the other.   They are now at full liberty simply to follow the Scriptures and the primitive church.   And we judge it best that they should stand fast in that liberty wherewith God has so strangely made them free.   JOHN WESLEY."

At the same time, Mr. Wesley prepared and printed, for the use of the church in America, a Liturgy, abridged from that of the Church of England, and a collection of psalms and hymns.   The former was entitled, " The Sunday Service of the Methodists in North America.   With other occasional Services. London.   Printed in the year 1784 ;" and contained, among other things, " The Form and Manner of making and ordaining of Superintendents, Elders, and Deacons," and the " Articles of Religion."   The latter was entitled, " A Collection of Psalms and Hymns for the Lord's Day.   Published by John Wesley, M. A., late Fellow of Lincoln College, Oxford; and

Charles Wesley, M. A., late Student of Christ Church Oxford. London. Printed in the year 1784."

To carry into effect the proposed organization, a General Conference of preachers was called, to meet in Baltimore at Christmas, 1784. Sixty out of the eighty-three preachers, then in the travelling connection, attended at the appointed time. "At this conference," say the Annual Minutes for 1785, "it was unanimously agreed that circumstances made it expedient for us to become a separate body, under the denomination of 'The Methodist Episcopal Church.'" And again they say, "We formed ourselves into an independent church; and following the counsel of Mr. John Wesley, who recommended the Episcopal mode of church government, we thought it best to become an Episcopal church, making the Episcopal office elective, and the elected superintendent or bishop amenable to the body of ministers and preachers." They adopted a Form of Discipline for the government of the church. This was substantially the same with the Large Minutes, the principal alterations being only such as were necessary to adapt it to the state of things in America. As this was the first Discipline of the Methodist Episcopal Church, it is here republished entire, together with the portions of the Large Minutes which were left out or altered. Those parts of the Large Minutes which were left out of the Discipline of 1784 are here enclosed in brackets, and, when the passages are long, are printed in smaller type, while what was contained in the latter, and not in the former, is printed in italics. Where there has been merely a substitution of one passage for another, the language of the Large Minutes is given at the foot of the page. The figures in parentheses refer to the Large Minutes.

" *Minutes of several Conversations between the Rev. Thomas Coke, LL.D., the Rev. Francis Asbury and others, at a Conference, begun in Baltimore*

2

*in the State of Maryland, on Monday the 27th of
December, in the Year 1784. Composing a Form
of Discipline for the Ministers, Preachers, and
other Members of the Methodist Episcopal Church
in America.*[1]

" It is desired that all things be considered as in the
immediate presence of God ; that every person speak
freely whatever is in his heart.

" *Quest.* 1. How may we best improve the time
of *our conferences ?*[2]

" *Ans.* 1. While we are conversing, let us have an
especial care to set God always before us.

" 2. In the intermediate hours, let us redeem all the
time we can for private exercises.

" 3. Therein let us give ourselves to prayer for
one another, and for a blessing on [this] our labour.

[" *Quest.* (2.) Have our conferences been as useful as they
might have been !

" *Ans.* No : we have been continually straitened for time.
Hence scarce any thing has been searched to the bottom. To
remedy this, let every conference last nine days, concluding on
Wednesday in the second week.]

" *Quest. 2. What can be done in order to the future
union of the Methodists ?*

" *Ans. During the life of the Rev. Mr. Wesley, we
acknowledge ourselves his sons in the gospel, ready in*

---

[1] The title of the Large Minutes reads, " Minutes of several Conversations between the Rev. Mr. Wesley and others ; from the Year
1744 to the Year 1789." They are here printed as found in Wesley's Works, vol. v, pp. 211–239. The English editor observes in a
note, " This tract, which is usually denominated, ' The Large Minutes,' contains the plan of Discipline as practised in the Methodist
connection during the life of Mr. Wesley. As its title intimates, it
underwent several alterations and enlargements from the year 1744
to 1789, when the last revision took place. It is here reprinted from
a copy which bears the date of 1791—the year in which Mr. Wesley
died—collated with the edition of 1789." Although the edition,
which is here quoted, was revised four years after the organization of
the Methodist Episcopal Church, yet it is ascertained, by comparison
with the Annual Minutes of the English Conference, that little alteration was made in the Large Minutes subsequently to 1784.

[2] " this conference."—*Large Minutes.*

matters belonging to church government, to obey his commands. And we do engage, after his death, to do every thing that we judge consistent with the cause of religion in America and the political interests of these States, to preserve and promote our union with the Methodists in Europe.

"*Quest.* 3. *As the ecclesiastical as well as civil affairs of these United States have passed through a very considerable change by the revolution, what plan of church government shall we hereafter pursue?*

"*Ans. We will form ourselves into an Episcopal Church, under the direction of superintendents, elders, deacons, and helpers, according to the forms of ordination annexed to our Liturgy, and the Form of Discipline set forth in these Minutes.*

"*Quest.* 4. (3.) What may we reasonably believe to be God's design in raising up the preachers called Methodists?

"*Ans.* [Not to form any new sect; but] to reform the *continent*,[1] [particularly the Church;] and to spread Scriptural holiness over *these lands*.[2]

"*Quest.* 5. (4.) What was the rise of Methodism, so called?

"*Ans.* In 1729, two young men, reading the Bible, saw they could not be saved without holiness, followed after it, and incited others so to do. In 1737 they saw holiness comes by faith. They saw likewise, that men are justified before they are sanctified; but still holiness was their point. God then thrust them out, utterly against their will, to raise an holy people. When Satan could no otherwise hinder this, he threw Calvinism in the way; and then Antinomianism, which strikes directly at the root of all holiness.

"*Quest.* 6. (5.) Is it advisable for us to preach in as many places as we can, without forming any societies?

"*Ans.* By no means. We have made the trial in

---

[1] "nation."—*Large Minutes.*   [2] "the land."—*Ib.*

various places; and that for a considerable time. But all the seed has fallen as by the [high] way side. There is scarce any fruit remaining.

"*Quest.* 7. (6.) Where should we endeavour to preach most?

"*Ans.* 1. Where there is the greatest number of quiet and willing hearers. 2. Where there is most fruit.

"*Quest.* 8. (7.) Is field preaching unlawful?

"*Ans.* We conceive not. We do not know that it is contrary to any law either of God or man.

"*Quest.* 9. (8.) Have we not used it too sparingly?

"*Ans.* It seems we have; 1. Because our call is, to save that which is lost. Now, we cannot expect them to seek us. Therefore we should go and seek them. 2. Because we are particularly called, by ' going into the highways and hedges,' [which none else will do,] ' to compel them to come in.' 3. Because that reason against it is not good, ' The house will hold all that come.' The house may hold all that come to the house; but not all that would come to the field.

"The greatest hinderance to this you are to expect from rich, or cowardly, or lazy Methodists. But regard them not, neither stewards, leaders, nor people. Whenever the weather will permit, go out in God's name into the most public places, and call all to repent and believe the gospel; every Sunday, in particular; especially where there are old societies, lest they settle upon their lees.

["The stewards will frequently oppose this, lest they lose their usual collection. But this is not a sufficient reason against it. Shall we barter souls for money?]

"*Quest.* 10. (9.) Ought we not diligently to observe in what places God is pleased at any time to pour out his Spirit more abundantly?

"*Ans.* We ought; and at that time to send more labourers than usual into that part of the harvest.

["But whence shall we have them? 1. So far as we can afford it, we will keep a reserve of preachers at Kingswood.

9. Let an exact list be kept of those who are proposed for trial
but not accepted.]

" *Quest.* 11. (10.) How often shall we permi
strangers to be present at the meeting of the society?

" *Ans.* At every other meeting of the society i
every place let no stranger be admitted. At othe
times they may; but the same person not above twic
or thrice. In order to this, see that all in every plac
shew their tickets before they come in. If the steward
and leaders are not exact herein, employ others tha
have more resolution.

" *Quest. 12. How often shall we permit stranger
to be present at our love-feasts?*

" *Ans. Let them be admitted with the utmost cau
tion; and the same person on no account above twice
unless he becomes a member.*

" *Quest.* 13. (11.) How may the leaders of classe
be made more useful?

" *Ans.* 1. Let each of them be diligently examine
concerning his method of meeting a class. Let this b
done with all possible exactness at the [next] quarterl
visitation. And in order to this, allow sufficient tim
for the visiting of each society.

" 2. Let each leader carefully inquire how ever
soul in his class prospers; not only how each perso
observes the outward rules, but how he grows in th
knowledge and love of God.

" 3. Let the leaders converse with the assistant fre
quently and freely.

" *Quest.* 14. (12.) Can any thing farther be done
in order to make the meetings of the classes lively an
profitable?

" *Ans.* 1. Change improper leaders.

" 2. Let the leaders frequently meet each other'
classes.

" 3. Let us observe which leaders are the most useful
and let these meet the other classes as often as possible

" 4. See that all the leaders be not only men o
sound judgment, but men truly devoted to God.

" *Quest.* 15. (13.) How can we farther assist those under our care ?

" *Ans.* 1. By meeting the married men and women together, the first Sunday after the *quarterly meeting*,[1] —the single men and women apart, on the two following,—in all the large societies : [this has been much neglected.]

" 2. By instructing them at their own houses. What unspeakable need is there of this ! The world say, ' The Methodists are no better than other people.' This is not true. But it is nearer the truth than we are willing to believe.

" [N. B.] For 1. Personal religion either toward God or man is amazingly superficial among us.

" We[2] can but just touch on a few generals. How little faith is there among us ! How little communion with God ! How little living in heaven, walking in eternity, deadness to every creature ! How much love of the world ; desire of pleasure, of ease, *of praise*,[3] of getting money ! How little brotherly love ! What continual judging one another ! What gossiping, evil speaking, tale bearing ! What want of moral honesty ! To instance only [in] one or two particulars : who does as he would be done by, in buying and selling, particularly in selling horses ! Write him a knave that does not. And the Methodist knave is the worst of all knaves.

" 2. Family religion is shamefully wanting, and almost in every branch.

" And the Methodists in general will be little the better, till we take quite another course with them. For what avails public preaching alone, though we could preach like angels ? We must, yea, every travelling preacher must, instruct them from house to house. Till this is done, and that in good earnest, the Methodists will be little better than other people. Our reli-

---

[1] " visitation."—*Large Minutes.*   [2] " I."—*Ib.*
[3] " of praise" is in the original English Minutes, though not in the Large Minutes.

gion is not deep, universal, uniform; but superficia
partial, uneven. It will be so, till we spend half a
much time in this visiting, as we now do in talkin
uselessly.

"Can we find a better method of doing this than M
Baxter's? If not, let us adopt it without delay. Hi
whole tract, intitled, 'Gildas Salvianus' is well worth
careful perusal. [A short extract from it I will subjoin
Speaking of this visiting from house to house, h
says, p. 351:—

"We shall find many hinderances, both in ourselve
and in the people.

"1. In ourselves there is much dulness and laziness
so that there will be much ado to get us to be faithfu
in the work.

"2. We have a base, man-pleasing temper; so tha
we let men perish, rather than lose their love. W
let them go quietly to hell, lest we should anger them

"3. Some of us have also a foolish bashfulness
We know not how to begin, and blush to contradic
the devil.

"4. But the greatest hinderance is, weakness o
faith. Our whole motion is weak, because the sprin
of it is weak.

"5. Lastly, we are unskilful in the work. Hov
few know how to deal with men, so as to get withi
them, and suit all our discourse to their several condi
tions and tempers; to choose the fittest subjects, an
follow them with a holy mixture of seriousness, an
terror, and love, and meekness!"

"[And we have many difficulties to grapple with in our peopl

"1. Too many of them will be unwilling to be taught, till w
conquer their perverseness by the force of reason and the powe
of love.

"2. And many are so dull that they will shun being taugl
for fear of showing their dulness. And indeed you will find it ex
tremely hard to make them understand the very plainest points

"3. And it is still harder to fix things on their hearts, withou
which all our labour is lost. If you have not, therefore, grea
seriousness and fervency, what good can you expect? And
after all, it is grace alone that must do the work.

" 4. And when we have made some impressions on their hearts, if we look not after them, they will soon die away.

" But as great as this labour of private instruction is, it is absolutely necessary. For, after all our preaching, many of our people are almost as ignorant as if they had never heard the gospel. I speak as plain as I can, yet I frequently meet with those who have been my hearers many years, who know not whether Christ be God or man. And how few are there that know the nature of repentance, faith, and holiness! Most of them have a sort of confidence that God will save them, while the world has their hearts. I have found by experience, that one of these has learned more from one hour's close discourse, than from ten years' public preaching.]

" But[1] undoubtedly this private application is implied in those solemn words of the apostle : 'I charge thee, before God and the Lord Jesus Christ, who shall judge the quick and dead at his appearing, preach the word, be instant in season, out of season ; reprove, rebuke, exhort, with all long suffering.'

" O brethren, if we could but set this work on foot in all our societies, and prosecute it zealously, what glory would redound to God ! If the common *lukewarmness*[2] were banished, and every shop and every house busied in speaking of the word and works of God, surely God would dwell in our habitations, and make us his delight.

" And this is absolutely necessary to the welfare of our people, many of whom neither believe nor repent to this day. Look round and see how many of them are still in apparent danger of damnation. And how can you walk, and talk, and be merry with such people, when you know their case ? Methinks, when you look them in the face, you should break forth into tears, as the prophet did when he looked upon Hazael ; and then set on them with the most vehement and importunate exhortations. O, for God's sake, and for the sake of poor souls, bestir yourselves, and spare no pains that may conduce to their salvation !

" What cause have we to bleed before the Lord this

---

1 " And."—*Large Minutes.*   2 " ignorance."—*Ib.*

day, that we have so long neglected this good work
If we had but set upon it sooner, how many more
might have been brought to Christ ! And how much
holier and happier might we have made our societies
before now ! And why might we not have done i
sooner ? There were many hinderances ; and so there
always will be. But the greatest hinderance was in
ourselves, in our littleness of faith and love.

"But it is objected, 1. ·' This will take up so much
time, that we shall not have *leisure*[1] to follow our
studies.'

" *We*[2] answer, 1. Gaining knowledge is a good thing
but saving souls is a better. 2. By this very thing you
will gain the most excellent knowledge, that of God
and eternity. 3. You will have time for gaining other
knowledge too, [if you spend all your mornings therein.
Only sleep not more than you need ; and never be idle
or triflingly employed. But, 4. If you can do but one
let your studies alone. *We*[3] would throw by all the
libraries in the world, rather than be guilty of the loss
of one soul.

[" I allow, in some of the country circuits, where you have
only a day to spend in each place, you have not time for this
excellent work. But you have, wherever you spend several
days together in one town.]

" It is objected, 2. 'The people will not submit to
it.' If some will not, others will. And the success
with them will repay all your labour. O let us herein
follow the example of St. Paul !

" 1. For our general business, ' Serving the Lord
with all humility of mind.' 2. Our special work,
'Take heed to yourselves and to all the flock.' 3. Our
doctrine, ' Repentance toward God, and faith in our
Lord Jesus Christ.' 4. The place, ' I have taught you
publicly, and from house to house.' 5. The object and
manner of teaching, ' I ceased not to warn every one,
night and day, with tears.' 6. His innocence and self-
denial herein, ' I have coveted no man's silver or gold.'

---

[1] " time."—*Large Minutes.*   [2] " I."—*Ib.*   [3] " I."—*Ib.*

2*

7. His patience, 'Neither count I my life dear unto myself.' And among all our motives, let these be ever before our eyes : 1. 'The church of God, which he hath purchased with his own blood.' 2. 'Grievous wolves shall enter in ; yea, of yourselves shall men arise, speaking perverse things.' Write this upon your hearts, and it will do you more good than twenty years' study.

" Let every preacher, having a catalogue of those in each society, go to each house ; and deal gently with them, that the report of it may move others to desire your coming.

["Give the children the 'Instructions for Children,' and encour-. age them to get them by heart. Indeed, you will find it no easy matter to teach the ignorant the principles of religion. So true is the remark of Archbishop Usher : ' Great scholars may think this work beneath them. But they should consider, the laying the foundation skilfully, as it is of the greatest importance, so it is the masterpiece of tho wisest builder. And let the wisest of us all try, whenever we please, we shall find, that to lay this groundwork rightly, to make the ignorant understand the grounds of religion, will put us to the trial of all our skill.'

" Perhaps in doing this it may be well, 1. After a few loving words spoken to all in the house, to take each person singly into another room, where you may deal closely with him, about his sin, and misery, and duty. Set these home, or you lose all your labour. (At least, let none be present but those who are famil-iar with each other.)

" 2. Hear what the children have learned by heart.

" 3. Choose some of the weightiest points, and try if they under-stand them. As, ' Do you believe you have sin in you? What does sin deserve ? What remedy has God provided for guilty, helpless sinners ?'

" 4. Often with the question suggest the answer. As, ' What is repentance ? Sorrow for sin, or a conviction that we are guilty, helpless sinners.' ' What is faith ? A divine conviction of things not seen.'

" 5. Where you perceive they do not understand the stress of your question, lead them into it by other questions. For in-stance, you ask, ' How do you think your sins will be pardoned ?' They answer, ' By repenting and amending my life.' You ask farther, ' But will your amendment make satisfaction for your past sins ?' They will answer, ' I hope so, or I know not what will.' One would think, these had no knowledge of Christ at all. And some have not. But others have ; and give such answers, only because they do not understand the scope of the question. Ask them farther, 'Can you be saved without the death of Christ?' They immediately say, 'No.' And if you ask, 'What has he suffered for you?' they will say, 'He shed his blood for us.' But many cannot express even what they have some conception of; no, not even when expressions are put into their mouths. With these you are to deal exceeding tenderly, lest they be discouraged.

" 6. If you perceive them troubled, that they cannot answer step in yourself, and take the burden off them; answering the question yourself. And do it thoroughly and plainly, making a full explication of the whole business to them.

" 7. When you have tried their knowledge, proceed to instruct them, according to their several capacities. If a man understand the fundamentals, speak what you perceive he most needs, either explaining farther some doctrines, or some duty, or showing him the necessity of something which he neglects. If he still understands not, go over it again till he does.

" 8. Next inquire into his state, whether convinced or unconvinced, converted or unconverted. Tell him, if need be, what conversion is; and then renew and enforce the inquiry.

" 9. If unconverted, labour with all your power to bring his heart to a sense of his condition. Set this home with a more earnest voice than you spoke before. Get to the heart, or you do nothing.

" 10. Conclude all with a strong exhortation, which should enforce, 1. The duty of the heart, in order to receive Christ 2. The avoiding former sins, and constantly using the outward means. And be sure, if you can, to get their promise, to forsake sin, change their company, and use the means. And do this solemnly, reminding them of the presence of God, who hears their promises, and expects the performance.

" 11. Before you leave them, engage the head of each family to call all his family together every Sunday before they go to bed and hear what they can repeat, and so continue, till they have learned the 'Instructions' perfectly; and afterward let him take care that they do not forget what they have learned.]

" Do this in earnest, and you will soon find what a work you take in hand, in undertaking to be a travelling preacher!

" *Quest.* 16. (14.) How shall we prevent improper persons from insinuating into the society?

" *Ans.* 1. Give tickets to none till they are recommended by a leader, with whom they have met at least two months on trial.

" 2. Give notes to none but those who are recommended by one you know, or till they have met three or four times in a class.

"3. Give them the rules the first time they meet. [See that this be never neglected.]

" *Quest.* 17. (15.) When shall we admit new members ?

" *Ans.* In large towns, admit them into the bands at the quarterly love-feast following the *quarterly meeting :*[1] into the society, on the Sunday following the *quarterly meeting.*[1]   Then also read the names of them that are excluded.

" *Quest.* 18. (16.) Should we insist on the rules *concerning dress ?*[2]

" *Ans.* By all means.   This is no time to give any encouragement to superfluity of apparel.   Therefore give no [band] tickets to any till they have left off superfluous ornaments.   In order to this, 1. Let every assistant read the ' Thoughts upon Dress' at least once a year, in every large society.   2. In visiting the classes, be very mild, but very strict.   3. Allow no exempt case, not even of a married woman.   Better one suffer than many.   4. Give no ticket to any that wear [calashes,] high heads, [or] enormous bonnets, *ruffles or rings.*

" *Quest.* 19. *What can be done* to encourage meeting in band ?

" *Ans.* 1. In every large society have a love-feast quarterly for the bands only.   2. Never fail to meet them once a week.   3. Exhort every believer to embrace the advantage.   4. Give a band ticket to none till they have met a quarter on trial.

[" Observe ! You give none a band ticket before he meets, but after he has met.

" *Quest.* (17.) Have those in band left off snuff and drams !

" *Ans.* No.   Many are still enslaved to one or the other.   In order to redress this, 1. Let no preacher touch either on any account.   2. Strongly dissuade our people from them.   3. Answer their pretences, particularly curing the colic.]

[1] " visitation."—*Large Minutes.*
[2] the band rules, particularly with regard to dress ?"—*Ib*

" *Quest.* 20. (18.) Do we observe any evil whicl has lately prevailed among our societies ?

" *Ans.* Many of our members have married [with un believers, yea,] with unawakened persons. This ha: had fatal effects. They had either a cross for life, o turned back to perdition.

" *Quest.* 21. (19.) What can be done to put a stop t this ?

" *Ans.* 1. Let every preacher publicly enforce th apostle's caution, ' Be not unequally yoked with un believers.' 2. Let him openly declare, whoever doe: this will be expelled the society. 3. When any sucl is expelled, let a suitable exhortation be subjoined And, 4. Let all be exhorted to take no step in s weighty a matter without advising with the most seriou: of their brethren.

" *Quest.* 22. (20.) Ought any woman to marry with out the consent of her parents ?

" *Ans.* In general, she ought not. Yet there may b an exception. For if, 1. A woman be under the[1] neces sity of marrying ; if, 2. Her parents absolutely refus to let her marry any Christian ; then she may, nay ought to, marry without their consent. Yet, even then a Methodist preacher ought not to marry her.

" *Quest.* 23. *May our ministers or travellin preachers drink spirituous liquors ?*

" *Ans. By no means, unless it be medicinally.*

" *Quest.* 24. (21.) Do not sabbath breaking, [dran drinking,] evil speaking, unprofitable conversation lightness, expensiveness, or gayety of apparel, and con tracting debts without due care to discharge them, stil prevail in several places ? How may these evils b remedied ?

" *Ans.* 1. Let us preach expressly on each of thes heads. 2. Read in every society the ' Sermon on Evi Speaking.' 3. Let the leaders closely examine an exhort every person to put away the accursed thing

---

[1] " a."—*Large Minutes.*

4. Let the preacher warn every society, that none who is guilty herein can remain with us. 5. Extirpate smuggling, buying or selling uncustomed goods, out of every society.

" Let none remain with us, who will not totally abstain from every kind and degree of it.

[" Speak tenderly, but earnestly, and frequently of it, in every society near the coasts ; and read to them, and diligently disperse among them, the ' Word to a Smuggler.']

" 6. Extirpate bribery, receiving any thing, directly or indirectly, for voting in any election. Show no respect of persons herein, but expel all that touch the accursed thing.

[" Largely show, both in public and private, the wickedness of thus selling our country. And everywhere read the ' Word to a Freeholder,' and disperse it with both hands.]

" *Quest.* 25. (22.) What shall we do to prevent scandal, when any of our members becomes a bankrupt ?

" *Ans.* Let the assistant talk with him at large ; and if he has not kept fair accounts, [or has been concerned in that base practice of raising money by coining notes, (commonly called the bill trade,)] let him be expelled immediately."

" *Quest. 26. What is the office of a superintendent ?*

" *Ans. To ordain superintendents, elders, and deacons ; to preside as a moderator in our conferences ; to fix the appointments of the preachers for the several circuits ; and, in the intervals of the conference, to change, receive or suspend preachers, as necessity may require ; and to receive appeals from the preachers and people, and decide them.*

" *N. B. No person shall be ordained a superintendent, elder, or deacon, without the consent of a majority of the conference, and the consent and imposition of hands of a superintendent ; except in the instance provided for in the 29th minute.*

" *Quest. 27. To whom is the superintendent amenable for his conduct ?*

" *Ans. To the conference : who have power to expel him for improper conduct, if they see it necessary.*

" *Quest.* 28. *If the superintendent ceases from tra-velling at large among the people, shall he still exer-cise his office in any degree?*

"*Ans. If he ceases from travelling without the con-sent of the conference, he shall not thereafter exercise any ministerial function whatsoever in our church.*

" *Quest.* 29. *If by death, expulsion or otherwise, there be no superintendent remaining in our church, what shall we do?*

"*Ans. The conference shall elect a superintendent, and the elders, or any three of them, shall ordain him according to our Liturgy.*

" *Quest.* 30. *What is the office of an elder?*

" *Ans. To administer the sacraments of baptism and the Lord's supper, and to perform all the other rites prescribed by our Liturgy.*

" *Quest.* 31. *What is the office of a deacon?*

" *Ans. To baptize in the absence of an elder, to assist the elder in the administration of the Lord's sup-per, to marry, bury the dead, and read the Liturgy to the people as prescribed, except what relates to the ad-ministration of the Lord's supper.*

[" *Quest.* (23.) What is the office of a Christian minister ?

" *Ans.* To watch over souls, as he that must give account.

" *Quest.* (24.) In what view may we and our helpers be con-sidered ?

" *Ans.* Perhaps as extraordinary messengers, (that is, out of the ordinary way,) designed, 1. To provoke the regular minis-ters to jealousy. 2. To supply their lack of service toward those who are perishing for want of knowledge. But how hard is it to abide here ! Who does not wish to be a little higher ? suppose, to be ordained !*]

" *Quest.* 32. (25.) What is the office of a helper ?

[" *Ans.* In the absence of a minister, to feed and guide the flock ; in particular,]

" 1. To preach.

[" Morning and evening. (But he is never to begin later in the evening than seven o'clock, unless in particular cases.)]

---

* This and similar passages in other parts of Mr. Wesley's writ-ings refer to the Methodists in England, whom he desired still to re-main as societies within the Church of England. See pp. 22–24.

" 2. To meet the society and the bands weekly.

" 3. *To visit the sick.*

" 4. (3.) To meet the leaders weekly.

" Let every preacher be particularly exact in this, and in morning preaching. If he has twenty hearers, let him preach. [If not, let him sing and pray.]

"N. B. We are fully determined never to drop morning preaching ; and to *preach*[1] at five, wherever it is practicable, [particularly in London and Bristol.]

" *Quest.* 33. (26.) What are the rules of a helper ?

"*Ans.* 1. Be diligent. Never be unemployed [a moment.] Never be triflingly employed. Never while away time ; neither spend any more time at any place than is strictly necessary.

" 2. Be serious. Let your motto be, ' Holiness to the Lord.' Avoid all lightness, jesting, and foolish talking.

" 3. Converse sparingly and cautiously with women ; particularly with young women.

" 4. Take no step toward marriage, without first consulting with your brethren.

" 5. Believe evil of no one ; unless you see it done, take heed how you credit it. Put the best construction on every thing. You know the judge is always supposed to be on the prisoner's side.

" 6. Speak evil of no one ; else your word especially would eat as doth a canker. Keep your thoughts within your own breast till you come to the person concerned.

" 7. Tell every one *who is under your care*, what you think wrong in *his conduct and tempers*,[2] and that plainly, as soon as may be ; else it will fester in your heart. Make all haste to cast the fire out of your bosom.

" 8. Do not affect the gentleman. You have no more to do with this character than with that of a dancing master. A preacher of the gospel is the servant of all.

---

[1] " continue preaching."—*Large Minutes.*   [2] " him."—*Ib.*

" 9. Be ashamed of nothing but sin : not of fetching wood (if time permit) or drawing water ; not of clean ing your own shoes, or your neighbour's.

" 10. Be punctual. Do every thing exactly at the time. And [in general] do not mend our rules, but keep them ; not for wrath, but for conscience' sake.

" 11. You have nothing to do but to save souls. Therefore spend and be spent in this work. And go always, not only to those that want you, but to those that want you most.

" Observe : It is not your business to preach so many times, and to take care of this or that society ; but to save as many souls as you can ; to bring as many sinners as you possibly can to repentance, and with all your power to build them up in that holiness without which they cannot see the Lord. And remember ! A Methodist preacher is to mind every point, great and small, in the Methodist discipline ! Therefore you will need all the sense you have, and to have all your wits about you !

" 12. Act in all things, not according to your own will, but as a son in the gospel. As such, it is your part to employ your time in the manner which we direct ; partly in preaching and visiting from house to house ; partly in reading, meditation, and prayer. Above all, if you labour with us in our Lord's vineyard, it is needful that you should do that part of the work which we advise, at those times and places which we judge most for his glory.

" *N. B. No helper, or even deacon, shall on any pretence at any time whatsoever administer the Lord's supper.*

" *Quest.* 34. *Will it be expedient to appoint some of our helpers to read the morning and evening service out of our Liturgy on the Lord's day.*

" *Ans. It will. And every helper who receives a written direction under the hand of a superintendent, may regularly read the morning and evening service on the Lord's day.*

" *Quest.* 35. *How are we to proceed with tho*
elders or deacons who cease from travelling?

" *Ans. Unless they have the permission of the co*
ference declared under the hand of a superintenden
they are on no account to exercise any of the peculi
functions of those offices among us. And if they d
they are to be expelled immediately.

" *Quest.* 36. *What method shall we take to preve*
improper persons from preaching among us as trave
ling preachers?

" *Ans. Let no person be employed as a travellir*
preacher, unless his name be printed in the Minutes
the conference preceding, or a certificate be given hi
under the hand of one or other of the superintendent
or, in their absence, of three assistants, as is hereaft
provided. And, for this purpose, let the Minutes
the conference be always printed.

" *Quest.* 37. *What shall be the regular annu*
salary of the elders, deacons, and helpers?

" *Ans. Twenty-four pounds, (Pennsylvania curre*
cy,) and no more.

" *Quest.* 38. *What shall be annually allowed t*
wives of the married preachers?

" *Ans. Twenty-four pounds (Pennsylvania cu*
rency) if they need it, and no more.

" *Quest.* 39. *How is this to be provided?*

" *Ans. By the circuits proportionably.*

" *Quest.* 40. *What shall be allowed the marrie*
preachers for the support of their children?

" *Ans. For each of their children under the age o*
six years, let them be allowed six pounds, (Pennsylve
nia currency:) and for each child of the age of si
and under the age of eleven, eight pounds.

" *Quest.* 41. *Are there any directions to be give*
concerning the negroes?

" *Ans. Let every preacher, as often as possibl*
meet them in class. And let the assistant always a
t a proper white person as their leader. Let t
ts also make a regular return to the conferen

e *number of negroes in society* 'the *same time be*
its. _____ *'anding or*

uest. 42. *What methods can we take to extir*
lavery?

s. *We are deeply conscious of the impropriety*
ng new terms of communion for a religious so-
eady established, excepting on the most press-
ion: and such we esteem the practice of hold-
'ellow-creatures in slavery. We view it as
'o the golden law of God on which hang all
d the prophets, and the unalienable rights of
's well as every principle of the revolution,
. the deepest debasement, in a more abject
.y than is perhaps to be found in any part of the
world except America, so many souls that are all
capable of the image of God.

"*We therefore think it our most bounden duty to*
take immediately some effectual method to extirpate
this abomination from among us: and for that purpose
we add the following to the rules of our society, viz.:

"1. *Every member of our society who has slaves in*
his possession, shall, within twelve months after notice
given to him by the assistant, (which notice the assist-
ants are required immediately, and without any delay,
to give in their respective circuits,) legally execute and
record an instrument, whereby he emancipates and sets
free every slave in his possession who is between the
ages of forty and forty-five immediately, or at farthest
when they arrive at the age of forty-five.

"*And every slave who is between the ages of twenty-*
five and forty immediately, or at farthest at the expi-
ration of five years from the date of the said instru-
ment.

"*And every slave who is between the ages of twenty*
and twenty-five immediately, or at farthest when they
arrive at the age of thirty.

"*And every slave under the age of twenty, as soon*
as they arrive at the age of twenty-five at farthest.

"*And every infant born in slavery after the above-*

" *Quest.* ~~2. .... ~~*re complied with, immediately on its* ~~elders or~~

" 2. *Every assistant shall keep a journal, in which he shall regularly minute down the names and ages of all the slaves belonging to all the masters in his respective circuit, and also the date of every instrument executed and recorded for the manumission of the slaves, with the name of the court, book, and folio, in which the said instruments respectively shall have been recorded : which journal shall be handed down in each circuit to the succeeding assistants.*

" 3. *In consideration that these rules form a new term of communion, every person concerned, who will not comply with them, shall have liberty quietly to withdraw himself from our society within the twelve months succeeding the notice given as aforesaid : otherwise the assistant shall exclude him in the society.*

" 4. *No person so voluntarily withdrawn, or so excluded, shall ever partake of the supper of the Lord with the Methodists, till he complies with the above requisitions.*

" 5. *No person holding slaves shall, in future, be admitted into society or to the Lord's supper, till he previously complies with these rules concerning slavery.*

" *N. B. These rules are to affect the members of our society no farther than as they are consistent with the laws of the states in which they reside.*

" *And respecting our brethren in Virginia that are concerned, and after due consideration of their peculiar circumstances, we allow them two years from the notice given, to consider the expedience of compliance or non-compliance with these rules.*

" *Quest.* 43. *What shall be done with those who buy or sell slaves, or give them away ?*

" *Ans. They are immediately to be expelled : unless they buy them on purpose to free them.*

" *Quest.* 44. *Are there any directions to be given concerning the administration of the Lord's supper ?*

" *Ans.* 1. *Let it be recommended to the people to*

receive it kneeling: but let them at the same time be informed that they may receive it either standing or sitting.

"2. Let no person who is not a member of the society be admitted to the communion without a sacrament ticket, which ticket must be changed every quarter. And we empower the elder or assistant, and no others, to deliver these tickets.

"*Quest.* 45. Is there any direction to be given concerning the administration of baptism?

"*Ans.* Let every adult person, and the parents of every child, to be baptized, have their choice either of immersion or sprinkling, and let the elder or deacon conduct himself accordingly.

"*Quest.* 46. What shall be done with those who were baptized in their infancy, but have now scruples concerning the validity of infant baptism?

"*Ans.* Remove their scruples by argument, if you can; if not, the office may be performed by immersion or sprinkling, as the person desires.

"*Quest.* 47. Shall persons who continue to attend divine service and partake of the Lord's supper with other churches, have liberty at the same time to be members of our society?

"*Ans.* They shall have full liberty, if they comply with our rules.

"*Quest.* 48. Are there any directions to be given concerning the fees of office?

"*Ans.* We will on no account whatsoever suffer any elder or deacon among us to receive a fee or present for administering the ordinance of marriage, baptism, or the burial of the dead. Freely we have received, and freely we will give.

["*Quest.* (37.) What power is this which you exercise over both the preachers and the societies?

"*Ans.* Count Zinzendorf loved to keep all things close: I love to do all things openly. I will therefore tell you all I know of the matter, taking it from the very beginning.

"1. In November, 1738, two or three persons who desired ' to flee from the wrath to come,' and then a few more, came to me

ı London, and desired me to advise and pray with them. I said,
If you will meet me on Thursday night, I will help you as well
s I can.' More and more then desired to meet with them, till
ıey were increased to many hundreds. The case was after-
ıard the same at Bristol, Kingswood, Newcastle, and many
ther parts of England, Scotland, and Ireland. It may be ob-
erved, the desire was on their part, not mine. My desire was,
ı live and die in retirement. But I did not see that I could re-
ıse them my help, and be guiltless before God.

" Here commenced my power; namely, a power to appoint
ıhen, and where, and how they should meet; and to remove
ıose whose lives showed that they had not a desire ' to flee from
ıe wrath to come.' And this power remained the same, whether
ıe people meeting together were twelve, or twelve hundred, or
ıvelve thousand.

" 2. In a few days some of them said, ' Sir, we will not sit
nder you for nothing; we will subscribe quarterly.' I said, ' I
ıill have nothing; for I want nothing. My fellowship supplies me
ıith all I want.' One replied, ' Nay, but you want a hundred
nd fifteen pounds to pay for the lease of the Foundry; and like-
ıise a large sum of money to put it into repair.' On this conside-
ıtion, I suffered them to subscribe. And when the society met,
ıasked, ' Who will take the trouble of receiving this money, and
ıaying it where it is needful ?' One said, ' I will do it, and keep
ıe account for you.' So here was the first steward. After-
ıard, I desired one or two more to help me, as stewards, and, in
ıocess of time, a greater number.

" Let it be remarked, it was I myself, not the people, who
ıhose these stewards, and appointed to each the distinct work
ıherein he was to help me, as long as I desired. And herein I
egan to exercise another sort of power; namely, that of appoint-
ıg and removing stewards.

" 3. After a time a young man, named Thomas Maxfield,
ıame and desired to help me as a son in the gospel. Soon after
ıame a second, Thomas Richards; and then a third, Thomas
Vestell. These severally desired to serve me as sons, and to
ıbour when and where I should direct. Observe : these like-
ıise desired me, not I them. But I durst not refuse their
ıssistance. And here commenced my power, to appoint each of
ıese when, and where, and how to labour; that is, while he
ıhose to continue with me. For each had a power to go away
ıhen he pleased; as I had also, to go away from them, or any
f them, if I saw sufficient cause. The case continued the same
ıhen the number of preachers increased. I had just the same
ıower still, to appoint when, and where, and how each should
elp me; and to tell any, (if I saw cause,) ' I do not desire your
elp any longer.' On these terms, and no other, we joined at

first : on these we continue joined. But they do me no favou in being directed by me. It is true, my 'reward is with th Lord :' but at present I have nothing from it but trouble and care and often a burden I scarce know how to bear.

"4. In 1744 I wrote to several clergymen, and to all wh then served me as sons in the gospel, desiring them to meet m in London, and to give me their advice concerning the bes method of carrying on the work of God. And when their num ber increased, so that it was not convenient to invite them al. for several years I wrote to those with whom I desired to confei and they only met me at London, or elsewhere ; till at length gave a general permission, which I afterward saw cause t retract

"Observe : I myself sent for these of my own free choice And I sent for them to advise, not govern, me. Neither did at any time divest myself of any part of the power above de scribed, which the providence of God had cast upon me, withou any design or choice of mine.

"5. What is that power ? It is a power of admitting into, an excluding from, the societies under my care ; of choosing an removing stewards ; of receiving or not receiving helpers ; o: appointing them when, where, and how to help me, and of de siring any of them to confer with me when I see good. And a it was merely in obedience to the providence of God, and for th good of the people, that I at first accepted this power, which newer sought ; so it is on the same consideration, not for profit honour, or pleasure, that I use it at this day.

"6. But 'several gentlemen are offended at your having s much power.' I did not seek any part of it. But when it wa come unawares, not daring to 'bury that talent,' I used it to th best of my judgment. Yet I never was fond of it. I alway did, and do now, bear it as my burden ;—the burden which Go lays upon me, and therefore I dare not lay it down.

"But if you can tell me any one, or any five men, to whom may transfer this burden, who can and will do just what I d now, I will heartily thank both them and you.

"7. But some of our helpers say, 'This is shackling freebor Englishmen ;' and demand a free conference, that is, a meetin of all the preachers, wherein all things shall be determined b most votes. I answer, It is possible, after my death, somethin of this kind may take place ; but not while I live. To me th preachers have engaged themselves to submit, to serve me a sons in the gospel ; but they are not thus engaged to any ma or number of men besides. To me the people in general wil submit ; but they will not thus submit to any other.

"It is nonsense, then, to call my using this power, ' shack ling freeborn Englishmen.' None needs to submit to it unles

will; so that there is no shackling in the case. Every
eacher and every member may leave me when he pleases.
.t while he chooses to stay, it is on the same terms that he
.ned me at first.
" 'But this is making yourself a pope.' This carries no face
truth. The pope affirms that every Christian must do all he
.s, and believe all he says, under pain of damnation. I never
.rmed any thing that bears any the most distant resemblance to
s. All I affirm is, the preachers who choose to labour with
., choose to serve me as sons in the gospel. And the people
.o choose to be under my care, choose to be so on the same
.ms they were at first.
" Therefore all talk of this kind is highly injurious to me, who
.r the burden merely for your sake. And it is exceeding
schievous to the people, tending to confound their understand-
., and to fill their hearts with evil surmisings and unkind tem-
.rs toward me ; to whom they really owe more, for taking all
.s load upon me, for exercising this very power, for shackling
.rself in this manner, than for all my preaching put together;
.ause preaching twice or thrice a day is no burden to me at
. ; but the care of all the preachers and all the people is a bur-
.n indeed !
" *Quest.* (28.) What reason can be assigned why so many of
.r preachers contract nervous disorders ?
" *Ans.* The chief reason, on Dr. Cadogan's principles, is
.her indolence or intemperance. 1. Indolence. Several of
.m use too little exercise, far less than when they wrought at
.ir trade. And this will naturally pave the way for many,
.pecially nervous, disorders. 2. Intemperance,—though not in
. vulgar sense. They take more food than they did when they
.oured more : and let any man of reflection judge how long this
.ll consist with health. Or they use more sleep than when
.y laboured more : and this alone will destroy the firmness of
. nerves. If, then, our preachers would avoid nervous disor-
.rs, let them, 1. Take as little meat, drink, and sleep as na-
.e will bear ; and, 2. Use full as much exercise daily as they
.l before they were preachers.]

" *Quest.* 49. (29.) What general method of employ-
.z our time would you advise us to ?
" *Ans.* We advise you, 1. As often as possible to
.e at four. 2. From four to five in the morning,
.d from five to six in the evening, to meditate, pray,
.d read, partly the Scriptures with *Mr. Wesley's*
.ptes,[1] partly the closely practical parts of what *he*

---

[1] " the Notes."—*Large Minutes.*

has[1] published.   3. From six in the morning ti
twelve, (allowing an hour for breakfast,) to read i
order, with much prayer, [first,] 'The Christian Li
brary,' and *other pious books.*[2]

[" *Quest.* (30.) Should our helpers follow trades ?

" *Ans.* The question is not, whether they may occasionall
work with their hands, as St. Paul did, but whether it be prope
for them to keep shop or follow merchandise. After long consi
deration, it was agreed by all our brethren, that no preacher wh
will not relinquish his trade of buying and selling, (though it wer
only pills, drops, or balsams,) shall be considered as a travellin
preacher any longer.]

" *Quest.* 50. (31.) Why is it that the people unde
our care are no better ?

" *Ans.* Other reasons may concur ; but the chief is
because we are not more knowing and more holy.

" *Quest.* 51. (32.) But why are we not more know
ing ?

"*Ans.* Because we are idle. We forget our very firs
rule, ' Be diligent. Never be unemployed [a moment.
Never be triflingly employed. Never while awa
time ; neither spend any more time at any place tha
is strictly necessary.'

" I fear there is altogether a fault in this matter, an
that few of us are clear. Which of you spends a
many hours a day in God's work, as you did formerl
in man's work ? We talk,—or read history, or wha
comes next to hand. We must, absolutely must, cur
this evil, or betray the cause of God.

" But how ? 1. Read the most useful books, an
that regularly and constantly. Steadily spend all th
morning in this employ, or, at least, five hours in fou
and twenty.

[" ' But I read only the Bible.' Then you ought to teac
others to read only the Bible, and, by parity of reason, to hea
only the Bible : but if so, you need preach no more. Just s
said George Bell. And what is the fruit ? Why, now he nei

---

[1] " we have."—*Large Minutes.*

[2] " the other books which we have published in prose and vers
and then those which we recommended in our rules of Kingswoo
school."—*Ibid.*

3

ther reads the Bible, nor any thing else.   This is rank enthusi-
asm.   If you need no book but the Bible, you are got above St.
Paul.   He wanted others too.   'Bring the books,' says he, 'but
especially the parchments,' those wrote on parchment.]

" ' But I have no taste for reading.'   Contract a
taste for it by use, or return to your trade.

" ' But I have no books.'   [I will give each of you,
as fast as you will read them, books to the value of five
pounds.]   And *we*[1] desire the assistants *will*[2] take
care that all the large societies provide *Mr. Wesley's*[3]
Works, [or at least the Notes,] for the use of the
preachers.

" 2. In the afternoon follow Mr. Baxter's plan.
Then you will have no time to spare : you will have
work enough for all your time.   Then, likewise, no
preacher will stay with us who is as salt that has lost
its savour.   For to such this employment would be
mere drudgery.   And in order to it, you will have need
of all the knowledge you [have, or] can procure.

" The sum is, Go into every house in course, and
teach every one therein, young and old, if they belong
to us, to be Christians inwardly and outwardly.

" Make every particular plain to their understanding;
fix it in their memory ; write it on their heart.   In order to this, there must be ' line upon line, precept upon
precept.'   What patience, what love, what knowledge
is requisite for this !

[" *Quest.* (33.) In what particular method should we instruct
them ?

" *Ans.* You may, as you have time, read, explain, enforce,
1. ' The Rules of the Society.'   2. ' Instructions for Children.'   3. The fourth volume of ' Sermons.'   And, 4. Philip
Henry's ' Method of Family Prayer.']

" We must needs do this, were it only to avoid idleness.   Do we not loiter away many hours in every
week ?   Each try himself : no idleness *is consistent*[4]
with growth in grace.   Nay, without exactness in re-

---

[1] " I."—*Large Minutes.*   [2] " would."—*Ibid.*   [3] " our."—*Ibid.*
[4] " can consist."—*Ibid.*

deeming time, you cannot retain the grace you received
in justification.

"But what shall we do for the rising generation?
[Unless we take care of this, the present revival will be
res unius ætatis; it will last only the age of a man.]
Who will labour *for them?*[1] Let him who is zealous
for God and the souls of men begin now.

"1. Where there are ten children, *whose parents
are in society,*[2] meet them at least an hour every week.

"2. Talk with them every time you see any at
home.

"3. Pray in earnest for them.

"4. Diligently instruct and vehemently exhort all
parents at their own houses.

"5. Preach expressly on education, [particularly at
midsummer, when you speak of Kingswood.] 'But I
have no gift for this.' Gift or no gift, you are to do it;
else you are not called to be a Methodist preacher. Do
it as you can, till you can do it as you would. Pray
earnestly for the gift, and use the means for it. [Par-
ticularly, study the 'Instructions' and 'Lessons' for
Children.']

"*Quest.* 52. (34.) Why are not we more holy?
Why do not we live in eternity; walk with God all
the day long? Why are we not all devoted to God;
breathing the whole spirit of missionaries?

"*Ans.* Chiefly because we are enthusiasts; looking
for the end without using the means. To touch only
upon two or three instances: Who of you rises at four
[in summer;] or even at five, when he does not preach?
Do you recommend to all our societies the five o'clock
hour for private prayer? Do you observe it, or any
other fixed time? Do not you find, by experience, that
any time is no time? Do you know the obligation and
the benefit of fasting? How often do you practise it?
The neglect of this alone is sufficient to account for
our feebleness and faintness of spirit. We are con-

---

[1] "herein."—*Large Minutes.*   [2] "in a society."—*Ibid.*

tinually grieving the Holy Spirit of God by the habitual neglect of a plain duty ! Let us amend from this hour.

" *Quest.* 53. (35.) But how can I fast, since it hurts my health ?

• " *Ans.* There are several degrees of fasting which cannot hurt your health. *We*[1] will instance in one : Let *us*[2] every Friday (beginning on the next) avow this duty throughout the *continent,*[3] by touching no tea, coffee, or chocolate in the morning ; but (if we want it) half a pint of milk or water gruel. Let us dine on *vegetables,*[4] and (if we need it) eat three or four ounces of flesh in the evening. At other times let us eat no flesh suppers : these exceedingly tend to breed nervous disorders.

" *Quest.* 54. (36.) What is the best general method of preaching ?

" *Ans.* [1. To invite.] 1. (2.) To convince. 2. (3.) To offer Christ. 3. (4.) To build up ; and to do this in some measure in every sermon.

" *Quest.* 55. (37.) Are there any smaller advices relative to preaching which might be of use to us ?

" *Ans.* Perhaps these : 1. Be sure never to disappoint a congregation, unless in case of life or death.

" 2. Begin [and end] precisely at the time appointed.

" 3. Let your whole deportment before the congregation be serious, weighty, and solemn.

" 4. Always suit your subject to your audience.

" 5. Choose the plainest texts you can.

" 6. Take care not to ramble ; but keep to your text, and make out what you take in hand.

[" (7.) Be sparing in allegorizing or spiritualizing.]

" 7. (8.) Take care of any thing awkward or affected, either in your gesture, phrase, or pronunciation.

" 8. (9.) Sing no hymns of your own composing.

" 9. (10.) Print nothing without *the approbation of one or other of the superintendents.*[5]

---

[1] " I."—*Large Minutes.*   [2] " you and I."—*Ib.*   [3] " nation."—*Ib.*
[4] " potatoes."—*Ib.*   [5] " my approbation."—*Ib.*

" 10. (11.) Do not usually pray *ex tempore* above eight or ten minutes (at most) without intermission.

" 11. (12.) Frequently read and enlarge upon a portion of the Notes. And let young preachers often exhort, without taking a text.

[" (13.) In repeating the Lord's prayer, remember to say 'hallowed,' not *hollowed ;* 'trespass against *us ;*' 'amen.'

" (14.) Repeat this prayer aloud after the minister, as ofte⟨ as he repeats it. (15.) Repeat after him aloud every confession, and both the doxologies in the communion service.]

" 12. (16.) Always kneel during public prayer.

" 13. (17.) Everywhere avail yourself of the grea⟨ festivals, by preaching on the occasion,

[" And sing the hymns, which you should take care to hav⟨ in readiness.

" (18.) Avoid quaint words, however in fashion, as *object, ori⟨ ginate, very, high,* &c.

" (19.) Avoid the fashionable impropriety of leaving out the ⟨ in many words, as honor, vigor, &c. This is mere childish af⟨ fectation.]

" 14. (20.) Beware of clownishness, [either in speecʰ or dress. Wear no slouched hat.] *Be courteous to all*

" 15. (21.) Be merciful to your beast. Not only rid⟨ moderately, but see with your own eyes that your hors⟨ be rubbed, *and fed.*[1]

" *Quest.* 56. (38.) Have not some of us been led off from practical preaching by what was called preachinǥ Christ ?

" *Ans.* Indeed we have. The most effectual wa⟨ of preaching Christ, is to preach him in all his offices and to declare his law as well as his gospel, both t⟨ believers and unbelievers. Let us strongly and closel⟨ insist upon inward and outward holiness in all it⟨ branches.

" *Quest.* 57. (39.) How shall we guard against for⟨ mality [in public worship ; particularly] in singing ?

" *Ans.* [1. By preaching frequently on the head 2. By taking care to speak only what we feel.] 1. (3.) B⟨

---

[1] " fed and bedded."—*Large Minutes.* The American preacheɾ of that day could not always find beds for themselves, much less fo their horses.

hoosing such hymns as are proper for the congrega-
on.   2. (4.) By not singing too much at once ; sel-
om more than five or six verses.   3. (5.) By suiting
ie tune to the words.   4. (6.) By often stopping short
nd asking the people, ' Now, do you know what you
aid last ?   Did you speak no more than you felt ?'

[" Is not this formality creeping in already by those complex
mes, which it is scarcely possible to sing with devotion ? Such
i, ' Praise the Lord, ye blessed ones :' such the long quavering
allelujah annexed to the morning song tune, which I defy any
ian living to sing devoutly.   The repeating the same words so
ften, (but especially while another repeats different words, the
orrid abuse which runs through the modern church music,) as
shocks all common sense, so it necessarily brings in dead
ormality, and has no more of religion in it than a Lancashire
ornpipe.   Besides, it is a flat contradiction to our Lord's com-
iand, ' Use not vain repetitions.' For what is a vain repetition,
' this is not ?   What end of devotion does it serve ?   Sing no
nthems.]

" 5. (7.) Do not suffer the people to sing too slow.
`his naturally tends to formality, and is brought in by
hem who have either very strong or very weak voices.
i. (8.) In every large society let them learn to sing ; and
et them always learn our own tunes first.   7. (9.) Let
he women constantly sing their parts alone.   Let no
nan sing with them, unless he understands the notes,
nd sings the bass, as it is pricked down in the *tune*-
ook.   8. (10.) Introduce no new tunes, till they are
erfect in the old.   [(11.) Let no organ be placed any-
vhere, till proposed in the conference.]   9. (12.) Re-
ommend our tune-book everywhere ; and if you can-
iot sing yourself, choose a person or two in each place
o pitch the tune for you.   10. (13.) Exhort every
ne in the congregation to sing, not one in ten only.
1. (14.) If a preacher be present, let no singer give
ut the words.   12. (15.) When they would teach a
une to the congregation, they must sing only the tenor.

[" After preaching, take a little lemonade, mild ale, or can-
ied orange-peel.   All spirituous liquors, at that time especially,
re deadly poison.]

" *Quest.* 58. (40.) Who is the assistant ?

" *Ans.* That preacher in each circuit who is appointed, from time to time, *to assist the superintendents i the*[1] charge of the societies and the other preacher therein.

"*Quest.* 59. (41.) How should an assistant be qua lified for his charge?

"*Ans.* By walking closely with God, and havin, his work greatly at heart; and by understanding an loving discipline, ours in particular;

["And by loving the Church of England, and resolving no to separate from it. Let this be well observed. I fear, whe the Methodists leave the Church, God will leave them. But i they are thrust out of it, they will be guiltless.*]

"*Quest.* 60. (42.) What is the business of an as sistant?

"*Ans.* 1. To see that the other preachers in his cir cuit behave well, and want nothing. 2. *To renew th tickets quarterly, and regulate the bands.*[2] 3. To tak in or put out of the society or the bands. 4. *To appoin all the stewards and leaders, and change them whe he sees it necessary.* 5. (4.) To keep watch-night and love-feasts. 6. (5.) To hold quarterly meetings, an therein diligently to inquire both into the temporal an spiritual state of each society. 7. (6.) To take care tha every society be duly supplied with books; particularl with 'Kempis,' 'Instructions for Children,' and th 'Primitive Physic,' which ought to be in every house [O why is not this regarded! (7.) To send from ever quarterly meeting a circumstantial account to Londo of every remarkable conversion and remarkable death. 8. To take exact lists of his societies, *and bring the to the conference.*[3] 9. *To send an account of his cir*

---

[1] "to take."—*Large Minutes.*

* This passage is found in the original Minutes for 1749. The fac that it was continued in an edition of the Large Minutes, which wa revised four years after the organization of the Methodist Episcopa Church, affords conclusive evidence that Mr. Wesley did not conside that the Methodists in America had *separated* from or *left* the Churol of England; but that the connection between them was providen tially *dissolved.* (See above, pp. 22–25.)

[2] "To visit the classes quarterly, regulate the bands, and delive tickets."—*Ib.* [3] "every quarter, and send them up to London."—*Ib*

cuit every half year to one of the superintendents.
10. (9.) To meet the married men and women, and
the single men and women, in the large societies once
a quarter. 11. (10.) To overlook the accounts of all
the stewards.

["*Quest.* (43.) Has the office of an assistant been well executed?

"*Ans.* No, not by half the assistants. 1. Who has sent me
word, whether the other preachers behave well or ill? 2. Who
has visited all the classes, and regulated the bands quarterly?
3. Love-feasts for the bands have been neglected : neither have
persons been duly taken in and put out of the bands. 4. The
societies are not half supplied with books ; not even with those
above mentioned. O exert yourselves in this! Be not weary!
Leave no stone unturned! 5. How few accounts have I had,
either of remarkable deaths, or remarkable conversions!
6. How few exact lists of the societies! 7. How few have met
the married and single persons once a quarter!]

"*Quest.* 61. (44.) Are there any other *directions*[1]
which you would give the assistants?

"*Ans.* Several. 1. Take a regular catalogue of
your societies, as they live in house-row. 2. Leave
your successor a particular account of the state of the
circuit. 3. See that every band leader has the rules
of the bands. 4. Vigorously, but calmly, enforce the
rules concerning needless ornaments, *and drams.*[2]
[Give no band ticket to any man or woman who does
not promise to leave them off.] 5. As soon as there are
four men or women believers in any place, put them into
a band. 6. Suffer no love-feast to last above an hour and
a half; [and instantly stop all breaking the cake with
one another.] 7. Warn all, from time to time, that
none are to remove from one society to another without a certificate from the assistant in these words : (else
he will not be received in other societies :) ' A. B., the
bearer, is a member of our society in C. : I believe he
has sufficient cause for removing.' [I beg every assistant to remember this.] 8. Everywhere recommend decency and cleanliness : [cleanliness is next to

---

[1] " advices."—*Large Minutes.*
[2] " drams, snuff, and tobacco."—*Ibid.*

godliness.]   9. *Read the rules of the society, with the aid of your helpers, once a year in every congregation, and once a quarter in every society.*

["(9.) Exhort all that were brought up in the Church, to continue therein.   Set the example yourself; and immediately change every plan that would hinder their being at church at least two Sundays in four.   Carefully avoid whatever has a tendency to separate men from the Church; and let all the servants in our preaching houses go to church once on Sunday at least.

"Is there not a cause?   Are we not unawares, by little and little, sliding into a separation from the Church?   O use every means to prevent this!   1. Exhort all our people to keep close to the Church and sacrament.   2. Warn them all against niceness in hearing—a prevailing evil.   3. Warn them also against despising the prayers of the Church.   4. Against calling our society, 'the Church.'   5. Against calling our preachers 'ministers;' our houses, 'meeting houses:' call them plain preaching houses or chapels.   6. Do not license them as dissenters.   The proper paper to be sent in at the assizes sessions, or bishop's court, is this: 'A. B. has set apart his house in C. for public worship, of which he desires a certificate. N. B. The justice does not license the house, but the act of parliament.   7. Do not license yourself till you are constrained and then, not as a dissenter, but a Methodist.   It is time enough when you are prosecuted to take the oaths.   And by so doing you are licensed.

"*Quest.* (45.) But are we not dissenters?

"*Ans.* No: although we call sinners to repentance in all places of God's dominion; and although we frequently use extemporary prayer, and unite together in a religious society; yet we are not dissenters in the only sense which our law acknowledges, namely, those who renounce the service of the Church We do not, we dare not, separate from it.   We are not seceders, nor do we bear any resemblance to them.   We set out upon quite opposite principles.   The seceders laid the very foundation of their work in judging and condemning others: we laid the foundation of our work in judging and condemning ourselves They begin everywhere with showing their hearers how fallen the Church and ministers are: we begin everywhere with showing our hearers how fallen they are themselves.   What they do in America, or what their Minutes say on this subject, is nothing to us.*   We will keep in the good old way.

---

* This sentence was obviously introduced into the **Large Minutes** subsequently to 1784, and seems to refer to the Minutes, or **Discipline**

"And never let us make light of going to church, either by word or deed. Remember Mr. Hook, a very eminent and a zealous Papist. When I asked him, 'Sir, what do you do for public worship here, where you have no Romish service?' he answered, 'Sir, I am so fully convinced it is the duty of every man to worship God in public, that I go to church every Sunday. If I cannot have such worship as I would, I will have such worship as I can.'

"But some may say, 'Our own service is public worship.' Yes; but not such as supersedes the Church service; it presupposes public prayer, like the sermons at the university. If it were designed to be instead of the Church service, it would be essentially defective; for it seldom has the four grand parts of public prayer, deprecation, petition, intercession, and thanksgiving.

"If the people put ours in the room of the Church service, we hurt them that stay with us, and ruin them that leave us; for then they will go nowhere, but lounge the sabbath away without any public worship at all.

"*Quest.* (46.) Nay, but is it not our duty to separate from the Church, considering the wickedness both of the clergy and the people?

"*Ans.* We conceive not: 1. Because both the priests and the people were full as wicked in the Jewish Church; and yet it was not the duty of the holy Israelites to separate from them. 2. Neither did our Lord command his disciples to separate from them; he rather commanded the contrary. 3. Hence it is clear that could not be the meaning of St. Paul's words: 'Come out from among them, and be ye separate.'

"*Quest.* (47.) But what reasons are there why we should not separate from the Church?

"*Ans.* Among others, those which were printed above twenty years ago, entitled, 'Reasons against a Separation from the Church of England.'

"We allow two exceptions: 1. If the parish minister be a notoriously wicked man. 2. If he preach Socinianism, Arianism, or any other essentially false doctrine.*]

"*Quest. 62. Are there any directions to be given the assistant concerning the decision of disputes among the people?*

"*Ans. On any dispute of importance, or difficult*

of 1789, (1787?) in which very strong language was used with reference to the condition of the Church of England. (See below, part i, chap. i, sec. 1; and above, pp. 22–25.)
    * See note, p. 39.

to be settled, let the assistant inquire into the circum
stances, and, having consulted the stewards and lead
ers, appoint referees, whose decision shall be final, and
the party expelled that refuses to abide by it : unless
there appear to the assistant some fraud or gross mis
take in the decision, in which case he shall appoin
new referees, for a rehearing of the cause, whose de
cision shall be absolutely final.

" *Quest.* 63. Are there any further directions need
ful for the preservation of good order among the
preachers ?

" *Ans.* In the absence of a superintendent, a tra
velling preacher or three leaders shall have power to
lodge a complaint against any preacher in their cir
cuit, whether elder, assistant, deacon, or helper, before
three neighbouring assistants ; who shall meet at an
appointed time, (proper notice being given to the par
ties,) hear, and decide the cause. And authority is
given them to change or suspend a preacher, if they
see it necessary, and to appoint another in his place
during the absence of the superintendents.

" *Quest.* 64. If there happen to be a vacancy in a
circuit by the death of a preacher, by his withdraw
ing himself from the work, or otherwise, in the
absence of a superintendent, who are to fill up the
vacancy ?

" *Ans.* Three neighbouring assistants, called and
assembled according to the preceding minute.

" *Quest.* 65. What shall we do with those members
of our society who wilfully and repeatedly neglect to
meet their class ?

" *Ans.* 1. Let the assistant or one of his helpers
visit them, wherever it is practicable, and explain to
them the consequence, if they continue to neglect,
namely, exclusion.

" 2. If they do not amend, let the assistant exclude
them in the society, informing it that they are laid
aside for a breach of our rules of Discipline, and not
for immoral conduct.

" *Quest.* 66. (48.) Do we sufficiently watch over ich other ?[1]

" *Ans. We do not.*[2] Should we not frequently ask ich other, Do you walk closely with God ? Have ou now fellowship with the Father and the Son ? t what hour do you rise ? Do you punctually ob-rve the morning and evening hour of retirement ? o you spend the day in the manner which *the con-erence advises ?*[3] Do you converse seriously, use-lly, and closely ? To be more particular : Do you se all the means of grace yourself, and enforce the se of them on all other persons ?

" They are either instituted or prudential :—

" I. The instituted are,

" 1. Prayer ; private, family, public ; consisting of eprecation, petition, intercession, and thanksgiving. o you use each of these ? Do you use private ayer every morning and evening ? if you can, at five the evening ; and the hour before or after morning eaching ? Do you forecast daily, wherever you are, ow to secure these hours ? Do you avow it every-here ? Do you ask everywhere, ' Have you family ayer?' Do you retire at five o'clock ?

" 2. Searching the Scriptures by,

" i. Reading : constantly, some part of every day ; gularly, all the Bible in order ; carefully, with *Mr. Vesley's*[4] Notes ; seriously, with prayer before and ter ; fruitfully, immediately practising what you arn there ?

" ii. Meditating : At set times ? by any rule ?

" iii. Hearing : Every morning ? carefully ; with ayer before, at, after ; immediately putting in prac-ce ? Have you a New Testament always about ou ?

" 3. The Lord's supper : Do you use this at every

---

[1] " our helpers."—*Large Minutes.*
[2] " We might consider those that are with us as our pupils ; into hose behaviour and studies we should inquire every day."—*Ib.*
[3] " we advise."—*Ib.*   [4] " the."—*Ib.*

opportunity? with solemn prayer before; with earnest and deliberate self-devotion?

" 4. Fasting: How do you fast every Friday?

" 5. Christian conference: Are you convinced how important and how difficult it is to ' order your conversation aright?'   Is it ' always in grace? seasoned with salt? meet to minister grace to the hearers?   Do not you converse too long at a time?   Is not an hour commonly enough?   Would it not be well always to have a determinate end in view; and to pray before and after it?

" II. Prudential means we may use either as common Christians, as Methodists, as preachers, or as assistants.

" 1. As common Christians.   What particular rules have you in order to grow in grace?   What arts of holy living?

" 2. As Methodists.   Do you never miss your class, or band?

" 3. As preachers.   Do you meet every society; also the leaders and bands, if any?

" 4. As assistants.   Have you throughly considered your office; and do you make a conscience of executing every part of it?

" These means may be used without fruit: but there are some means which cannot; namely, watching, denying ourselves, taking up our cross, exercise of the presence of God.

" 1. Do you steadily watch against the world, the devil, yourselves, your besetting sin?

" 2. Do you deny yourself every useless pleasure of sense, imagination, honour?   Are you temperate in all things? instance in food: do you use only that kind and that degree which is best both for your body and soul?   Do you see the necessity of this?   Do you eat no flesh suppers? no late suppers?   Do you eat no more at each meal than is necessary?   Are you no heavy or drowsy after dinner?   Do you use only that kind and that degree of drink which is best both for

our body and soul? Do you drink water? Why
ot? Did you ever? Why did you leave it off? If
ot for health, when will you begin again? to-day?
low often do you drink wine [or ale?] every day?
)o you want it?

"3. Wherein do you 'take up your cross daily?'
)o you cheerfully bear your cross (whatever is griev-
us to nature) as a gift of God, and labour to profit
1ereby?

"4. Do you endeavour to set God always before
ou; to see his eye continually fixed upon you?
Jever can you use these means but a blessing will
nsue. And the more you use them, the more will
ou grow in grace.

" *Quest.* 67. (49.) What can be done, in order to a
loser union of our helpers with each other?

"*Ans.* 1. Let them be deeply convinced of [the
rant there is of it at present, and] the absolute neces-
ity of it.

"2. Let them pray for a desire of union.

"3. Let them speak freely to each other.

"4. When they meet let them never part without
irayer.

"5. Let them beware how they despise each other's
jifts.

"6. Let them never speak slightingly of each other
n any kind.

"7. Let them defend one another's characters in
very thing, so far as consists with truth: and,

"8. Let them labour in honour each to prefer the
ther before himself.

" *Quest.* 68. (50.) How shall we try those who
hink they are moved by the Holy Ghost to preach?

"*Ans.* Inquire, 1. Do they know God as a pardon-
ig God? Have they the love of God abiding in
hem? Do they desire and seek nothing but God?
.nd are they holy in all manner of conversation?
!. Have they gifts (as well as grace) for the work?
lave they (in some tolerable degree) a clear, sound

understanding? Have they a right judgment in the
things of God? Have they a just conception of salvation by faith? And has God given them any degree
of utterance? Do they speak justly, readily, clearly?
3. Have they fruit? Are any truly convinced of sin,
and converted to God, by their preaching?

"As long as these three marks concur in any one,
we believe he is called of God to preach. These we
receive as sufficient proof that he is 'moved thereto
by the Holy Ghost.'

"*Quest.* 69. (51.) What method may we use in
receiving a new helper?

"*Ans.* A proper time for doing this is at a conference, after solemn fasting and prayer.

"Every person proposed *shall then be asked (with
any other questions which may be thought necessary by
the conference) the following,*[1] namely, Have you faith
in Christ? Are you 'going on to perfection?' Do you
expect to be 'perfected in love' in this life? Are you
groaning after it? Are you resolved to devote yourself wholly to God and to his work? Do you know
the Methodist plan? [Have you read the 'Plain Account?' the 'Appeals?'] Do you know the rules of
the society? of the bands? Do you keep them? Do
you take no [snuff, tobacco,] drams? Do you constantly attend the [church and] sacrament? Have you
read the 'Minutes of the Conference?' Are you willing to conform to them? Have you considered the
rules of a helper; especially the first, tenth, and
twelfth? Will you keep them for conscience' sake?
Are you determined to employ all your time in the work
of God? Will you preach every morning *at five o'clock
wherever you can have twenty hearers? Will you
endeavour*[2] not to speak too long or too loud? Will
you diligently instruct the children in every place?
Will you visit from house to house? Will you recom-

---

[1] "is then to be present; and each of them may be asked."—
Large Minutes.
[2] " and evening; endeavouring."—*Ib.*

mend fasting, both by precept and example ?   Are you
in debt ?

["Are you engaged to marry ?

"N. B. A preacher who marries while on trial is thereby
set aside.]

"We may then, *if he gives satisfaction,* receive him
as a probationer, by giving him the 'Minutes of the
Conference,' inscribed thus :—

" 'TO A. B.

" 'You think it your duty to call sinners to repent
ance.   Make full proof hereof, and we shall rejoice to
receive you as a fellow-labourer.'

"Let him then read and carefully weigh what is
contained therein, that if he has any doubt it may be
removed.

"Observe : taking on trial is entirely different from
admitting a preacher.   One on trial may be either admitted or rejected, without doing him any wrong,
otherwise it would be no trial at all.   Let every assistant explain this to them that are on trial.

"*After two years' probation, being recommended
by the assistant, and examined by the conference,*[1] he
may be received into full connection, by giving him
the 'Minutes,' inscribed thus :—'As long as you freely
consent to, and earnestly endeavour to walk by, these
rules, we shall rejoice to acknowledge you as a fellow-
labourer.'   Meantime, let none *preach or* exhort in any
of our societies, without a note of permission from the
assistant.   Let every *preacher or* exhorter take care
to have this renewed yearly ; and let every assistant
insist upon it.

"*Quest.* 70. (52.) What is the method wherein we
usually proceed in our conferences ?

"*Ans.* We inquire, 1. What preachers are admitted ?
Who remain on trial ?   Who are admitted on trial ?
Who desist from travelling ?

---

[1] "When he has been on trial four years, if recommended by the
assistant."—*Large Minutes.*

" 2. Are there any objections to any of the preach
ers ? who are named one by one.

" 3. How are the preachers stationed this year ?

" 4. What numbers are in the society ?

[" (5.) What is the Kingswood collection ?

" (6.) What boys are received this year ?

" (7.) What girls are assisted ?]

" 5. (8.) What was contributed for the contingen
expenses?

" 6. (9.) How was this expended ?

" 7. (10.) What is contributed toward the fund fo:
*the superannuated preachers and the widows anc
orphans of the preachers* ?[1]

" 8. (11.) What demands are there upon it ?

" 9. (12.) How many preachers' wives are to be provided for ? By what *circuits and in what proportion ?'*

" 10. (13.) Where and when may our next conference begin ?

" *Quest.* 71. *What provision can we make for c
proper supply of preachers in the circuits during the
sitting of the conference ?*

" *Ans. Let as many local preachers as are necessary
be provided by the assistant in every circuit, as far as
possible ; and let them be paid in proportion to their
work as travelling preachers out of the yearly collection.*

" *Quest.* 72. (53.) How can we provide for *superannuated preachers and the widows and orphans of
preachers* ?[3]

" *Ans.* [Those who can preach four or five times a week are
supernumerary preachers. As for those who cannot,] .

" 1. Let every travelling preacher contribute *two
dollars*[4] yearly at the conference.

" 2. Let every one when first admitted as a travelling
preacher pay *twenty shillings (Pennsylvania currency.*[5])

---

[1] " superannuated and supernumerary preachers."—*Large Minutes.*
[2] " societies."—*Ib.*
[3] " superannuated and supernumerary preachers."—*Ib.*
[4] " half a guinea."—*Ib.*   [5] " a guinea."—*Ib.*

" 3. Let this *money* be lodged in the hands of the treasurers.[1]

[" 4. The present stewards are John Murlin and John Pawson.]

" 4. *Let there be three treasurers ; three clerks, each of whom shall keep a separate account ; and three inspectors, who shall annually lay before the conference an exact state of the fund.*

" 5. *Let these nine form a committee for the management of the fund. Three of whom shall be competent to proceed on any business, provided one be a treasurer, another an inspector, and a third a clerk.*

" 6. (5.) Out of this *fund* let provision be made, first for the worn-out preachers, and then for the widows and children of those that are dead.

" 7. (6.) Every worn-out preacher shall receive, if he wants it, *twenty-four pounds a year,* (*Pennsylvania currency.[2]*)

" 8. (7.) Every widow of a preacher shall receive, yearly, if she wants it, during her widowhood, *twenty pounds.[3]*

" 9. (8.) Every child *of[4]* a preacher shall receive, once for all, *if he wants it, twenty pounds.[5]*

" 10. (9.) But none *shall be[6]* entitled to any thing from this fund, till he has *paid fifty shillings.[7]*

" 11. (10.) Nor any who neglects paying his subscription for *three[8]* years together, *unless he be sent by the conference out of these United States.*

[" (11.) Let every preacher who does not bring or send his subscription to the conference, be fined two shillings and sixpence.]

" 12. Let the fund never be reduced to less than a hundred pounds.

[" (13.) Let a committee be named to see these rules duly executed. The present committee are,—Christopher Hopper,

---

" stewards."—*Large Minutes.*
least ten pounds a year."—*Ib.*
n not usually exceeding ten pounds."—*Ib.*
.."—*Ib.* [6] " a sum not usually exceeding ten pounds."—*Ib.*
-*Ib.* [7] " subscribed two guineas."—*Ib.*
"—*Ib.*

Thomas Coke, Thomas Hanby, John Allen, Robert Roberts
Henry Moore, Thomas Taylor, William Thompson, Andrew Blair.

"(14.) Let an exact account of all receipts and disbursements
be produced at the conference.]

"13. (15.) Let every assistant *as far as possible*
bring to the conference the contribution of every preacher
left behind in his circuit.

[" *Quest.* (54.) Are not many of the preachers' wives still straitened for the necessaries of life ?

"*Ans.* Some certainly have been.   To prevent this for the
time to come, 1. Let every circuit either provide each with a
lodging, coals, and candles, or allow her fifteen pounds a year
2. Let the assistant take this money at the quarterly meeting
before any thing else be paid out of it.   Fail not to do this.

" *Quest.* (55.) How can we account for the decrease of the
work of God in some circuits, both this year and the last ?

"*Ans.* It may be owing either, 1. To the want of zeal and
exactness in the assistant, occasioning want of discipline throughout : or 2. To want of life and diligence in the preachers : or
3. To our people's losing the life of God, and sinking into the
spirit of the world.

" It may be owing, farther, to the want of more field preaching
and of trying more new places.]

" *Quest.* 73. (56.) What can be done in order to revive the work of God where it is decayed ?

"*Ans.* [1. Let every preacher read carefully over the ' Life
of David Brainerd.'   Let us be followers of him, as he was of
Christ, in absolute self-devotion, in total deadness to the world
and in fervent love to God and man.   Let us but secure this
point, and the world and the devil must fall under our feet.]

" 1. (2.) Let both assistants and preachers be conscientiously exact in the whole Methodist discipline.

" 2. (3.) See that no circuit be at any time without
preachers.   Therefore let no preacher, who does not
attend the conference, leave the circuit, at that time
on any pretence whatever.   This is the most improper
time in the whole year.   Let every assistant see to
this, and require each of these to remain in the circuit
till the new preachers come.

" Let not all the preachers in any circuit come to
the conference.

" Let those who do come, set out as late and return
as soon as possible.

"3. (4.) Wherever you can, appoint prayer meetings, and particularly on Friday.

"4. (5.) Let a fast be *published at every quarterly meeting for the Friday following. And let a memorandum of it be written on all the class papers.*[1]

"5. (6.) Be [more] active in dispersing *Mr. Wesley's*[2] books, [particularly the sermon on 'The Good Steward,' on 'Indwelling Sin,' 'The Repentance of Believers,' and 'The Scripture Way of Salvation.'] Every assistant [may give away small tracts: and he] may beg money of the rich to buy books for the poor.

"6. (7.) Strongly and explicitly exhort all believers to 'go on to perfection.' That we may 'all speak the same thing,' *we*[3] ask, once for all, Shall we defend this perfection, or give it up? *we*[4] all agree to defend it, meaning thereby, (as we did from the beginning,) salvation from all sin, by the love of God and man filling our heart. The Papists say, 'This cannot be attained, till we have been refined by the fire of purgatory.' The Calvinists say, 'Nay, it will be attained as soon as the soul and body part.' The old Methodists say, 'It may be attained before we die: a moment after is too late.' Is it so or not? *We*[5] are all agreed, we may be saved from all sin before death. The substance then is settled; but, as to the circumstance, is the change gradual or instantaneous? It is both the one and the other.

[" From the moment we are justified, there may be a gradual sanctification, a growing in grace, a daily advance in the knowledge and love of God. And if sin cease before death, there must, in the nature of the thing, be an instantaneous change; there must be a last moment wherein it does exist, and a first moment wherein it does not.]

"' But should we in preaching insist both on one and the other?' Certainly we must insist on the gradual

---

[1] " observed in all our societies, the last Friday in August, November, February, and May."—*Large Minutes.*
[2] " the."—*Ib.*
[3] " I."—*Ib.*   [4] " You."—*Ib.*   [5] " You."—*Ib.*

change ; and that earnestly and continually. And are
there not reasons why we should insist on the instantaneous also ?   If there be such a blessed change before death, should we not encourage all believers to
expect it ? and the rather, because constant experience
shows, the more earnestly they expect this, the more
swiftly and steadily does the gradual work of God go
on in their souls ; the more watchful they are against all
sin, the more careful to grow in grace, the more zealous of good works, and the more punctual in their attendance on all the ordinances of God.   Whereas, just
the contrary effects are observed whenever this expect-
ation ceases.   They are ' saved by hope,' by this hope
of a total change, with a gradually increasing salvation.
Destroy this hope, and that salvation stands still, or
rather, decreases daily.   Therefore whoever would advance the gradual change in believers, should strongly
insist on the instantaneous.

[" *Quest.* (57.) What can be done to increase the work of God
in Scotland ?

" *Ans.* 1. Preach abroad as much as possible.   2. Try every
town and village.   3. Visit every member of the society at
home.

" *Quest.* (58.) How many circuits are there now ?

" *Ans.* Of America we have no late account.   There are
seventy-four circuits in England, Wales, and the Isle of Man,
seven in Scotland, and twenty-eight in Ireland.

" *Quest* (59.) Are our preaching houses safe ?

" *Ans.* Not all ; for some of them are not settled on trustees.
Several of the trustees for others are dead.

" *Quest.* (60.) What then is to be done ?

" *Ans.* 1. Let those who have debts on any of the houses
give a bond, to settle them as soon as they are indemnified.
2. Let the surviving trustees choose others without delay, by
endorsing their deed thus :—

" ' WE, the remaining trustees of the Methodist preaching
house in ——, do, according to the power vested in us by this
deed, choose —— to be trustees of the said house, in the place
of ——.

' Witness our hands ——.'

" N. B. The deed must have three new stamps, and must be
enrolled in chancery within six months.

" *Quest.* (61.) In what form may a house be settled ?

"*Ans.* In the following, which was drawn by three of the most eminent lawyers in London. Whoever therefore objects to it only betrays his own ignorance.

" 'The Indenture made ——— ———, between Benjamin Heap of ———, in the county of ———, on the one part, and Thomas Philips, hatter, &c., on the other part, WITNESSETH, That in consideration of five shillings, lawful money of Great Britain, by the said T. P., &c, to the said B. H., truly paid, before the sealing and delivering hereof, (the receipt whereof the said B. H. doth hereby acknowledge,) and for divers other considerations him thereunto moving, the said B. H. hath granted, bargained, and sold, and by these presents doth bargain and sell unto the said T. P., &c, their heirs and assigns for ever, all that lately erected house or tenement, with the yard thereunto adjoining, situate ———, in ———, aforesaid, now in the tenure or occupation of ———, together with all the ways, drains, and privileges to the said premises appertaining, and all the profits thereof, with all the right, title, and interest in law and equity : To HAVE AND TO HOLD, the said house, yard, and other premises, to the said T. P., &c., their heirs and assigns for ever. NEVERTHELESS, upon special trust and confidence, and to the intent that they and the survivors of them, and the trustees for the time being, do, and shall permit John Wesley, of the City Road, London, clerk, and such other persons as he shall from time to time appoint, at all times, during his natural life, and no other persons, to have and enjoy the free use and benefit of the said premises ; that the said John Wesley, and such other persons as he appoints, may therein preach and expound God's holy word. And after his decease, upon farther trust and confidence, and to the intent, that the said T. P., &c., or the major part of them, or the survivors of them, and the major part of the trustees of the said premises for the time being, shall, from time to time, and at all times for ever, permit such persons as shall be appointed at the yearly conference of the people called Methodists, in London, Bristol, Leeds, Manchester, or elsewhere, specified by name in a deed enrolled in chancery, under the hand and seal of the said John Wesley, and bearing date the 28th day of February, 1784, and no others, to have and to enjoy the said premises, for the purposes aforesaid : provided always, that the persons preach no other doctrine than is contained in Mr. Wesley's ' Notes upon the New Testament,' and four volumes of ' Sermons.' And upon farther trust and confidence, that, as often as any of these trustees, or the trustees for the time being, shall die, or cease to be a member of the society commonly called Methodists, the rest of the said trustees, or of the trustees for the time being, as soon as conveniently may be, shall and may choose another trustee or trustees, in order to keep up the number of ——— trustees for ever.

In witness whereof the said B. H. hath hereunto set his hand and seal, the day and year above written.'

" In this form the proprietors of the house are to make it over to five, seven, or nine trustees.

" *Quest.* (62.) But is this form asafe one ? Should we not have the opinion of counsel upon it ?

" *Ans.* I think this would be throwing money away ; 1. Because this form was drawn up by three eminent counsellors : But, 2. It is the way of almost every lawyer to blame what another has done. Therefore, you cannot at all infer, that they think a thing wrong, because they say so. 3. If they did in reality think it wrong, this would not prove it was so. 4. If there was (which I do not believe) some defect therein, who would go to law with the body of Methodists ? But, 5. If they did, would any court in England put them out of possession ; especially when the intent of the deed was plain and undeniable ?

" *Quest.* 74. (63.) Is any thing [farther] advisable with regard to building ?

" *Ans.* [1. Build all preaching houses, where the ground will permit, in the octagon form. It is best for the voice, and, on many accounts, more commodious than any other. 2. Why should not any octagon house be built after the model of Yarm ? any square house after the model of Bath or Scarborough ? Can we find any better model ? 3. Let the roof rise only one-third of its breadth : this is the true proportion. 4. Have doors and windows enough ; and let all the windows be sashes, opening downward. 5. Let there be no Chinese paling, and no tub pulpit, but a square projection with a long seat behind. 6. Let there be no pews, and no backs to the seats, which should have aisles on each side, and be parted in the middle by a rail running all along, to divide the men from the women ; just as at Bath.]

" (7.) Let all *our chapels*[1] be built plain and decent ; but not more expensive than is absolutely unavoidable : otherwise the necessity of raising money will make rich men necessary to us. But if so, we must be dependant upon them, yea, and governed by them. And then farewell to the Methodist discipline, if not doctrine too.

[" (8.) Wherever a preaching house is built, see that lodgings for the preachers be built also.]

" *Quest.* 75. (64.) Is there any exception to the rule ' Let the men and women sit apart ?'

---

[1] " the preaching houses."—*Large Minutes.*

"*Ans. There is no exception.   Let them sit apart
n all our chapels.*¹

["*Quest.* (65.) But how can we secure their sitting apart there ?
"*Ans.* I must do it myself.   If I come into any new house,
nd see the men and women together, I will immediately go out.
hereby give public notice of this : pray let it be observed.]

" *Quest.* 76. (66.) But there is not a worse indecency
han this [creeping in among us]—talking in the *chapels*²
efore and after service.   How shall this be cured ?

"*Ans.* Let all the *ministers and* preachers join as
ne man, and [the very next Sunday they preach in
ny place] enlarge on the impropriety of talking before
r after service, and strongly exhort them to do it no
nore.   In three months, if we are in earnest, this vile
ractice will be banished out of every Methodist con-
regation.   Let none stop till he has carried his point.

["*Quest.* (67.) Is there not another shocking indecency fre-
uently practised by filthy men against the wall of a preaching
ouse ; enough to make any modest woman blush !

"*Ans.* There is : but I beg any one who sees another do this
vill give him a hearty clap on the back.

" *Quest.* (68.) Complaint has been made that sluts spoil our
ouses.   How may we prevent this ?

" *Ans.* Let none that has spoiled one, ever live in another. But
vhat a shame is this !   A preacher's wife should be a pattern of
leanliness, in her person, clothes, and habitation.   Let nothing
latternly be seen about her ; no rags, no dirt, no litter.   And she
hould be a pattern of industry ; always at work, either for her-
elf, her husband, or the poor.   I am not willing any should live
n the orphan house at Newcastle, or any preaching house, who
oes not conform to this rule.

" *Quest.* (69.) It has been complained also, that people crowd
nto the preachers' houses, as into coffee houses, without any in-
itation.   Is this right ?

"ˡAns. It is utterly wrong.   Stop it at once.   Let no person
ome into the preacher's house, unless he wants to ask a ques-
ion ?

" *Quest.* (70.) May any new preaching houses be built ?
" *Ans.* Not unless, 1. They are proposed at the conference.
No, nor 2. Unless two-thirds of the expense be subscribed.

¹ " In those galleries where they have always sat together, they
nay do so still.   But let them sit apart everywhere below, and in all
ew erected galleries."—*Large Minutes.*
² " preaching houses."—*Ib.*

And if any collection be made for them, it must be made between the conference and the beginning of February.

"*Quest.* (71.) What can be done to make the Methodists sensible of the excellency of Kingswood school?

"*Ans.* Let every assistant read the following account of it yearly in every congregation:—

"1. The wisdom and love of God have now thrust out a large number of labourers into his harvest; men who desire nothing on earth but to promote the glory of God, by saving their own souls and those that hear them. And those to whom they minister spiritual things are willing to minister to them of their carnal things; so that they 'have food to eat, and raiment to put on,' and are content therewith.

"2. A competent provision is likewise made for the wives of married preachers. These also lack nothing, having a weekly allowance over and above for their little children; so that neither they nor their husbands need to be 'careful about many things,' but may 'wait upon the Lord without distraction.'

"3. Yet one considerable difficulty lies on those that have boys, when they grow too big to be under their mother's direction. Having no father to govern and instruct them, they are exposed to a thousand temptations. To remedy this we have a school on purpose for them, wherein they have all the instruction they are capable of, together with all things necessary for the body, clothes only excepted. And it may be, if God prosper this labour of love, they will have these too, shortly.

"4. In whatever view we look upon this, it is one of the noblest charities that can be conceived. How reasonable is the institution! Is it fit that the children of those who leave wife and all that is dear, to save souls from death, should want what is needful either for soul or body? Ought not we to supply what the parent cannot, because of his labours in the gospel? How excellent are the effects of this institution! The preacher eased of this weight, can the more cheerfully go on in his labour. And perhaps many of these children may hereafter fill up the place of those that shall 'rest from their labours.'

"5. It is not strange, therefore, considering the excellence of this design, that Satan should have taken much pains to defeat it, particularly by lies of every kind, which were plentifully invented and handed about for several years. But truth now generally prevails, and its adversaries are put to silence. It is well known that the children want nothing; that they scarce know what sickness means; that they are well instructed in whatever they are capable of learning; that they are carefully and tenderly governed; and that the behaviour of all in the house elder and younger, is 'as becometh the gospel of Christ.'

4

he beginning of February.

hat can be done to make the Methodists
lency of Kingswood school?

assistant read the following account of it
regation :—

and love of God have now thrust out a large
into his harvest ; men who desire nothing
note the glory of God, by saving their own
near them.   And those to whom they minis-
e willing to minister to them of their carnal
' have food to eat, and raiment to put on,'
with.

provision is likewise made for the wives
s.   These also lack nothing, having a
er and above for their little children ;
nor their husbands need to be 'careful
ut may 'wait upon the Lord without dis-

derable difficulty lies on those that have
too big to be under their mother's direc-
er to govern and instruct them, they are
temptations.   To remedy this we have a
them, wherein they have all the instruc-
of, together with all things necessary for
excepted.   And it may be, if God prosper
ey will have these too, shortly.
iew we look upon this, it is one of the
an be conceived.   How reasonable is the
at the children of those who leave wife,
save souls from death. should want what
soul or body ?   Ought not we to supply
t, because of his labours in the gospel ?
effects of this institution !   The preacher,
an the more cheerfully go on in his labour.
these children may hereafter fill up the
ll 'rest from their labours.'
e, therefore, considering the excellence of
a should have taken much pains to defeat
s of every kind, which were plentifully in-
out for several years.   But truth now ge-
its adversaries are put to silence.   It is
children want nothing ; that they scarce
means ; that they are well instructed in
apable of learning ; that they are carefully
d ; and that the behaviour of all in the house,
s 'as becometh the gospel of Christ.'

4

" 6. But the expense of such an undertaking is very large, so that we are ill able to defray it.   The best means we could think of at our conference to supply the deficiency, is, once a year to desire the assistance of all those in every place who wish well to the work of God ; who long to see sinners converted to God, and the kingdom of Christ set up in all the earth.

" 7. All of you who are thus minded have an opportunity now of showing your love to the gospel.   Now promote, as far as in you lies, one of the noblest charities in the world.   Now forward, as you are able, one of the most excellent designs that ever was set on foot in this kingdom.   Do what you can to comfort the parents who give up their all for you, and to give their children cause to bless you.   You will be no poorer for what you do on such an occasion.   God is a good paymaster.   And you know, in doing this, you lend unto the Lord.   In due time he shall pay you again.

" *Quest.* (72.) But how can we keep out of debt ?

" *Ans.* Let a collection be made for this school, the Sunday before or after midsummer, in every preaching house, great and small, throughout England, Scotland, and Ireland.]

" *Quest. 77.* (73.) How may we raise a general fund for carrying on the whole work of God ?

" *Ans. By a yearly collection, and if need be a quarterly one, to be raised by every assistant in every principal congregation in his circuit.*[1]

" To this end he may then read and enlarge upon the following hints in every *such congregation :*[2]—

" (1.) How shall we send labourers into those parts where they are most of all wanted ? [suppose the north-west of Ireland, and the north of Scotland.]   Many are willing to hear, but not to bear the expense.   Nor can it as yet be expected of them : stay till the word of God has touched their hearts, and then they will gladly provide for them that preach it.   Does it not lie upon us, in the mean time, to supply their lack of service ? to raise a general fund, out of which, from time to time, that expense may be defrayed ?   By this means, those who willingly offer themselves may travel through every

---

[1] " By a yearly subscription to be proposed by every assistant when he visits the classes at Christmas, and received at the visitation following."—*Large Minutes.*
[2] " society."—*Ib.*

part, *whether there are societies or not,*[1] and stay
wherever there is a call, without being burdensome to
any. Thus may the gospel, in the life and power
thereof, be spread from sea to sea. Which of you will
not rejoice to throw in your mite to promote this glorious work?

"(2.) Besides this, in carrying on so large a work
through the *continent,*[2] there are calls for money in various ways, and we must frequently be at considerable expense, or the work must be at a full stop.
Many too are the occasional distresses of our preachers
or their families, which require an immediate supply
Otherwise their hands would hang down, if they were
not constrained to depart from the work.

["(3.) Let then every member of our society once a year set
his shoulder to the work; contributing more or less, as God hath
prospered him, at the Lady-day visitation of the classes. Let
none be excluded from giving something,—be it a penny, a half-
penny, a farthing. Remember the widow's two mites! And let
those who are able to give shillings, crowns, and pounds, do it
willingly.]

"The money contributed will be brought to the ensuing conference.

"(4.) Men and brethren, help! Was there ever a call
like this, since you first heard the gospel sound? Help
to relieve your companions in the kingdom of Jesus,
who are pressed above measure.

"'Bear ye one another's burdens, and so fulfil the
law of Christ.' Help to send forth able, willing labourers into your Lord's harvest: so shall ye be assistant in saving souls from death, and hiding a multitude
of sins. Help to spread the gospel of your salvation
into the remotest corners of the *earth,*[3] till 'the
knowledge of our Lord shall cover the land, as the
waters cover the sea.' So shall it appear to ourselves,
and all men, that we are indeed one body, united by one

[1] This clause is in the original Minutes of 1749, but not in the
Large Minutes.
[2] "three kingdoms."—*Large Minutes.*
[3] "kingdom."—*Ib.*

spirit; so shall the baptized heathens be yet again constrained to say, 'See how these Christians love one another!'

["In this, may not even the Romanists provoke us to jealousy? They have a general fund at Rome, and another at Paris, which bears all the expenses of their missionaries throughout the world.]

"*Quest.* 78. *What can be done towards erecting new chapels, and discharging the debts on those already built?*

"*Ans. Let every assistant raise a yearly subscription through his circuit: and let every member who is not supported by charity, give something. Let them subscribe the first quarter, and pay the second. And let the money be applied where it is most wanted, by a committee of lay-members annually appointed by the assistant, one of whom shall be chosen out of each society concerned.*

"*Quest.* 79. *Is it not right that the assistant, and not the stewards or leaders, should receive the quarterly collections in the classes?*

"*Ans. Certainly it is. This has been the general practice among the Methodists in Europe. And therefore let every assistant look to it, and ask every person, who can afford it, for his quarterly subscription, when he changes the tickets; and in due time let him deliver the whole into the hands of the stewards, to carry on the work of God in the circuit.*

["*Quest.* (74.) What is the direct antidote to Methodism, the doctrine of heart holiness?

"*Ans.* Calvinism: all the devices of Satan, for these fifty years, have done far less toward stopping this work of God, than that single doctrine. It strikes at the root of salvation from sin, previous to glory, putting the matter on quite another issue.

"*Quest.* (75.) But wherein lie the charms of this doctrine? What makes men swallow it so greedily?

"*Ans.* 1. It seems to magnify Christ; although in reality it supposes him to have died in vain. For the absolutely elect must have been saved without him; and the non-elect cannot be saved by him.

"2. It is highly pleasing to flesh and blood, final perseverance in particular.]

"*Quest.* 80. (76.) What can be done to guard against Antinomianism?[1]

"*Ans.* 1. Let all our preachers carefully read over *Mr. Wesley's*[2] and *Mr.* Fletcher's tracts.

"2. Let them frequently and explicitly preach the truth, though not in a controversial way. But let them take care to do it in love and gentleness; not in bitterness, not returning railing for railing.

["Let those who preach it have all this to themselves.

"3. Do not imitate them in screaming, allegorizing, boasting; rather mildly expose these things when time serves.

"4. Imitate them in this: they readily seize upon any one that is newly convinced or converted. Be diligent to prevent them, and to guard those tender minds against the predestinarian poison.]

"3. (5.) Answer all *the objections of our people,*[3] as occasion offers, [both in public and private.] But take care to do this with all possible sweetness both of look and of accent.

["(6.) Very frequently, both in public and private, advise our people not to hear them.

"(7.) Make it a matter of constant and earnest prayer, that God would stop the plague.]

"*Quest.* 81. (77.) *Wherein lies our danger of it.*[4]

"*Ans.* 1. With regard to man's faithfulness. Our Lord himself taught us to use the expression: therefore we ought never to be ashamed of it. We ought steadily to assert upon his authority, that if a man is not 'faithful in the unrighteous mammon, God will not give him the true riches.'

"2. With regard to 'working for life,' which our Lord expressly commands us to do. 'Labour,' εργαζεσθε, literally, 'work, for the meat that endureth to everlasting life.' And in fact, every believer, till he comes to glory, works for as well as from life.

"3. We have received it as a maxim, that 'a man is to do nothing in order to justification.' Nothing can

---

[1] "it."—*Large Minutes.*   [3] "ours."—*Ib.*
[2] "their objections."—*Ib.*
[4] "*Quest.* (77.) We said in 1744, 'We have leaned too much toward Calvinism.' Wherein?"—*Ib.*

ie more false.   Whoever desires to find favour with
3od should 'cease from evil, and learn to do well.'
3o God himself teaches by the prophet Isaiah.   Who-
ver repents, should 'do works meet for repentance.'
And if this is not in order to find favour, what does he
lo them for?

"Once more review the whole affair :

" 1. Who of us is now accepted of God ?

" He that now believes in Christ with a loving, obe-
lient heart.

" 2. But who among those that never heard of
Christ ?

" He that, according to the light he has, 'feareth
3od and worketh righteousness.'

" 3. Is this the same with ' he that is sincere ?'

" Nearly, if not quite.

" 4. Is not this salvation by works?

" Not by the merit of works, but by works as a
ondition.

[" (5.) What have we then been disputing about for these
hirty years?

" I am afraid about words, namely, in some of the foregoing
nstances.

" (6.) As to merit itself, of which we have been so dreadfully
ifraid : we are rewarded according to our works, yea, because
if our works.   How does this differ from, 'for the sake of our
vorks?'   And how differs this from *secundum merita operum?*
vhich is no more than, 'as our works deserve.'   Can you split
his hair?   I doubt I cannot.]

" 5. (7.) The grand objection to one of the preceding
propositions is drawn from matter of fact.   God does
n fact justify those who, by their own confession,
ieither ' feared God' nor ' wrought righteousness.'   Is
his an exception to the general rule ?

" It is a doubt whether God makes any exception
it all.   But how are we sure that the person in ques-
ion never did fear God and work righteousness?   His
>wn thinking so is no proof.   For we know how all
hat are convinced of sin undervalue themselves in
very respect.

" 6. (8.) Does not talking, without proper caution, of

a justified or sanctified state, tend to mislead men ; almost naturally leading them to trust in what was done in one moment ?   Whereas we are every moment pleasing or displeasing to God, according to our works; according to the whole of our present inward tempers and outward behaviour."

While the number of preachers in America was small, there was but one conference held in the year. By 1779, however, they had increased so as to render it inconvenient to meet in one place.   From that time, therefore, till 1784, two conferences, in reality, were held annually, though the second was considered as an adjournment of the first.   Their respective powers are thus stated by the Rev. Jesse Lee :—" As the conference in the north was of the longest standing, and withal composed of the oldest preachers, it was allowed greater privileges than that in the south ; especially in making rules, and forming regulations for the societies. Accordingly, when any thing was agreed to in the Virginia Conference, and afterward disapproved of in the Baltimore Conference, it was dropped.   But if any rule was fixed and determined on at the Baltimore Conference, the preachers in the south were under the necessity of abiding by it.   The southern conference was considered at that time as a convenience, and designed to accommodate the preachers in that part of the work, and to do all the business of a regular conference, except that of making or altering particular rules."*

The Christmas Conference, at which the church was organized, was, as already stated, a General Conference.   None such was held again until November, 1792.   The alterations of the Discipline, therefore, during that interval, seem to have been made in the same informal manner as prior to 1784 :—Bishop Asbury submitting the proposed amendments to the annual

---

* History of the Methodists, pp. 78, 79.

conferences, in succession ; and, when adopted, publishing them, either in the Annual Minutes, (which were printed regularly after 1784,) or in new editions of the General Minutes or Discipline.

1785. At the annual conferences for 1785, it was concluded that the rule on slavery, adopted at the Christmas Conference, would do harm. It was, therefore, resolved to suspend its execution for the present,[*] and a note to that effect[†] was added to the Annual Minutes for that year. The conferences, however, still expressed "the deepest abhorrence" of "the practice," and a determination "to seek its destruction by all wise and prudent means."

1786. The first edition of the Discipline was printed in Philadelphia, in 1785, and is found bound up with "the Sunday Service," and "the Collection of Psalms and Hymns" which had been sent over to America in sheets."[‡] In 1786 a new edition of the whole, in one book, was printed in London. In this the following questions of the first edition, with their answers, are omitted, namely : Quest. 23. (Of preachers' drinking spirituous liquors ;) Quest. 42. (Of extirpating slavery ;) Quest. 63. (Of the trial of travelling preachers ;) and Quest. 64. (Of supplying vacancies on circuits.)

This appears to have been the last edition of "the Sunday Service" for the use of the Methodists in America. The General Minutes, or Discipline proper, were published, the next year, in a separate pamphlet; the Articles of Religion, and the Forms for administering the sacraments, for solemnizing matrimony, for burying the dead, and for ordinations, were subsequently incorporated into the Discipline ; and "the

---

[*] See Lee's History of the Methodists, p. 102.
[†] For the note, see below, part ii, sec. 10.
[‡] "Defence of our Fathers," sec. 8.

Collection of Psalms and Hymns" has been trans
formed into the present Hymn-book ; but the Sunda\
Service proper was laid aside soon after its introduc
tion, forms of prayer for public worship not bein(
popular with the church in America.

1787. In 1787 the Discipline underwent an entir
change in its form. It will have been perceived, tha
the first and second editions consisted of a series o!
questions and answers, arranged with very little me
thod. The book was now divided into sections, wit!
appropriate heads. This appears to have been done
almost entirely, by Bishop Asbury, with the aid of th(
Rev. John Dickins ; though the work was, no doubt
revised, before publication, by Dr. Coke.   In the latte
part of the year 1785, while Bishop Asbury was con
fined, with a swollen foot, at James' City, in Vir
ginia, he writes, under date of November 27 : " Fo
some time past I had not been quite satisfied with th(
order and arrangement of our Form of Discipline ; and
persuaded that it migh. be improved without difficulty
we accordingly set about it, and, during my confine
ment in James' City, completed the work, arrangin(
the subject matter thereof under their proper heads
divisions, and sections."*   That the " we," in this ex
tract, refers to the Rev. John Dickins, may be infer
red from the fact that he was then stationed in tha
part of the country, and from the following entry i!
Bishop Asbury's Journal, under date of April 25
1786 : " Read our Form of Discipline in manuscript
which brother Dickins has been preparing for th(
press."†

The publication of this revised Discipline was delayec
until May, 1787, probably with a view of obtainin(
the concurrence of Dr. Coke, who made his secon(
visit to America in March of that year.

The author has not been able to obtain a copy o!

---

* Journal, vol. i, p. 391.   † Ibid., p. 396.

4*

this edition, and, as it was published in pamphlet form, it is likely that none is extant. Its loss, however, is the less to be regretted, since by the aid of Lee's History of the Methodists, and the Discipline of 1789, we are enabled to arrive at a pretty accurate knowledge of its contents. We learn, from the former,* that it contained thirty-one sections, embracing sixty-three questions ; and that its last, or thirty-first section, corresponded with the thirty-first section of the Discipline of 1789.† It is also known that the latter contained four additional sections, embracing six questions ; and that two of these were the thirty-first section, (Of the trial of members,) and the thirty-second, (Of the trial of ministers.)‡ It is probable, therefore, that the other two were the thirty-fourth (Of stewards) and the thirty-fifth, (The General Rules) :—a conclusion which is further confirmed by the fact, that these four sections embrace precisely six questions. If these inferences be correct, then the Discipline of 1787 was substantially the same as the first thirty-one sections of that of 1789, and all the alterations in those sections which are assigned in this work to the latter year, may have been made in the former, but they are not referred to 1787, because the author is unwilling to rely on any mere presumption, however strong.

It was in the Discipline of 1787 that the superintendents were first called *bishops.*§

It was the leaving out, in this year, the second question and answer of the former Discipline, that is called, in Methodist history, " leaving Mr. Wesley's name off the Minutes."

In the Annual Minutes for the same year we find several regulations relating to discipline, namely, Quest. 17. (Of the spiritual welfare of the coloured people.)∥ Quest. 18. (Of the salaries of married preachers.)¶

---

* Lee's History of the Methodists, pp. 127, 128.   † Ibid., p. 129.
‡ See Asbury's Journal, vol. ii, pp. 29, 30.
§ Lee's Hist. of the Methodists, p. 128.
∥ See below, book ii, part ii, sec. 10.   ¶ Ibid., sec. 4.

Quest. 19. (Of register books ;)* and Quest. 20. (Of the rising generation.)†

1788. No edition of the Discipline for 1788 has been found. That no material alterations, however, were made in that year, may be reasonably inferred from the silence of contemporary writers, especially of Lee, who says that he "inserted all the Minutes of importance," and who mentions, in his History, alterations in 1787 and 1789, but none in 1788.

1789. In March, 1789, the fifth edition of the Discipline was published. The correspondence between it and the edition of 1787 has already been noticed under the latter date. Two of the new sections (thirty-first and thirty-second) appear to have been prepared by Bishop Asbury nearly a year previously. Under date of April 2, 1788, he writes : "I rested and compiled two sections, which I shall recommend to be put into our Form of Discipline, in order to remove from society, by regular steps, either preachers or people that are disorderly."‡

To this Discipline was prefixed an Address, by the bishops, "to the members of the Methodist Societies in the United States." There were also appended the Articles of Religion, and certain Doctrinal Tracts, both printed as distinct parts. The former were entitled "The Articles of Religion as received and taught in the Methodist Episcopal Church throughout the United States of America. 'If any man will *do his will*, he shall know of the *doctrine*, whether it be of God,' John vii, 17. 'Prove all things : *hold fast* that which is *good*,' 1 Thess. v. 21." The Doctrinal Tracts were severally entitled, "The Scripture Doctrine of Predestination, Election, and Reprobation, by the Rev. John Wesley, &c." "Serious Thoughts on the Infallible

---

* See below, book ii, part ii, sec. 3. † Ibid., part i, chap. i, sec. 16
‡ Journal, vol. ii, p. 29.

Unconditional Perseverance of all that have once experienced Faith in Christ;" and "A Plain Account of Christian Perfection, as believed and taught by the Rev. John Wesley, from the Year 1725 to the Year 1765." These tracts were inserted in the subsequent editions of the Discipline, (except that of 1796,) until 1812, when they were omitted. They may now be found in the volume entitled, "Doctrinal Tracts," and in Wesley's Works, vol. vi, pp. 81, 483.*

1790. In the edition of 1790 the Articles of Religion and the Doctrinal Tracts, instead of being published as an appendix to the Discipline, were inserted in the body of it, and a new tract was added, "On the Nature and Subjects of Christian Baptism." These constituted, in the order they have been cited, sections thirty-five to thirty-nine of this edition.

1791. In the Discipline of 1791 was inserted a new section, namely, "§ 9. Of Band Societies."

1792. Another General Conference having been convened in 1792, the Discipline of the church was revised and somewhat altered. The sections were now distributed into three chapters, of which the first, containing twenty-six sections, related to the ministry; the second, containing eight sections, to the membership; and the third, containing ten sections, embraced the temporal economy of the church, the Doctrinal Tracts, and the Forms.

A General Conference having been held regularly, every four years from this time, no alterations were made in the Discipline, except at its successive sessions.

1796. The Discipline of 1796 is distinguished from all others, by containing notes on the respective

---

* In Dr. Bangs's History of the Methodist Episcopal Church, vol. i, pp. 175–215, the Discipline of 1789 is published entire, excepting the first section, for which see below, book ii, "The Bishops' Address."

sections, prepared by the bishops. The origin and design of these are thus stated in the " Advertisement to the Reader :"—" The last General Conference desired the bishops to draw up Annotations on the Form of Discipline, and to publish them with the present edition The bishops have accordingly complied, and have proved or illustrated every thing by quotations from the word of God, agreeably also to the advice of the conference : and they sincerely pray that their labour of love may be made a blessing to many. 1797."

In this edition we find, in the first chapter, two new sections ; the one, Section 21. " Of the Local Preachers ;" the other, Section 28. "Of the Chartered Fund. In the second chapter there are also two additiona sections ; the one, Section 9. " Of Slavery ;" the other Section 10. " Of the Sale and Use of Spirituous Liquors. The Doctrinal Tracts and the Forms are omitted.

1800. The Discipline of 1800 omits the bishops' Notes, which were ordered to be printed " by themselves, but in such a manner that the Notes may be conveniently bound up with the Form of Discipline."[*] In this edition the section on " The Plan of Education recommended to all our Seminaries of Learning" is omitted ; and the Doctrinal Tracts (except that on baptism) and the Forms are restored.

1804. In 1804 the Discipline was divided int two parts, as now, the second relating to the " temporal economy" of the church. There has been n change in the order of the sections from that time.

1808. In 1808 an important change was mad in the constitution of the church, by the establishment of a delegated General Conference. In this year th word " salary" was changed throughout to " allowance."

---

[*] See below, book ii, part 2, sec. 8.

1812. Since 1812 the Doctrinal Tracts have been omitted.

1816. In 1816 the Forms, instead of being embraced, as before, in one chapter, (the third,) were divided into two, of which one (the third) contained the order for administering the sacraments, and the forms for solemnizing matrimony and burying the dead ; and the other (the fourth) contained the forms of ordination. In this year the word " society" was very generally changed to " church," the latter term having occurred occasionally before.

1832. In 1832 a new section was added to part ii, namely, " Section 6. Of the Support of Missions."

1840. In 1840 a new section was added to part i, chap. 1, namely, " Section 8. Of the reception of Preachers from the Wesleyan Connection, and from other Denominations ;" and the eighth section of chapter 2, " Of the Sale and Use of Spirituous Liquors," was omitted.*

---

* Some of the first copies of the 24mo. edition of the Discipline of 1840 were imperfect. (See below, book ii, part i, chap. i, sec. 4 and 16.) The correct copies may be known by having pp. 61—4 in smaller type than the others.

BOOK II.

HISTORY OF THE SEVERAL SECTIONS.

In this book it is proposed to trace the modifications which the respective sections of the Discipline have undergone from time to time. Every material alteration is noticed; ar.d, in the Articles of Religion and the Forms, even the most minute verbal changes. When a section is long and complicated, its parts are considered separately. To avoid unnecessary repetition, it will be understood that the first date under any head indicates when a rule on the subject was first introduced; and the others, in succession, show the changes which it subsequently underwent, until it assumed its present form. The title of the Discipline and the Bishops' Address will first be considered.

The Title.

1784. The original title was, as already stated, " Minutes of several Conversations between the Rev. Thomas Coke, LL.D., the Rev. Francis Asbury, and others, at a Conference, begun in Baltimore, in the State of Maryland, on Monday the 27th of December, in the Year 1784. `Composing a Form of Discipline for the Ministers, Preachers, and other Members of the Methodist Episcopal Church in America."

1786. The title was altered to the following :— " The General Minutes of the Conferences of the Methodist Episcopal Church in America, forming the Constitution of the said Church."

1787. The following was the title :—" A Form of Discipline for the Ministers, Preachers, and Members of the Methodist Episcopal Church in America ;

:onsidered and approved at a Conference held in Bal imore, in the State of Maryland, on Monday, the 27th lay of December, 1784. In which the Reverend Thomas Coke, LL.D., and the Reverend Francis Asbury presided. Arranged under proper Heads, and methodized in a more acceptable and easy Manner."

1789. The names were printed simply,—" Thomas Coke and Francis Asbury."

1790. The Articles of Religion and the Doctrinal Tracts having been incorporated into the Discipline, the following clause was inserted before the words " of the Methodist Episcopal Church," namely, " now comprehending the Principles and Doctrines.")

1792. The title was altered so as to read,— ' The Doctrine and Discipline of the M. E. Church n America, revised and approved at the General Conference held at Baltimore, in the State of Maryland, in November, 1792 : in which Thomas Coke and Francis Asbury presided."

1796. All after " America" was struck out, and he following substituted :—" with Explanatory Notes, by Thomas Coke and Francis Asbury."

1804. The present title was adopted, namely : ' The Doctrines and Discipline of the Methodist Episcopal Church."

The Bishops' Address.

1789. This appears first in the Discipline of 1789,* as follows :—

----

* All references to the edition of 1789 are made, in view of what has been stated, p. 82.

" *To the Members of the Methodist Societies in the United States.*

" Dearly Beloved Brethren,—We esteem it our duty and privilege most earnestly to recommend to you, as members of our church, our Form of Discipline, which has been founded on the experience of fifty years in Europe, and of twenty years in America; as also on the observations and remarks we have made on ancient and modern churches. We have made some little alterations in the present edition, yet such as affect not in any degree the essentials of our doctrines and discipline. We think ourselves obliged to view and review annually the whole order of our church, always aiming at perfection, standing on the shoulders of those who have lived before us, and taking the advantage of our former selves.

" We wish to see this little publication in the house of every Methodist, and the more so as it contains our plan of collegiate and Christian education, and the Articles of Religion maintained more or less, in part or in the whole, by every reformed church in the world. We would likewise declare our real sentiments concerning the Scripture doctrine of election and reprobation; as also on the infallible, unconditional perseverance of all that ever have believed, or ever shall; and, lastly, on the doctrine of Christian perfection.

" Far from wishing you to be ignorant of any of our doctrines, or any part of our Discipline, we desire you to read, mark, learn, and inwardly digest the whole. We know you are not, in general, able to purchase many books; but you ought, next to the word of God, to procure the Articles and Canons of the church to which you belong. This present edition is small and cheap, and we can assure you that the profits of the sale of it shall be applied to charitable purposes.

" We remain your very affectionate brethren and

pastors, who labour night and day, both in public and private, for your good,

"THOMAS COKE,
"FRANCIS ASBURY.

" Charlestown, [S. C.,] March 20, 1789."

1790. In the Discipline of 1790 the following additional paragraphs are inserted at the beginning of the Address :—

"We think it expedient to give you a brief account of the rise of Methodism, (so called,) both in Europe and America. In 1729 two young men in England, reading the Bible, saw they could not be saved without holiness, followed after it, and incited others so to do. In 1737 they saw, likewise, that men are justified before they are sanctified : but still holiness was their object. God then thrust them out to raise a holy people.

" And during the space of thirty years past certain persons, members of the society, emigrated from England and Ireland, and settled in various parts of this country. About twenty years ago Philip Embury, a local preacher from Ireland, began to preach in the city of New-York, and formed a society of his own countrymen and the citizens. About the same time Robert Strawbridge, a local preacher from Ireland, settled in Frederic county, in the state of Maryland, and, preaching there, formed some societies. In 1769 Richard Boardman and Joseph Pilmoor came to New-York, who were the first regular Methodist preachers on the continent. In the latter end of the year 1771 Francis Asbury and Richard Wright, of the same order, came over.

" And we humbly believe that God's design, in raising up the preachers called Methodists in America, was to reform the continent, and spread Scripture holiness over these lands. As a proof hereof we have seen, in the course of twenty-two years, a great and glorious work of God, from New-York, through the Jerseys

Pennsylvania, Maryland, Virginia, North and South Carolina, and Georgia; as also the extremities of the western settlements."

These paragraphs were taken, with but little alteration, from the Discipline of 1789, where they constituted the first section. A portion of them may also be found in the Discipline of 1784, in the answer to questions four and five.

1791. The following alterations were made:—In the second paragraph, second sentence, (1790,) for " About twenty years ago," we have, " In the latter end of the year 1766." The following was inserted as the next sentence:—" In the same year Thomas Webb preached in a hired room near the barracks; and in the year 1767 the rigging-house was occupied." The following was also inserted:—" The first Methodist church in New-York was built in 1768 or 1769."

1792. The clause relating to "the rigging-house" is omitted. And, in the last paragraph but one, (1789,) reference is made to a tract " On the Nature and Subjects of Christian Baptism," which was inserted in this edition, as it had been in those of 1790 and 1791. The Address is dated, " Baltimore, Nov. 16, 1792."

1796. The following alterations appear:—In the first paragraph (1790) the sentences from " In 1729" to " a holy people" are marked with quotations, and this note added at the foot of the page, " These are the words of the Messrs. Wesley themselves." In the second paragraph the first sentence is omitted, and the next begins, " In the year 1766, &c." In the third paragraph, " Delaware," and " the extremities of the western and eastern states," are included among the subjects of the work of God. In the fourth paragraph (1st of 1789) all after " modern churches" is struck out. In the fifth paragraph (2d of 1789) the words " collegiate and" are struck out; the college (Cokesbury) having then been destroyed. The clause referring to the extract on baptism is struck out. The reference to the other tracts, however, is retained, though they were not published in the Discipline of 1796.

1812.   In 1812 the reference to the plan of education and the Doctrinal Tracts was omitted, the former having been struck from the Discipline, and the latter no longer published in connection with it.

1840.   In the last line of the last paragraph (1789) the words "and religious" were inserted after "charitable."

The signatures to the Address have, of course, varied from time to time with the changes in the episcopacy. Until 1800 it was signed by "Thomas Coke" and "Francis Asbury." In 1800 and 1804 the name of "Richard Whatcoat" was added. In 1808 and 1812 it was signed by "Francis Asbury" and "William M'Kendree." In 1816 and 1820 by "William M'Kendree, Enoch George," and "Robert R. Roberts." In 1824 and 1828, "Joshua Soule" and "Elijah Hedding" are added. In 1832 "Enoch George" omitted, and "James O. Andrew" and "John Emory" added. In 1836 "William M'Kendree" and "John Emory" omitted, and "Beverly Waugh" and "Thomas A. Morris" added.

CHAPTER I.

SECTION I.

Of the Origin of the Methodist Episcopal Church.

The only notice of the subject in 1784 is contained in the answer to question 3, p. 27. The title is first found in 1792, but the substance of the section is contained in the Discipline of 1789, sections three and four, as follows :—

1789. " Sec. 3.   On the Nature and Constitution of our Church.

" We are thoroughly convinced that the Church of England, to which we have been united, is deficient in several of the most important parts of Christian discipline ;   and that (a few ministers and members excepted) it has lost the life and power of religion. We are not ignorant of the spirit and design it has ever discovered in Europe, of rising to pre-eminence and worldly dignities by virtue of a national establishment, and by the most servile devotion to the will of temporal governors :   and we fear the same spirit will lead the same Church in these United States (though altered in its name) to similar designs and attempts, if the number and strength of its members will ever afford a probability of success ;   and particularly to obtain a national establishment, which we cordially abhor as the great bane of truth and holiness, and consequently a great impediment to the progress of vital Christianity.

" For these reasons we have thought it our duty to form ourselves into an independent church.   And as the most excellent mode of church government, according to our maturest judgment, is that of a moderate episcopacy, and as we are persuaded that the uninterrupted succession of bishops from the apostles can be proved neither from Scripture nor antiquity, we therefore have constituted ourselves into an Episcopal Church, under the direction of bishops, elders, deacons, and preachers, according to the forms of ordination annexed to our Prayer-book, and the regulations laid down in this Form of Discipline."

" Sec. 4. On constituting of Bishops, and their Duty.

" *Quest.* 1. What is the proper origin of the Episcopal authority in our church ?

" *Ans.* In the year 1784 the Rev. John Wesley, who, under God, has been the father of the great revival of religion now extending over the earth by the means of the Methodists, determined, at the intercession of multitudes of his spiritual children on this con-

tinent, to ordain ministers for America, and for this
purpose sent over three regularly-ordained clergy; but
preferring the Episcopal mode of church government
to any other, he solemnly set apart, by the imposition
of his hands and prayer, one of them, namely, Thomas
Coke, doctor of civil law, late of Jesus College, in the
University of Oxford, for the episcopal office; and
having delivered to him letters of episcopal orders,
commissioned and directed him to set apart Francis
Asbury, then general assistant of the Methodist Society in America, for the same Episcopal office, he, the
said Francis Asbury, being first ordained deacon and
elder. In consequence of which, the said Francis
Asbury was solemnly set apart for the said Episcopal
office by prayer and the imposition of the hands of the
said Thomas Coke, other regularly-ordained ministers
assisting in the sacred ceremony. At which time the
General Conference held at Baltimore did unanimously
receive the said Thomas Coke and Francis Asbury as
their bishops, being fully satisfied of the validity of
their Episcopal ordination."

1792. These sections were condensed into one,
with the present title and number. Section 3, of 1789,
was struck out, and the following paragraph substituted:

"The preachers and members of our society, in
general, being convinced that there was a great deficiency of vital religion in the Church of England in
America, and being in many places destitute of the
Christian sacraments, as several of the clergy had for-
saken their churches, requested the late Rev. John
Wesley to take such measures, in his wisdom and
prudence, as would afford them suitable relief in their
distress."

The remainder of the section reads as in the answer
of section 4, 1789, except that the first sentence begins:—" In consequence of this our venerable friend,
who, under God, had been the father of the great revival
of religion now extending over the earth, by the means

of the Methodists, determined to ordain ministers foɪ America; and for this purpose, in the year 1784 sent over, &c.;" and after the other titles of Dr Coke it is added "and a presbyter of the Church oɪ England."

SECTION II.

Articles of Religion.

THE Articles of Religion were originally preparec by Mr. Wesley, and printed in "the Sunday Service' which he sent over to America. They were not incorporated into the body of the Discipline until 1790, when they constituted the thirty-fifth section. In 1791 they were the thirty-sixth section, and in 1792 they took their present place as the second section.

1784. The original articles are here compared with the Thirty-nine Articles of the Church of England, on the same plan that the first Discipline was compared with the Large Minutes.*

"I. *Of Faith in the Holy Trinity.*

"There is but one living and true God, everlasting, without body, parts, or passions; of infinite power, wisdom, and goodness; the Maker and Preserver of all things both visible and invisible. And in unity of this Godhead there *are*[1] three Persons of one substance, power, and eternity; the Father, the Son, and the Holy Ghost.

"II. *Of the Word, or Son of God, who*[2] *was made very Man.*

"The Son, *who*[3] is the Word of the Father, begotten from everlasting of the Father, the very and eternal God, of one substance with the Father, tooɪ

---

* See page 25.
[1] " be."—*Thirty-nine Articles.*
[2] " which."—*Ib.*
[3] " which."—*Ib*

man's nature in the womb of the blessed Virgin, [of her substance ;] so that two whole and perfect natures, that is to say, the Godhead and manhood, were joined together in one Person, never to be divided, whereof is one Christ, very God, and very man, who truly suffered, was crucified, dead, and buried, to reconcile his Father to us, and to be a sacrifice, not only for original guilt, but also for actual sins of men.

[" (III.) *Of the going down of Christ into Hell.*

" As Christ died for us, and was buried ; so also is it to be believed that he went down into hell.]

" III. (IV.) *Of the Resurrection of Christ.*

" Christ did truly rise again from the dead, and took again his body, with [flesh, bones, and] all things appertaining to the perfection of man's nature, wherewith he ascended into heaven, and there sitteth until he return to judge all men at the last day.

" IV. (V.) *Of the Holy Ghost.*

" The Holy Ghost, proceeding from the Father and the Son, is of one substance, majesty, and glory, with the Father and the Son, very and eternal God.

" V. (VI.) *Of the Sufficiency of the Holy Scriptures for Salvation.*

" Holy Scripture containeth all things necessary to salvation : so that whatsoever is not read therein, or[1] may be proved thereby, is not to be required of any man, that it should be believed as an Article of the Faith, or be thought requisite or necessary to salvation. In the name of the Holy Scripture we do understand those canonical Books of the Old and New Testament, of whose authority was never any doubt in the church.

---

[1] " nor."—*Thirty-nine Articles.*

"*Of the Names [and Number] of the Canonical Books.*

"Genesis, Exodus, Leviticus, Numbers, Deuteronomy, Joshua, Judges, Ruth, The First Book of Samuel The Second Book of Samuel, The First Book of Kings The Second Book of Kings, The First Book of Chronicles, The Second Book of Chronicles, *The Book of Ezra*,[1] *The Book of Nehemiah*,[2] The Book of Hester The Book of Job, The Psalms, The Proverbs, Ecclesiastes, or the Preacher, Cantica, or Songs of Solomon, Four Prophets the greater, Twelve Prophets the less.

["And the other books (as Hierome saith) the Church doth read for example of life and instruction of manners; but yet doth it not apply them to establish any doctrine : such are these following :—

"The Third Book of Esdras, The Fourth Book of Esdras, The Book of Tobias, The Book of Judith, The rest of the Book of Esther, The Book of Wisdom, Jesus the Son of Sirach, Baruch the Prophet, The Song of the three Children, The Story of Susanna, Of Bel and the Dragon, The Prayer of Manasses, The First Book of Maccabees, The Second Book of Maccabees.]

"All the books of the New Testament, as they are commonly received, we do receive and account [them] canonical.

"VI. (VII.) *Of the Old Testament.*

"The Old Testament is not contrary to the New; for both in the Old and New Testament everlasting life is offered to mankind by Christ, who is the only Mediator between God and man, being both God and man. Wherefore they are not to be heard, *who*[3] feign that the old fathers did look only for transitory promises. Although the law given from God by Moses, as touching ceremonies and rites, *doth*[4] not bind *Chris-*

---

[1] "The First Book of Esdras."—*Thirty-nine Articles.*
[2] "The Second Book of Esdras."—*Ib.*
[3] "which."—*Ib.*   [4] "do."—*Ib.*

ians,[1] *nor ought the civil precepts thereof*[2] of necessity to be received in any commonwealth : yet notwithstanding, no Christian [man] whatsoever is free
from the obedience of the commandments which are
called moral.

[" (VIII.) *Of the three Creeds.*

" The three creeds, Nicene Creed, Athanasius' Creed, and
that which is commonly called the Apostles' Creed, ought
thoroughly to be received and believed : for they may be proved
by most certain warrants of Holy Scripture.]

" VII. (IX.) *Of Original or Birth Sin.*

" Original sin standeth not in the following of Adam,
as the Pelagians do vainly talk,) but it is the [fault
and] corruption of the nature of every man, that naturally is engendered of the offspring of Adam, whereby
man is very far gone from original righteousness, and
is] of his own nature inclined to evil, *and that continually,*[3]

[" and therefore in every person born into this world, it de-
serveth God's wrath and damnation. And this infection of
nature doth remain ; yea, in them that are regenerated ; whereby
the lust of the flesh, called in Greek, Φρόνημα σαρκός, which some
do expound the wisdom, some sensuality, some the affection,
some the desire of the flesh, is not subject to the law of God.
And although there is no condemnation for them that believe
and are baptized, yet the apostle doth confess, that concupiscence
and lust hath of itself the nature of sin.]

" VIII. (X.) *Of Free Will.*

" The condition of man after the fall of Adam is
such, that he cannot turn and prepare himself by his
own natural strength and [good] works, to faith, and
calling upon God : wherefore we have no power to do
good works pleasant and acceptable to God, without
the grace of God by Christ preventing us, that we may

---

[1] " Christian men."—*Thirty-nine Articles.*
[2] " nor the civil precepts thereof ought."—*Ib.*
[3] " so that the flesh lusteth always contrary to the Spirit."—*Ib.*

have a good will, and working with us, when we have that good will.

"IX. (XI.) *Of the Justification of Man.*

"We are accounted righteous before God, only for the merit of our Lord and Saviour Jesus Christ, by faith, and not for our own works or deservings : wherefore, that we are justified by faith only, is a most wholesome doctrine, and very full of comfort, [as more largely is expressed in the Homily of Justification.]

"X. (XII.) *Of good Works.*

"*Although*[1] good works, which are the fruits of faith, and follow after justification, cannot put away our sins, and endure the severity of God's judgment; yet are they pleasing and acceptable to God in Christ, and [do] spring out [necessarily] of a true and lively faith, insomuch that by them a lively faith may be as evidently known, as a tree discerned by *its*[2] fruit.

[" (XIII.) *Of Works before Justification.*

"Works done before the grace of Christ, and the inspiration of his Spirit, are not pleasant to God ; forasmuch as they spring not of faith in Jesus Christ, neither do they make men meet to receive grace, or (as the school authors say) deserve grace of congruity ; yea, rather, for that they are not done as God hath willed and commanded them to be done, we doubt not but they have the nature of sin.]

"XI. (XIV.) *Of Works of Supererogation.*

"Voluntary works, besides, over and above God's commandments, which they call works of supererogation, cannot be taught without arrogancy and impiety. For by them men do declare, that they do not only render unto God as much as they are bound to do, but that they do more for his sake than of bounden duty is required : whereas Christ saith plainly, When ye have

---

[1] "Albeit that."—*Thirty-nine Articles.*   [2] "the."—*Ib.*

done all that is[1] commanded [to] you, say, We are unprofitable servants.

[" (XV.) *Of Christ alone without Sin.*

" Christ, in the truth of our nature, was made like unto us in all things, sin only except, from which he was clearly void, both in his flesh and in his spirit. He came to be the Lamb without spot, who, by sacrifice of himself once made, should take away the sins of the world ; and sin (as St. John saith) was not in him. But all we the rest (although baptized and born again in Christ) yet offend in many things ; and if we say we have no sin, we deceive ourselves, and the truth is not in us.]

" XII. (XVI.) *Of Sin after* Justification.[2]

" Not every *sin willingly committed after justification is the*[3] sin against the Holy Ghost, and unpardonable. Wherefore the grant of repentance is not to be denied to such as fall into sin, after *justification :*[4] after we have received the Holy Ghost, we may depart from grace given, and fall into sin, and by the grace of God [we may] rise again, and amend our lives. And therefore they are to be condemned *who*[5] say they can no more sin as long as they live here, or deny the place of forgiveness to such as truly repent.

[" (XVII.) *Of Predestination and Election.*

" Predestination to life is the everlasting purpose of God, whereby (before the foundations of the world were laid) he hath constantly decreed by his counsel, secret to us, to deliver from curse and damnation those, whom he hath chosen in Christ out of mankind, and to bring them by Christ to everlasting salvation, as vessels made to honour. Wherefore they which be endued with so excellent a benefit of God, be called according to God's purpose by his Spirit working in due season : they through grace obey the calling : they be justified freely : they be made sons of God by adoption : they be made like the image of his only-begotten Son Jesus Christ : they walk religiously in good works, and, at length, by God's mercy, they attain to everlasting felicity.

---

[1] " are."—*Thirty-nine Articles.*   [2] " Baptism."—*Ib.*
[3] " deadly sin willingly committed after baptism is."—*Ib.*
[4] " baptism."—*Ib.*   [5] " which."—*Ib.*

" As the godly consideration of predestination and our election in Christ is full of sweet, pleasant, and unspeakable comfort to godly persons, and such as feel in themselves the working of the Spirit of Christ, mortifying the works of the flesh, and their earthly members, and drawing up their mind to high and heavenly things ; as well because it doth greatly establish and confirm their faith of eternal salvation, to be enjoyed through Christ, as because it doth fervently kindle their love towards God : so for curious and carnal persons, lacking the Spirit of Christ, to have continually before their eyes the sentence of God's predestination, is a most dangerous downfall, whereby the devil doth thrust them either into desperation, or into wretchlessness of most unclean living, no less perilous than desperation.

"Furthermore, we must receive God's promises in such wise as they be generally set forth to us in Holy Scripture : and in our doings, that will of God is to be followed, which we have expressly declared unto us in the word of God.

" (XVIII.) *Of obtaining eternal Salvation only by the Name of Christ.*

" They also are to be had accursed, that presume to say, that every man shall be saved by the law or sect which he professeth, so that he be diligent to frame his life according to that law, and the light of nature. For Holy Scripture doth set out unto us only the name of Jesus Christ, whereby men must be saved.]

" XIII. (XIX.) *Of the Church.*

" The visible church of Christ is a congregation of faithful men, in the which the pure word of God is preached, and the sacraments [be] duly *ad*ministered according to Christ's ordinance, in all those things that of necessity are requisite to the same.

[" As the Church of Hierusalem, Alexandria, and Antioch, have erred ; so also the Church of Rome hath erred, not only in their living and manner of ceremonies, but also in matters of faith.

" (XX.) *Of the Authority of the Church.*

" The Church hath power to decree rites or ceremonies, and authority in controversies of faith ; and yet it is not lawful for the Church to ordain any thing that is contrary to God's word written ; neither may it so expound one place of Scripture, that it be repugnant to another. Wherefore, although the Church be a witness and a keeper of holy writ, yet, as it ought not to

lecree any thing against the same, so besides the same ought
t not to enforce any thing to be believed for necessity of sal-
ration.

" (XXI.) *Of the Authority of General Councils.*

" General councils may not be gathered together without the
:ommandment and will of princes.   And when they be gathered
ogether (forasmuch as they be an assembly of men, whereof all
e not governed with the Spirit and word of God) they may err,
nd sometimes have erred, even in things pertaining unto God.
Wherefore things ordained by them as necessary to salvation,
ave neither strength nor authority, unless it may be declared
hat they be taken out of Holy Scripture.]

" XIV. (XXII.) *Of Purgatory.*

" The Romish doctrine concerning purgatory, par-
lons, worshipping, and adoration, as well of images,
us of reliques, and also invocation of saints, is a fond
hing vainly invented, and grounded upon no warrant[y]
of Scripture, but [rather] repugnant to the word of
God.

[" (XXIII.) *Of Ministering in the Congregation.*

" It is not lawful for any man to take upon him the office of
ublic preaching, or ministering the sacraments in the congre-
ation, before he be lawfully called, and sent to execute the
ame.   And those we ought to judge lawfully called and sent,
which be chosen and called to this work by men who have public
uthority given unto them in the congregation to call and send
ninisters into the Lord's vineyard.]

' XV. (XXIV.) *Of speaking in the Congregation in such a tongue as the people understand[eth.]*

" It is a thing plainly repugnant to the word of God,
nd the custom of the primitive church, to have public
orayer in the church, or to minister the sacraments in
a tongue not *understood by*[1] the people.

" XVI. (XXV.) *Of the Sacraments.*

" Sacraments ordained of Christ, *are*[2] not only badges
ir tokens of Christian men's profession ; but rather they

---

[1] " understanded of."—*Thirty-nine Articles.*   [2] " be."—*Ib.*

are[1] certain [sure witnesses and effectual] signs of grace, and God's good will toward us, by the which he doth work invisibly in us, and doth not only quicken, but also strengthen and confirm our faith in him.

" There are two sacraments ordained of Christ our Lord in the gospel ; that is to say, baptism, and the supper of the Lord.

" Those five commonly called sacraments ; that is to say, confirmation, penance, orders, matrimony, and extreme unction, are not to be counted for sacraments of the gospel, being such as have grown, partly of the corrupt following of the apostles, partly are states of life allowed in the Scriptures : but yet have not *the* like nature of [sacraments with] baptism and the Lord's supper, *because*[2] they have not any visible sign or ceremony ordained of God.

" The sacraments were not ordained of Christ to be gazed upon, or to be carried about ; but that we should duly use them. And in such only as worthily receive the same, they have a wholesome effect or operation : but they that receive them unworthily, purchase to themselves *condemnation*,[3] as St. Paul saith.

[" (XXVI.) *Of the Unworthiness of the Ministers, which hinders not the Effect of the Sacrament.*

" Although in the visible church the evil be ever mingled with the good, and sometimes the evil have chief authority in the ministration of the word and sacraments : yet forasmuch as they do not the same in their own name, but in Christ's, and do minister by his commission and authority, we may use their ministry, both in hearing the word of God, and in the receiving of the sacraments. Neither is the effect of Christ's ordinance taken away by their wickedness, nor the grace of God's gifts diminished from such, as by faith, and rightly, do receive the sacraments ministered unto them, which be effectual, because of Christ's institution and promise, although they be ministered by evil men.

" Nevertheless, it appertaineth to the discipline of the Church, that inquiry be made of evil ministers, and that they be accused by those that have knowledge of their offences : and finally, being found guilty, by just judgment, be deposed.]

---

[1] " be."—*Thirty-nine Articles.*   [2] " for that."—*Ib.*
[3] " damnation."—*Ib.*

"XVII. (XXVII.) *Of Baptism.*

"Baptism is not only a sign of profession, and mark of ifference, whereby *Christians*[1] are *distinguished*[2] from thers that *are*[3] not *baptized;*[4] but it is also a sign of egeneration, or the new birth, [whereby, as by an nstrument, they that receive baptism rightly are grafted nto the Church : the promises of the forgiveness of in, and of our adoption to be the sons of God by the Ioly Ghost, are visibly signed and sealed : faith is onfirmed, and grace increased by virtue of prayer nto God.] The baptism of young children is [in any vise] to be retained in the Church [as most agreeable vith the institution of Christ.]

"XVIII. (XXVIII.) *Of the Lord's Supper.*

"The supper of the Lord is not only a sign of the ove that Christians ought to have among themselves ne to another, but rather is a sacrament of our re- lemption by Christ's death : insomuch, that to such as ightly, worthily, and with faith receive the same, the read which we break is a partaking of the body of Christ ; and likewise the cup of blessing is a partaking f the blood of Christ.

"Transubstantiation, or the change of the substance f bread and wine in the supper of the Lord, cannot be roved by holy writ ; but is repugnant to the plain vords of Scripture, overthroweth the-nature of a sacra- nent, and hath given occasion to many superstitions.

"The body of Christ is given, taken, and eaten in he supper, only after an heavenly and spiritual manner. And the mean whereby the body of Christ is received nd eaten in the supper, is faith.

"The sacrament of the Lord's supper was not by Christ's ordinance reserved, carried about, lifted up, or vorshipped.

---

[1] " Christian men."—*Thirty-nine Articles.*   [2] " discerned."—*Ib.*
[3] " be."—*Ib.*   [4] " christened."—*Ib.*

[" **(XXIX.)** *Of the wicked, which eat not the Body of Christ in the Use of the Lord's Supper.*

" The wicked, and such as be void of a lively faith, although they do carnally and visibly press with their teeth (as St. Augustine saith) the sacrament of the body and blood of Christ; yet in no wise are they partakers of Christ; but rather to their condemnation do eat and drink the sign or sacrament of so great a thing.]

" XIX. (XXX.) *Of both Kinds.*

" The cup of the Lord is not to be denied to the lay people; for both the parts of the Lord's *supper*[1] by Christ's ordinance and commandment, ought to be ministered to all *Christians*[2] alike.

"XX. (XXXI.) *Of the one Oblation of Christ, finished upon the Cross.*

" The offering of Christ once made, is that perfect redemption, propitiation, and satisfaction for all the sins of the whole world, both original and actual; and there is none other satisfaction for sin but that alone. Wherefore the sacrifice of masses, in the which it *is*[3] commonly said that the priest *doth*[4] offer Christ for the quick and the dead, to have remission of pain or guilt, *is a blasphemous fable, and dangerous deceit.*[5]

" XXI. (XXXII.) *Of the Marriage of* Ministers.[6]

" *The ministers of Christ*[7] are not commanded by God's law either to vow the estate of single life, or to abstain from marriage; therefore it is lawful for them, as for all other *Christians*,[8] to marry at their own discretion, as they shall judge the same to serve *best*[9] to godliness.

---

[1] " sacrament."—*Thirty-nine Articles.*   [2] " Christian men."—*Ib.*
[3] " was."—*Ib.*   [4] " did."—*Ib.*
[5] " were blasphemous fables, and dangerous deceits."—*Ib.*
[6] " Priests."—*Ib.*   [7] " Bishops, priests, and deacons."—*Ib.*
[8] " Christian men."—*Ib.*   [9] " better."—*Ib.*

5*

["(XXXIII.) *Of excommunicate Persons, how they are to be avoided.*

" That person which by open denunciation of the Church is rightly cut off from the unity of the Church, and excommunicated, ought to be taken of the whole multitude of the faithful as a heathen and publican, until he be openly reconciled by penance, and received into the Church by a judge that hath authority thereunto.]

" XXII. (XXXIV.) Of the Rites and Ceremonies of Churches.[1]

" It is not necessary that *rites and ceremonies should in all places be the same, or exactly alike ; for they have been always different,*[2] and may be changed according to the diversity of countries, times, and men's manners, so that nothing be ordained against God's word. Whosoever, through his private judgment, willingly and purposely doth openly break the *rites*[3] and ceremonies of the church *to which he belongs,* which *are*[4] not repugnant to the word of God, and *are*[5] ordained and approved by common authority, ought to be rebuked openly, that others may fear to do the like, as *one*[6] that offendeth against the common order of the church, [and hurteth the authority of the magistrate,] and woundeth the consciences of [the] weak brethren.

" Every particular [or national] church *may*[7] ordain, change, *or*[8] abolish *rites and ceremonies, so that all things may be done to edification.*[9]

[" (XXXV.) *Of the Homilies.*

" The second Book of Homilies, the several titles whereof we have joined, under this article, doth contain a godly and whole-

---

[1] " Of the Traditions of the Church."—*Thirty-nine Articles.*
[2] " traditions and ceremonies be in all places one, or utterly like; for at all times they have been divers."—*Ib.*
[3] " traditions."—*Ib.*   [4] " be."—*Ib.*   [5] " be."—*Ib.*   [6] " he."—*Ib.*
[7] " hath authority to ordain."—*Ib.*   [8] " and."—*Ib.*
[9] " ceremonies, or rites of the church, ordained only by man's aurity, so that all things be done to edifying."—*Ib.*

some doctrine, and necessary for these times, as doth the former
Book of Homilies, which were set forth in the time of Edward
the Sixth, and therefore we judge them to be read in churches
by the ministers diligently and distinctly, that they may be understanded of the people.

Of the Names of the Homilies.

" 1. Of the Right Use of the Church. 2. Against Peril of
Idolatry. 3. Of repairing and keeping clean of Churches. 4. Of
Good Works : first of Fasting. 5. Against Gluttony and Drunkenness. 6. Against excess of Apparel. 7. Of Prayer. 8. Of
the Place and Time of Prayer. 9. That Common Prayers and
Sacraments ought to be ministered in a known Tongue. 10. Of
the reverent Estimation of God's Word. 11. Of Alms-doing.
12. Of the Nativity of Christ. 13. Of the Passion of Christ.
14. Of the Resurrection of Christ. 15. Of the worthy receiving of the Sacrament of the Body and Blood of Christ. 16. Of
the Gifts of the Holy Ghost. 17. For the Rogation-days.
18. Of the State of Matrimony. 19. Of Repentance. 20. Against
Idleness. 21. Against Rebellion.

" (XXXVI.) *Of Consecration of Bishops and Ministers.*

" The Book of Consecration of Archbishops and Bishops, and
Ordering of Priests and Deacons, lately set forth in the time of
Edward the Sixth, and confirmed at the same time by authority
of parliament, doth contain all things necessary to such consecration and ordering : neither hath it any thing that of itself is
superstitious and ungodly. And therefore whosoever are consecrated or ordered according to the rites of that book, since the
second year of the forenamed King Edward, unto this time, or
hereafter shall be consecrated or ordered according to the same
rites ; we decree all such to be rightly, orderly, and lawfully
consecrated and ordered.

(" XXXVII.) *Of the Civil Magistrates.*

" The king's majesty hath the chief power in this realm of
England, and other his dominions, unto whom the chief government of all estates of this realm, whether they be ecclesiastical
or civil, in all causes doth appertain, and is not, nor ought to be,
subject to any foreign jurisdiction.
" Where we attribute to the king's majesty the chief government, by which titles we understand the minds of some slander-
ous folks to be offended ; we give not to our princes the ministering either of God's word, or of the sacraments, the which
thing the injunctions also lately set forth by Elizabeth our queen
do most plainly testify ; but that only prerogative, which we see

o have been given always to all godly princes in Holy Scriptures by God himself; that is, that they should rule all estates and degrees committed to their charge by God, whether they be ecclesiastical or temporal, and restrain with the civil sword the stubborn and evil doers.

"The bishop of Rome hath no jurisdiction in this realm of England.

"The laws of the realm may punish Christian men with death, for heinous and grievous offences.

"It is lawful for Christian men, at the commandment of the magistrate, to wear weapons, and serve in the wars.]*

'XXIII. [XXIV.] (XXXVIII.) *Of Christian men's Goods, [which are not common.]*

"The riches and goods of Christians are not common as touching the right, title, and possession of the same, as *some*[1] do falsely boast. Notwithstanding, every man ought, of such things as he possesseth, liberally to give alms to the poor according to his ability.

'XXIV. [XXV.] (XXXIX.) *Of a Christian Man's Oath.*

"As we confess that vain and rash swearing is forbidden Christian men by our Lord Jesus Christ, and James his apostle; so we judge that *the* Christian reli-

---

* Although Mr. Wesley inserted, in the Liturgy which he prepared for the American Methodists, a prayer for "the supreme rulers of the United States," yet he probably did not think himself sufficiently familiar with the subject to draw up an article respecting "the civil magistrates." Such an article was framed, however, at the Christmas Conference, when the church was organized. It could not be printed with the others, because they had been previously printed in England. It was inserted, however, in the next edition of the Prayer-book, in 786, (see "Defence of our Fathers," sec. 8,) and read as follows:—

"XXIII. *Of the Rulers of the United States of America.*

"The congress, the general assemblies, the governors, and the councils of state, *as the delegates of the people*, are the rulers of the United States of America, according to the division of power made to them by the general Act of Confederation, and by the Constitutions of their respective states. And the said states ought not to be subject to any foreign jurisdiction."

[1] "certain Anabaptists."—*Thirty-nine Articles.*

gion doth not prohibit, but that a man may swear when
the magistrate requireth, in a cause of faith and charity, so it be done according to the prophet's teaching,
in justice, judgment, and truth."

The following alterations have been made in the
Articles, from time to time. It will be perceived that
they are almost all typographical errors, or substitutions
of modern forms of expression ; but, on account of the
importance of the subject, it has been thought best to
notice them all.

1786. Article I, l. 2. For " without body, parts,
or passions," read " without body or parts."

Article II, ll. 1, 2, " begotten from everlasting of
the Father," omitted.

Article XIII, l. 2. For " in the which"—" in which."

" Article XVI, l. 15. For "grown partly"—"partly
grown."

1789. Article V, l. 4, " the" omitted.

Article XIV, l. 2. For " pardons"—" pardon."

1790. Article V, l. 9. For " Of the names"—
" The names."

Article XXIII, (in the note,) l. 1. Before " The
Congress," insert " The President."

1791. Article XIX, l. 4. For " ministered"—
" administered."

1796. Article XVIII, l. 10. For " the Lord"—
" our Lord."

1804. Article XXIII, (in the note.) For " the
general Act of Confederation"—"the Constitution of the
United States." After " said states," the following inserted—" are a sovereign and independent nation, and.'

1808. Article V, l. 3. For " or"—" nor."

Article XVIII, l. 15. For " spiritual"—" scriptural,'
a misprint which has been continued in every subsequent edition.

1812. Article VI, l. 10, " to" omitted.

Article X, l. 7, " is" inserted after " tree."

Article XVIII, ll. 1, 2. The words, " of the love,'

omitted—a misprint which was not corrected until 1840.

1816.   Article V, l. 1. For "Holy Scripture con taineth"—"The Holy Scriptures contain."

Article XI, l. 2. For "they call"—"are called."

Article XVI, end. "1 Cor. xi, 29" added.

1820.   Article I, l. 4, "both" omitted.

Article XVIII. l. 16. For "mean"—"means."

Article XXIII, end The following note was added: "As far as it respects civil affairs, we believe it the duty of Christians, and especially all Christian ministers, to be subject to the supreme authority of the country where they may reside, and to use all laudable means to enjoin obedience to the *powers that be ;* and therefore it is expected that all our preachers and people, who may be under the British or any other government, will behave themselves as peaceable and orderly subjects."*

1824.   Article VI, l. 8. For "rites"—"rights," a misprint which was continued until 1836.

SECTION III.

Of the General and Annual Conferences.

The section corresponding to this in 1789 was the second, entitled—"On the Method of holding a Conference, and the Business to be done therein."   In 1792 it was made the third section, with the title, "Of the General and District Conferences," and in 1796, "District"† was changed to "Yearly" and that, in 1816, to "Annual."

---

* This note was added especially to meet the peculiar case of the brethren in Canada, against whom unfounded suspicions had been created, because the Methodist Episcopal Church, of which they were then a part, was regarded as a foreign ecclesiastical authority.

† To avoid repetition it is here stated, once for all, that throughout the Discipline of 1792 the annual conferences are called "District Conferences," there being then one held for every presiding elder's district.   But the term was never afterward thus employed; though it was subsequently (1820–1836) applied to the conferences of local preachers appointed for each presiding elder's district.

The introductory part of this section is found in the first Discipline, (Question 1,) and as it has undergone no material alteration since, it will be sufficient to refer to it.* The remainder of the section was not divided until 1808, but for convenience, the whole will be treated under the heads then adopted, namely, "Of the General Conference" and "Of the Annual Conference."

Of the General Conference.

Nothing appears, on this subject, until 1792, when the first General Conference, after the organization of the church, was held. We then find the following:—

1792. "*Quest.* 2. Who shall compose the General Conference?

"*Ans.* All the travelling preachers who shall be in full connection at the time of holding the conference.

"*Quest.* 3. When and where shall the next General Conference be held?

"*Ans.* On the first day of November, in the year 1796, in the town of Baltimore."

1796. Question 3, struck out.

1800. An additional qualification for membership was added, namely:—to "have travelled four years."

1804. It was provided that the "four years" should date "from the time that they were received on trial by an annual conference."

1808. This was the last meeting of a General Conference, composed of all the preachers who had travelled four years. It was then resolved to have, in future, a delegated General Conference, and the following was adopted as its constitution, in lieu of the former.

"*Quest.* 2. Who shall compose the General Conference, and what are the regulations and powers belonging to it?

"*Ans.* 1. The General Conference shall be com-

---

* See above, p. 26.

posed of one member for every five members of each
annual conference, to be appointed either by seniority
or choice, at the discretion of such annual conference :
yet so that such representatives shall have travelled at
least four full calendar years from the time that they
were received on trial by an annual conference, and
are in full connection at the time of holding the conference.

" 2. The General Conference shall meet on the first
day of May, in the year of our Lord 1812, in the city
of New-York, and thenceforward on the first day of
May, once in four years perpetually, in such place or
places as shall be fixed on by the General Conference
from time to time : but the general superintendents,
with or by the advice of all the annual conferences, or
if there be no general superintendent, all the annual
conferences respectively shall have power to call a
General Conference, if they judge it necessary at any
time.

" 3. At all times when the General Conference is
met, it shall take two-thirds of the representatives of all
the annual conferences to make a quorum for transacting business.

" 4. One of the general superintendents shall preside
in the General Conference ; but in case no general superintendent be present, the General Conference shall
choose a president pro tem.

" 5. The General Conference shall have full powers
to make rules and regulations for our church, under the
following limitations and restrictions, namely :—

" 1. The General Conference shall not revoke, alter,
or change our Articles of Religion, nor establish any
new standards or rules of doctrine contrary to our present existing and established standards of doctrine.

" 2. They shall not allow of more than one representative for every five members of the annual conference,
nor allow of a less number than one for every seven.

" 3. They shall not change or alter any part or rule
ͫr government, so as to do away episcopacy, or

destroy the plan of our itinerant general superintend ency.

"4. They shall not revoke or change the general rules of the United Societies.

" 5. They shall not do away the privileges of our ministers or preachers of trial by a committee, and of an appeal : neither shall they do away the privileges of our members of trial before the society, or by a committee, and of an appeal.

" 6. They shall not appropriate the produce of the Book Concern, nor of the Chartered Fund, to any purpose other than for the benefit of the travelling, supernumerary, superannuated and worn-out preachers, their wives, widows, and children.

"Provided, nevertheless, that upon the joint recommendation of all the annual conferences, then a majority of two-thirds of the General Conference succeeding, shall suffice to alter any of the above restrictions."

1816. The ratio of representation, in Ans. 1, was altered to one for every seven.

1832. The former proviso, at the close of the restrictive rules, was struck out, and the following substituted : " Provided, nevertheless, that upon the concurrent recommendation of three-fourths of all the members of the several annual conferences, who shall be present and vote on such recommendation, then a majority of two-thirds of the General Conference succeeding shall suffice to alter any of the above restrictions excepting the first article : and also, whenever such alteration or alterations shall have been first recommended by two-thirds of the General Conference, so soon as three-fourths of the members of all the annual conferences shall have concurred as aforesaid, such alteration or alterations shall take effect."

1836. The ratio of representation was altered to one for every twenty-one ; and to allow this, the second of the restrictive rules was changed to the following :—

" 2. They shall not allow of more than one repre-

sentative for every fourteen members of the annual
conference, nor allow of a less number than one for
every thirty : provided, nevertheless, that when there
shall be in any annual conference a fraction of two-
thirds the number which shall be fixed for the ratio of
representation, such annual conference shall be entitled
to an additional delegate for such fraction ; and provided, also, that no conference shall be denied the
privilege of two delegates."

Of the Annual Conferences.

First, as to who compose them, when and where held.

There was nothing in relation to these points in the
Discipline of 1784, or 1789 ; but in 1792 we have the
following :—

1792. " *Quest.* 4. Who are the members of the
district conferences ?

" *Ans.* All the travelling preachers of the district or
districts respectively who are in full connection.

" *Quest.* 5. How often are the district conferences
to be held ?

" *Ans.* Annually.

" *Quest.* 6. How many circuits shall send preachers
in order to form a district conference ?

" *Ans.* Not fewer than three, nor more than twelve.

" *Quest.* 7. Shall the bishop be authorized to unite
two or more districts together, where he judges it expedient, in order to form a district conference ?

" *Ans.* He shall, as far as is consistent with the rule
immediately preceding.

" *Quest.* 8. Who shall appoint the times of holding
the district conferences ?

" *Ans.* The bishop."

1796. Instead of question 4, above, we have

" *Quest.* 3. Who shall attend the yearly conferences?

" *Ans.* All the travelling preachers who are in full
connection, and those who are to be received into full
connection."

The 5th, 6th, and 7th questions struck out.

1804. The answer to Question 4 (Question 8,

1792) reads :—" The bishops ; but they shall allow the annual conference to sit a week at least."

The following added :—" *Quest.* 5. Who shall appoint the place of holding the annual conference. *Ans.* Each annual conference shall appoint the place of its own sitting."

Second, as to the order of business.

1784. The following order was adopted.*
" *Quest.* 70. What is the method wherein we usually proceed in our conferences ?

" *Ans.* We inquire, 1. What preachers are admitted ? Who remain on trial ? Who are admitted on trial ? Who desist from travelling ? 2. Are there any objections to any of the preachers ?—who are named one by one. 3. How are the preachers stationed this year ? 4. What numbers are in the society ? What was contributed for the contingent expenses ? 6. How was this expended ? 7. What is contributed toward the fund for the superannuated preachers and the widows and orphans of the preachers ? 8. What demands are there upon it ? 9. How many preachers' wives are to be provided for ? By what circuits and in what proportion ? 10. Where and when may our next conference begin ?"

1789. Item 9 was omitted.

---

* According to the Annual Minutes, the order of business, prior to the organization of the church, was as follows :—
1773. " 1. How are the preachers stationed ?
" 2. What numbers are there in the society ?"
The following questions were subsequently added, at the dates prefixed to them respectively :—
1774. " 1. Who are admitted this year ?
" 2. Who are admitted on trial ?
" 3. Who are assistants this year ?
" 4. Are there any objections to any of the preachers ?"
1779. " Who desist from travelling ?"
1780. " What preachers are admitted into full connection ?"
1782. " What is the yearly collection ?" " How was it expended ?"
" Where and when shall our next conferences be held ?"
1783. " What sum is to be raised for the support of the preachers' wives ?"
1784. " What preachers have died this year ?"

1792. The order of business was thus modified:—

"*Quest.* 9. What is the method wherein we usually proceed in the district conferences?

"*Ans.* We inquire,—

" 1. What preachers are admitted on trial?

" 2. Who remain on trial?

" 3. Who are admitted into full connection?

" 4. Who are the deacons?

" 5. Who are the elders?

" 6. Who have been elected by the unanimous suffrages of the General Conference to exercise the Episcopal office, and superintend the Methodist Episcopal Church in America?

" 7. Who are under a location, through weakness of body, or family concerns?

" 8. Who are the supernumeraries?*

" 9. Who have died this year?

" 10. Are all the preachers blameless in life and conversation?

" 11. Who are expelled from the connection?

" 12. Where are the preachers stationed this year?

" 13. What numbers are in society?

" 14. What has been collected for the contingent expenses?

" 15. How has this been expended?

" 16. What is contributed toward the fund for the superannuated preachers, and the widows and orphans of the preachers?

" 17. What demands are there upon it?

" 18. Where and when shall our next conference be held?"

1800. The fourteenth item reads, "What has been collected for the contingent expenses, for the making up the allowance of the preachers, &c." The sixteenth and seventeenth items are omitted.

---

* " A supernumerary preacher is one so worn out in the itinerant service, as to be rendered incapable of preaching constantly: but at the same time is willing to do any work in the ministry which the conference may direct, and his strength enable him to perform."

1804. The eighth item reads, "Who are the supernumerary, superannuated, and worn-out preach ers?"

1812. The seventh item reads, "Who have lo cated this year?" The eighth item of 1804 is divided so as to read,—"8. Who are the supernumeraries 9. Who are the superannuated or worn-out preachers? The following item was added:—"11. Who have with drawn from the connection this year?"

1832. After the ninth item, (1812,) the following was added:—"Every superannuated preacher, who may reside without the bounds of the conference of which he is a member, shall annually forward to his conference a certificate of his Christian and ministeria conduct, together with an account of the number and circumstances of his family, signed by the presiding elder of the district, or the preacher in charge of the circuit or station within whose bounds he may reside without which the conference shall not be required to allow his claim."

The fifteenth item (fourteenth, 1800) was thus ex pressed:—"What amounts are necessary for the super annuated preachers, and the widows and orphans of preachers, and to make up the deficiencies of those who have not obtained their regular allowance on the cir cuits?" The sixteenth (fifteenth, 1792) thus:—"Wha has been collected on the foregoing accounts, and how has it been applied?" A new item was also inserted namely, "17. What has been contributed for the sup port of missions, and what for the publication of Bibles tracts, and Sunday-school books?"

1840. After the eighth item, (1812,) the follow ing was added:—"A supernumerary preacher, who refuses to attend to the work assigned him, unless in case of sickness, or other unavoidable cause or causes shall not be allowed to exercise the functions of his office, nor even to preach among us; nevertheless, the final determination of the case shall be with the annua conference of which he is a member, who shall have power to acquit, suspend, locate, or expel him, as the case may be."

Third, Miscellaneous Questions.

1787.   The following was added :—

"*Quest.* 3. Is there any other business to be done in the conference?

"*Ans.* The electing and ordaining of bishops,* elders, and deacons."

1792.   The following was added :—

"*Quest.* 11. How are the districts to be formed?

"*Ans.* According to the judgment of the bishop.

"N. B. In case that there be no bishop to travel through the district, and exercise the Episcopal office, on account of death, the districts shall be regulated in every respect by the district conferences and the presiding elders till the ensuing General Conference, (ordinations only excepted.")†

1796.   The following question was inserted :—

"*Quest.* 7. Are there any other directions to be given concerning the yearly conferences?

"*Ans.* There shall be six conferences in the year, as follows, namely :" [The boundaries of the annual conferences are given, in this and in subsequent editions until 1804, in this connection ; but as this

---

* It will be remembered that this was prior to the distinction between general and annual conferences. When that took place, (in 1792,) the word "bishops" was struck out of this answer. This was the first time that the title " bishop" was applied to the "superintendents" in the Discipline. Afterward it was generally substituted for the latter.

† It will be perceived that in 1792 the Discipline contemplated the holding of an annual conference in each presiding elder's district. And such was the practice of that day, as many as four such conferences being held in a month, and twenty of them in a year, by a single bishop. In 1796 the yearly conferences, as they were now called, were reduced in number to six, each including a number of districts, and their boundaries were fixed by the General Conference. Nevertheless, the above question and note were still retained, only changing the name " district conferences," in the note, to " yearly conferences." But as a presiding elder's district was now but a fraction of a conference, the provisions of this clause were, of course, more limited in their application.

portion of the Discipline was afterward transferred to Part ii, Sec. 1, we shall there present a connected view of the whole.]

1800. The following was added at the close of the section :—" A record of the proceedings of each annual conference shall be kept by a secretary, chosen for that purpose ; and let a copy of the said record be sent to the General Conference.

" Each annual conference is to pay its proportionable part toward the allowances of the bishops."

1804. The following portions of this section were transferred to Part ii, and constituted its first section, namely, the boundaries of the annual conferences, (1796) Question 11 and the note (1792,) and the last sentence added in 1800. These have been the subjects of Section 1, Part ii, from that time to the present.

The number and order of the questions relating to the annual conferences have not been altered since 1804.

SECTION IV.

*Of the Election and Consecration of Bishops, and of their Duty.**

1784. At the organization of the church the following provisions were introduced respecting the superintendency :—

" *Quest.* 26. What is the office of a superintendent ?

" *Ans.* To ordain superintendents, elders, and deacons ; to preside as a moderator in our conferences ; to fix the appointments of the preachers for the several circuits ; and, in the intervals of the conference, to

---

* Prior to the organization of the church, the superintendence of the societies was committed to the general assistant. In 1779 we find the following minute as to his authority :—

" *Quest.* 13. How far shall his power extend ?

" *Ans.* On hearing every preacher for and against what is in debate, the right of determination shall rest with him according to the Minutes."

change, receive, or suspend preachers, as necessity may
require ; and to receive appeals from the preachers and
people, and decide them.

"N. B. No person shall be ordained a superintendent, elder, or deacon, without the consent of a majority
of the conference, and the consent and imposition of
hands of a superintendent ; except in the instance provided for in the twenty-ninth minute.

"*Quest.* 27. To whom is the superintendent amenable for his conduct ?

"*Ans.* To the conference ; who have power to expel him for improper conduct, if they see it necessary.

"*Quest.* 28. If the superintendent ceases from travelling at large among the people, shall he exercise his
office in any degree ?

"*Ans.* If he ceases from travelling without the consent of the conference, he shall not thereafter exercise
any ministerial function whatsoever in our church.

"*Quest.* 29. If by death, expulsion, or otherwise,
there be no superintendent remaining in our church,
what shall we do ?

"*Ans.* The conference shall elect a superintendent,
and the elders or any three of them shall ordain him,
according to our Liturgy."

1789. This subject was treated in the fourth
section, entitled, "On the constituting of Bishops, and
their Duty."

The following was substituted for the "N. B.,"
1784 :—

"*Quest.* 2. How is a bishop to be constituted in
future ?

"*Ans.* By the election of a majority of the conference, and the laying on of the hands of a bishop."

The following is added to the duties of a bishop,
(Question 26, 1784):—"To travel through as many circuits as he can, and to direct in the spiritual business
of the societies ;" and he was now deprived of the power
" to receive appeals from the preachers and people, and
to decide them."

Question 29, (1784,) struck out.

1792. The section took the place and the title which it now holds, and read as follows :—

" *Quest.* 1. How is a bishop to be constituted in future ?

" *Ans.* By the election of the General Conference, and the laying on of the hands of three bishops, or at least of one bishop and two elders.

" *Quest.* 2. If by death, expulsion, or otherwise, there be no bishop remaining in our church, what shall we do ?

" *Ans.* The General Conference shall elect a bishop ; and the elders, or any three of them, that shall be appointed by the General Conference for that purpose, shall ordain him according to our office of ordination.

" *Quest.* 3. What is the bishop's duty ?

" *Ans.* 1. To preside in our conferences.

" 2. To fix the appointments of the preachers for the several circuits.

" 3. In the intervals of the conferences to change, receive, or suspend preachers, as necessity may require.

" 4. To travel through the connection at large.

" 5. To oversee the spiritual and temporal business of the societies.

" 6. To ordain bishops, elders, and deacons.

" *Quest.* 4. To whom is the bishop amenable for his conduct ?

" *Ans.* To the General Conference, who have power to expel him for improper conduct, if they see it necessary.

" *Quest.* 5. What provision shall be made for the trial of an immoral bishop, in the interval of the General Conference ?

" *Ans.* If a bishop be guilty of immorality, three travelling elders shall call upon him, and examine him on the subject : and if the three elders verily believe that the bishop is guilty of the crime, they shall call to their aid two presiding elders from two districts in the neigh-

6

At the close is added, " And also to appoint an agent or agents for the benefit of our literary institutions."

In 1840, also, the two following were added to the duties of a bishop, (Question 3.)

" 7. To decide all questions of law in an annual conference, subject to an appeal to the General Conference ; but in all cases the application of law shall be with the conference.

" 8. The bishops may, when they judge it necessary, unite two or more circuits or stations together, without affecting their separate financial interests or pastoral duties."

SECTION V.

Of the Presiding Elders, and of their Duty.

The origin of this office is thus explained by the bishops in their Notes to the Discipline of 1796 :—

" When Mr. Wesley drew up a plan of government for our church in America, he desired that no more elders should be ordained, in the first instance, than were absolutely necessary, and that the work on the continent should be divided between them, in respect the duties of their office. The General Conference accordingly elected twelve elders for the above purposes. Bishop Asbury and the district conferences afterward found that this order of men was so necessary, that they agreed to enlarge the number, and give them the *name** by which they are at present called, and which is perfectly Scriptural, though not *the word* used in our translation : and this proceeding afterward received the approbation of Mr. Wesley.

" In 1792 the General Conference, equally conscious of the necessity of having such an office among us, not only confirmed every thing that Bishop Asbury and the district conferences had done, but also drew up or

* The title does not occur in the Annual Minutes, however, till 1797.

agreed to the present section for the explanation of the nature and duties of the office."

As then all elders were, at first, presiding elders, we shall notice, under this head, all the rules in reference to them prior to 1792, when the distinction was introduced into the Discipline between "presiding elders" and "travelling elders"—a distinction, not of order, but of office.

1784. "*Quest.* 30. What is the office of an elder?

"*Ans.* To administer the sacraments of baptism and the Lord's supper, and to perform all the other rites prescribed by our Liturgy."

"*Quest.* 35. How are we to proceed with those elders or deacons who cease from travelling?

"*Ans.* Unless they have the permission of the conference declared under the hand of a superintendent they are on no account to exercise any of the peculiar unctions of those offices among us. And if they do they are to be expelled immediately."

1786. The following added to the duties of an elder:—

"2. To exercise within his own district, during the absence of the superintendents, all the powers invested in them for the government of our church. Provided that he never act contrary to an express order of the superintendents."

1789. The following section on the subject was substituted for the previous provisions:—

"Sec. V. On the constituting of Elders, and their Duty.

"*Quest.* 1. How is an elder constituted?

"*Ans.* By the election of a majority of the conference, and by the laying on of the hands of a bishop and of the elders that are present.

"*Quest.* 2. What is his duty?

"*Ans.* 1. To travel through his appointed district.

"2. To administer baptism and the Lord's supper, and to perform all parts of divine service.

" 3. In the absence of a bishop to take charge of all
he deacons, travelling and local preachers, and ex-
orters.

" 4. To change, receive, or suspend preachers.

" 5. To direct in the transaction of the spiritual busi-
ess of his circuit.

" 6. To take care that every part of our Discipline
e enforced.

" 7. To aid in the public collections.

" 8. To attend his bishop, when present, and give
im, when absent, all necessary information, by letter,
f the state of his district.*

" N. B. No elder that ceases to travel, without the
onsent of the conference, certified under the hand of a
ishop, shall, on any account, exercise the peculiar
unctions of his office among us."

1792.   The rules relating to the eldership as an
rder in the church were transferred to a distinct sec-
:on, and the following section, with its present title,
ras framed, respecting the presiding elders.

" *Quest.* 1. By whom are the presiding elders to be
hosen?

" *Ans.* By the bishop.

" *Quest.* 2. What are the duties of the presiding elder?

" *Ans.* 1. To travel through his appointed district.

" 2. In the absence of a bishop to take charge of all
ie elders, deacons, travelling and local preachers, and
xhorters in his district.

" 3. To change, receive, or suspend preachers in his
istrict during the intervals of the conferences, and in
ie absence of the bishop.

" 4. In the absence of a bishop to preside in the
onference of his district.

" 5. To be present, as far as practicable, at all the
uarterly meetings; and to call together, at each quar-

* In 1773 it was ordered, " Every preacher who acts as an assistant
send an account of the work once in six months to the general
sistant."—*Annual Minutes.*

terly meeting, all the travelling and local preachers
exhorters, stewards, and leaders of the circuit, to hea
complaints, and to receive appeals.

" 6. To oversee the spiritual and temporal busines
of the societies in his district.

" 7. To take care that every part of our Disciplin(
be enforced in his district.

" 8. To attend the bishop when present in his dis
trict ; and to give him when absent all necessary in
formation, by letter, of the state of his district.

" *Quest.* 3. By whom are the presiding elders to b(
stationed and changed ?

" *Ans.* By the bishop.

" *Quest.* 4. How long may the bishops allow a
elder to preside in the same district ?

" *Ans.* For any term not exceeding four years succes
sively.*

" *Quest.* 5. How shall the presiding elders be sup
ported ?

" *Ans.* If there be a surplus of the public money i
one or more circuits in his district, he shall receiv
such surplus, provided he do not receive more than hi
annual salary.   In case of a deficiency in his salary
after such surplus is paid him, or if there be no sur
plus, he shall share with the preachers of his distric
in proportion with what they have respectively received
so that he receive no more than the amount of hi
salary upon the whole."

1804. To the third item of the presiding elder'
duties (Quest. 2) is added, " as the Discipline directs.
In the fourth item, the words, " of his district," strucl
out, and the following added, " but in case there ar
two or more presiding elders belonging to one confei

---

* This restriction (for originally there was none) is said to hav
been introduced in consequence of the evil results of a more protrac
ed term, in the case of James O'Kelly, who had been presidin
elder in the southern part of Virginia, ever since the organization o
the church, besides having been stationed there several years before
and who thus acquired a power to injure the church by his secessiot
which otherwise he would not have possessed.

nce, the bishop or bishops may, by letter or otherwise,
ppoint the president ; but if no appointment be made,
r if the presiding elder appointed do not attend, the
onference shall, in either of these cases, elect the pre-
ident by ballot, without debate, from among the pre-
iding elders."

In the fifth item, after " quarterly meeting," is in-
erted, " a quarterly meeting conference,* consisting
f ;" after " circuit," the words " and none else ;" and
fter " receive," the words " and try." At the close is
dded, " The quarterly meeting conference shall
ppoint a secretary to take down the proceedings of
he quarterly meeting conference, in a book kept by
ne of the stewards of the circuit for that purpose."

The following new question was inserted :—

" *Quest.* 5. Shall the presiding elder have power to
mploy a preacher who has been rejected at the pre-
ious annual conference ?

"*Ans.* He shall not, unless the conference should
ive him liberty under certain conditions."

At the close of the answer to Quest. 6, (Quest. 5,
792,) is added the following: " he shall be accounta-
le to the annual conference for what he receives as his
alary."

1832. To the sixth item of the presiding elder's
uties (Quest. 2, 1792) is added, " and to promote, by
ll proper means, the cause of missions and Sunday
chools, and the publication, at our own press, of Bibles,
racts, and Sunday-school books."

1840. To the same item is added, " and care-
ully to inquire, at each quarterly meeting conference,
vhether the rules respecting the instruction of children
ave been faithfully observed."

To the seventh item is added, " And to decide all
uestions of law in a quarterly meeting conference,
ubject to an appeal to the president of the next annual

---

* The terms " quarterly meeting," " quarterly conference," and
quarterly meeting conference," are frequently used as synonymous.

conference ; but in all cases the application of law shal
be with the conference."

SECTION VI.

*Of the Election and Ordination of Travelling Elders
and of their Duty.**

1792. " *Quest.* 1. How is an elder constituted
" *Ans.* By the election of a majority of the distric
conference, and by the laying on of the hands of ;
bishop, and of the elders that are present.
" *Quest.* 2. What is the duty of a travelling elder ?
" *Ans.* 1. To administer baptism and the Lord'
supper, and to perform the office of matrimony and al
parts of divine worship.
" 2. To do all the duties of a travelling preacher.
" N. B. No elder, that ceases to travel, without the
consent of the district conference, certified under the
hand of the president of the conference, shall, on any
account, exercise the peculiar functions of his offic(
among us."
1804. In the note, after "president of the con
ference," is inserted, " except in case of sickness, de
bility, or other unavoidable circumstance ;" and, at the
close, is added, " or even be allowed to preach amon{
us ; nevertheless, the final determination in all such
cases is with the yearly conference."

SECTION VII.

*Of the Election and Ordination of Travelling Dea
cons, and of their Duty.*

1784. " *Quest.* 31. What is the office of a deacon
" *Ans.* To baptize in the absence of an elder, to assis
the elder in the administration of the Lord's supper, t(
marry, bury the dead, and read the Liturgy to the peo

---

* For the rules on this subject prior to 1792, see Sec. 5.
6*

ple as prescribed, except what relates to the administration of the Lord's supper."

1789.   In the place of the above we have the following :—

" Section 6. On the constituting of Deacons, and their Duty.

" *Quest.* 1. How is a deacon constituted ?

" *Ans.* By the election of a majority of the conference, and the laying on of the hands of a bishop.

" *Quest.* 2. What is the duty of a deacon ?

" *Ans.* 1. To baptize, and perform the office of matrimony, in the absence of the elder.

" 2. To assist the elder in administering the Lord's supper.

[Here follows a long list of other duties, which were afterward transferred to a new section on the duties of those who have the charge of circuits. See Sec. 10.]

The following note was added, being a modification of the rule of 1784, Quest. 35. (See p. 125.)

" N. B. No deacon that ceases to travel without the consent of the conference, certified under the hand of a bishop, shall on any account exercise the peculiar functions of his office."

1792.   This was made the seventh section, with the present title.   The epithet " travelling" is prefixed to " deacon," throughout : and at the close of the section the following is added to the duties of a deacon:—

" 3. To do all the duties of a travelling preacher."

1796.   The following new question was inserted:

" *Quest.* 3. What shall be the time of probation of a travelling deacon for the office of an elder ?

" *Ans.* Every travelling deacon shall exercise that office for two years, before he be eligible to the office of an elder ; except in the case of missions, when the yearly conferences shall have authority to elect for the elder's office sooner, if they judge it expedient."

1804.   The same changes made in the note respecting deacons who cease to travel], as in the case of elders (p. 129.)

1832. The following was added at the close of this section :—

" Provided always, that when a preacher shall have passed his examination, and been admitted into full connection, and elected to deacon's office, but fails of his ordination through the absence of the bishop, his eligibility to the office of elder shall run from the time of his election to the office of a deacon."

SECTION VIII.

Of the Reception of Preachers from the Wesleyan Connection, and from other Denominations.

This section was inserted in 1840, and is as follows :

" *Quest.* 1. In what manner shall we receive those ministers who may come to us from the Wesleyan connection in Europe or Canada ?

" *Ans.* If they come to us properly accredited from either the British, Irish, or Canada Conference, they may be received according to such credentials, provided they give satisfaction to an annual conference of their willingness to conform to our church government and usages.

" *Quest.* 2. How shall we receive those ministers who may offer to unite with us from other Christian churches ?

" *Ans.* Those ministers of other evangelical churches, who may desire to unite with our church, whether as local or itinerant, may be received according to our usages, on condition of their taking upon them our ordination vows, without the reimposition of hands, giving satisfaction to an annual conference of their being in orders, and of their agreement with us in doctrine, discipline, government, and usages ; provided the conference is also satisfied with their gifts, grace, and usefulness.   Whenever any such minister is received, he shall be furnished with a certificate, signed by one of our bishops, in the following words, namely :—

" This is to certify, that   has been admitted into   conference as a travelling preacher, [or has been admitted as a local preacher on   circuit,] he having been ordained to the office of a deacon, (or an elder, as the case may be,) according to the usages of the   church, of which he has been a member and minister ; and he is hereby authorized to exercise the functions pertaining to his office in the Methodist Episcopal Church, so long as his life and conversation are such as become the gospel of Christ.

" Given under my hand and seal, at   this day of   in the year of our Lord,

" *Quest.* 3. How shall we receive preachers of other denominations who are not in orders ?

" *Ans.* They may be received as licentiates, provided they give satisfaction to a quarterly, or an annual conference, that they are suitable persons to exercise the office, and of their agreement with the doctrines, discipline, government, and usages of our church."

SECTION IX.

Of the Method of receiving Travelling Preachers, and of their Duty.

Quest. 1. How is a preacher to be received?

1784. " *Quest.* 36. What method shall we take to prevent improper persons from preaching among us as travelling preachers ?*

" *Ans.* Let no person be employed as a travelling preacher, unless his name be printed in the Minutes of the conference preceding, or a certificate be given him under the hand of one or other of the superintendents, or, in their absence, of three assistants, as is hereafter

---

* In 1780 it was required that all the travelling preachers should take a license from every conference, signed by Mr. Asbury.

In 1782, the more effectually to " guard against disorderly travelling preachers," it was ordered—" Write at the bottom of every certificate :—' The authority this conveys is limited to next conference.' "

provided.   And for this purpose, let the Minutes of the conference be always printed."*

1786.   For "three assistants, as is hereafter provided," we have "the elder of his district."

1789.   The following was substituted :—

" *Quest.* 1. How is a preacher to be received ?

" *Ans.* 1. By the conference.

" 2. In the interval of the conference by the bishop, or an elder, until the sitting of the conference.

" 3. When his name is not printed in the Minutes, he must receive a written license from his elder or bishop."

1792.   "Presiding elder of the district" substituted for " elder."

1816.   A new paragraph was inserted as follows :—

" 3. It shall be the duty of the bishops or of a committee which they may appoint, at each annual conference, to point out a course of reading and study proper to be pursued by candidates for the ministry ; and the presiding elder, whenever such are presented to him, shall direct them to those studies which have been thus recommended.—And before any such candidate is received into full connection, he shall give satisfactory evidence respecting his knowledge of those particular subjects which have been recommended to his consideration."

Quest. 2. What is the duty of a preacher !

1784.   " *Quest.* 32. What is the office of a helper ?

" *Ans.* 1. To preach.

" 2. To meet the society and the bands weekly.†

" 3. To visit the sick.

" 4. To meet the leaders weekly.

---

* They had not been printed previously.—See Lee's Hist. of the Methodists, p. 45.

† In the Annual Minutes for 1779 we find the following question " Ought not every travelling preacher to meet the class wherever he preaches ?   *Ans.* Yes, if possible."

"Let every preacher be particularly exact in this, and in morning preaching. If he has twenty hearers, let him preach. N. B. We are fully determined never to drop morning preaching, and to preach at five wherever it is practicable."

1786. The morning preaching ordered to be "at five in the summer, and at six in the winter, wherever it is practicable."

1789. The second item of a preacher's duty reads: "To meet the societies or classes and bands." In the fourth, the word "weekly" was struck out, and the following was added: 5. To preach in the morning, where he can get hearers."

1792. Item 4, struck out.

1804. In item 2, before "bands" was inserted "general." The hours of morning preaching were now only "recommended."*

Quest. 3. What are the directions given to a preacher?

The rules on this subject are found under Quest. 33, 1784, and, as there has been little alteration in them since, it will be sufficient to refer to them. (See pp. 40–1.)

1786. The following sentences were struck out of the answer; namely, (item 8.) "You have no more to do with this character [that of a gentleman] than with that of a dancing master." (9.) "Not of cleaning your own shoes or your neighbour's."

1789. The question reads as now. The following clauses struck out: (3.) "particularly with young

---

* In 1784 the following was included among the duties of helpers:
" *Quest.* 34. Will it be expedient to appoint some of our helpers to read the morning and evening service out of our Liturgy on the Lord's day?

" *Ans.* It will. And every helper who receives a written direction under the hand of a superintendent, may regularly read the morning and evening service on the Lord's day.

" In 1789 this was modified so as to read—*Quest.* 3. Are the preachers to read our Liturgy? *Ans.* All that have received a written direction for that purpose, under the hand of a bishop or elder, may read the Liturgy as often as they think it expedient."

In 1792 the whole was struck out.

women."—(9.) " Not of fetching wood, (if time permit,) or drawing water ;" and the note at the end of the answer was also omitted.

1792. In item 5, after, " Believe evil of no one," was inserted "without good evidence." In item 8, the first sentence was modified so as to read, " Avoid all affectation."

Quest. 4. What method do we use in receiving a preacher at the conference ?*

1784. The original provisions on this subject may be found in the Discipline of 1784, under Question 69. (See pp. 63–4.) By reference to them, the alterations they have undergone will be understood without quoting them here.

1789. The question assumed its present form ; and the following were left out of the interrogatories to be proposed to the candidate, namely :—" Do you know the Methodist plan ?" " Do you take no drams ?" and, " Will you preach every morning at five o'clock, wherever you can have twenty hearers ?" It was now provided that a preacher may be received into full connection, "after two years' probation, being recommended by the elders and deacons present, and examined by the bishop." The " note of permission from the assistant" was now required only in the case of *local* preachers or exhorters.

1792. In regard to receiving on trial, it was provided, " But no one shall be received unless he first procure a recommendation from the quarterly meeting of his circuit."

It was now provided that the candidates for admission into full connection should be " approved by the district [annual] conference, and examined by the president of the conference."

The rule about licensing local preachers and exhorters was transferred to the close of the section " On the

---

* This portion of the Discipline has reference, in all the editions, to receiving on trial ; but in practice, it is believed, it is always applied to admission into full connection.

Duties of those who have the Charge of Circuits," and the following introduced :—

" N. B. If any preacher absent himself from his circuit without the leave of the presiding elder, the presiding elder shall, as far as possible, fill his place with another preacher who shall be paid for his labours out of the salary of the absent preacher, in proportion to the usual allowance."

1804.   It was provided that the two years' probation of a preacher " is to commence from his being received on trial at the yearly conference."

1836.   The following note was added to the section :—

" N. B. Whenever a preacher on trial is selected by the bishop for a mission, he may, if elected by an annual conference, ordain him a deacon before his probation ends, and a missionary employed on a foreign mission may be admitted into full connection, if recommended by the superintendent of the mission where he labours, without being present at the annual conference for examination.

" At each annual conference, those who are received on trial, or are admitted into full connection, shall be asked whether they are willing to devote themselves to the missionary work ; and a list of the names of all those who are willing to do so shall be taken and reported to the corresponding secretary of the Missionary Society ; and all such shall be considered as ready and willing to be employed as missionaries whenever called for by either of the bishops.

" It shall be the duty of all our missionaries, except those who are appointed to labour for the benefit of the slaves, to form their circuits into auxiliary missionary societies, and to make regular quarterly and class collections wherever practicable, and report the amount collected every three months, either by endorsing it on their drafts, or by transmitting the money to the treasurer of the parent society.

" It shall be the duty of each annual conference to

examine strictly into the state of the domestic missions within its bounds, and to allow none to remain on the list of its missions which, in the judgment of the conference, is able to support itself."

1840. It was now provided that a candidate, instead of being received into full connection, "after two years' probation, &c.," should only be received "after he has been employed two successive years in the regular itinerant work, &c." In the "N. B.," 1792 the words, "without the leave of the presiding elder," struck out.

SECTION X.

Of the Duties of those who have the Charge of Circuits

This subject was treated, in 1784, under the Questions 60, 61 and 62 : and, in 1789, under the duties of a deacon.   In 1792 it was made a distinct section with its present title and number.   The duties will be taken up one by one.

Quest. 1. What are the duties of the elder, deacon, or preacher, who has the special charge of a circuit?

1.   **1784.** "To see that the other preachers in his circuit behave well and want nothing."

2.   **1784.** "To renew the tickets quarterly and regulate the bands."

1820. After "tickets" was inserted "for the admission of members into love-feast."

3.   **1792.** "To meet the stewards and leaders as often as possible."

4.   **1784.** "To appoint all the stewards and leaders, and change them when he sees it necessary."

1812.   The power to *appoint* stewards taken away

5.   **1792.**   "To receive, try, and expel members according to the form of Discipline." *

---

* This was a substitute for the original rule, which was struck out in 1789, namely :—" To take in or put out of the society or the bands."

6. **1784.** "To keep watch-nights and love feasts."

7. **1784.** "To hold quarterly meetings, and therein diligently to inquire both into the temporal and spiritual state of each society."

1792. It was changed so as to read, "To hold quarterly meetings in the absence of the presiding elder."

8. **1784.** "To take care that every society be duly supplied with books : particularly with Kempis, the Instructions for Children, and the Primitive Physic, which ought to be in every house."

1792. All after "with books," struck out.

9. **1784.** "To take exact lists of his societies, and bring them to the conference."

1789. It reads, "To take an exact account of the numbers in society, and bring it to the conference."

1800. It was, "To take an exact account of the numbers in society, and a regular account of all the deaths in the societies, in their respective circuits, and deliver in such accounts to the annual conference, that they may be printed in the Minutes."

1836. It was altered so as to read, "To take an exact account of the members in society in their respective circuits and stations, keeping the names of all local elders, deacons, and preachers, properly distinguished, and deliver in such account to the annual conference, that their number may be printed in the Minutes."

10. **1784.** "To send an account of his circuit every half year to one of the superintendents."

1789. It was to be done "every quarter to his elder."

11. **1784.** "To meet the married men and women, and the single men and women, in the large societies, once a quarter."

1789. It reads, "To meet the men and women apart, in the large societies, once a quarter."

1792. "wherever it is practicable," is added.

12. **1784.** " To overlook the accounts of all the stewards."

13. **1789.** " To appoint a person to receive the quarterly collection *in the classes,* and to be present at the time of receiving it."*

1792. All after " *classes*" struck out.

14. **1789.** " To see that *public* collections be made quarterly, if need be."

15. **1832.** " To encourage the support of missions and Sunday schools, and the publication and distribution of Bibles, tracts, and Sunday-school books, by forming societies and making collections for these objects, in such way and manner as the annual conference to which he belongs shall from time to time direct."

16. **1832.** " To lay before the quarterly conference, at its last meeting annually, to be entered on its journal, a written statement of the number and state of the Sunday schools in the circuit or station, and to report the same, together with the amount raised for the support of missions, and for the publication of Bibles, tracts, and Sunday-school books, to his annual conference."

1840. For " at its last meeting annually," we have " at each quarterly meeting, as far as practicable.'

17. **1789.** " To move a yearly subscription through those circuits that can bear it, for building churches."

1792. It is added, " and paying the debts of those which have been already erected."

18. **1789.** " To choose a committee of lay members to make a just application of the money where it is most needed."

Quest. 2. What other directions shall we give him ?

1. **1784.** " Several, 1. Take a regular catalogue of your societies as they live in house-row."

1789. This was to be done in " the societies in towns and cities."

---

* For the previous usage see Quest. 79, 1784, p. 76.

1792. This, as well as the subsequent answers, put into the infinitive form instead of the imperative.

2. **1784.** "Leave your successor a particular account of the state of the circuit."

1832. It is added, "including an account of the subscribers for our periodicals."

3. **1784.** "See that every band leader have the rules of the bands."

4. **1784.** "Vigorously but calmly enforce the rules concerning needless ornaments and drams."

1792. This was to be done in reference to "all the rules of the society."

5. **1784.** "As soon as there are four men or women believers in any place, put them into a band."

6. **1784.** "Suffer no love-feast to last above an hour and a half."

7. **1784.** "Warn all from time to time, that none are to remove from one society to another, without a certificate from the assistant, in these words, (else he will not be received in other societies,) 'A. B., the bearer, is a member of our society in C. I believe he has sufficient cause for removing.' "*

1789. It reads, "Warn all from time to time, that none are to remove from one circuit to another without a note of recommendation from the elder or deacon, in these words :—'A. B., the bearer, has been an acceptable member of our society in C.,' and inform them, that without such a certificate, they will not be received into other societies."

1792. The note was to be "from a preacher of the circuit."

8. **1784.** "Everywhere recommend decency and cleanliness."

9. **1784.** "Read the rules of the society, with the aid of your helpers, once a year in every congregation, and once a quarter in every society."

* It had been ordered by the annual conference in 1782, "Let no person remove from north to south without a certificate from the assistant preacher; and let no one be received into society without."

10. This contains several provisions : *first*, about *arbitrations.*

1784. " *Quest.* 62. Are there any directions to be given the assistant concerning the decision of disputes among the people ?

" *Ans.* On any dispute of importance, or difficult to be settled, let the assistant inquire into the circumstances, and having consulted the stewards and leaders, appoint referees, whose decision shall be final, and the party expelled that refuses to abide by it ; unless there appear to the assistant some fraud or gross mistake in the decision, in which case he shall appoint new referees, for a rehearing of the cause, whose decision shall be absolutely final."*

1789. The following was substituted :—

" On any dispute between two or more of the members of our society, which cannot be settled by the parties concerned, the deacon shall inquire into the circumstances of the case, and having consulted the stewards and leaders, shall, if agreeable to their advice, recommend to the contending parties a reference, consisting of one arbiter chosen by the plaintiff, and another by the defendant ; which two arbiters, so chosen, shall nominate a third, (the three arbiters being members of our society,) and the decision of any two of them shall be final. But if either of the parties refuse to abide by such decision, he shall be immediately expelled.

" N. B. If any member of our society enter into a lawsuit with another member before these measures are taken, he shall be expelled."

1792. The dispute in question is stated to be " concerning the payment of debts or otherwise ;" and the subject is committed to " the preacher who has the charge of the circuit," instead of " the deacon." For the note the following paragraph was substituted:—

" And if any member of our society shall refuse, in cases of debt or other disputes, to refer the matter to

---

* A similar rule had been adopted in 1781. See pp. 17, 18.

arbitration, when recommended by him who has the charge of the circuit, with the approbation of the stewards and leaders, or shall enter into a lawsuit with another member before these measures are taken, he shall be expelled."

1796. It was provided that the decision of the arbiters should not be final, as before ; " But if one of the parties be dissatisfied with the judgment given, such party may apply to the ensuing quarterly meeting of the circuit, for allowance to have a *second* arbitration appointed ; and if the quarterly meeting see sufficient reason, they shall grant a *second* arbitration ; in which case each party shall choose two arbiters, and the four arbiters shall choose a fifth, the judgment of the majority of whom shall be final ; and any party refusing to abide by such judgment, shall be excluded the society."

1808. The clauses directing the preacher to consult the stewards and leaders about the arbitration, struck out.   To the paragraph (1792) relating to those who enter into a lawsuit before arbitration, the following clause was added : " excepting the case be of such a nature as to require and justify a process at law."

The *second* part of Answer 10 relates to *insolvencies*, &c., and was originally as follows :—

1784. " *Quest*. 25. What shall we do to prevent scandal, when any of our members becomes a bankrupt?

" *Ans*. Let the assistant talk with him at large. And if he has not kept fair accounts, let him be expelled immediately."

It has since undergone the following changes :—

1789. The provision on this subject was placed in the section about " Visiting from House to House, &c.," and was as follows :—

" *Quest*. 4. What shall we do to prevent scandal, when any of our members fail in business, or contract debts which they are not able to pay ?

" *Ans*. Let the elder or deacon desire two or three judicious members of the society to inspect the ac-

counts of the supposed delinquents ; and if they have
behaved dishonestly, or borrowed money without a probability of paying, let them be suspended until their
credit is restored."

1796. The following additional provision on the
subject was introduced into the section on " The Duties
of those who have Charge of Circuits."

" The preachers who have the oversight of circuits
are required to execute all our rules fully and strenu-
ously against all frauds, and particularly against dis-
honest insolvencies ; suffering none to remain in our
society, on any account, who are found guilty of any
fraud."

1800. The question and answer, which had
been inserted in the section on " Visiting, &c.," were
combined into one paragraph and transferred to this section, as follows :—" To prevent scandal, when any of
our members fail in business, or contract debts which
they are not able to pay, let two or three judicious members of the society inspect the accounts of the supposed
delinquent, and if he have behaved dishonestly, or borrowed money without a probability of paying, let him
be expelled."

1832. After " inspect accounts," in the preceding
paragraph, was added, " contracts and circumstances
of the case."

The *third* part of Answer 10 relates to the *non-payment of debts.* It was added in

1812. " Whenever a complaint is made against
any member of our church for non-payment of debt ;
when the accounts are adjusted, and the amount ascertained, the preacher having the charge shall call the
debtor before a committee of at least three, to show
cause why he does not make payment.   The committee
shall determine what further time shall be granted him
for payment, and what security, if any, shall be given
for payment, and in case the debtor refuse to comply,
he shall be expelled ; but in such case he may appeal
to the quarterly meeting conference, and their decision

hall be final.   And in case the creditor complains that
ustice is not done him, he may lay his grievance be-
ore the quarterly meeting conference, and their decision
hall be final ; and if the creditor refuse to comply he
hall be expelled."

11. **1789.**   (Sec. 17.)   "Wherever you can, in
arge societies, appoint prayer meetings."

1792.   " The preacher who has the charge of a
:ircuit, shall appoint prayer meetings wherever he can,
n his circuit."

12. **1789.**   (Sec. 17.)   " Let a fast be published at
:very quarterly meeting, for the Friday following ; and
₁ memorandum of it be written on all the class papers."*

1792.   The fast to be " on the Friday preceding
:very quarterly meeting."

13. **1784.**   " Meantime let none preach or exhort
n any of our societies without a note of permission
:rom the assistant.   Let every preacher or exhorter
:ake care to have this renewed yearly ; and let every
issistant insist upon it."†

1789.   For " none," we have, " none who are
ocal ;" for " preacher," " local preacher;" and for "as-
iistant," where it first occurs, " deacon," and in the
iecond, " elder."

1792.   The whole was remodelled thus,—" He
ihall also take care, that no ordained local preacher or
:xhorter in his circuit shall officiate in public, without
irst obtaining a license from the presiding elder or him-
ielf.   Let every unordained local preacher and exhorter
:ake care to have this renewed yearly ; and let him who
ias the charge of the circuit insist upon it."

1816.   It was altered as follows :—" To license
iuch persons as he may judge proper to officiate as
:xhorters in the church, provided no person shall be so
icensed without the consent of the leaders' meeting, or

---

* A similar rule found in 1780.   See p. 15.
† For the provisions on this subject prior to 1784, see pp. 12, 14, 18.

of the class of which he is a member, where no leaders'
meeting is held ; and the exhorters so authorized shall
be subject to the annual examination of character, in the
quarterly meeting conference, and have their license annually renewed by the presiding elder, or the preacher
having the charge, if approved by the quarterly meeting
conference."

SECTION XI.

Of the Trial of those who think they are moved by the
Holy Ghost to preach.

This section remains substantially as it was in 1784,
and therefore it will be sufficient to refer to it under
question 68, pp. 62–3.

SECTION XII.

Of the Matter and Manner of Preaching, and of
other public Exercises.

The original of this section may be seen under
Questions 54, 56, and 55, of 1784. The alterations
can be understood by referring to them, (pp. 52–3.)
1789. This was the fifteenth section, with the
same title as now. Of the " smaller advices," (Quest.
55,) item 8 was transferred to another section (see Sec.
25,) and items 12, 14, and 15, were struck out. But
the principal alterations have been in item 9, namely
" Print nothing without the approbation of one or other
of the superintendents." In 1789 it was, " Print
nothing without the approbation of the conference and
one of the bishops." Its subsequent modifications have
been as follows :—
1792. " Print nothing without the approbation
of the conference, *or* of one of the bishops."
1800. " Do not print or circulate any books or
pamphlets, without the consent of the conference ; ex-
7

cepting as an agent or assistant to the superintendent of the Book Concern."

1804. "It is recommended to the yearly conferences to caution and restrict our preachers from improper publications."

1812. This direction was transferred to Part ii. (See Sec. 8.)

SECTION XIII.

Of the Duty of Preachers to God, themselves, and one another.

The original of this section may be found in the Discipline of 1784, under Questions 59 and 66. (See pp. 55, 60–2.) It has undergone no material alteration since then; and none of any kind since 1792.

SECTION XIV.

Rules by which we should continue or desist from Preaching at any Place.

The original of this section may be found in the first Discipline, under Questions 6, 7, and 10. The intervening questions, 8 and 9, about field preaching, were left out in 1789.

SECTION XV.

Of visiting from House to House, guarding against those Things that are so common to Professors, and enforcing practical Religion.

The original of this section may be found in the Discipline of 1784, in the answer to Quest. 15, part of the answer to Quest. 51 (from, "Then you will have, &c.," to " in justification,") and the answers to Questions 52 and 24. (See pp. 30, 50–2, 37–8.) The only material alterations which have been made in it are the following :—

1789. The first item (p. 30) of the answer to

Quest. 15 (Quest. 1, 1840) omitted, as also, from the same answer, the following clause :—" Particularly in selling horses ?   Write him knave that does not.   And the Methodist knave is the worst of all knaves."   In the paragraph beginning, " The sum is, &c.," (p. 50,' the words, " if they belong to us," struck out.

From the answer to Quest. 52 (p. 51) the questions relating to the hour of private prayer were struck out.

From the answer (p. 38) to Quest. 24 (Quest. 3 1840) " smuggling" struck out.

1792.   The following clause was added to this last answer :—" And strongly advise our people to discountenance all treats given by candidates before or at elections, and not to be partakers in any respect of such iniquitous practices."

SECTION XVI.

Of the Instruction of Children.

The original of this section was as follows :—

1784.   "(*Quest.* 51.) But what shall we do for the rising generation ?*   Who will labour for them ' Let him who is zealous for God and the souls of men begin now.   1. Where there are ten children whose parents are in society, meet them at least an hour every week : 2. Talk with them every time you see any at home : 3. Pray in earnest for them : 4. Diligently in-struct and vehemently exhort all parents at their own houses :   5. Preach expressly on education.   ' But I have no gift for this.'   Gift or no gift, you are to do it ; else you are not called to be a Methodist preacher: do it as you can, till you can do it as you would.   Pray earnestly for the gift, and use the means for it."

1789.   The following alterations and additions were made :—In regard to meeting the children, " at

* In the Annual Minutes for 1779 we find the following provision on the same subject :—" *Quest.* 11. What shall be done with the children ?   *Ans.* Meet them once a fortnight, and examine the parents with regard to their conduct toward them."

least an hour every week," was altered to "an hour
once a week ; but where this is impracticable, meet
them once in two weeks." The following new items
were inserted :—" Procure our ' Instructions' for them,
and let all who can, read and commit them to memory.
Explain and impress them upon their hearts." "Let
the elders, deacons, and preachers take a list of the
names of the children : and if any of them be truly
awakened, let them be admitted into society."* The
following clause omitted :—" Gift or no gift, you are
to do it ; else you are not called to be a Methodist
preacher. Do it as you can, till you can do it as you`
would."

1796. No alterations were made in the section,
but the bishops, in their Notes, earnestly urge the
" people in the cities, towns, and villages," to " establish sabbath schools, wherever practicable, for the
benefit of the children *of the poor.*"

1824. For the former rule, (1789,) beginning,
" Let the elders, &c.," the following was substituted :—

" As far as practicable, it shall be the duty of every
preacher of a circuit or station to obtain the names of
the children belonging to his congregations, to form
them into classes, for the purpose of giving them religious instruction, to instruct them regularly himself, as
much as his other duties will allow, to appoint a suitable leader for each class, who shall instruct them in
his absence, and to leave his successor a correct account of each class thus formed, with the name of its
leader."

1828. In the above rule of 1824, the following

---

* A fuller provision on the same subject had been made in the
Annual Minutes for 1787, as follows :—" *Quest.* 20. What can we
do for the rising generation ? *Ans.* Let the elders, deacons, and
helpers class the children of our friends in proper classes, as far as
it is practicable ; meet them as often as possible, and commit them,
during their absence, into the care of proper persons, who may meet
them at least weekly ; and if any of them be *truly awakened,* let
them be admitted into society."

was inserted as the first duty of the preacher, on this subject, " to form Sunday schools."

1836. In the same rule the following was inserted, respecting the course of instruction :—" The course of instruction shall not only embrace the nature of experimental religion, but also the nature, design, privileges, and obligations of their baptism." And it was made the duty of the leader of the children to " recommend to the preacher such among them as he may think suitable to be received among us on trial."

1840.* The whole was remodelled as follows :—

" *Quest.* What shall we do for the rising generation ?

" *Ans.* 1. Let Sunday schools be formed in all our congregations where ten children can be collected for that purpose. And it shall be the special duty of preachers having charge of circuits and stations, with the aid of the other preachers, to see that this be done ; to engage the co-operation of as many of our members as they can ; to visit the schools as often as practicable ; to preach on the subject of Sunday schools and religious instruction in each congregation at least once in six months ; to lay before the quarterly conference at each quarterly meeting, to be entered on its journal, a written statement of the number and state of the Sunday schools within their respective circuits and stations, and to make a report of the same to their several annual conferences. Each quarterly conference shall be deemed a board of managers, having supervision of all the Sunday schools and Sunday-school societies within its limits, and shall be auxiliary to the Sunday-School Union of the Methodist Episcopal Church ; and each annual conference shall report to said Union the number of auxiliaries within its bounds,

---

* The first copies of the 24mo. edition of the Discipline for this year were incorrect in this section. The correct copies may be known by having pp. 61–4 in smaller type than the others.

together with other facts presented in the annual reports of the preachers, as above directed.

" 2. It is recommended that each annual conference, where the general state of the work will allow, request the appointment of a special agent, to travel throughout its bounds, for the purpose of promoting the interests of Sunday-schools ; and his expenses shall be paid out of collections which he shall be directed to make, or otherwise, as shall be ordered by the conference.

" 3. Let our catechisms be used as extensively as possible, both in our Sunday schools and families; and let the preachers faithfully enforce upon parents and Sunday-school teachers the great importance of instructing children in the doctrines and duties of our holy religion.

" 4. It shall be the special duty of the preachers to form Bible classes wherever they can, for the instruction of larger children and youth ; and where they cannot superintend them personally, to appoint suitable leaders for that purpose.

" 5. It shall be the duty of every preacher of a circuit or station to obtain the names of the children belonging to his congregations, and leave a list of such names for his successor ; and in his pastoral visits he shall pay special attention to the children, speak to them personally, and kindly, on experimental and practical godliness, according to their capacity, pray earnestly for them, and diligently instruct and exhort all parents to dedicate their children to the Lord in baptism as early as convenient ; and let all baptized children be faithfully instructed in the nature, design, privileges, and obligations of their baptism. Those of them who are well disposed may be admitted to our class meetings and love-feasts, and such as are truly serious, and manifest a desire to flee the wrath to come, shall be advised to join society as probationers."*

* It may be proper here to notice "the Plan of Education" which was inserted in the Discipline, from 1789 to 1796 inclusive. As found in the Discipline of 1789 it is as follows :—

" SECTION XXX. *On the Plan of Education established in Cokesbury College.*

" The college is built at Abingdon, in Maryland, on a healthy spot, enjoying a fine air, and very extensive prospect.   It is to receive for education and board the sons of the elders and preachers of the Me. thodist Church, poor orphans, and the sons of the subscribers, and of other friends.   It will be expected that all our friends who send their children to the college will, if they be able, pay a moderate sum for their education and board : the rest will be taught and boarded, and, if our finances will allow of it, clothed gratis.   The institution is also intended for the benefit of our young men who are called to preach, that they may receive a measure of that improvement which is highly expedient as a preparative for public service.   A teacher of the lan- guages, with an assistant, will be provided, as also an English master, to teach, with the utmost propriety, both to read and speak the Eng. lish language : nor shall any other branch of literature be omitted, which may be thought necessary for any of the students.   Above all, especial care shall be taken that due attention be paid to the religion and morals of the children, and to the exclusion of all such as con- tinue of an ungovernable temper.   The college will be under the presidentship of the bishops of our church for the time being : and is to be supported by yearly collections throughout our circuits, and any endowments which our friends may think proper to give and be. queath.

" Three objects of considerable magnitude we have in view in the instituting of this college.

" The first is a provision for the sons of our married ministers and preachers.

" The wisdom and love of God hath now thrust out a large number of labourers into his harvest : men who desire nothing on earth but to promote the glory of God, by saving their own souls and those that hear them.   And those to whom they minister spiritual things are willing to minister to them of their temporal things ; so that they have food to eat, and raiment to put on, and are content therewith.

" A competent provision is likewise made for the wives of married preachers.

" Yet one considerable difficulty lies on those that have boys, when they grow too big to be under their mother's direction.   Having no father to govern and instruct them, they are exposed to a thousand temptations.   To remedy this is one motive that induces us to lay before our friends the intent of the college, that these little ones may have all the instruction they are capable of, together with all things necessary for the body.

" In this view our college will become one of the noblest charities that can be conceived.   How reasonable is the institution ?   Is it fit that the children of those who leave wife and all that is dear, to save souls from death, should want what is needful either for soul or body ' Ought not we to supply what the parent cannot, because of his labour in the gospel ?   How excellent will be the effect of this institution ' The preacher, eased of this weight, can the more cheerfully go on in his labour. And perhaps many of these children may hereafter fill up the place of those that shall rest from their labours.

" The second object we have in view is the education and support of poor orphans; and surely we need not enumerate the many happy consequences arising from such a charity. Innumerable blessings concenter in it; not only the immediate relief of the objects of our charity, but the ability given them, under the providence of God, to provide for themselves through the remainder of their lives.

" The last, though not perhaps the least, object in view is the establishment of a seminary for the children of our competent friends, where learning and religion may go hand in hand: where every advantage may be obtained which may promote the prosperity of the present life, without endangering the morals and religion of the children through those temptations to which they are too much exposed in most of the public schools. This is an object of importance indeed: and here all the tenderest feelings of a parent's heart range on our side.

" But the expense of such an undertaking will be very large: and the best means we could think of at our late conference to accomplish our design was, to desire the assistance of all those in every place who wish well to the work of God: who long to see sinners converted to God, and the kingdom of Christ set up in all the earth.

" All who are thus minded, and more especially our own friends who form our congregations, have an opportunity now of showing their love to the gospel. Now promote, as far as in you lies, one of the noblest charities in the world. Now forward, as you are able, one of the most excellent designs that ever was set on foot in this country. Do what you can to comfort the parents, who give up their all for you, and to give their children cause to bless you. You will be no poorer for what you do on such an occasion. God is a good paymaster. And you know in doing this you lend unto the Lord: in due time he shall repay you.

" The students will be instructed in English, Latin, Greek, logic, rhetoric, history, geography, natural philosophy, and astronomy. To these languages and sciences shall be added, when the finances of our college will admit of it, the Hebrew, French, and German languages.

" But our first object shall be, to answer the design of Christian education, by forming the minds of the youth, through divine aid, to wisdom and holiness, by instilling into their tender minds the principles of true religion, speculative, experimental, and practical, and training them in the ancient way, that they may be rational, Scriptural Christians. For this purpose we shall expect and enjoin it, not only on the president and tutors, but also upon our elders, deacons, and preachers, to embrace every opportunity of instructing the students in the great branches of the Christian religion.

" And this is one principal reason why we do not admit students indiscriminately into our college. For we are persuaded that the promiscuous admission of all sorts of youth into a seminary of learning is pregnant with many bad consequences. For are the students likely (suppose they possessed it) to retain much religion in a college where

all that offer are admitted, however corrupted already in principle a
well as practice ? And what wonder, when (as too frequently it hap
pens) the parents themselves have no more religion than their off
spring.

"For the same reason we have consented to receive children of
seven years of age, as we wish to have the opportunity of ' teachin;
their young ideas how to shoot,' and gradually forming their mind
through the divine blessing, almost from their infancy, to holiness an
heavenly wisdom, as well as human learning. And we may add
that we are thoroughly convinced, with the great Milton, (to whos
admirable treatise on education we refer you,) that it is highly expe
dient for every youth to begin and finish his education at the sam
place : that nothing can be more irrational and absurd than to breal
this off in the middle, and to begin it again at a different place, an
perhaps in a quite different manner. And on this account we earn
estly desire that the parents, and others who may be concerned, wil
maturely consider the last observation, and not send their children t
our seminary if they are not to complete their education there, or a
least make some considerable proficiency in the languages, and in th
arts and sciences.

"It is also our particular desire that all who shall be educated i
our college, may be kept at the utmost distance as from vice in gene
ral, so in particular from softness and effeminacy of manners.

"We shall therefore inflexibly insist on their rising early in th
morning; and we are convinced, by constant observation and expe
rience, that this is of vast importance both to body and mind. It i
of admirable use either for preserving a good, or improving a bad
constitution. It is of peculiar service in all nervous complaints, botl
in preventing and in removing them. And by thus strengthening th
various organs of the body, it enables the mind to put forth its utmos
exertions.

"On the same principle we prohibit play in the strongest terms : an
in this we have the two greatest writers on the subject that perhap
any age has produced (Mr. Locke and Mr. Rousseau) of our senti
ments : for though the latter was essentially mistaken in his religiou
system, yet his wisdom in other respects, and extensive genius, ar
indisputably acknowledged. The employments, therefore, which w
have chosen for the recreation of the students are such as are of th
greatest public utility, agriculture and architecture—studies more espe
cially necessary for a new-settled country ; and of consequence th
instructing of our youth, in all the practical branches of those import
ant arts, will be an effectual method of rendering them more useful t
their country. Agreeably to this idea, the greatest statesman tha
perhaps ever shone in the annals of history, Peter, the Russian em
peror, who was deservedly styled the Great, disdained not to stoop t
the employment of a ship carpenter. Nor was it rare, during th
purest times of the Roman republic, to see the conquerors of nation
and deliverers of their country return with all simplicity and cheerful
ness to the exercise of the plough. In conformity to this sentimen
one of the completest poetic pieces of antiquity (the Georgics of Virgil
is written on the subject of husbandry ; by the perusal of which, an

7*

submission to the above regulations, the students may delightfully unite the theory and the practice together. We say delightfully, for we do not entertain the most distant thought of turning these employ. ments into drudgery or slavery, but into pleasing recreations for the mind and body.

"In teaching the languages, care shall be taken to read those authors, and those only, who join together the purity, the strength, and the elegance of their several tongues. And the utmost caution shall be used, that nothing immodest be found in any of our books.

"But this is not all. We shall take care that our books be not only inoffensive, but useful : that they contain as much strong sense and as much genuine morality as possible. As far therefore as is consistent with the foregoing observations, a choice and universal library shall be provided for the use of the students.

"Our annual subscription is intended for the support of the charitable part of the institution. We have in the former part of this address enlarged so fully on the nature and excellency of the charity, that no more need be said. The relieving our travelling ministers and preachers, by educating, boarding, and clothing their sons, is a charity of the most noble and extensive kind, not only toward the immediate subjects of it, but also toward the public in general; enabling those ' flames of fire,' who might otherwise be obliged to confine themselves to an exceedingly contracted sphere of action for the support of their families, to carry the savour of the gospel to the remotest corners of these United States.

"The four guineas a year for tuition, we are persuaded, cannot be lowered, if we give the students that finished education which we are determined they shall have. And though our principal object is to instruct them in the doctrine, spirit, and practice of Christianity, yet we trust that our college will in time send forth men that will be blessings to their country in every laudable office and employment of life, thereby uniting the two greatest ornaments of intelligent beings, which are too often separated, deep learning and genuine religion.

"The rules and regulations with which you are here presented have been weighed and digested in our conference : but we also submit them to your judgment, as we shall be truly thankful for your advice, as well as your prayers for the success of the college, even where the circumstances of things will not render it expedient to you to favour us with your charity. And we shall esteem ourselves happy if we be favoured with any new light, whether from the members of our own church or any other, whereby they may be abridged, enlarged, or in any other way improved, that the institution may be as near perfection as possible.

" General Rules concerning the College.

"I. A president and two tutors shall be provided for the present.

"II. The students shall consist of

"First. The sons of travelling preachers.

"Secondly. The sons of annual subscribers, the children recommended by those annual subscribers who have none of their own, and the sons of members of our society.

" Thirdly. Orphans.   But,

" 1. The sons of the annual subscribers shall have the preference
to any others, except those of the travelling preachers.

" 2. An annual subscriber who has no sons of his own shall have
a right to recommend a child ; and such child so recommended shall
have the preference to any other, except the sons of travelling
preachers and annual subscribers.

" 3. As many of the students as possible shall be lodged and
boarded in the town of Abingdon, among our pious friends ; but those
who cannot be so lodged and boarded, shall be provided for in the
college.

" 4. The price of education shall be four guineas.

" 5. The sons of the travelling preachers shall be boarded, educated
and clothed gratis, except those whose parents, according to the judg
ment of the conference, are of ability to defray the expense.

" 6. The orphans shall be boarded, educated, and clothed gratis.

" 7. No travelling preacher shall have the liberty of keeping his son
on the foundation any longer than he travels, unless he be superan
nuated, or disabled by want of health.

" 8. No travelling preacher, till he has been received into full con
nection, shall have a right to place his son on the foundation of this
institution.

" 9. No student shall be received into the college under the age of
seven years.

" *Rules for the Economy of the College and Students.*

" 1. The students shall rise at five o'clock in the morning, summer
and winter, at the ringing of the college bell.

" 2.. All the students, whether they lodge in or out of the college
shall assemble together in the college at six o'clock, for public prayer
except in cases of sickness ; and on any omission shall be responsible
to the president.

" 3. From morning prayer till seven they shall be allowed to recre
ate themselves, as is hereafter directed.

" 4. At seven they shall breakfast.

" 5. From eight to twelve they are to be closely kept to their re
spective studies.

" 6. From twelve to three they are to employ themselves in recrea
tion and dining—dinner to be ready at one o'clock.

" 7. From three to six they are again to be kept closely to their
studies.

" 8. At six they shall sup.

" 9. At seven there shall be public prayer.

" 10. From evening prayer till bed-time they shall be allowed re
creation.

" 11. They shall all be in bed at nine o'clock, without fail.

" 12. Their recreations shall be gardening, walking, riding, and
bathing, without doors ; and the carpenter's, joiner's, cabinet maker's
or turner's business, within doors.

" 13. A large plot of land, of at least three acres, shall be appropri

ated for a garden, and a person skilled in gardening be appointed to
overlook the students when employed in that recreation.

" 14. A convenient bath shall be made for bathing.

" 15. A master, or some proper person by him appointed, shall be
always present at the time of bathing. Only one shall bathe at a
time ; and no one shall remain in the water above a minute.

" 16. No student shall be allowed to bathe in the river.

" 17. A *Taberna Lignaria** shall be provided on the premises,
with all proper instruments and materials, and a skilful person be
employed to overlook the students at this recreation.

" 18. The students shall be indulged with nothing which the world
calls play. Let this rule be observed with the strictest nicety ; for
those who play when they are young, will play when they are old.

" 19. Each student shall have a bed to himself, whether he boards
in or out of the college.

" 20. The students shall lie on mattresses, not on feather beds,
because we believe the mattresses to be more healthy.

" 21. The president and tutors shall strictly examine, from time to
time, whether our friends who board the students comply with these
rules as far as concern them.

" 22. A skilful physician shall be engaged to attend the students
on every emergency, that the parents may be fully assured that proper care shall be taken of the health of their children, without any
expense to them.

" 23. The bishops shall examine by themselves, or their delegates,
into the progress of all the students in learning, every half year, or
oftener, if possible.

" 24. The elders, deacons, and preachers, as often as they visit
Abingdon, shall examine the students concerning their knowledge of
God and religion.

" 25. The students shall be divided into proper classes for that
purpose.

" 26. A pupil who has a total incapacity to attain learning, shall,
after sufficient trial, be returned to his parents.

" 27. If a student be convicted of any open sin, he shall, for the
first offence, be reproved in private ; for the second offence he shall
be reproved in public ; and for the third offence he shall be punished
at the discretion of the president : if incorrigible, he shall be expelled.

" 28. But if the sin be exceedingly gross, and a bishop see it necessary, he may be expelled for the first, second, or third offence.

" 29. Idleness, or any other fault, may be punished with confine-
ment, according to the discretion of the president.

" 30. A convenient room shall be set apart as a place of confine-
ment.

" 31. The president shall be the judge of all crimes and punishments, in the absence of the bishops.

" 32. But the president shall have no power to expel a student
without the advice and consent of three of the trustees : but a bishop
shall have that power."

---

* It is explained, in 1796, as " a place for working in wood."

In 1792 the following changes were made :—The price of tuition which had been before four guineas for the year, was altered to eigh. teen dollars and two-thirds.   The rate of boarding in the college was fixed at sixty dollars per annum, which was an increase on what it had been before.

In the " Rules for the Economy of the College and Students," the thirty-first and thirty-second were altered to the following :—

" 31. The president shall be the judge of all crimes and punish ments, in the absence of the bishops and the presiding elder : and with the concurrence of two of the tutors, shall have power to dismiss a student, if he judge it highly necessary, for any criminal conduct, or for refusing to submit to the discipline of the college, or to such pun ishment as the president and tutors judge he deserves.

" 32. A committee of five respectable friends, entitled, *The Com mittee of Safety*, shall be appointed, who shall meet once in every fortnight.   Three of these meeting at the appointed time shall be sufficient to enter upon business, and shall have full powers to inspec and regulate the whole economy of the college, and to examine the characters and conduct of all the servants, and to fix their wages, and change them as they may think proper.   The committee shall deter mine every thing by a majority."

In 1796, Cokesbury College having been previously burnt down, the section was considerably modified. It was then entitled, " The Plan of Education recommended to all our Seminaries of Learning." The Ad dress to the public was greatly abridged.   The " General Rules con cerning the College" are omitted ; as also the twenty-eighth, thirty first, and thirty-second of the " Rules for the Economy of the College and Students."   The other alterations are not material.

From this time the interest of the Methodist Episcopal Church, in the cause of liberal education, seems for a number of years to have gradually declined ; and after 1796 no notice is taken of it in the Discipline.   As the church has since taken hold of this work with greater zeal than ever, it may be a question, whether some provisions on the subject might not again, with propriety, be introduced.

SECTION XVII.

Of employing our Time profitably, when we are no travelling or engaged in public Exercises.

The original of this section may be found in the Dis cipline of 1784, in the answers to Questions 49 and 50 and the first part of the answer to Question 51—to the words, " use of the preachers." (See pp. 48–9.)   I has undergone no material alteration.

SECTION XVIII.

Of the Necessity of Union among ourselves.

The original of this section may be found in the Disci-
line of 1784, in the answer to Question 67. (See p. 62.)
The only material alterations have been the following:—

1789. This paragraph was prefixed to the section:
 Let us be deeply sensible (from what we have known)
f the evil of a division in principle, spirit, or practice,
nd the dreadful consequences to ourselves and others.
f we are united, what can stand before us? If we
ivide, we shall destroy ourselves, the work of God, and
he souls of our people."

1792. The following was added at the close :—
'We recommend a serious perusal of ' The Causes,
Evils, and Cures of Heart and Church Divisions.' "

SECTION XIX.

Of the Method by which immoral Travelling Ministers
or Preachers shall be brought to Trial, found guilty,
and reproved or suspended in the Intervals of the
Conferences.

The only provision on the subject in the first Disci-
line was the following :—

1784. " *Quest.* 63. Are there any further direc-
ions needful for the preservation of good order among
he preachers ?

" *Ans.* In the absence of a superintendent, a travel-
ng preacher or three leaders shall have power to lodge
 complaint against any preacher in their circuit,
hether elder, assistant, deacon, or helper, before
hree neighbouring assistants ; who shall meet at an ap-
ointed time, (proper notice being given to the parties,)
ear and decide the cause. And authority is given
hem to change or suspend a preacher, if they see it
ecessary, and to appoint another in his place, during
he absence of the superintendents."*

---

* A previous provision on the same subject is found in the Annual
Minutes for 1784.   (See p. 20.)

The original of the present section was prepared by Bishop Asbury,* and introduced in 1789. It then constituted the thirty-third section, with the same title as now, except the words "reproved and suspended" instead of " and reproved or suspended." The questions will be taken up in order.

Quest. 1. What shall be done when an elder, deacon, or preacher is under report of being guilty of *some crime*, expressly forbidden in the word of God, as an unchristian practice, sufficient to exclude a person from the kingdom of grace and glory?

1789. The original was as follows:—

" *Quest.* 1. What shall be done when an elder deacon, or preacher, is under the report of being guilty of some capital crime, expressly forbidden in the word of God, as an unchristian practice, sufficient to exclude a person from the kingdom of grace and glory, and to make him a subject of wrath and hell?

" *Ans.* Let the presiding elder call as many ministers to the trial as he shall think fit, at least three, and if possible bring the accused and accuser face to face. If the person is clearly convicted, he shall be suspended from official services in the church, and not be allowed the privileges of a member. But if the accused be a *presiding* elder, the preachers must call in the presiding elder of the neighbouring district, who is required to attend and act as judge.   -

" If the persons cannot be brought face to face, but the supposed delinquent flees from trial, it shall be received as a presumptive proof of guilt, and out of the mouth of two or three witnesses he shall be condemned. Nevertheless, he may then demand a trial face to face, or he may appeal to the next conference in that district.'

1792. The section took its present title and number. In the question, the word "capital" before " crime," omitted. It was now provided that only " in the absence of a bishop," the presiding elder was to summon the committee of trial. The punishment, in case of conviction, was now, " he shall be suspended

---

* Journal, vol. ii, p. 29.

from all official services in the church till the ensuing district conference, at which his case shall be fully considered and determined."   " Act as judge," changed to " preside at the trial."   In the next paragraph, " persons" changed to " accused and accuser."   And for the last sentence, the following is substituted :—"Nevertheless, even in that case the district conference shall reconsider the whole matter, and determine."

1836.   The following provision was added :—

" And if the accused be a superannuated preacher, living out of the bounds of the conference of which he is a member, the presiding elder, in whose district he may reside, shall bring him to trial, and in case of suspension, shall forward to the ensuing annual conference, of which the accused is a member, exact minutes of the charges, testimony, and decision of the committee in the case."

1840.   All the foregoing clause, after " of which he is a member," was struck out, and the following substituted,—" he shall be held responsible to the annual conference within whose bounds he may reside, who shall have power to try, acquit, suspend, locate, or expel him, in the same manner as if he were a member of said conference."

Quest. 2. What shall be done in cases of improper tempers, words, or actions !

Quest. 3. What shall be done with those ministers or preachers who hold and disseminate, publicly or privately, doctrines which are contrary to our Articles of Religion ?

These questions were originally embraced under one head, as follows :—

1789.   " *Quest.* 2. What shall be done in cases of improper tempers, words, or actions, or a breach of the Articles and Discipline of the church ?

" *Ans.* The person so offending shall be reprehended by his bishop, elder, deacon, or preacher that has the charge of the circuit ; or if he be a bishop, he shall be reprehended by the conference. Should a second transgression take place, one, two, or three preachers may be called in; if not cured then, he shall be tried at the quarterly meeting by the elder and preachers present; if still incurable, he shall be brought before the conference, and if found guilty and impenitent, he shall be expelled from the connection, and his name so returned in the Minutes.

" N. B. Any preacher suspended at a quarterly meeting from preaching, shall not resume that employment again, but by the order of the conference.   But it is to be observed, that a preacher shall be tried by a deacon, a deacon by an elder, an elder by a presiding elder, and a presiding elder by the presiding elder of a neighbouring district."

1792.   These cases were divided thus :—

" *Quest.* 2. What shall be done in case of improper tempers, words, or actions ?

" *Ans.* The person so offending shall be reprehended by his senior in office.   Should a second transgression take place, one, two, or three ministers or preachers are to be taken as witnesses.   If he be not then cured he shall be tried at the conference of his district, [annual conference] and, if found guilty and impenitent, shall be expelled from the connection, and his name so returned in the Minutes of the conference.

" *Quest.* 3. What shall be done with those ministers or preachers who hold and preach doctrines which are contrary to our Articles of Religion ?

" *Ans.* Let the same process be observed as in cases of gross immorality : but if the minister or preacher so offending do solemnly engage neither to preach nor defend such erroneous doctrines in public or in private, he shall be borne with till his case be laid before the next district conference, which shall determine the matter.'

1816.   The question reads as now.   " Neither to preach nor defend," altered to " not to disseminate.'

Quest. 4. What shall be done with a member of an annual conference who conducts himself in a manner which renders him unacceptable to the people as a travelling preacher ?

This question and answer remain as first introduced in

1836. "*Ans.* When any member of an annual onference shall be charged with having so conducted imself as to render him unacceptable to the people as travelling preacher, it shall be the duty of the confernce to which he belongs to investigate the case; and f it appear that the complaint is well founded, and he o not give the conference satisfaction that he will mend or voluntarily retire, they may locate him without his consent : provided that he shall be at liberty to efend himself before the conference in person or by is representative ; and if he be located in his absence vithout having been previously notified of an intention hus to proceed against him, he may apply to the conerence, at its next session, to be heard in his defence, n which case they shall reconsider the matter for that urpose."

Appeal to the General Conference.

The following provision was introduced in

1792. "Provided nevertheless, that in all the bove-mentioned cases of trial and conviction, an appeal ɔ the ensuing General Conference shall be allowed."

1820. The following clauses added:—" If the ondemned person signify his intention to appeal, at the ime of his condemnation, or at any time thereafter, rhen he is informed thereof.

" In all the above-mentioned cases, it shall be the uty of the secretary of the annual conference to keep egular minutes of the trial, including all the questions roposed to the witnesses, and their answers, together rith the crime with which the accused is charged, the pecification or specifications, and also preserve all the ocuments relating to the case ; which minutes and ocuments only, in case of an appeal from the decision f an annual conference, shall be presented to the Geeral Conference, in evidence on the case. And in all ases, when an appeal is made, and admitted by the ieneral Conference, the appellant shall either state peronally, or by his representative, (who shall be a member of the conference,) the grounds of his appeal, show-

ing cause why he appeals, and he shall be allowed tc
make his defence without interruption.   After which
the representatives of the annual conference from whose
decision the appeal is made, shall be permitted tc
respond in presence of the appellant, who shall have
the privilege of replying to such representatives, which
shall close the pleadings on both sides.   This done, the
appellant shall withdraw, and the conference shal
decide."

1836.   To which, in 1836, the following clause
added: "And after such form of trial and expulsion, the
person so expelled shall have no privileges of society ol
sacraments in our church, without confession, contrition, and proper trial."

Trial of a preacher on probation.

1836.   "A preacher on trial who may be accused
of crime shall be accountable to the quarterly conference
of the circuit on which he travels.   The presiding
elder shall call a committee of three local preachers,
who may suspend him.   And the quarterly conference
may expel him.   Nevertheless, he shall have a right to
an appeal to the next annual conference."

Restoring credentials.

1836.   "When any travelling elder or deacon is
deprived of his credentials, by expulsion or otherwise,
they shall be filed with the papers of the annual conference of which he was a member ; and should he at any
future time give satisfactory evidence to said conference
of his amendment, and procure a certificate of the quarterly conference of the circuit or station where he
resides, or of an annual conference who may have admitted him on trial, recommending to the annual conference of which he *was* a member formerly the restoration of his credentials, the said conference may restore
them."

Iow to provide for the Circuits in time of Conference,
and to preserve and increase the Work of God.

The original provision on this subject may be found
1 the answer to Question 71.* (See p. 65.) The fol-
>wing was substituted for it in

1789. " *Quest.* What can be done to supply the
ircuits during the sitting of the conference ?

"*Ans.* 1. Let all the appointments stand according to
he plan of the circuit.

" 2. Engage as many local preachers and exhorters
s will supply them ; and let them be paid for their
ime in proportion to the salary of the travelling
reachers.

" 3. If preachers and exhorters cannot attend, let
ome person of ability be appointed in every society, to
ing, pray, and read one of Mr. Wesley's sermons.

" 4. And if that cannot be done, let there be prayer
neetings.

" 5. Wherever you can, in large societies, appoint
rayer meetings.

" Lastly, let a fast be published at every quarterly
neeting for the Friday following ; and a memorandum
f it be written on all the class papers. Also be active
n dispersing the books among the people."

1792. The last two paragraphs were struck out,
he same duties being prescribed elsewhere. (See Sec.
0.) But the clause in the title, (" and to preserve and
ncrease the work of God,") which seems to refer to
hem, has been retained.

SECTION XXI.

Of Local Preachers.

This subject was not treated in a distinct section
ntil 1796.

---

* A similar provision was made in 1783. (See p. 20.)

Quest. 1. What directions shall be given concerning loca preachers ?

Until 1816 this question read, "What directions shall be given concerning our brethren the loca preachers, in respect to their being received as preachers, or admitted into the order of deacons?' As a variety of provisions have been embraced unde1 it, they will be treated separately under the following heads :—1. *Licensing* ; 2. *Election to deacon's orders* ; 3. *Election to elder's orders* ; 4. *Sundry requisitions.*

1. *Licensing.*—For the original provisions on this subject, see under the thirteenth direction to those who have charge of circuits, (p. 144.) Those of 1796 were as follows :—

1796. "1. No local preacher shall receive a license to preach till he has been examined and approved at the quarterly meeting of his circuit ; which license shall be drawn up in the following words, signed by the president of the meeting, namely :—' N. M. has applied to us for liberty to preach as a local preacher in our circuit : and after due inquiry concerning his gifts, grace, and usefulness, we judge he is a proper person to be licensed for this purpose ; and we accordingly authorize him to preach.'

" 2. Before any person shall be licensed as a local preacher by a quarterly meeting, he shall bring a recommendation from the society of which he is a member."

1816. Answers 1 and 2 were combined into one, and modified so as to read as follows :—

" 1. Before any person shall be licensed to preach as a local preacher among us, he shall bring a recommendation from the society or class of which he is a member, and be personally examined before the quarterly meeting conference, by the presiding elder, or, in his absence, by the preacher having the charge, touching his acquaintance with the doctrines of our church, (to which he shall declare his assent,) together with his gifts and grace for preaching; and if he be approved by the quarterly meeting conference in these respects, and they believe that he will be generally acceptable and useful as a preacher, he shall then receive a license, signed by the presiding elder, or, in his absence, by the preacher having the charge, in these words, namely: —' N. M. has applied to us for liberty to preach as a local preacher in our circuit; and after due inquiry concerning his gifts, grace, and usefulness, we judge he is a proper person to be licensed for this purpose; and we accordingly authorize him to preach,' which license it shall be the duty of such local preacher to have annually renewed."

1820. In consequence of the controversies which were then agitating the church, as to the rights of the laity and the local preachers, new regulations were made respecting the latter, by the organization of *district conferences.*

Answer 1 (1816) was struck out, and the following substituted:—

" 1. There shall be held annually, in each presiding elder's district, a district conference, of which all the local preachers in the district, who shall have been licensed two years, shall be members; and of which the presiding elder of the district for the time being shall be president; or, in case of his absence, the conference shall have authority to elect a president pro tem. It shall be the duty of the presiding elder of each district to appoint the time and place of the first conference, after which the presiding elder shall appoint the time, and the conference the place of its own sitting.

" 2. The said district conference shall have authority to license proper persons to preach, and renew their license; to recommend suitable candidates to the annual conference for deacon's or elder's orders, in the local connection, for admission on trial in the travelling connection; and to try, suspend, expel, or acquit any local preacher in the district, against whom charges may be brought, *provided*, that no person shall be licensed without being first recommended by the quarterly conference of the circuit or station to which he belongs, nor shall any one be licensed to preach, or recommended to the annual conference for ordination without first being examined in the district conference on the subjects of doctrine and discipline.

"3. The district conference shall take cognizance of all the local preachers in the district, and shall inquire into the gifts, labours, and usefulness of each preacher by name."

In these provisions the following alterations were afterward made :—

1824. At the end of Answer 1, was added the following:—"*Provided*, that if any district conference shall refuse or neglect to hold its regular sessions, then the quarterly meeting conferences of the circuits and stations respectively, shall have authority to transact the business of the district conference."

The renewal of licenses in the district conference was to be " annually, when, in the judgment of the said conference, their gifts, grace, and usefulness will warrant such renewal."

In the proviso to Answer 2, a clause was inserted which provided that no person should be " recommended for admission into the travelling connection without being first recommended by the quarterly conference."

1828. It was provided that a majority of the members of a district conference should " be a quorum to do business." The words " refuse or neglect to," in the proviso of 1824, were changed to " not."

At the end of Answer 1 the following sentence was added :—" Provided that no person shall be licensed to preach without the recommendation of the society of which he is a member, or of a leaders' meeting."

1836. The plan of district conferences had proved an entire failure, the local preachers themselves, for whose sake it was adopted, not approving

of it. It was therefore abolished, and matters restored, for the most part, to the condition in which
they were prior to 1820.

The provisions of 1820, and all the subsequent
modifications of them, were struck out, and the following substituted :—

" 1. The quarterly meeting conference shall take
cognizance of all the local preachers in the circuit or
station, and shall inquire into the gifts, labours, and
usefulness of each preacher by name.

" 2. The quarterly conference shall have authority
to license proper persons to preach, and renew their
license annually, when in the judgment of said conference their gifts, grace, and usefulness will warrant such
renewal ; to recommend suitable candidates to the annual conference for deacons' or elders' orders in the
local connection, for admission on trial in the travelling
connection, and to try, suspend, expel, or acquit any
local preacher in the circuit or station against whom
charges may be brought. *Provided*, that no person
shall be licensed to preach without the recommendation of the society of which he is a member, or of a
leaders' meeting. Nor shall any one be licensed to
preach, or recommended to the annual conference to
travel, or for ordination, without first being examined
in the quarterly conference on the subject of doctrines
and discipline."

2. *Election to deacon's orders.*

1789. The following provision on this subject
was inserted under the duty of a bishop :—

" The bishop has obtained liberty, by the suffrages
of the conference, to ordain local preachers to the
office of deacons, provided they obtain a testimonial
from the society to which they belong, and from the
stewards of the circuit, signed by three travelling
preachers, three deacons, and three elders, (one of
them being a presiding elder ;) the names of those
nominated being read in the conference previous to
their ordination."

1792. The clause about reading the names was struck out, and it was only required that the testimonial should be signed " by three elders, three deacons, and three travelling preachers."

1796. The following paragraph on the subject was inserted in this section :—

" 3. A local preacher shall be eligible to the office of a deacon after he has preached for four years from the time he has received a regular license, and has obtained the testimonial" [specified above.]

1804. It was required that the testimonial should be " from the society to which he belongs, and from the stewards of the circuit, signed also by nine travelling preachers ; three of whom shall be elders, three others elders or deacons ; and the other three elders, deacons, or preachers."

1808. The testimonial was to be " from the quarterly meeting of the circuit to which he belongs, after proper examination, signed by the president, and countersigned by the secretary." It was also required, for ordination, that " his character has passed in examination before, and he has obtained the approbation of the yearly conference."

1816. The word " licensed" was inserted before " local preacher," (1796.)

1836. The words " to which he belongs" (of 1808) omitted.

3. *Election to elder's orders.*

1812. We find the first provision on this subject as follows :—

" A local deacon shall be eligible to the office of an elder after he has preached four years from the time he was ordained a deacon, and has obtained a recommendation from two-thirds of the quarterly meeting conference of which he is a member, certifying his qualifications in doctrine, discipline, talents, and usefulness, and the necessity of his official services as an elder in the circuit where he resides ; signed by the president, and countersigned by the secretary. He

8

shall, if he cannot attend, send to the annual conference such recommendation, and a note certifying his belief in the doctrine and discipline of our church :— the whole being examined by the annual conference, and, if approved, he may be ordained ; *provided,* nevertheless, that no slaveholder shall be eligible to the office of an elder, where the laws will admit of emancipation, and permit the liberated slave to enjoy freedom."

1816. "or deacon" inserted after "elder," in the clause respecting the eligibility of a slaveholder.

1820. The recommendation for orders no longer required to be by "two-thirds" of the conference.

1824. The clause requiring the recommendation to certify "the necessity of his official services as an elder in the circuit where he resides," omitted.

4. *Sundry requisitions.*

1800. It was required that

"Every local preacher shall have his name enrolled on a class paper, and meet in class, if the distance of his place of residence from any class be not too great; or, in neglect thereof, shall forfeit his license."

1812. The penalty for neglecting to meet in class was changed to the following : "The quarterly meeting conference, if they judge it proper, may deprive him of his ministerial office."

It was further required, that "every local elder, deacon, and preacher, shall have his name recorded on the journal of the quarterly meeting conference of which he is a member."

1820. The following paragraphs were added :—

"Whenever a local preacher shall remove from one circuit to another, he shall procure from the presiding elder of the district, or the preacher having the charge of the circuit, a certificate of his official standing in the church at the time of his removal, without which he shall not be received as a local preacher in other places.

"No preacher among us shall distil or retail spirituous liquors, without forfeiting his official standing."

1824. The requisition for meeting in class was restricted to "licensed" local preachers.

1836. The words "retail spirituous liquors" changed to "vend spirituous liquors;" and the requisitions to meet in class, to obtain a certificate on removal and to abstain from distilling or vending spirituous liquors, extended to every "elder, deacon, or preacher."

Quest. 2. What shall be done when a local elder, deacon or preacher, is reported to be guilty of some crime expressly forbidden in the word of God, sufficient to exclude a person from the kingdom of grace and glory ?

Quest. 3. What shall be done in cases of improper tempers words, or actions !

A distinct provision for the trial of local preachers was first introduced in 1796, as follows :—

1796. *Quest.* 3. "What directions shall be given concerning the trial of local preachers, local deacons, or local elders ?

"*Ans.* If a charge be brought against a local preacher, or local deacon, or elder, the preacher who has the oversight of the circuit shall summon three or more local preachers of the neighbourhood, or, for want of local preachers, so many leaders, or exhorters. And if they, or a majority of them, on due examination, judge that the local preacher, deacon, or elder, aforesaid, has been guilty of such a crime, or has preached such false doctrines, as require his suspension from all public offices in our church till the ensuing quarterly meeting, the preacher who has the oversight of the circuit shall accordingly suspend him from all public offices till the ensuing quarterly meeting.

"And in such case, and in every case where a meeting, assembled as above described, shall deem the said local preacher, deacon, or elder, culpable, the next quarterly meeting shall proceed upon his trial, and shall have authority to clear, censure, suspend, or expel him, according to their judgment. And the presiding elder, or the preacher who has the oversight of the circuit, shall, at the commencement of the trial, appoint a secretary, who shall take down regular minutes of the evidence and proceedings of the trial, which minutes, when read and approved, shall be signed by the said presiding elder, or preacher, and also by the members of the said quarterly meeting, or by the majority of them.

"And in case of condemnation, the local preacher, deacon, or elder condemned, shall be allowed an appeal to the next yearly conference, provided that he signify to the said quarterly meeting his determination to appeal; in which case the said presiding elder, or the preacher who has the oversight of the circuit, shall lay the minutes of the trial above-mentioned before the said yearly conference, at which the local preacher, deacon, or elder so appealing, may appear; and the said yearly conference shall judge, and finally determine, from the minutes of the said trial so laid before them."

1812. After "all public offices" was inserted "and privileges."

1816. The word "licensed" inserted before "local preachers," in the first paragraph, to distinguish such from deacons and elders. For "has preached such false doctrine," we have, "has publicly or privately disseminated such false doctrine."

1820. The mode of trial was remodelled as follows:—

"When charges are preferred against any local preacher, it shall be the duty of the preacher in charge to call a committee, consisting of three or more local preachers within the station, circuit, or district, before whom it shall be the duty of the accused to appear, and by whom he shall be acquitted, or, if found guilty, be suspended until the meeting of the next district conference. And the president of the said district conference shall, at the commencement of the trial, appoint a secretary, who shall take down regular minutes of the evidence and proceedings of the trial; which minutes, when read and approved, shall be signed by the said president, and also by the members of the said district conference, or by a majority of them.

" And in case of condemnation, the local preacher, deacon, or elder condemned, shall be allowed an appeal to the next annual conference, provided that he signify to the said district conference his determination to appeal ; in which case the said president shall lay the minutes of the trial above-mentioned before the said annual conference, at which the local preacher, deacon, or elder so appealing, may appear ; and the said annual conference shall judge, and finally determine, from the minutes of the said trial so laid before them."

1824. The following clause inserted after the first sentence, (1820) :—

" And the preacher in charge shall cause exact minutes of the charges, testimony, and examination, together with the decision of the committee, to be laid before the district conference, where it shall be the duty of the accused to appear."

The following new paragraph inserted :—

" When a local elder or deacon shall be expelled, the president of the conference shall require of him the credentials of his ordination, to be filed with the papers of the annual conference within the limits of which the expulsion has taken place.   And should he, at any future time, produce to the annual conference a certificate of his restoration, signed by the president, and countersigned by the secretary of the district conference, his credentials shall be restored to him."

1836. Prior to this time no distinction had been made in the mode of procedure, according to the nature of the offence.   Now, however, instead of one general course for all kinds of charges, the subject was treated under two questions, one relating to " crimes," and the other to " improper tempers, words, or actions."

The introductory words, (1820,) namely, " When charges are preferred against any local preacher, it shall be the duty of the preacher in charge to call," were struck out, and the following substituted :—

" *Quest.* 2. What shall be done when a local elder, deacon, or preacher, is reported to be guilty of some crime expressly forbidden in the word of God, sufficient to exclude a person from the kingdom of grace and glory?

"*Ans.* 1. The preacher having charge shall call."

The local preachers on the committee were no longer required to be of "the station, circuit, or district." The minutes of the trial are to be signed by the members "who are present," or a majority of them. "District conference," here, as in other parts of the section, changed to " quarterly conference."

The following was added at the close of the section:

" *Quest.* 3. What shall be done in cases of improper tempers, words, or actions?

"*Ans.* The person so offending shall be reprehended by the preacher having charge. Should a second transgression take place, one, two, or three faithful friends are to be taken as witnesses. If he be not then cured, he shall be tried at the next quarterly conference, and if found guilty, and impenitent, he shall be expelled from the church."*

1840. Instead of "his credentials shall be restored to him," (1824,) we have, "his credentials may be restored to him."

SECTION XXII.

Of Baptism.

The original provisions on this subject may be found under Questions 45, 46, and 48, (p. 45.) The provision under Question 46, about re-baptizing, was omitted after 1786. The others have been modified as follows:—

1786. "Pouring" was admitted as a mode of baptism, in addition to "immersion and sprinkling."

1789. The form of question and answer was laid

---

* From 1796 to 1804 there was comprised in this section a question (2.) relating to the compensation of local preachers, in certain cases; but as this was, in the latter year, transferred to Part II, we shall consider it there. (See Sec. 9.)

aside, and the following was added in place of Question 48, (1784) :—

"N. B. We will on no account whatever receive a present for administering baptism, or the burial of the dead."

1828.   The words "receive a present" changed to "make a charge."

SECTION XXIII.

Of the Lord's Supper

The original provisions on this subject may be found in the Discipline of 1784, under Questions 44 and 47. (See pp. 44–5.)

1789.   The answer read as follows :—

"1. Let those who choose, receive it kneeling, and let those who do not, either standing or sitting.

"2. Let no person that is not a member of our society be admitted to the communion, without examination, and some token given by an elder or deacon."

1792.   As follows :—

"1. Let those who have scruples concerning the receiving of it kneeling, be permitted to receive it either standing or sitting.

"2. [As in 1789.]

[3.] "N. B. No person shall be admitted to the Lord's supper among us who is guilty of any practice for which we would exclude a member of our society."

SECTION XXIV.

Of Public Worship.

This section was introduced in 1792, as follows :—

1792.   "*Quest.* What directions shall be given for the establishment of uniformity in public worship among us, on the Lord's day ?

"*Ans.* 1. Let the morning service consist of singing, prayer, the reading of a chapter out of the Old

Testament, and another out of the New, and preaching.

"2. Let the afternoon service consist of singing, prayer, the reading of one chapter out of the Bible, and preaching.

"3. Let the evening service consist of singing, prayer, and preaching.

"4. But on the days of administering the Lord's supper, the two chapters in the morning service may be omitted.

"5. Let the society be met, wherever it is practicable, on the sabbath day."

1804. It was provided that "one or two chapters" should be read in the afternoon service.

1824. The following clause was inserted :—" In administering the ordinances, and in the burial of the dead, let the form of Discipline invariably be used. Let the Lord's prayer also be used on all occasions of public worship in concluding the first prayer, and the apostolic benediction in dismissing the congregation."

SECTION XXV.

Of the Spirit and Truth of Singing.

The original provision on this subject may be found in the first Discipline, under Question 57, pp. 53–4.

1792. The following clauses added :—

" The preachers are desired not to encourage the singing of fugue tunes in our congregations.

" Let it be recommended to our people, not to attend the singing schools which are not under our direction.

" N. B. We do not think that fugue tunes are sinful, or improper to be used in private companies ; but we do not approve of their being used in our public congregations, because public singing is a part of divine worship, in which all the congregation ought to join."

CHAPTER II.

SECTION I.

The Nature, Design, and General Rules of our United Societies.

THE General Rules, as published by Mr. Wesley were as follows :—

"1. In the latter end of the year 1739, eight or ten persons came to me in London, who appeared to be deeply convinced of sin, and earnestly groaning for redemption. They desired (as did two or three more the next day) that I would spend some time with them in prayer, and advise them how to flee from the wrath to come; which they saw continually hanging over their heads. That we might have more time for this great work, I appointed a day when they might all come together, which from thenceforward they did every week, namely, on Thursday in the evening. To these, and as many more as desired to join with them, (for their number increased daily,) I gave those advices, from time to time, which I judged most needful for them; and we always concluded our meeting with prayer suited to their several necessities.

"2. This was the rise of the United Society, first in London, and then in other places. Such a society is no other than 'a company of men having the form and seeking the power of godliness, united in order to pray together, to receive the word of exhortation, and to watch over one another in love, that they may help each other to work out their salvation.'

"3. That it may the more easily be discerned, whether they are indeed working out their own salvation, each society is divided into smaller companies, called *classes*, according to their respective places of abode. There are about twelve persons in every class: one of whom is styled *the leader*. It is his business,

(1.) To see each person in his class once a week at least, in order to inquire how their souls prosper; to advise, reprove, comfort, or exhort, as occasion may require; to receive what they are willing to give toward the relief of the poor.   (2.) To meet the minister and the stewards of the society once a week; in order to inform the minister of any that are sick, or of any that walk disorderly, and will not be reproved; to pay to the stewards what they have received of their several classes in the week preceding; and to show their account of what each person has contributed.

"4. There is one only condition previously required in those who desire admission into these societies,—a desire 'to flee from the wrath to come, to be saved from their sins:' but, wherever this is really fixed in the soul, it will be shown by its fruits. It is therefore expected of all who continue therein, that they should continue to evidence their desire of salvation,

"First, by doing no harm, by avoiding evil in every kind; especially that which is most generally practised: such is, the taking the name of God in vain; the profaning the day of the Lord, either by doing ordinary work thereon, or by buying or selling; drunkenness, buying or selling spirituous liquors, or drinking them, unless in cases of extreme necessity; fighting, quarrelling, brawling; brother going to law with brother; returning evil for evil, or railing for railing; the using many words in buying or selling; the buying or selling uncustomed goods; the giving or taking things on usury, that is, unlawful interest; uncharitable or unprofitable conversation, particularly speaking evil of magistrates or of ministers; doing to others as we would not they should do unto us; doing what we know is not for the glory of God, as the 'putting on of gold or costly apparel;' the taking such diversions as cannot be used in the name of the Lord Jesus; the singing those songs, or reading those books, which do not tend to the knowledge or love of God; softness, and needless self-indulgence; laying up treasures upon

earth ; borrowing without a probability of paying ; o:
taking up goods without a probability of paying fo:
them.

" 5. It is expected of all who continue in these societies, that they should continue to evidence their desire
of salvation,

" Secondly, by doing good, by being, in every kind
merciful after their power ; as they have opportunity
doing good of every possible sort, and as far as is possible, to their bodies, of the ability which
God giveth, by giving food to the hungry, by clothing
the naked, by visiting or helping them that are sick, o:
in prison ;—to their souls, by instructing, reproving, o:
exhorting all they have any intercourse with ; trampling
under foot that enthusiastic doctrine of devils, that ' we
are not to do good unless our heart be free to it :' by
doing good especially to them that are of the household
of faith, or groaning so to be ; employing them prefera-
bly to others, buying one of another ; helping each
other in business ; and so much the more, because the
world will love its own, and them only : by all possible diligence and frugality, that the gospel be no:
blamed : by running with patience the race that is se:
before them, ' denying themselves, and taking up their
cross daily ;' submitting to bear the reproach of Christ
to be as the filth and offscouring of the world ; and
looking that men should ' say all manner of evil of
them falsely for the Lord's sake.'

" 6. It is expected of all who desire to continue in
these societies, that they should continue to evidence
their desire of salvation,

" Thirdly, by attending upon all the ordinances of
God.   Such are, the public worship of God ; the ministry of the word, either read or expounded ; the supper of the Lord ; family and private prayer ; searching
the Scriptures ; and fasting, or abstinence.

" 7. These are the General Rules of our societies; al:
which we are taught of God to observe, even in his
written word, the only rule, and the sufficient rule, both

of our faith and practice.   And all these, we know, his
Spirit writes on every truly awakened heart.   If there
be any among us who observe them not, who habitually break any of them, let it be made known unto
them who watch over that soul as they that must give
an account.   We will admonish him of the error of his
ways; we will bear with him for a season : but then
f he repent not, he hath no more place among us.
We have delivered our own souls.

" JOHN WESLEY,

"*May* 1, 1743."   " CHARLES WESLEY."*

These Rules, as thus drawn up by the Wesleys,
were adopted without alteration by the first Methodist
societies in America.†   They do not seem, however, to
have been published in any edition of the Discipline
until 1789,‡ when we find the following alterations :—
The historical introduction, which precedes the definition of the United Society, is omitted, and the section
begins, " Our society is nothing more than 'a company,
&c.'"   Under the duty of a leader, for " relief of the
poor," it reads, " relief of the preachers, church, and
poor," and it is added in a note, " This part refers
wholly to town and cities, where the poor are generally
numerous, and church expenses considerable."   It
omits the requisition that the leaders shall " show their
account of what each person has contributed."   Under
the rule about drunkenness, it omits the clause, " unless
in cases of extreme necessity."   It is in this Discipline
that we find, for the first time, among the General Rules,
one respecting slaves.   It reads, " The buying or selling the bodies and souls of men, women, or children,
with an intention to enslave them."
    In the expression of the original rules,—" that en-
thusiastic doctrine of devils," the words "of devils" are
omitted.   After the direction about " buying one of

---

* Wesley's Works, vol. v, pp. 190–2.
† See Lee's Hist. of the Meth., pp. 29–33.   ‡ See above, p. 82

another," it is added, (" unless you can be served better elsewhere,") but this clause was omitted in 1792. The only rules that have since undergone any change are those which relate to spirituous liquors and slavery. The various alterations in them are presented below.

Spirituous liquors.

The rule on this subject has been at different times as follows :—

1743. Mr. Wesley's original rule,—" Drunkenness, buying or selling spirituous liquors, or drinking them, unless in cases of extreme necessity."

1789. " Drunkenness, buying or selling spirituous liquors, or drinking them."

1790. " Drunkenness, or drinking spirituous liquors, unless cases of necessity."

1791. "Drunkenness, or drinking spirituous liquors, unless in cases of necessity."

Slaves.

There is nothing on this subject in the General Rules of Mr. Wesley. But we find the following in

1789. " The buying or selling the bodies and souls of men, women, or children, with an intention to enslave them."

1792. It reads, " The buying or selling of men, women, or children, with an intention to enslave them."

1808. It reads, " The buying and selling of men, women, and children, with an intention to enslave them."*

SECTION II.

Of Class Meetings.

This section contains five questions, the changes in which will be noticed in order.

Quest. 1. How may the leaders of classes be rendered more useful ?

The answer to this question remains substantially the same as in 1784. (See Quest. 13, p. 29.)

---

* For this alteration (if indeed it be not a purely typographical error) no authority is found in the journal of the General Conference.

Quest. 2. Can any thing more be done in order to make the class meetings lively and profitable ?

The answer to this remains precisely the same as in 1784. (See Quest. 14, p. 29.)

Quest. 3. How shall we prevent improper persons from insinuating themselves into the church ?

1784. " *Quest.* 16. How shall we prevent improper persons from insinuating into the society ?

" *Ans.* 1. Give tickets to none till they are recommended by a leader, with whom they have met at least two months on trial.

" 2. Give notes to none but those who are recommended by one you know, or till they have met three or four times in a class.

" 3. Give them the rules the first time they meet."

1789. The probation was extended to " six months."

1836. "Give tickets to none," was changed to, " Let none be received into the church ;" and, " Give notes to none," into, " Let none be admitted on trial." It was now made a requisite for admission into the church, that the candidates " have been baptized." For admission on trial, it was now made sufficient to have met "twice or thrice" in a class, instead of " three or four times."

1840. The following was added to the requisites for admission into the church :—

"And shall on examination by the minister in charge, before the church, give satisfactory assurances both of the correctness of their faith, and their willingness to observe and keep the rules of the church. Nevertheless, if a member in good standing in any other orthodox church shall desire to unite with us, such applicant may, by giving satisfactory answers to the usual inquiries, be received at once into full fellowship."

Quest. 4. How shall we be more exact in receiving and excluding members ?

1784. " *Quest.* 17. When shall we admit new members ?

" *Ans.* In large towns, admit them into the bands a the quarterly love-feast following the quarterly meeting into the society,*on the Sunday following the quarterl meeting. Then also read the names of them that ar< excluded."

1789. The following was substituted :—

" How shall we be more strict in receiving an< excluding members ?

" *Ans.* In large societies, we may read the name of those that are received and excluded, once a quarter.'

1792. The answer is, " The official minister o preacher shall, at every quarterly meeting, read th< names of those that are received and excluded."

1836. The last clause of the answer reads " those that are received into the church and also thos< that are excluded therefrom."

Quest. 5. What shall we do with those members of ou: church who wilfully and repeatedly neglect to meet their class.

The answer to this question remained substantiall; the same as in 1784, (see Quest. 65, p. 59,) until

1836, when the second answer was changed s< as to read, " If they do not amend, let him who has th< charge of the circuit or station bring their case befor< the society or a select number, before whom they shal have been cited to appear ; and if they be found guilt; of wilful neglect by the decision of a majority of th< members before whom their case is brought, let them be laid aside, and let the preacher show that they ar< excluded for a breach of our rules, and not for immora conduct."

SECTION III.

Of the Band Societies.

The rules for the bands were drawn up by Mr. Wes ley at the dates prefixed to them severally. But the; were not introduced into our Discipline until 1791.' The original rules were as follows :—

---

* Wesley's Works, vol. v, pp. 192–4.

Rules of the Band Societies, drawn up Dec. 25, 1738.

" The design of our meeting is, to obey that command of God, ' Confess your faults one to another, and pray one for another, that ye may be healed.'

" To this end, we intend,—

" 1. To meet once a week, at the least.

" To come punctually at the hour appointed, without some extraordinary reason.

" 3. To begin (those of us who are present) exactly at the hour, with singing or prayer.

" 4. To speak each of us in order, freely and plainly, the true state of our souls, with the faults we have committed in thought, word, or deed, and the temptations we have felt, since our last meeting.

" 5. To end every meeting with prayer, suited to the state of each person present.

" 6. To desire some person among us to speak his own state first, and then to ask the rest, in order, as many and as searching questions as may be, concerning their state, sins, and temptations.

" Some of the questions proposed to every one before he is admitted among us may be to this effect :—

" 1. Have you the forgiveness of your sins ?

" 2. Have you peace with God, through our Lord Jesus Christ ?

" 3. Have you the witness of God's Spirit with your spirit, that you are a child of God ?

" 4. Is the love of God shed abroad in your heart ?

" 5. Has no sin, inward or outward, dominion over you ?

" 6. Do you desire to be told your faults ?

" 7. Do you desire to be told all your faults, and that plain and home ?

" 8. Do you desire that every one of us should tell you, from time to time, whatsoever is in his heart concerning you ?

" 9. Consider ! Do you desire we should tell you whatsoever we think, whatsoever we fear, whatsoever we hear, concerning you ?

" 10. Do you desire that, in doing this we should come as close as possible, that we should cut to the quick, and search your heart to the bottom ?

" 11. Is it your desire and design to be on this, and all other occasions, entirely open, so as to speak every thing that is in your heart without exception, without disguise, and without reserve ?

" Any of the preceding questions may be asked as often as occasion offers ; the four following at every meeting :—

" 1. What known sins have you committed since our last meeting ?

" 2. What temptations have you met with?

" 3. How were you delivered ?

" 4. What have you thought, said, or done, of which you doubt whether it be sin or not ?

" Directions given to the Band Societies, Dec. 25, 1744.

" You are supposed to have the faith that ' overcometh the world.' To you, therefore, it is not grievous,—

" I. Carefully to abstain from doing evil; in particular,

" 1. Neither to buy nor sell any thing at all on the Lord's day.

" 2. To taste no spirituous liquor, no dram of any kind, unless prescribed by a physician.

" 3. To be at a word both in buying and selling.

" 4. To pawn nothing, no, not to save life.*

" 5. Not to mention the fault of any behind his back, and to stop those short that do.

" 6. To wear no needless ornaments, such as rings, earrings, necklaces, lace, ruffles.

" 7. To use no needless self-indulgence, such as taking snuff or tobacco, unless prescribed by a physician.

" II. Zealously to maintain good works ; in particular,

" 1. To give alms of such things as you possess, and that to the uttermost of your power.

---

* In publishing this rule, Mr. Crowther adds the following note :— " There was a fund at that time established to assist the poor, either by loan or donation, which accounts for the rigour of the rule."—*Portraiture of Methodism*, p. 256.

" 2. To reprove all that sin in your sight; and that in love and meekness of wisdom.

" 3. To be patterns of diligence and frugality, of self-denial, and taking up the cross daily.

" III. Constantly to attend on all the ordinances of God ; in particular,—

"1. To be at church and at the Lord's table every week, and at every public meeting of the bands.

" 2. To attend the ministry of the word every morning, unless distance, business, or sickness prevent.

" 3. To use private prayer every day ; and family prayer, if you are at the head of a family.

" 4. To read the Scriptures, and meditate therein, at every vacant hour. And,—

" 5. To observe, as days of fasting or abstinence, all Fridays in the year."*

1791. The section was introduced, as now, by a definition of a band, namely,

" Two, three, or four true believers, who have full confidence in each other, form a band. Only it is to be observed, that in one of these bands all must be men, or all women ; and all married, or all single."

The following was added to the questions at the close of the Rules, namely, " 5. Have you nothing you desire to keep secret ?" which was omitted in 1792. In Direction I, 6, " earrings" included among the needless ornaments.

Under the " Directions, &c.," I, 4, the rule is simply, " To pawn nothing," omitting the clause, " no, not to save life."

1792. In Question 11, the words, " every thing that is in your heart, without exception," are omitted.

Under the " Directions, &c.," that about " pawning" is omitted. The last under that head reads, " To use no needless self-indulgence," omitting the words " such as taking snuff or tobacco, unless prescribed by a phy-

---

* In 1784, some directions were given, " how to encourage meeting in band." (See Quest. 19, p. 36.)

sician." Direction III, 1, was altered to the follow
ing :—" To be at church, and at the Lord's table, an
at every public meeting of the bands, at every oppor
tunity." Direction III, 2, was omitted ; and III, 4, (3
changed to the following :—" Frequently to read th
Scriptures, and meditate thereon."

SECTION IV.

*Of the Privileges granted to Serious Persons wh
are not of our Church.*

The only material alterations in the Rules on thi
subject since 1784 (see Questions 11 and 12, p. 29
are the following :—

1789. In the answer to the first question, th
last two sentences struck out ; and in the second, afte
" twice," was inserted " or thrice."*

1808. The first question reads, " How often
shall we permit those who are not of our society t
meet in class or society ?"

1816. The rule was made to refer only to meet
ing in class.

SECTION V.

Of Marriage.

The title in 1789 was, " On unlawful Marriages,'
which was changed for the present in 1804.

Quest. 1. Do we observe any evil which has prevailed in
our church with respect to marriage ?

There has been no material change in the answer to
this question since 1784. (See Question 20, p. 37.
The question assumed its present form in 1796.

Quest 2. What can be done to discourage this ?

The original provisions on the subject may be seer
under Question 21, p. 37.

1804. The words, " put a stop to," in the ques
tion, were changed to " discourage ;" and the punish

---

* The rule had been thus in 1773. (See p. 10.)

ment for violating the rule was changed from expulsion
to " putting back on trial for six months."

1836. The penalty was done away with, by
striking out entirely Answers 2 and 3.

Quest. 3. Ought any woman to marry without the consent
of her parents ?

The original answer may be found under Question
22, p. 37. The alterations in it have been as follows :—

1789. The last three words, " to marry her,"
were changed to " to be married to her."

1800. The words, " if a woman be under the
necessity of marrying," were changed to, " if a woman
believe it to be her duty to marry."

1792. The following note was added :—

" N. B. By the word ' unawakened,' as used above,
we mean one whom we could not in conscience admit
into society." To this, in

1796, the following sentence was added :—
" We do not prohibit our people from marrying persons
who are not of our society, provided such persons have
the form, and are seeking the power, of godliness ; but
if they marry persons who do not come up to this
description, we shall be obliged to purge our society
of them ; and even in a doubtful case the member of
our society shall be put back upon trial."

1800. The definition of an " unawakened" person was omitted.

1804. For " but if they marry persons who do
not come up to this description, we shall be obliged to
purge our society of them," it reads, ' but we are
determined to discourage their marrying persons who
do not come up to this description."

1836. The last clause, (1796,) " And even in a
doubtful case the member shall be put back on trial,"
omitted.

SECTION VI.

Of Dress.

The original provision on this subject* may be found under Question 18, p. 36.

1792. The words, "not even of a married woman" struck out.

1836. The words, " give no tickets," where they first occur, were changed to " receive none into the church ;" but they were retained in the last sentence. The word " any," before " encouragement," and the word " large," before " society," were omitted.

SECTION VII.

Of bringing to Trial, finding guilty, and reproving, suspending, or excluding disorderly Persons from Society and Church Privileges.

The original draft of this section was prepared by Bishop Asbury in 1788,† and introduced into the Discipline of 1789. It was as follows :—

" On bringing to Trial, finding guilty, reproving, suspending, and excluding disorderly Persons from Society and Church Privileges.

" *Quest.* How shall a suspected member be brought to trial ?

" *Ans.* Before the society of which he is a member, or a select number of them, in the presence of a bishop, elder, deacon, or preacher, in the following manner :— Let the accused and accuser be brought face to face : if this cannot be done, let the next best evidence be procured. If the accused person be found guilty, and the crime be such as is expressly forbidden by the word of God, sufficient to exclude a person from the kingdom of grace and glory, and to make him a subject of

---

* The subject is also noticed in the Annual Minutes for 1784. (See above, page 21, Question 11.)

† See p. 83.

wrath and hell, let him be expelled. If he evade a trial by absenting himself, after sufficient notice given him, and the circumstances of the accusation be strong and presumptive, let him be esteemed as guilty, and accordingly excluded. And without evident marks and fruits of repentance, such offenders shall be solemnly disowned before the church. Witnesses from without shall not be rejected, if a majority believe them to be honest men.

"But in cases of neglect of duties of any kind, imprudent conduct, indulging sinful tempers or words, disobedience to the order and Discipline of the church, first, let private reproof be given by a leader or preacher : if there be an acknowledgment of the fault, and proper humiliation, the person may remain on trial. On a second offence, a preacher may take one or two faithful friends. On a third failure, if the transgression be increased or continued, let it be brought before the society, or a select number : if there be no sign of humiliation, and the church is dishonoured, the offender must be cut off. If there be a murmur or complaint that justice is not done, the person shall be allowed an appeal to the quarterly meeting, and have his case reconsidered before a bishop, presiding elder, or deacon, with the preachers, stewards, and leaders who may be present. After such forms of trial and expulsion, such persons as are thus excommunicated shall have no privileges of society and sacrament in our church, without contrition, confession, and proper trial.*

"N. B. From this time forward, no person shall be owned as a member of our church without six months' trial."†

---

* For a provision on this point in 1781, see p. 17.

† In the same year the following explanation of this section was published in the Minutes :—

"As a very few persons have in some respect mistaken our meaning, in the thirty-second section of our Form of Discipline, on bringing to trial disorderly persons, &c., we think it necessary to explain it.

"When a member of our society is to be tried for any offence, the officiating minister or preacher is to call together all the members, if

1792. The title was changed to its present form
The words, " let him be expelled," changed to " let
the minister or preacher who has charge of the circui
expel him." The last sentence but one of the firs
paragraph, beginning, " And without, &c.," omitted
The last sentence made to read as now, " witnesse:
from without shall not be rejected."

The latter part of the second paragraph read as fol
lows :—" On a second offence, the preacher or leade
may take one or two faithful friends. On a thir
offence, let the case be brought before the society, or ?
select number ; and if there be no sign of real humilia
tion, the offender must be cut off.

" If there be a murmur or complaint from any ex
cluded person in any of the above-mentioned instances
that justice has not been done, he shall be allowed ar
appeal to the next quarterly meeting ; and the majorit)
of the ministers, travelling and local preachers, exhort
ers, stewards, and leaders present shall finally deter
mine the case." The words, " as are thus excommu
nicated," in the last sentence, are omitted, as also the
note.

The following new note was added :—

" N. B. If a member of our church shall be clearl)
convicted of endeavouring to sow dissensions in any ol
our societies, by inveighing against either our doctrine:
or discipline, such person so offending shall be firs
reproved by the senior minister or preacher of his cir
cuit, and, if he afterward persist in such perniciou;
practices, he shall be expelled the society."

1800. The word " suspected," in the question
changed to " accused."

In Answer 1, (1789,) after the words " found guilty,'

---

the society be small, or a select number if it be large, to take know
ledge and give advice, and bear witness to the justice of the whol
process ; that improper and private expulsions may be prevented fo
the future."

This note is not found in the reprint of the Minutes, but it is pub
lished in Lee's History of the Methodists, p. 143.

the following inserted :—" by the decision of a majority of the members before whom he is brought to trial." The words, " and to make him a subject of wrath and hell," omitted.

The following new provision added :—

" Nevertheless, if in any of the above-mentioned cases the minister or preacher differ in judgment from the majority of the society, or the select number, concerning the innocence or guilt of the accused person, the trial, in such case, may be referred by the minister or preacher to the ensuing quarterly meeting."

1808. The following inserted with reference to those who may appeal to the quarterly conferences (1792) :—" except such as exempt [absent] themselves from trial, after sufficient notice is given them."

1828. The words in the second paragraph, 1789, " the person may remain on trial," changed to " the person may be borne with."*

---

* In 1796 the following section was introduced on the sale and use of spirituous liquors. It was continued until 1840, when it was struck out, as seeming to sanction the practices for which it made regulations.

" Section 10. *Of the Sale and Use of Spirituous Liquors.*

" *Quest.* What directions shall be given concerning the sale and use of spirituous liquors ?

" *Ans.* If any member of our society retail or give spirituous liquors, and any thing disorderly be transacted under his roof on this account, the preacher who has the oversight of the circuit shall proceed against him as in the case of other immoralities : and the person accused shall be cleared, censured, suspended, or excluded, according to his conduct, as on other charges of immorality."

For the provisions on the subject prior to 1784, see pp. 15, 19.

CHAPTER III.

SACRAMENTAL SERVICES, &c.

As the Forms for the various services have undergone little alteration for many years, and can easily be
referred to, it will be sufficient here to show wherein
the present Forms differ from those recommended by
Mr. Wesley, and wherein the latter differed from those
of the Church of England, of which they were an
abridgment.

SECTION I.

The Order for the Administration of the Lord's Supper.

The original order, as recommended by Mr. Wesley, differed from that of the Church of England in the
following particulars :—It omitted the rubric requiring
communicants to signify their intention previously to
the curate, and those requiring the curate to repel improper persons from the table, the first prayer for
rulers ; the creed, the rubric respecting the publication
of notices, the verse in the offertory, taken from Tobi
iv, 7 ; the three exhortations preparatory to communion
that part of the rubric directing the people to kneel
while communing, (as well as the note in explanation
of the rule,) the third prayer after the communion, all
the collects at the close, and the rubrics, at the close
(of which the first prescribed how much of the order
was to be said when there was no communion, the
second and third, when there was to be no communion
the fourth regulated the communicating of priests and
deacons in cathedral and collegiate churches and colleges ; the fifth prescribed the kind of bread ; the sixth
what was to be done with the bread and wine that remained ; the seventh, how the bread and wine were
to be provided ; the eighth, how often parishes should
communicate and pay their ecclesiastical dues ; the

9

ninth, what was to be done with the money given at he offertory.)

Throughout, the title "elder" is substituted for "priest," and "the supreme rulers of the United States" for "the king," and "to all the ministers of thy gospel" for "to all bishops and curates."

The "absolution," after the Confession, in the order of the Church of England, is an address by the priest to the people, while, in the Methodist form, it is a prayer to God.

A provision was made, which is not found in the Church of England order, for extempore prayer at the close of the communion.

The order as prepared by Mr. Wesley contains the following portions that were afterward omitted :—

" *The Table at the Communion time, having a fair white Linen Cloth upon it, shall stand where morning and evening prayers are appointed to be said. And the Elder, standing at the Table, shall say the Lord's Prayer, with the Collect following, the People kneeling.*"

Then follows the Lord's Prayer. The Collect is the same that, in the present order, follows the prayer for absolution. After the Collect is inserted the following :—

" *Then shall the Elder, turning to the People, rehearse distinctly all the* TEN COMMANDMENTS : *and the People still kneeling shall, after every Commandment, ask God Mercy for their Transgression thereof for the Time past, and Grace to keep the same for the Time to come, as followeth :*

" *Minister.*

" God spake these words, and said, I am the Lord thy God : thou shalt have none other gods but me.

" *People*. Lord, have mercy upon us, and incline our hearts to keep this law.

" *Minist*. Thou shalt not make to thyself any graven image, nor the likeness of any thing that is in heaven above, or in the earth beneath, or in the water under the earth. Thou shalt not bow down to them, nor worship them : for I the Lord thy God am a jealous God, and visit the sins of the fathers upon the children, unto the third and fourth generation of them that hate.

me, and show mercy unto thousands in them that love me, and keep my commandments.

"*People.* Lord, have mercy upon us, and incline our hearts to keep this law.

"*Minist.* Thou shalt not take the name of the Lord thy God in vain : for the Lord will not hold him guiltless that taketh his name in vain.

"*People.* Lord, have mercy upon us, and incline our hearts to keep this law.

"*Minist.* Remember that thou keep holy the sabbath day. Six days shalt thou labour, and do all that thou hast to do : but the seventh day is the sabbath of the Lord thy God : in it thou shalt do no manner of work, thou, and thy son, and thy daughter, thy man-servant, and thy maid-servant, thy cattle, and the stranger that is within thy gates.   For in six days the Lord made heaven and earth, the sea, and all that in them is, and rested the seventh day ; wherefore the Lord blessed the seventh day, and hallowed it.

"*People.* Lord, have mercy upon us, and incline our hearts to keep this law.

"*Minist.* Honour thy father and thy mother, that thy days may be long in the land which the Lord thy God giveth thee.

"*People.* Lord, have mercy upon us, and incline our hearts to keep this law.

"*Minist.* Thou shalt do no murder.

"*People.* Lord, have mercy upon us, and incline our hearts to keep this law.

"*Minist.* Thou shalt not commit adultery.

"*People.* Lord, have mercy upon us, and incline our hearts to keep this law.

"*Minist.* Thou shalt not steal.

"*People.* Lord, have mercy upon us, and incline our hearts to keep this law.

"*Minist.* Thou shalt not bear false witness against thy neighbour.

"*People.* Lord, have mercy upon us, and incline our hearts to keep this law.

"*Minist.* Thou shalt not covet thy neighbour's house, thou shalt not covet thy neighbour's wife, nor his servant, nor his maid, nor his ox, nor his ass, nor any thing that is his.

"*People.* Lord, have mercy upon us, and write all these thy laws in our hearts, we beseech thee.

"*Then shall follow this Collect.*

"Almighty and everlasting God, we are taught by thy holy word, that the hearts of the princes of the earth are in thy rule and governance, and that thou dost dispose and turn them as it

seemeth best to thy godly wisdom ; we humbly beseech thee so
o dispose and govern the hearts of the supreme rulers of these
United States, our governors, that in all their thoughts, words,
and works, they may ever seek thy honour and glory, and study
o preserve thy people committed to their charge, in wealth,
peace, and godliness. Grant this, O merciful Father, for thy
dear Son's sake, Jesus Christ our Lord. Amen.

' *Then shall be said the Collect of the Day. And immediately
after the Collect, the Elder shall read the Epistle, saying,*
The Epistle [*or,* The Portion of Scripture appointed for the
Epistle] is written in the —— Chapter of ——, beginning at
the —— Verse. *And the Epistle ended, he shall say,* Here
endeth the Epistle. *Then shall be read the Gospel, (the
People all standing up,) saying,* The holy Gospel is written
in the —— Chapter of ——, beginning at the —— Verse.

" *Then shall follow the Sermon.*"

The offertory contains the following passages of
Scripture, which were afterward omitted, namely :——
1 Cor. ix, 7, 11, 13, 14 ; Gal. vi, 6, 7 ; Tobit iv, 8, 9.
After the offertory was the following prayer :——

"Let us pray for the whole state of Christ's church militant here on earth.

" Almighty and ever-living God, who by thy holy apostle hast
taught us to make prayers and supplications, and to give thanks
for all men ; we humbly beseech thee most
mercifully [*to accept our alms and oblations,
and*] to receive these our prayers, which we
offer unto thy divine Majesty ; beseeching
thee to inspire continually the universal church
with the spirit of truth, unity, and concord ;
and grant that all they that do confess thy
holy name may agree in the truth of thy holy word, and live in
unity and godly love. We beseech thee also to save and defend
all Christian kings, princes, and governors ; and especially thy
servants the supreme rulers of these United States ; that under
them we may be godly and quietly governed : and grant unto all
that are put in authority under them, that they may truly and indif-
ferently administer justice, to the punishment of wickedness and
vice, and to the maintenance of thy true religion and virtue. Give
grace, O heavenly Father, to all the ministers of thy gospel, that
they may both by their life and doctrine set forth thy true and
lively word, and rightly and duly administer thy holy sacraments.
And to all thy people give thy heavenly grace ; and especially
to this congregation here present ; that with meek heart and due
reverence they may hear and receive thy holy word, truly serv-

* If there be no alms
or oblations, then
shall the words [*of
accepting our alms
and oblations*] be left
unsaid.

ing thee in holiness and righteousness all the days of their life
And we most humbly beseech thee of thy goodness, O Lord, t
comfort and succour all them, who in this transitory life are i
trouble, sorrow, need, sickness, or any other adversity. An
we also bless thy holy name for all thy servants departed thi
life in thy faith and fear ; beseeching thee to give us grace a
to follow their good examples, that with them we may be par
takers of thy heavenly kingdom. Grant this, O Father, fo
Jesus Christ's sake, our only Mediator and Advocate. Amen.'

After the prayer for absolution the following was
inserted :—

> " *Then all standing, the Elder shall say,*

" Hear what comfortable words our Saviour Christ saith unto
all that truly turn to him :

" Come unto me, all ye that are burdened and heavy-laden,
and I will refresh you. Matt. xi, 28.

" So God loved the world, that he gave his only-begotten Son,
to the end that all that believe in him, should not perish, but
have everlasting life. John iii, 16.

" Hear also what St. Paul saith :

" This is a true saying, and worthy of all men to be received,
That Christ Jesus came into the world to save sinners. 1 Tim.
i, 15.

" Hear also what St. John saith :

" If any man sin, we have an Advocate with the Father, Jesus
Christ the righteous : and he is the propitiation for our sins.
1 John ii, 1, 2.

> " *After which the Elder shall proceed, saying,*

" Lift up your hearts.
" *Ans.* We lift them up unto the Lord.
" *Elder.* Let us give thanks unto our Lord God.
" *Ans.* It is meet and right so to do."

Before the passage beginning—" Therefore with
angels, &c.," was inserted this rubric :—

" *Here shall follow the proper Preface, according to the Time,
if there be any especially appointed ; or else immediately shall
follow :*

The prefaces were inserted as follows :—

> " *Upon Christmas-Day.*

" Because thou didst give Jesus Christ thine only Son to be
born as at this time for us, who, by the operation of the Holy

Ghost, was made very man, and that without spot of sin, to make us clean from all sin.   Therefore with angels, &c.

" *Upon Easter-Day.*

" But chiefly we are bound to praise thee for the glorious resurrection of thy Son Jesus Christ our Lord : for he is the very Paschal Lamb, which was offered for us, and hath taken away the sin of the world ; who by his death hath destroyed death, and by his rising to life again, hath restored to us everlasting life.   Therefore with angels, &c.

" *Upon Ascension-Day.*

" Through thy most dearly beloved Son, Jesus Christ our Lord ; who, after his most glorious resurrection, manifestly appeared to all his apostles, and in their sight ascended up into heaven, to prepare a place for us ; that where he is, thither we might also ascend, and reign with him in glory.   Therefore with angels, &c.

" *Upon Whitsunday.*

" Through Jesus Christ our Lord ; according to whose most true promise the Holy Ghost came down, as at this time, from heaven with a sudden great sound, as it had been a mighty wind, in the likeness of fiery tongues, lighting upon the apostles, to teach them, and to lead them into all truth ; giving them both the gift of divers languages, and also boldness, with fervent zeal, constantly to preach the gospel unto all nations, whereby we have been brought out of darkness and error into the clear light and true knowledge of thee, and of thy Son Jesus Christ.   Therefore with angels, &c.

" *Upon the Feast of Trinity.*

" Who art one God, one Lord ; not one only person, but three persons in one substance.   For that which we believe of the glory of the Father, the same we believe of the Son, and of the Holy Ghost, without any difference or inequality.   Therefore with angels, &c."

The forms immediately following the prayer of absolution being said standing, the rubric prefixed to the prayer before that of consecration was as follows :—

" *Then shall the Elder, kneeling down at the Table, say in the Name of all them that shall receive the Communion, this Prayer following ; the People also kneeling :*

The original order in the Sunday service has since undergone the following alterations :—

1786.   The first rubric, instead of directing that the table should " stand where morning and evening prayers are appointed to be said," directed that it should " stand in some convenient place."   In the collect after the commandments, " princes of the earth" was changed to " rulers of the earth," and "supreme" omitted before "rulers of the United States."   In the offertory the verses from Tobit iv, 8, 9, were omitted.   In the prayer after the offertory, the words " kings, princes, and" before " governors," and " supreme" before " rulers," struck out.

1792.   In this year the Forms were first incorporated in the book of Discipline.   The order for the communion as prepared by Mr. Wesley was abridged by the omission of all the parts quoted above in small type, and the passages of the offertory from 1 Cor. and Gal.

The following changes were also made.   The first collect was transferred so as to follow the prayer for absolution.   In the addresses to the communicants, on delivering the elements, the words " body" and "soul' were transposed, and the words " thee" and " thy soul' and " body" were printed in italics, (as they have been ever since,) indicating that if there be more than one communicant, the plural form is to be used ;—which is a departure from the original usage.

In the prayer immediately preceding the prayer of consecration, the original words, "that our sinful bodies may be made clean by his body, and our souls washed through his most precious blood," were changed to "that our sinful souls and bodies may be made clean by his death, and washed through his most precious blood."

At the close of the order, the following note was added:—

" N. B. If the elder be straitened for time, he may omit any part of the service except the prayer of consecration."

The order has undergone no alteration since 1792.

The Ministration of Baptism of Infants.

The order recommended by Mr. Wesley differed from that of the Church of England, in the following particulars. It omits the four introductory rubrics, (the first of which relates to the periods at which baptism should be administered; the second, to godfathers and godmothers; the third, to the preparatory arrangements for baptism; and the fourth, to ascertaining whether the child has been baptized before.) It also omits the exhortation after the Gospel, all the addresses to the god fathers and godmothers, and the two concluding notes (the first of which declares that baptized children, dying before they commit actual sin, are undoubtedly saved and the second relates to the use of the sign of the cross in baptism.)

The whole service for " the ministration of baptism of children in private houses" is omitted.

In regard to the mode of baptizing, the English rubric directed—" (if they shall certify him that the child may well endure it) he shall dip it in the water discreetly and warily,"—" But, if they certify that the child is weak, it shall suffice to pour water upon it." The Sunday service directed, " He shall dip it in the water or sprinkle it therewith." The English form declared of the child, after baptism—" this child is regenerate,' —" it hath pleased thee to regenerate this infant with thy Holy Spirit." These expressions, with the corresponding ones in the baptism of adults, were omitted

The following parts of the original order have been subsequently omitted.

This prayer was to be said before reading the Gospel :—

A " Almighty and immortal God, the aid of all that need, the helper of all that flee to thee for succour, the life of them that believe, and the resurrection of the dead; we call upon thee for infant, that he, coming to thy holy baptism, may receive remission of his sins by spiritual regeneration. Receive him

O Lord, as thou hast promised by thy well-beloved Son, saying, ask, and ye shall have ; seek, and ye shall find ; knock, and it shall be opened unto you : so give now unto us that ask ; let us that seek find ; open the gate unto us that knock ; that *this infant* may enjoy the everlasting benediction of thy heavenly washing, and may come to the eternal kingdom which thou hast promised by Christ our Lord.   *Amen.*"

And immediately after the Gospel, the following :—

" Almighty and everlasting God, heavenly Father, we give thee humble thanks, that thou hast vouchsafed to call us to the knowledge of thy grace and faith in thee : increase this knowledge, and confirm this faith in us evermore.   Give thy Holy Spirit to *this infant ;* that *he* may be born again, and be made *an heir* of everlasting salvation, through our Lord Jesus Christ, who liveth and reigneth with thee and the Holy Spirit, now and for ever.   *Amen.*"

After baptizing the child, the minister was to say :—

" We receive this child into the congregation of Christ's flock, and do* sign *him* with the sign of the cross ; in token that hereafter *he* shall not be ashamed to confess the faith of Christ crucified, and manfully to fight under *** Here the priest shall make a cross upon the child's forehead.** his banner against sin, the world, and the devil ; and to continue Christ's faithful soldier and servant unto his life's end.   *Amen.*

" *Then shall the Minister say,*

" Seeing now, dearly beloved brethren, that *this child is* grafted into the body of Christ's church ; let us give thanks unto Almighty God for these benefits, and with one accord make our prayers unto him, that *this child* may lead the rest of *his life* according to this beginning."

And at the close of the service, this prayer :—

" We yield thee hearty thanks, most merciful Father, that it hath pleased thee to receive *this infant* for thine own *child* by adoption, and to incorporate *him* into thy holy church.   And humbly we beseech thee to grant, that *he,* being dead unto sin, and living unto righteousness, and being buried with Christ in his death, may crucify the old man, and utterly abolish the whole body of sin ; and that as *he is* made *partaker* of the death of thy Son, *he* may also be *partaker* of his resurrection ; so that finally, with the residue of thy holy church, *he* may be *an inheritor* of thine everlasting kingdom, through Christ our Lord.   *Amen.*"

9*

The changes in the original order have been as follows :—

1786. The first three forms quoted above in small type were omitted. In the first prayer, the words, "didst sanctify water to the mystical washing away of sin," were altered to "didst sanctify water for his holy sacrament." And in the prayer immediately before baptizing, the clause in the original—"sanctify this water to the mystical washing away of sin" was left out. The rubric of 1784 directed, as to the mode of baptizing, "he shall dip it in the water or sprinkle it therewith." That of 1786 directed—"he shall dip it in the water or pour water upon it, or sprinkle it therewith." At the close was now added a new rubric, namely, "The minister, if he see it expedient, may conclude with a prayer extempore."

1792. The following rubric was inserted at the beginning :—"The minister coming to the font shall use the following or some other exhortation suitable to his sacred office." The rubric respecting the mode of baptizing now read—"he shall sprinkle or pour water upon it, or if desired, immerse it in water." The Gospel was transposed so as immediately to precede the baptizing ; and in the prayer before the Gospel, the words "sanctify this water for this holy sacrament" were inserted in place of "sanctify this water to the mystical washing away of sin," which had been left out altogether in 1786. The last two of the forms quoted above in small type were now omitted.

There has been no alteration in the order since 1792.

*The Ministration of Baptism to such as are of Riper
Years.*

The order of the Church of England contains the following parts, which are not in that recommended by Mr. Wesley, namely :—Three introductory rubrics respecting the preparations for baptism, and inquiring whether the person has been baptized before ; an address connected with the use of the sign of the cross, corresponding with that in the case of infants, (see p. 201 ;) an exhortation to the godfathers and godmothers, and one to the new baptized persons ; and two concluding rubrics, one respecting confirmation and the other respecting the baptism of those who have passed infancy but have not arrived at years of discretion.

The order prepared by Mr. Wesley contained the following parts, which are omitted in later editions, namely :

The first prayer was :—

" Almighty and everlasting God, who of thy great mercy didst save Noah and his family in the ark from perishing by water ; and also didst safely lead the children of Israel thy people through the Red Sea, figuring thereby thy holy baptism ; and by the baptism of thy well-beloved Son Jesus Christ in the river Jordan, didst sanctify the element of water, to the mystical washing away of sin ; we beseech thee for thine infinite mercies, that thou wilt mercifully look upon *these* thy *servants ;* wash *them* and sanctify *them* with the Holy Ghost ; that *they* being delivered from thy wrath, may be received into the ark of Christ's church ; and being steadfast in faith, joyful through hope, and rooted in charity, may so pass the waves of this troublesome world, that finally *they* may come to the land of everlasting life ; there to reign with thee world without end, through Jesus Christ our Lord. *Amen.*"

After baptizing, the minister was to say,—

" Seeing now, dearly beloved brethren, that *these persons are* grafted into the body of Christ's church ; let us give thanks unto Almighty God for these benefits, and with one accord make our prayers unto him, that *they* may lead the rest of *their* life according to this beginning."

And at the close of the service this prayer,—

" We yield thee humble thanks, O heavenly Father, that thou hast vouchsafed to call us to the knowledge of thy grace and faith in thee : increase this knowledge, and confirm this faith in us evermore.   Give thy Holy Spirit to *these persons ;* that being born again, and made *heirs* of everlasting salvation, through our Lord Jesus Christ, *they* may continue thy *servants*, and attain thy promises, through the same Lord Jesus Christ thy Son ; who liveth and reigneth with thee, in the unity of the same Holy Spirit, everlastingly. *Amen.*"

The alterations in this order have been as follows :—
1786.   The prayer which now immediately precedes the Gospel was omitted.

There was now prefixed to the prayers this rubric:
" Then shall the minister use as many of the following
prayers as the time will permit."   And immediately
before the ceremony of baptizing was inserted this
rubric, " The congregation may here sing a hymn suitable to the occasion."   In the first prayer, the words,
" didst sanctify the element of water to the mystical
washing away of sin," are changed to "didst sanctify
the element of water for this holy sacrament."   In the
creed, " that he went down into hell," omitted.   In the
prayer just before baptizing, the words, " sanctify this
water to the mystical washing away of sin," are left
out.

The rubric of 1784, respecting the mode of baptizing,
was, " shall dip him in the water, or pour water upon
him."   That of 1786 was, " shall dip him in the
water, or pour water upon him, or sprinkle him therewith."

1792.   The following rubric was prefixed to the
service : " The minister shall use the following, or some
other exhortation, suitable to this holy office."   The
forms quoted above, in small type, were left out ;
and the prayer which now precedes the Gospel, and
which was left out in 1786, was restored and placed in
its present position.   It originally followed the Gospel.
The rubric respecting the mode of baptizing now read,
" shall sprinkle or pour water upon him, (or if he shall
desire it, shall immerse him in water.")   The following
rubric was added at the close : " Then let the minister
conclude with extemporary prayer."

The only alteration in the order since 1792 was in
1836.   A note was added to the creed, defining
' holy catholic church" to be " the church of God in
general."

SECTION III.

The Form of Solemnization of Matrimony.

The form recommended by Mr. Wesley omits the following portions of that of the Church of England namely, the rubric directing what is to be done in case an impediment be alleged ; the ceremony of giving the woman to the man, and of putting on the ring, as also all allusion to it in other parts of the service ; the psalms after the blessing ; the address on the duties of husbands and wives, and the rubric at the close about the new married persons receiving the holy communion

The original form contains the following portions which were subsequently omitted, namely, in the introductory address, after the word " unadvisedly," it reads

" Lightly or wantonly to satisfy men's carnal lusts and appetites, like brute beasts that have no understanding," &c.

And after the words, " fear of God," was the following passage :—

" Duly considering the causes for which matrimony was ordained.

" First. It was ordained for the procreation of children, to be brought up in the fear and nurture of the Lord, and to the praise of his holy name.

" Secondly. It was ordained for a remedy against sin, and to avoid fornication ; that such persons as have not the gift of continency, might marry, and keep themselves undefiled members of Christ's body.

" Thirdly. It was ordained for the mutual society, help, and comfort that the one ought to have of the other, both in prosperity and adversity."

The following was to be said before the Lord's prayer :—

" *Then shall the minister say,* Lord, have mercy upon us.

" *Ans.* Christ, have mercy upon us.

" *Minister.* Lord, have mercy upon us.

And the following after it :—

" *Minister.* O Lord, save thy servant and thy handmaid.

" *Answer.* And let them put their trust in thee.

" *Minister.* O Lord, send them help from thy holy place.

"*Answer.* And evermore defend them.

"*Minister.* Be unto them a tower of strength.

"*Answer.* From the face of their enemy.

"*Minister.* O Lord, hear our prayer.

"*Answer.* And let our cry come unto thee."

The following was included among the closing prayers :—

' *This Prayer next following shall be omitted, where the Woman is past child-bearing.*

"O merciful Lord and heavenly Father, by whose gracious gift mankind is increased ; we beseech thee assist with thy blessing these two persons, that they may both be fruitful in the procreation of children, and also live together so long in godly love and honesty, that they may see their children Christianly and virtuously brought up, to thy praise and honour, through Jesus Christ our Lord. *Amen.*"

The only alterations in this form have been the following :—

1786. The following qualifying clause was inserted in the rubric, requiring the publication of the banns :—"(unless a license be procured from the proper authority.)"

1792. The preceding clause was changed to the following :—" (unless they be otherwise qualified according to law.)"

In the introductory address the original had these words, " in the face of this congregation." They were now changed to, " in the presence of these witnesses." The passages in the original form, quoted above in small type, were now left out.

There have been no alterations since.

" The Communion of the Sick."

The next form in the Sunday service was, "The Communion of the Sick." It was the same with that of the Church of England, omitting only the first and the three last rubrics. It was as follows :—

" The Collect.

" Almighty, ever-living God, maker of mankind, who dost correct those whom thou dost love, and chastise every one whom thou dost receive ; we beseech thee to have mercy upon this thy servant visited with thine hand ; and to grant that *he* may take *his* sickness patiently, and recover *his* bodily health, if it be thy gracious will ; and that whenever *his* soul shall depart from the body, it may be without spot presented unto thee, through Jesus Christ our Lord.   *Amen.*

" *The Epistle.*   Heb. xii, 5, 6.

" My son, despise not thou the chastening of the Lord, nor faint when thou art rebuked of him : for whom the Lord loveth he chasteneth, and scourgeth every son whom he receiveth.

" *The Gospel.*   John v, 24.

" Verily, verily, I say unto you, he that heareth my word, and believeth on him that sent me, hath everlasting life, and shall not come into condemnation ; but is passed from death unto life.

" *After which, the elder shall proceed according to the form before prescribed for the holy communion, beginning at these words* [Ye that do truly, &c.]

" *At the time of the distribution of the holy sacrament, the elder shall first receive the communion himself, and after minister unto them that are appointed to communicate with the sick, and last of all to the sick person.*"

1792.   This form was left out altogether.

SECTION IV.

The Order of the Burial of the Dead.

The order in the Sunday service omits the following portions found in that of the Church of England, namely,—the first rubric, forbidding the office " to be used for any that die unbaptized, or excommunicate, or have laid violent hands on themselves ;" one of the Psalms, (thirty-ninth ;) the words to be spoken while the earth is cast upon the body ; and the prayer following the Lord's Prayer.

It contains the following parts, which were omitted in 1792, namely, the Psalm (nineteeth) and the Lesson, (1 Cor. xi, 20, to end.)

1792.   This note was prefixed to the order :— " N. B. The following or some other solemn service shall be used."

There have been no alterations since 1792.

CHAPTER IV.

THE FORM AND MANNER OF MAKING AND ORDAINING BISHOPS, ELDERS, AND DEACONS.

THE title in the form of the Church of England is, —" The Form and Manner of making, ordaining, and consecrating of Bishops, Priests, and Deacons." In the Sunday service it was,—" The Form and Manner of making and ordaining of Superintendents, Elders, and Deacons;" and throughout, "superintendents" was used for "bishops," and "elders" for "priests." In the ordering of deacons and priests, the English rubric directed the bishop to surcease ordaining, "if any great crime or impediment" was objected; the Sunday service, " if any crime or impediment."

SECTION I.

The Form and Manner of making of Deacons.

The form recommended by Mr. Wesley omitted the following portions of that of the Church of England, namely,—the preface, the address of the bishop to the archdeacon, and the reply; the passage from Acts vi, 2–7; the oath of the king's supremacy; and the closing rubric, respecting the qualifications for the priesthood.

The English form directs the bishop to deliver to the ordained deacon "the New Testament;" the Sunday service, "the Holy Bible."

1786. The rubric in this edition directs the superintendent, in saying the litany, to insert a petition for the candidates, when he prays for the ministers of the gospel; and to omit the last prayer and the blessing. This was to be done also in ordaining elders and superintendents.

1792. The rubric, with reference to saying the litany and the service for the communion, was omitted in all the forms.   In the first question proposed to the candidate, the words " this office and ministration" changed to " the office of the ministry."   The following question and answer were also omitted :—

" *The Superintendent.*

" Do you think that you are truly called, according to the will of our Lord Jesus Christ, to the ministry of the church ?
" *Ans.* I think so."

In the third question, the words " or expound" inserted after " read."

There have been no changes since 1792.

SECTION II.

The Form and Manner of ordaining Elders.

The form recommended by Mr. Wesley omitted the following portions of the form of the Church of England, namely,—the address of the archdeacon to the bishop, and his reply ; one of the Gospels ; (Matt. ix, 36 ;) the oath of the king's supremacy ; the second form,—" Come, Holy Ghost, eternal God, &c. ;" and the Nicene Creed.

1792.   The original address to the congregation began,—" Good people ;" it now began,—" Brethren." The original form for the ordination began,—" Receive the Holy Ghost for the office, &c." It was now changed to,—" The Lord pour upon thee the Holy Ghost for the office, &c. ;" though the original form has been retained in ordaining a bishop.   The rubric directing the persons ordained to receive the communion was omitted here, although it has been retained in the ordination of deacons.

There have been no changes in this form since 1792.

SECTION III.

The Form of ordaining a Bishop.

The title in the form of the Church of England is, —" The Form of ordaining or consecrating of an

Archbishop or Bishop ;" in Mr. Wesley's it is,—"The Form of ordaining of a Superintendent." The latter omits the following portions of the former, namely,— the Epistle, (1 Tim. iii, 1–7 ;) one of the Gospels, (John xx, 19–23 ;) the Nicene Creed ; the oath of the king's supremacy, and the oath of obedience to the archbishop ; the form, " Come, Holy Ghost, eternal God, &c."

1792.   The rubric respecting the communion service was omitted.

1808.   When the elders presented the elected person for ordination, the original form was,—" We present unto you this godly man to be ordained a bishop."   In 1808 " godly" was changed to " holy."

PART II.

THE TEMPORAL ECONOMY OF THE METHODIST EPISCOPAL CHURCH.*

SECTION I.

Of the Boundaries of the Annual Conferences.

THE first question of this section originally belonged to Part i, Sec. 3, " Of the General and Yearly Conferences," where the boundaries of the conferences were given in **1796,** as follows :—†

" 1. The New-England Conference, under the direction of which shall be the affairs of our church in New-England, and in that part of the state of New-York which lies on the east side of Hudson's River. *Provided*, that if the bishops see it necessary, a conference may be held in the province of Maine.

" 2. The Philadelphia Conference, for the direction of our concerns in the remainder of the state of New-York, in New-Jersey, in all that part of Pennsylvania which lies on the east side of the Susquehannah River, the state of Delaware, and all the rest of the peninsula.

" 3. The Baltimore Conference, for the remainder of Pennsylvania, the remainder of Maryland, and the Northern Neck of Virginia.

" 4. The Virginia Conference, for all that part of Virginia which lies on the south side of the Rappahannock River, and for all that part of North Carolina which lies on the north side of Cape Fear River, including also the circuits which are situated on the branches of the Yadkin.

---

* The title of Part i, according to the division ordered in 1804, was, " The Doctrines and Discipline of the Methodist Episcopal Church," but in publishing, this has been applied to the whole book.
† For the previous arrangement respecting the conferences, see p. 118.

" 5. The South Carolina Conference, for South Carolina, Georgia, and the remainder of North Carolina.

" 6. The Western Conference, for the states of Kentucky and Tennessee : *Provided*, that the bishops shall have authority to appoint other yearly conferences in the interval of the General Conference, if a sufficiency of new circuits be anywhere formed for that purpose."

1800.   The boundaries were fixed as follows :—

" 1. The New-England Conference shall include the district of Maine, and all the circuits eastward and northward from the bounds of the New-York Conference.

" 2. The New-York Conference shall include that part of the state of New-York east of the Hudson River, all Connecticut, and those parts of Massachusetts, New-Hampshire, and Vermont, which are included in the New-York and New-London districts.

" 3, 4, 5, 6, and 7. Philadelphia, Baltimore, Virginia, South Carolina, and Western Conferences"—as before.

The proviso added as before.

1804.   This subject was transferred to Part ii, Sec. 1, as follows :—

" 1. The New-England Conference shall include the district of Maine, and the Boston, New-London, and Vermont districts.

" 2. The New-York Conference comprehending the New-York, Pittsfield, Albany, and Upper Canada districts.

" 3. The Philadelphia Conference"—as before, only insert, after " Susquehannah River," " except what belongs to the Susquehannah district."

" 4. The Baltimore Conference"—as before, except the addition of " the Green Briar district."

" 5. The Virginia Conference"—as before, except, after " Rappahannock River" insert, " east of the Blue Ridge," after "Cape Fear River" insert, "except Wilmington."

" 6. The South Carolina Conference"—as before.

" 7. The Western Conference shall include the states of Tennessee, Kentucky, and Ohio, and that part of Virginia which lies west of the great river Kenhawa, with the Illinois and the Natchez."

The proviso added as before.

1808. The description of the boundaries was the same, with the following exceptions :—

In the New-York Conference, " Cayuga" is named as one of the districts.

The Susquehannah district is included in the Philadelphia Conference.

In the Baltimore Conference, " Carlisle district" is named.

The proviso added as before.

1812. The boundaries were altered as follows :—

" 1. The Ohio Conference shall include Ohio, Muskingum, Miami, Kentucky, and Salt River districts.

" 2. The Tennessee Conference shall include Holston, Nashville, Cumberland, Wabash, Illinois, and Mississippi districts.

" 3. The South Carolina Conference shall include Georgia, South Carolina, and that part of North Carolina not included in the Virginia and Tennessee Conferences.

" 4. The Virginia Conference shall include the circuits situated on the branches of the Yadkin, and that part of North Carolina on the north side of Cape Fear River, (except Wilmington,) and that part of Virginia on the south side of the Rappahannock, and east of the Blue Ridge.

" 5. The Baltimore Conference shall include the remaining part of Virginia not included in the Tennessee and Virginia Conferences, the Western Shore of Maryland, and that part of Pennsylvania east of the Ohio River, and west of the Susquehannah, not included in the Genesee Conference.

" 6. The Philadelphia Conference shall include the whole of the peninsula between the Chesapeake and Delaware Bays, and all that part of Pennsylvania lying between the Delaware and Susquehannah Rivers, (except what is included in the Genesee Conference,) and all the state of New-Jersey, with Staten Island.

" 7. The New-York Conference shall include all the state of New-York not included in the Genesee and Philadelphia Conferences, that part of Connecticut and Massachusetts west of the Connecticut River, and that part of Vermont lying west of the Green Mountain.

" 8. The New-England Conference shall include the remaining part of Vermont, and all the New-England states east of Connecticut River.

" 9. The Genesee Conference shall include the bounds of the Susquehannah, Cayuga, and Upper and Lower Canada districts. *Provided,* nevertheless, the bishops have authority, in the interval of the General Conference, to appoint another annual conference down the Mississippi, if they judge it necessary. *Provided,* also, that they have authority to appoint another annual conference, in the interval of the General Conference, if a sufficient number of new circuits be anywhere formed ; but no district or circuit shall be added to such new conference, without the consent of the old conference to which it belongs."

1816. The Ohio Conference—as before, except that part of Scioto district is substituted for Salt River.

" 2. The Missouri Conference shall be bounded by the Ohio Conference on the north, by the Ohio and Mississippi Rivers on the east, and by the Arkansas River on the south.

" 3. The Tennessee Conference"—as before, except that " Wabash, Illinois, and Mississippi districts" are struck out, and " Salt River and Green River" inserted.

" 4. The Mississippi Conference shall include all the state of Louisiana south of the Arkansas, and all the Mississippi Territory south of Tennessee River.

" 5. The South Carolina Conference"—as before.

" 6. The Virginia Conference"—as before, with the addition of these words at the end, " except Fredericksburg."

" 7. The Baltimore Conference"—as before.

" 8. The Philadelphia Conference"—as before, wit the addition of these words, " And so much of th state of New-York as now is, or at any time may be attached to the Bergen and Hamburg districts."

"9. The New-York Conference"—as before, with th addition of these words, " With that part of Lower Ca nada between Lake Champlain and Magog."

" 10. The New-England Conference"—as before with the addition of the following words, " And tha part of Lower Canada east of Lake Magog."

" 11. The Genesee Conference"—as before, excep that " Oneida, Genesee, and Chenango" districts ar substituted for " Cayuga."

The first proviso is struck out, and the other reads *"Provided,* that the bishops shall have authority to ap point other annual conferences, in the interval of th General Conference, if the number of circuits shoul increase so as, in their judgment, to require it."

1820. " 1. The Ohio Conference shall com mence at the town of Madison, on the Ohio River, stat of Indiana, thence, running due north to the neares point on Lake Michigan, shall include the whole of th Michigan Territory. Thence running down Lake Eri to the town of Erie, thence to Waterford, on Frencl Creek, thence down French Creek to the Alleghan River, thence down the Alleghany and Ohio Rivers t the place of beginning.

" 2. The Missouri Conference shall include tha part of the state of Indiana not included in the Ohi Conference, the states of Illinois and Missouri, and th Territory of Arkansas.

" 3. The Kentucky Conference shall include th Kentucky, Salt River, Green River, and Cumberlam districts, and that part of the state of Virginia include in the Green Briar and Munroe circuits, heretofore be longing to the Baltimore Conference, and the little Ken hawa and Middle Island circuits, heretofore belongin to the Ohio Conference.

" 4. The Tennessee Conference shall include the Nashville, French Broad, and Holston districts, together with the New River circuit, heretofore belonging to the Baltimore Conference, and that part of Tennessee district north of Tennessee River.

" 5. The Mississippi Conference shall include the states of Mississippi and Louisiana, and all that part of the state of Alabama south of Tennessee River.

" 6. The South Carolina Conference"—as before.

" 7. The Virginia Conference"—as before.

" 8. The Baltimore Conference shall include the remaining part of Virginia, not included in the Virginia, Philadelphia, Kentucky, and Tennessee Conferences, the Western Shore of Maryland, and that part of Pennsylvania east of the Ohio River, and west of the Susquehannah, together with the Bald Eagle, Lycoming, Northumberland, and Shamokin circuits, heretofore belonging to the Genesee Conference.

" 9. The Philadelphia Conference"—as before, except that " Baltimore and" is inserted before "Genesee."

" 10. The New-York Conference"—as before.

" 11. The New-England Conference"—as before.

" 12. The Genesee Conference shall include the Oneida, Genesee, Chenango, Seneca, and Upper and Lower Canada districts, the Chautauque and Lake circuits, heretofore belonging to the Ohio Conference, and that part of Susquehannah district not included in the Baltimore Conference."

The following provisos were added to the previous one :—

" *Provided*, 2d, that the bishops be, and are hereby authorized, by and with the advice and consent of the New-England Conference, to form a new conference in the eastern part of the New-England Conference, in the interval between this and the next General Conference, if they shall judge it to be expedient.

" *Provided*, 3d, that the episcopacy, by and with the advice and consent of the Genesee Conference, if 'y judge it expedient, previous to the sitting of the next General Conference, shall have authority to esta blish a conference in Canada."

1824. " 1. The Maine Conference shall includ all the state of Maine, and that part of the state o New-Hampshire lying east of the White Hills, an north of the waters of the Ossipie Lake.

" 2. The New-England Conference shall includ the remaining part of the state of New-Hampshire that part of Vermont lying east of the Green Moun tains, those parts of the states of Massachusetts an Connecticut lying east of Connecticut River, and all th state of Rhode Island.

" 3. The New-York Conference"—as before, excep the omission of these words, " And that part of Lowe Canada between Lakes Champlain and Magog."

" 4. The Genesee Conference shall include th Oneida, Black River, Chenango, Susquehannah, On tario, Genesee, and Erie districts, and Sharon circuit from New-York, except that part of Erie district south west of Cattaraugus Creek.

" 5. The Canada Conference shall include all th upper province of Canada.

" 6. The Pittsburgh Conference shall commence a the mouth of Cattaraugus Creek, on Lake Erie, thenc to Olean Point, on Alleghany River, thence eastwar to the top of the Alleghany Mountains, thence alon the said mountains southward to the head of Tygert' Valley, thence to the Ohio River, so as to include th Middle Island and Little Kenhawa circuits, thence u said river to the mouth of Little Muskingum, thenc to the mouth of White Woman, so as to include Mon roe, Barnesville, and Duck Creek circuits, thenc north-eastward between the waters of Tuscarawas an Mohicken to Lake Erie, near the mouth of Kuyahauga so as to include Tuscarawas and Canton circuits, thenc down the lake to the mouth of Cattaraugus.

" 7. The Ohio Conference shall include the remain ing part of the state of Ohio, the territory of Michigan and the Kenhawa.

10

" 8. The Illinois Conference shall include the states of Indiana and Illinois.

" 9. The Missouri Conference shall include the state of Missouri and Arkansas Territory.

" 10. The Kentucky Conference shall include the state of Kentucky, and that part of the state of Tennessee lying north of the Cumberland River.

" 11. The Tennessee Conference shall include all that part of the state of Tennessee lying south of Cumberland River, and west of the Cumberland Mountains, and that part of the state of Alabama lying north of the mountains which divide the waters of Mobile Bay from the Tennessee River.

" 12. The Holston Conference shall include the remaining part of the state of Tennessee lying east of the Cumberland Mountains, and that part of Virginia and North Carolina embraced in the Holston district, and the Black Mountain and French Broad circuits, formerly belonging to the South Carolina Conference.

" 13. The Mississippi Conference shall include the states of Mississippi and Louisiana, that part of Alabama not included in Tennessee Conference, and all West Florida.'

" 14. The South Carolina Conference shall include all South Carolina, Georgia, East Florida, and that part of North Carolina not included in the Virginia and Holston Conferences.

" 15. The Virginia Conference"—as before.

" 16. The Baltimore Conference shall include the remaining part of Virginia not included in the Virginia, Holston, Ohio, Pittsburgh, and Philadelphia Conferences, the Western Shore of Maryland, and that part of Pennsylvania lying east of the Alleghany Mountains, and west of Susquehannah River, including Northumberland district.

" 17. The Philadelphia Conference"—as before.

The provisos now read as follows :—

" *Provided,* that the bishops be, and they are hereby authorized, with the advice and consent of the South

Carolina and Mississippi Conferences, to form a new conference of such sections of country as may be included in those conferences.

"*Provided*, also, that the bishops shall have authority to appoint other annual conferences, if the number of circuits should so increase as, in their judgment, to require it."

1828.   The boundaries remained the same as in 1824, with the following exceptions :—

"10. The Kentucky Conference shall include the state of Kentucky, except so much of said state as lies west of the Tennessee River.

"11. The Tennessee Conference shall include all that part of the state of Tennessee lying west of the Cumberland Mountains, and that part of the state of Kentucky lying west of the Tennessee River, and that part of the state of Alabama"—&c., as before.

"15. Virginia Conference," Port Royal is mentioned, with Fredericksburg, as not included.

The following proviso was substituted for those of 1824 :—

"*Provided*, that the bishops or bishop attending the following conferences, with the advice and consent of the said conferences respectively, be, and hereby are authorized to form new conferences, as follows, namely :—

"From the South Carolina Conference, of any section of country included in said conference : from the Mississippi Conference, of any section of country included in said conference : or, on the joint recommendation of the South Carolina and Mississippi Conferences, to form one new conference, from any section of country within the bounds of the said conferences : also, at the joint request of the New-York and New-England Conferences, to form a new conference within the bounds of said conferences : and, with the advice and consent of the Genesee Conference, to form a new conference in any section of country now within the bounds of said conference."

1832. The boundaries were fixed as follows :—

" 1. The New-York Conference shall include the New-York, New-Haven, Rhinebeck, and Hudson River districts, Hudson station, and Ghent and Lee circuits.

" 2. The New-England Conference shall include all the state of Massachusetts lying east of the Green Mountains not included in the New-Hampshire Conference, and that part of Connecticut lying east of Connecticut River, and all the state of Rhode Island.

" 3. Maine Conference"—as before.

" 4. New-Hampshire Conference shall include all the state of New-Hampshire not included in the Maine Conference, that part of the state of Vermont east of the Green Mountains, and that part of the state of Massachusetts north-east of the Merrimack River.

" 5. Troy Conference shall include the Saratoga, Middlebury, and Plattsburg districts, and that part of Troy district not included in the New-York Conference.

" 6. Oneida Conference shall include that part of the state of New-York east of Cayuga Lake not included in the New-York and Troy Conferences, and the Susquehannah district in the state of Pennsylvania.

" 7. Genesee Conference shall include that part of the state of New-York west of Cayuga Lake not included in the Pittsburg, and the Tioga, Loyalsock and Wellsborough circuits, in the state of Pennsylvania.

" 8. Pittsburg Conference"—as before, with the following exceptions, namely :—

For " the Middle Island and Little Kenhawa circuits," read " Middleburn circuit." For " Monroe, Barnesville, and Duck Creek circuits," read " Woodfield, Summerfield, and Freeport circuits." For " Tuscarawas," read " Leesburg."

" 9. Ohio Conference shall include the remainder of the state of Ohio, except Elizabethtown, that part of Virginia contained in the Kenhawa district, and the Territory of Michigan, except St. Joseph's and Kalanazoo missions.

"10. Indiana Conference shall include the state of Indiana, (except so much as is included in the Illinois Conference,) Elizabethtown, in the state of Ohio, and the St. Joseph's and Kalamazoo missions in Michigan Territory.

"11. Illinois Conference shall include the state of Illinois, the Paris and Eugene circuits, in the state of Indiana, and the North Western Territory.

"12. Missouri Conference shall include the state of Missouri, the Missouri and Arkansas Territories.

"13. Kentucky Conference"—as before.

"14. Tennessee Conference shall include West Tennessee, and that part of Kentucky lying west of Tennessee River, and North Alabama.

"15. Holston Conference shall include East Tennessee, and that part of the state of Georgia lying north of the Blue Ridge, and also what is now embraced in the Tugulo and Pickens circuits, and those parts of South Carolina, North Carolina, and Virginia included in the Ashville and Abingdon districts.

"16. Mississippi Conference shall include the state of Louisiana, and that part of Mississippi lying west of the dividing ridge between Pearl and Leaf Rivers, and thence with the said ridge between Mississippi and Tombeckbee to the Tennessee line.

"17. Alabama Conference shall include South Alabama, that part of Mississippi not included in Mississippi Conference, and West Florida.

"18. Georgia Conference shall include the state of Georgia, (except what is embraced in the Holston Conference,) East and Middle Florida.

"19. South Carolina Conference shall include the state of South Carolina, (except so much as is included in the Tugulo, Greenville, and Pickens circuits,) and that part of North Carolina not included in the Virginia and Holston Conferences.

"20. Virginia Conference"—as before.

"21. Baltimore Conference"—as before, except that after the words "Western Shore of Maryland," *is* added, "except a small portion included in the Pittsburgh Conference."

"22. Philadelphia Conference"—as before, except for "Genesee," read "Oneida," and for "Bergen," read "Haverstraw."

The usual proviso is omitted from this time forward

1836. The boundaries were fixed as follows.—

"1. The New-York Conference shall embrace all that territory now included in the New-York, White-Plains, New-Haven, Poughkeepsie, Rhinebeck, Delaware, and Newburgh districts."

"2, 3, 4, New-England, Maine, and New-Hampshire Conferences"—as before.

"5. Troy Conference shall include the Albany, Middlebury, Plattsburgh, and Troy districts.

"6. Black River Conference shall include that part of the state of New-York west of the Troy Conference, not included in the Genesee Conference as far south as the Erie Canal, and all the societies on the immediate banks of said canal except Utica.

"7. Oneida Conference"—as before, except the insertion of "Black River" after "Troy."

"8. Genesee Conference"—as before, except that "Pittsburgh" is changed to "Erie." "Tioga" is struck out, and "Sugar Creek" and "Smethport" inserted.

"9. Erie Conference shall be bounded on the north by Lake Erie, on the east by a line commencing at the mouth of Cattaraugus Creek, thence to the Alleghany River at the mouth of Tunanquant Creek, thence up said creek eastward to the ridge dividing between the waters of Clarion and Sinnamahoning Creeks, thence east to the head of Mahoning Creek, thence down said creek to the Alleghany River, thence across said river in a north-westerly direction to the western reserve line, including the north part of Butler and New-Castle circuits, thence west to the Ohio Canal, thence along said canal to Lake Erie, including Ohio city.

"10. Pittsburgh Conference shall be bounded on the north by the Erie Conference, on the east by the

Alleghany Mountains, on the south by a line stretch
ing from the head of Tygert's Valley to the Ohio Rive
at the mouth of the Little Muskingum, embracing Mid
dleburn circuit and Hughes' River mission, thence ti
the Muskingum River, embracing Woodfield ani
M'Connelsville circuits, thence on the west to thi
mouth of White Woman Creek, embracing Summer
field and Freeport circuits, thence north-east to thi
Ohio Canal, embracing Dover circuit, and thence to thi
line of Erie Conference.

" 11. Michigan Conference shall embrace all tha
part of the state of Ohio not included in the Pittsburg
Erie, Ohio, and Indiana Conferences, and all the Terri
tory of Michigan, except so much as is included in thi
Laporte district, Indiana Conference.

" 12. Ohio Conference shall commence at the moutl
of the Great Miami River, thence running north witl
the state line, as far as the north line of Darke county
excluding Elizabethtown, thence eastwardly, so as ti
include Lebanon, Urbana, Columbus, and Zanesvilli
districts; thence down the Muskingum River so as ti
include Marietta circuit, and Kenhawa district in Vir
ginia, thence down the Ohio River to the place of be
ginning.

" 13. Indiana Conference shall include the state ol
Indiana, except so much as is included in the Illinoii
Conference, Elizabethtown in the state of Ohio, anc
that part of Michigan Territory now included in thi
Laporte district.

" 14. Illinois Conference shall include the state of
Illinois, and that part of Indiana included in the Dan
ville and Eugene circuits, the Wisconsin Territory
north of the state west of Lake Michigan, and also tha
part of said territory west of Mississippi, commonly
called the Black Hawk Purchase.

" 15. Missouri Conference shall include the state of
Missouri, and that part of Missouri Territory whicl
lies north of the Cherokee line.

" 16. Arkansas Conference shall include the Arkan

sas Territory, that part of Missouri Territory lying south of the Cherokee line ; also so much of the state of Louisiana as is now included in the Louisiana district."

" 17, 18. Kentucky and Tennessee Conferences"—as before.

" 19. Holston Conference"—as before, except for " lying north of the Blue Ridge," read, " now embraced in the Newtown district." " North Carolina" is struck out.

· " 20. Mississippi Conference shall include all the state of Mississippi, except what is embraced in the range of counties on the east boundary of the state, namely, Jackson, Greene, Wayne, Clarke, Lauderdale, Kemper, Noxaber, Lownds, and Munroe, and that part of the state of Louisiana not included in the Arkansas Conference."

" 21, 22. Alabama and Georgia Conferences"—as before.

" 23. South Carolina Conference"—as before, except for last clause read, " that part of North Carolina now included in the Wilmington and Lincolnton districts."

" 24. North Carolina Conference shall be bounded on the east by the Atlantic Ocean, on the north by Albemarle Sound, Roanoke and Staunton Rivers, on the west by the top of the Blue Ridge, including the counties of Wilks and Iredell, on the south by the south lines of Iredell, Rowan, Davidson, Randolph, and Chatham, thence by Cape Fear River, except those appointments now included in the Wilmington and Lincolnton districts.

" 25. Virginia Conference shall be bounded on the east by Chesapeake Bay and the Atlantic Ocean, on the south by Albemarle Sound, Roanoke and Staunton Rivers, on the west by the Blue Ridge, on the north by the Rappahannock River, except Fredericksburg and Port Royal.

" 26. Baltimore Conference"—as before.

" 27. Philadelphia Conference"—as before, except

that all after "conferences" is struck out, and "New-Jersey" inserted before it.

"28. New-Jersey Conference shall include the whole state of New-Jersey, Staten Island, and so much of the states of New-York and Pennsylvania as is now included in the Asbury district.

"29. There shall be an annual conference on the western coast of Africa, to be denominated The Liberia Mission Annual Conference, possessing all the rights, powers, and privileges of other annual confer ences, except that of sending delegates to the General Conference, and of drawing its annual dividend from the avails of the Book Concern and of the Chartered Fund."

1840. The boundaries were fixed as follows :—

" 1. The New-York Conference"—as before, except " Hartford" district inserted.

" 2. Providence Conference shall include that part of the state of Connecticut lying east of the Connecticut River, all the state of Rhode Island, and that part of the state of Massachusetts lying south-east of a line drawn from the north-east corner of the state of Rhode Island to the mouth of the Neponset River, which line shall so run as to leave the Walpole station within the bounds of the Providence Conference.

" 3. New-England Conference shall include all the state of Massachusetts lying east of the Green Mountains not embraced in the New-York, New-Hampshire, and Providence Conferences."

4, 5. Maine and New-Hampshire Conferences—as before.

" 6. Troy Conference shall include the Albany, Troy, Poultney, Burlington, and Plattsburg districts.

" 7. Black River Conference"—as before, except the addition, at the end, of the words, " and Canistota."

" 8. Oneida Conference"—as before.

" 9. Genesee Conference shall include that part of the state of New-York lying west of a line running south from Lake Ontario, by way of Cayuga Lake, to

10*

Pennsylvania, not embraced in the Erie Conference, and so much of the north part of the state of Pennsylvania as is included in Seneca Lake, Dansville, and Cattaraugus districts.

" 10. Erie Conference"—as before, except " Ohio city" changed to " Cleveland city."

" 11. Pittsburg Conference shall be bounded on the north by the Erie Conference, on the east by the Alleghany Mountains, on the south by a line stretching from the head of Tygert's Valley to the Ohio River, so as to embrace Middleburn circuit and Kenhawa mission, thence to the mouth of the Muskingum River, and up said river, exclusive of the towns of Marietta and Zanesville, to the Tuscarawas River, and thence up-said river to the line of the Erie Conference.

" 12. Ohio Conference shall commence at the mouth of the Great Miami River, running north with the state line to the line of Dark county, excluding Elizabethtown, thence eastwardly along the line of the North Ohio Conference, so as to exclude the circuits of Greenville, Sidney, (except Westville and M'Farlands,) Belfontaine, Allen mission, Richwood, Marion, Delaware, and Roscow, to the Muskingum River, thence down said river so as to include the towns of Zanesville and Marietta, and Kenhawa district, in Virginia, thence down the Ohio River to the place of beginning.

" 13. North Ohio Conference shall embrace all that part of the state of Ohio not included in the Ohio, Pittsburg, and Erie Conferences.

" 14. Michigan Conference shall include the state of Michigan.

" 15. Indiana Conference shall include all the state of Indiana, and Elizabethtown in Ohio.

" 16. Rock River Conference shall include that part of the state of Illinois not embraced in the Illinois Conference, and the Wisconsin and Iowa Territories.

" 17. Illinois Conference shall include the state of Illinois, except that part north of the following line, nely —Beginning at the mouth of Rock River, thence up said river to the mouth of Green River, thence up said river to the Winnebago Swamp, thence down the south branch of the Bureau River to the Illinois River, thence up said river to the mouth of the Kankakee, thence up the Kankakee River to the east line of the state of Illinois."

18, 19. Missouri and Kentucky Conferences—as before.

" 20. Holston Conference shall include East Tennessee and that part of the states of Georgia, South Carolina, North Carolina, and Virginia, now embraced in the Newtown, Ashville, Wytheville, Abingdon, and Greenville districts.

" 21. Tennessee Conference shall include Middle Tennessee and North Alabama.

" 22. Memphis Conference shall be bounded on the east by the Tombigbee River, Alabama state line, and Tennessee River, on the north by the Ohio and Mississippi Rivers, west by the Mississippi River, and south by a line running due east from the Mississippi River to the south-west corner of Tallahatchie county, thence due east to the south-eastern corner of Yallabusha county, thence in a straight line to the north-western corner of Oktibaha county, thence due east to the Tombigbee River.

" 23. Arkansas Conference shall include the state of Arkansas, that part of Missouri Territory south of the Cherokee line, and so much of Texas as is now embraced in the Red River district.

" 24. Texas Conference shall include the republic of Texas, except what is embraced in the Red River district, Arkansas Conference.

" 25. Mississippi Conference shall include all that part of the state of Mississippi not embraced in the Alabama and Memphis Conferences, and all the state of Louisiana.

" 26. Alabama Conference shall include South Alabama, West Florida, and the counties of Jackson Greene, Wayne, Clarke, Lauderdale, Kemper, Noxu-

ee, Lowndes, and that part of Monroe east of the
'ombigbee River, in the state of Mississippi."

27, 28. Georgia and South Carolina Conferences—
s before, the phraseology only being slightly altered.

29, 30, 31, and 32. North Carolina, Virginia, Balti-
ore, and Philadelphia Conferences—as before.

33. New-Jersey Conference—as before, except
Asbury district" changed to " Paterson district."

34. Liberia Mission Annual Conference—as before.

Quest. 2. How are the districts to be formed ?

The original answer to this question may be found
n p. 118. It was transferred to its present position
1 1804. The words, " or otherwise," were inserted
fter " death" in 1800 ; and " district conferences"
hanged to " yearly conference," in 1796.

The concluding note to this section about the allow-
nce of the bishops may be found on p. 119. It was
:ansferred to its present position in 1804, and the fol-
wing words were added in 1836 : " their widows and
rphans."

SECTION II.

)f building Churches, and the Order to be observed
*therein.**

Quest. 1. Is any thing advisable in regard to building ?

1784. "(*Quest.* 74.) *Ans.* Let all our chapels be
uilt plain and decent ; but not more expensive than is
bsolutely unavoidable: otherwise the necessity of
aising money will make rich men necessary to us.
ut if so, we must be dependant upon them, yea, and
overned by them. And then farewell to the Methodist
iscipline, if not doctrine too."

1789. The following clauses added :—

"(5.) That no person shall be eligible as a trustee
) any of our churches or colleges, nor act as a steward
r leader, that is not in constant church communion,
' a regular leader or member of a class.

provisions on this subject prior to 1784 see pp. 11, 13.

"(6.) That no person that is a trustee shall be ejected while he is in joint security for money, unless such relief be given him as is demanded, or the person who makes the loan will accept."

1792. "Schools" substituted for "colleges;" and the qualification for a trustee is that he be "a regular member of our society."

1800. "Houses" inserted before "churches."

1820. The words "and with free seats," inserted in Answer 1, after "decent;" and the following new clauses added :—

"2. In order more effectually to prevent our people from contracting debts which they are not able to discharge, it shall be the duty of the quarterly conference, of every circuit and station, where it is contemplated to build a house or houses of worship, to secure the ground or lot on which such house or houses are to be built, according to our deed of settlement, which deed must be legally executed ; and also said quarterly conference shall appoint a judicious committee of at least three members of our church, who shall form an estimate of the amount necessary to build ; and three-fourths of the money, according to such estimate, shall be secured or subscribed before any such building shall be commenced.

"3. In future we will admit no charter, deed, or conveyance, for any house of worship to be used by us, unless it be provided in such charter, deed, or conveyance, that the trustees of said house shall at all times permit such ministers and preachers belonging to the Methodist Episcopal Church as shall from time to time be duly authorized by the General Conference of the ministers of our church, or by the annual conferences, to preach and expound God's holy word, and to execute the discipline of the church, and to administer the sacraments therein, according to the true meaning and purport of our deed of settlement.

"4. As it is contrary to our economy to build houses with pews to sell or rent, it shall be the duty of the

several annual conferences to use their influence to
prevent houses from being so built in future ; and as
far as possible to make those houses free which have
already been built with pews."

Quest. 2. Is there any exception to the rule, " Let the men
and women sit apart ?"

The answer remains the same as in 1784, (see
Quest. 75, p. 72,) except that " chapels" was changed
in 1789 to " churches."

Quest. 3. Is there not a great indecency sometimes practised
among us, namely, talking in the congregation before and after
service ?

The answer remains substantially the same as in
1784. (See Quest. 76, p. 72.)

Quest. 4. What shall be done for the security of our preaching houses, and the premises belonging thereto ?

1796.   As follows :—

" *Quest.* 4. What shall be done for the security of
our preaching houses, and the premises belonging
thereto ?

" *Ans.* Let the following plan of a deed of settlement
be brought into effect in all possible cases, and as far
as the laws of the states respectively will admit of it,
namely :

" ' This INDENTURE, made this   day
of   in the year of our Lord one thousand
          hundred and   between
of the   in the state of   (if the
grantor be married, insert the name of his wife) of the
one part, and   trustees, in trust for the
uses and purposes hereinafter mentioned, all of the
                in the state of   aforesaid, of
the other part, WITNESSETH, that the said
(if married, insert the name of his wife) for and in consideration of the sum of   pounds, specie,
to   in hand paid, at and upon the sealing
and delivery of these presents, the receipt whereof is
hereby acknowledged, hath (or have) given, granted,
gained, sold, released, confirmed, and conveyed, and

by these presents doth (or do) give, grant, bargain, sell,
release, confirm, and convey unto them, the said
                                    and their successors,
(trustees, in trust for the uses and purposes hereinafter mentioned and declared,) all the estate, right, title,
interest, property, claim, and demand whatsoever, either
in law or equity, which he the said
(if married, here insert the name of his wife) hath (or
have) in, to, or upon all and singular a certain lot, or
piece of land, situate, lying, and being in the
and state aforesaid, bounded and butted as follows, to
wit, (here insert the several courses and distances of
the ground to the place of beginning,) containing and laid
out for   acres of ground, together with
all and singular the houses, woods, waters, ways, privileges, and appurtenances thereto belonging, or in any
wise appertaining : TO HAVE AND TO HOLD all and singular, the above-mentioned and described lot or piece of
ground, situate, lying, and being as aforesaid, together
with all and singular the houses, woods, waters, ways
and privileges thereto belonging, or in any wise appertaining unto them the said   ,   and their successors in office for ever in trust, that they shall erect
and build, or cause to be erected and built thereon, a
house or place of worship for the use of the members
of the Methodist Episcopal Church in the United States
of America, according to the rules and discipline which
from time to time may be agreed upon and adopted by
the ministers and preachers of the said church at their
General Conferences in the United States of America,
and in further trust and confidence that they shall at all
times, for ever hereafter, permit such ministers and
preachers belonging to the said church, as shall from
time to time be duly authorized by the General Conferences of the ministers and preachers of the said
Methodist Episcopal Church, or by the yearly conferences authorized by the said General Conference, and
none others, to preach and expound God's holy word
therein ; and in further trust and confidence, that a

often as any one or more of the trustees herein before
mentioned shall die, or cease to be a member or members of the said church according to the rules and discipline as aforesaid, then and in such case it shall be
the duty of the stationed minister or preacher (authorized as aforesaid) who shall have the pastoral charge
of the members of the said church, to call a meeting
of the remaining trustees as soon as conveniently may
be ; and when so met, the said minister or preacher
shall proceed to nominate one or more persons to fill
the place or places of him or them whose office or
offices has (or have) been vacated as aforesaid. *Provided*, the person or persons so nominated shall have
been one year a member or members of the said church
immediately preceding such nomination, and of at least
twenty-one years of age ; and the said trustees, so assembled, shall proceed to elect, and by a majority of
votes appoint, the person or persons so nominated to
fill such vacancy or vacancies, in order to keep up the
number of nine trustees for ever ; and in case of an
equal number of votes for and against the said nomination, the stationed minister or preacher shall have the
casting vote.

" ' *Provided nevertheless*, That if the said trustees, or
any of them, or their successors, have advanced, or
shall advance, any sum or sums of money, or are or
shall be responsible for any sum or sums of money, on
account of the said premises, and they the said trustees,
or their successors, be obliged to pay the said sum or
sums of money, they, or a majority of them, shall be authorized to raise the said sum or sums of money, by a
mortgage on the said premises, or by selling the said
premises, after notice given to the pastor or preacher who
has the oversight of the congregation attending divine
service on the said premises, if the money due be not
paid to the said trustees, or their successors, within one
year after such notice given : and if such sale take
place, the said trustees, or their successors, after paying the debt and all other expenses which are due from

the money arising from such sale, shall deposite th
remainder of the money produced by the said sale in
the hands of the steward or stewards of the societ
belonging to or attending divine service on the said pre
mises ; which surplus of the produce of such sale s
deposited in the hands of the said steward or stewards
shall be at the disposal of the next yearly conferenc
authorized as aforesaid ; which said yearly conferenc
shall dispose of the said money, according to the bes
of their judgment, for the use of the said society. An
the said   doth by these presents warrant
and for ever defend, all and singular the before men
tioned and described lot or piece of ground, with th
appurtenances thereto belonging unto them the said
                    and their successors, chosen and appointe
as aforesaid, from the claim or claims of him the sai
                    his heirs and assigns, and from the clain
or claims of all persons whatever. In testimony where
of, the said   (if married, insert the nam
of his wife) have hereto set their hands and seals, th
day and year aforesaid.
Sealed and delivered in ⎫
   the presence of us   ⎬
      (Two witnesses.)   ⎭

                                    Grantor's (L. S.)
                                    his wife's (L. S.)

Received the day of the date ⎫
   of   the   above-written   in- ⎬
   denture, the consideration ⎬
   therein mentioned in full.   ⎭
Witnesses.]   Grantor's (L S.)
         County, ss.

BE IT REMEMBERED, that on the   da
   of   in the year of our Lord one thousan
              personally appeared before me, one of th
   justices of the peace, in and for the county of
              and state of   the within named
   the grantor (if married, insert the name of his wife) an

acknowledged the within deed of trust to be their act and deed, for the uses and purposes therein mentioned and declared ; and she the said
wife of the said   being separate and apart from her said husband, by me examined, declared that she made the same acknowledgment, freely and with her own consent, without being induced thereto through fear or threats of her said husband.   In testimony whereof I have hereto set my hand and seal, the day and year first above written.
Here the justice's name.   (L. S.)'

"N. B. It is necessary that all our deeds should be recorded after execution, for prudential as well as legal reasons.

"2. Let nine trustees be appointed for preaching houses, where proper persons can be procured ; otherwise seven or five."

1812.   The following sentence was inserted just before the deed :—

"But each annual conference is authorized to make such modification in the deeds as they may find the different usages and customs of law require in the different states and territories, so as to secure the premises firmly by deed, and permanently to the Methodist Episcopal Church, according to the true intent and meaning of the following form of a deed of settlement; any thing in the said form to the contrary notwithstanding."

In the same year the words "and none others" were struck out of the deed, (p. 231, ll. 3, 2 from bottom.)

1820.   The note about recording the deed was struck out.

1828.   The following paragraph was added at the close of the section :—

"The board of trustees of every circuit or station shall be responsible to the quarterly meeting conference of said circuit or station, and shall be required to present a report of its acts during the preceding year; provided that in all cases, when a new board of trustees is to be created, it shall be done (except in those states and territories where the statutes provide differently) by the appointment of the preacher in charge, or the presiding elder of the district."

Of the Qualifications, Appointment, and Duty of the Stewards of Circuits.

Quest. 1. What are the qualifications necessary for stewards?

1789. "*Ans.* Let them be men of solid piety, who both know and love the Methodist doctrine and discipline, and of good natural and acquired abilities to transact the temporal business."

Quest. 2. How are the stewards to be appointed?

1812. "*Ans.* The preacher having the charge of the circuit shall have the right of nomination; but the quarterly meeting conference shall confirm or reject such nomination."

Quest. 3. What are the duties of steward?*

1789. "What is the duty of stewards?

"*Ans.* To take an exact account of all the money or other provision made for and received by any travelling or local preacher in the circuit; to make an accurate return of every expenditure of money, whether to the preacher, the sick, or the poor; to seek the needy and distressed in order to relieve and comfort them; to inform the preachers of any sick or dis-

---

* In the Annual Minutes for 1787 we find the following:—

"*Quest.* 19. Shall any directions be given concerning register books?

"*Ans.* Let register books be provided by all the societies, that the elders and deacons may enter the marriages and baptisms regularly in them; and let every such register book be kept in the hands of the steward, or any other proper person of each society respectively. Let one general register book be also kept in the hands of the general steward of every circuit, in which the contents of all the private register books in the circuit may be inserted at convenient times."

orderly persons; to tell the preachers what they think
wrong in them; to attend the quarterly meetings of their
circuit; to give advice, if asked, in planning the circuit; to attend committees for the application of money
to churches; to give counsel in matters of arbitration;
to provide elements for the Lord's supper; to write cir-
cular letters to the societies in the circuit to be more
liberal, if need be; as also to let them know the state
of the temporalities at the last quarterly meeting; to
register the marriages and baptisms, and to be subject
to the bishops, the presiding elder of their district, and
the elder, deacon, and travelling preachers of their
circuit."

1792. Instead of "made for and received by any
travelling or local preacher," we have "collected for
the support of preachers." The words "when occasion requires" inserted before "the state of the temporalities."

Quest. 4. To whom are the stewards accountable for the
faithful performance of their duties ?

1816. "*Ans.* To the quarterly meeting conference of the circuit or station."

1828. The following clause was added to the
preceding :—"which shall have power to dismiss or
change them at pleasure."

Quest. 5. What number of stewards are necessary in each
circuit ?

1789. "*Ans.* Not less than two, or more than
four."

1820. The answer was altered to the following :
—"Not less than three, or more than seven, one of
whom shall be the recording steward."

SECTION IV.

*Of the Allowance to the Ministers and Preachers, and
to their Wives, Widows, and Children.*

For the provisions on this subject prior to 1784, see
pp. 11–14, 18. The provisions of 1784 may be found

under Questions 37–40, (p. 42.*)   The subsequent changes have been as follows :—

1789.   The word "bishops" was inserted in the first question (37) before "elders."

The words " and no more," at the close of the first two answers, struck out ; as also the last two questions and answers.

The following note was added :—

" N. B. That no ministers or preachers, travelling or local, shall receive any support either in money or other provision for their services without the knowledge of the stewards of the circuits, and its being properly entered quarterly on the books."

1792.   The section was entitled, " Of the Salaries of the Ministers and Preachers," and the answers were as follows.   To the first question, (37th, of 1784,)—

" *Ans.* Sixty-four dollars, and their travelling expenses."

To the second question, (38th, of 1784,)—" Sixty-four dollars, if they be in want of it."

The following was added :—

" *Quest.* 3.   What plan shall we pursue in appropriating the money received by our travelling ministers for marriage fees ?

" *Ans.* In all the circuits where the preachers do not receive their full quarterage, let all such money be given into the hands of the stewards, and be equally divided between the travelling preachers of the circuit. In all other cases, the money shall be disposed of at the discretion of the district conference."

The note was also modified so as to read,—

" N. B. No minister or preacher whatsoever shall receive any money for deficiencies, or on any other

---

* In the Minutes for 1787 (see vol. i, pp. 28, 29) we find the following :—

" *Quest.* Are not many of our preachers and people dissatisfied with the salaries allowed our married preachers who have children ? *Ans.* They are.   Therefore, for the future, no married preacher shall demand more than £48, P. C."

account, out of any of our funds or collections, without
first giving an exact account of all the money, clothes,
and other presents of every kind, which he has received
the preceding year."

1796. The allowance to a preacher's wife is
made absolute, without the condition, " if she want it."

1800. The mode of questions and answers was
laid aside, and the section assumed its present form,
namely,—

" 1. The annual salary of the travelling preachers
shall be eighty dollars and their travelling expenses.

" 2. The annual allowance of the wives of travelling
preachers shall be eighty dollars.

" 3. Each child of a travelling preacher shall be
allowed sixteen dollars annually, to the age of seven
years, and twenty-four dollars annually from the age
of seven to fourteen years ; *nevertheless*, this rule shall
not apply to the children of preachers whose families
are provided for by other means in their circuits respectively.

" 4. The salary of the superannuated, worn-out, and
supernumerary preachers shall be eighty dollars annually.

" 5. The annual allowance of the wives of superannuated, worn-out, and supernumerary preachers shall
be eighty dollars.

" 6. The annual allowance of the widows of traveling, superannuated, worn-out, and supernumerary
preachers shall be eighty dollars.

" 7. The orphans of travelling, superannuated,
worn-out, and supernumerary preachers shall be
allowed by the annual conferences, if possible, by
such means as they can devise, sixteen dollars annually."

1804. The following inserted in clause 3, before
' *nevertheless*," " and those preachers whose wives are
dead shall be allowed for each child annually a sum
sufficient to pay the board of such child or children
during the above term of years."

The following added at the close of the section :—

" 8. Local preachers shall be allowed a salary in certain cases, as mentioned, p. 44." [Sec. 9.]

1816. The allowance of all preachers and their wives raised to one hundred dollars.

1824. Under clause 2, (allowance to wives,) it is added, " But this provision shall not apply to the wives of those preachers who were single when they were received on trial, and marry under four years, until the expiration of said four years."

1828. The seventh clause (relating to orphans) was altered so as to read as follows :—

" 7. The orphans of travelling, supernumerary, superannuated and worn-out preachers, shall be allowed by the annual conferences the same sums respectively which are allowed to the children of living preachers. And on the death of a preacher leaving a child or children, without so much of worldly goods as should be necessary to his, her, or their support, the annual conference, of which he was a member, shall raise, in such manner as may be deemed best, a yearly sum for the subsistence and education of such orphan child or children, until he, she, or they shall have arrived at fourteen years of age, the amount of which yearly sum shall be fixed by a committee of the conference at each session in advance."

1832. The following new clause was inserted :—

" 8. The more effectually to raise the amount necessary to meet the above-mentioned allowances, let there be made weekly class collections in all our societies where it is practicable ; and also for the support of missions and missionary schools under our care."

1836. The regulation respecting those who marry " under four years," struck out ; and bishops mentioned by name, as standing on the same footing with other travelling preachers. Clauses 1, 2, 4, and 5, thrown into two, as follows :—

" 1. The annual allowance of the married travelling, supernumerary, and superannuated preachers, and the ishops, shall be two hundred dollars, and their traveling expenses.

" 2. The annual allowance of the unmarried traveling, supernumerary, and superannuated preachers and bishops, shall be one hundred dollars, and their traveling expenses."*

SECTION V.

Of raising annual Supplies for the Propagation of the Gospel, making up the Allowance of the Preachers, &c.

The original provisions on this subject may be found under Question 77, (pp. 74–5.)†

From 1789 to 1800 the title of the section was, " Of raising a General Fund for the Propagation of the Gospel," and its provisions were the same as in 1784.

1800. The title was changed to the following :— " Of raising annual Supplies for the Propagation of the

---

* In 1789 the title of this section was, " Of the Collections that are to be made, and how the Money is to be expended ;" and there was another question connected with it, which was continued until 1792. It was as follows :—

" How many collections are to be made in a year ?

" *Ans.* 1. A quarterly collection from the members of the society, to supply the preachers : and when that is deficient, a public quarterly collection : if there be any overplus, let one-third of it be reserved for future deficiencies ; one-third be given to the poor in general : and one-third applied to the building or improving of our churches. If there is money left in the hands of the stewards at the close of the year, let it be sent to the conference.

" 2. A yearly collection from all our members that are of ability, for the building of convenient churches.*

" 3. A collection at love-feasts, and on sacramental occasions, for the poor of our own society.

" 4. An annual collection or subscription for the college.

" 5. An annual public collection for the contingencies of the conference ; which shall be applied,

" 1. To discharge the deficiencies of those preachers who shall not have received their full salary in their circuits. And

" 2. To defray the expenses of our missions to distant parts of the continent."

† For provisions on this subject prior to 1784, see pp. 11, 21.

* A provision for building new churches, &c , had been made in 1784. See ... . p. 76.

Gospel, for the making up the Salaries of the Preacher
and Allowances to the Wives, Widows, and Children o:
Preachers." The first sentence of the' former answe
was struck out, and the following clauses were sub
stituted :—

" 1. Every preacher, when first admitted into ful
connection, is to pay two dollars and sixty-seven cent
at the annual conference.

" 2. Every other preacher, in full connection, is t
contribute two dollars every year at the conference.

" 3. The moneys, which are accounted for to th
annual conferences for marriages, are also to be given in.

" 4. Every preacher who has the charge of a circu:

---

* These three paragraphs, which were struck out in 1804, took th
place of what was previously an entire section, under the title—" O
the Method of raising a Fund for the superannuated Preachers, and th
Widows and Orphans of Preachers." It may be found in substanc
under Question 72, (1784, pp. 65–7.)
1789. The following changes were made :—
In Answer 1, " travelling" omitted before " preacher." In Answe
3, for " treasurers," read " presiding elder, or lent to the college
and an account thereof kept by the deacon." Answers 4 and !
struck out, and the following note inserted : " N. B. The applicatio
of the money shall rest with the conference." In Answer 7, afte
" wants it," read " not usually more than." Answer 12, struck out
1792. The answers were modified, as follows :—
" 1. Let every preacher when first admitted into full connection pa
two dollars and two-thirds at the conference of his district.
" 2. Let every other preacher in full connection contribute two do
lars every year ; except the conference dispense with the payment i
cases of distress : in which instances, the preachers so indulged sha
be entitled to all the privileges of the fund, in the same manner as i
they had paid their subscription.
" 3. Let the money be lodged in the book fund, and for this pu:
pose be sent as soon as may be, from time to time, to the gener:
book steward : and the book fund shall pay interest for the same."
" 4." Same as 6, 1784.
" 5." Same as 7, 1784, except, " sixty-four dollars" for " twent;
four pounds, Pennsylvania currency."
" 6." Same as 8, 1784, except, " fifty-three dollars and one-third
for " twenty pounds."
" 7." Same as 9, 1784, except, " orphan" for " child," and " fift;
three dollars and one-third" for " twenty pounds."
" 8." Same as 10, 1784, except, " six dollars and two-thirds" fo
" fifty shillings."
" 9. Nor any one who neglects to pay his subscription and arrear

11

hall earnestly recommend to every class or society in is circuit to raise a quarterly or annual collection by oluntary contribution, or in such other way or manner as ley may judge most expedient from time to time ; and ie moneys so collected shall be lodged with the stew- rd or stewards of the circuit, to be brought or sent to ie annual conferences, with a regular account of the ums raised for this purpose in the classes or societies espectively.

" 5. Wherever there remains in the hands of the tewards a surplus of the moneys raised for the use of ie circuit preachers, after paying the allowances of the reachers in the circuit, let such surplus be brought or ent to the annual conference.

" 6. Every preacher who has the charge of a circuit

---

r three years together, unless he be employed on foreign missions, : has received a dispensation as above mentioned.
" 10. Let every preacher, who has the care of a circuit, bring, &c.," : before.
The following new paragraphs were added :—
" 11. Every person, who desires support from the fund, shall first ake his case known to the district conference, which shall determine ɔw far he is a proper subject of relief.
" 12. The president of the district conference shall give an order 1 the general steward of the book fund, or any of his agents, for any ım of money allowed by the conference, agreeably to these rules.
" 13. The receipts and disbursements of the fund shall be printed ınually in the Minutes of the conference.
" 14. The presiding elder of each district shall keep a regular ac- ɔunt of all the concerns of the fund, as far as they relate to his dis- ict, in a proper book, which he shall hand down to his successor.
" 15. The next district conferences shall give certificates to all eir members respectively for all the money which each preacher ıs already advanced to the fund, as far as it can be ascertained : ıd, in future, each member of the fund shall receive a certificate ɔm his district conference for the payment of his subscription.
" 16. The fund shall never be reduced to less than six hundred ɔllars."
1796. The following changes made :—Paragraph 3, about invest- g the money, struck out. In Answer 12, for " book fund," we have fund." In Answer 15, the first clause, to the word " ascertained," ·uck out. The following new paragraph was inserted :—
" 15. This fund shall be reserved for extraordinary cases, which the ıartered fund may not reach. And no travelling preacher shall have votr in the disposal of the travelling preachers' annual subscription, ıless he be himself an annual subscriber."

shall make a yearly collection, and, if expedient, a quarterly one, in every congregation where there is a probability that the people will be willing to contribute : and the money so collected shall be lodged in the hands of the steward or stewards, and brought or sent to the ensuing annual conference. To this end, he may read and enlarge upon the following hints." (See pp. 74–6.)

The following clauses were also added :—

" 7. A public collection shall be made at every annual and every General Conference, for the above purposes.

" 8. Let the annual produce of the chartered fund, as divided among the several conferences, be applied with the above contributions ; but so as not to militate against the rules of the chartered fund. Out of the moneys so collected, and brought to the respective annual conferences, let the various allowances agreed upon in the 10th section, be made up : and if at any conference there remain a surplus, after making up all such allowances, such surplus shall be carried forward to the next conference that shall meet."

1804. The first three paragraphs of 1800 were struck out. In paragraph 8, (5,) the following clauses were inserted, namely :—After " rules of the chartered fund,"—" and also the annual dividend arising from the profits of the Book Concern." And after "be made up," the following, " but in no case shall an allowance be made to any travelling preacher who has travelled in any circuit where he might in the judgment of the annual conference have obtained his full quarterage if he had applied for it."

1808. The following paragraphs were added :—

" 6. Every annual conference has full liberty to adopt and recommend such plans and rules as to them may appear necessary the more effectually to raise supplies for the respective allowances.

" 7. If the respective allowances are not raised as provided for, the connection shall not be accountable for the deficiency, as in a case of debt."

1819. The following sentence added to paragraph 6, of 1808 :—"Each annual conference is authorized to raise a fund, if they judge it proper, and under such regulations as their wisdom may direct, for the relief of the distressed travelling, superannuated, and supernumerary preachers, their wives, widows, and children, as also for missionary purposes."

1816. At the end of paragraph 8, (5,) of 1800, for "to the next conference that shall meet" read "to that conference they judge to be the most necessitous." In paragraph 6, (1812,) after the words "judge it proper," was inserted, "subject to its own control."

1824. The following new paragraph was added :—
"8. To defray the expenses of the delegates composing the General Conference, a collection shall be taken up in each circuit and station some time previously to the sitting of the conference, and the sums so collected shall be brought up to the General Conference, and applied to the object herein contemplated in proportion to the expenses of the several delegates."

1832. The following new paragraph inserted :—
"7. It shall be the duty of each annual conference to take measures, from year to year, to raise moneys in every circuit and station within its bounds, for the relief of its necessitous superannuated and supernumerary ministers, widows, and orphans.—And the conference shall annually appoint a committee to estimate the several sums necessary to be allowed for the extra expenses of such necessitous claimants, who shall be paid in proportion to the estimates made and the moneys in hand."

Quest. What advice or direction shall be given concerning the building or renting of dwelling houses for the use of the married travelling preachers ?

1800. "*Ans.* 1. It is recommended by the General Conference to the travelling preachers, to advise our friends in general to purchase a lot of ground in each circuit, and to build a preacher's house thereon, and to furnish it with, at least, heavy furniture, and to settle the same on trustees appointed by the official members of the quarter meeting, according to the deed of settlement published in our Form of Discipline.

"2. The General Conference recommend to the country circuits, in cases where they are not able to comply with the above request, to rent a house for the married preacher and his family, (when such are stationed upon their circuits respectively,) and that the annual conferences do assist to make up the rents of such houses as far as they can, when the circuit canno do it."

1816. The following new paragraphs were added namely :—

"3. It shall be the duty of the presiding elders and preachers to use their influence to carry the above rule respecting building and renting houses for the accom modation of preachers and their families into effect In order to this, each quarterly meeting conference shall appoint a committee, (unless other measures have been adopted,) who, with the advice and aid of the preachers and presiding elders, shall devise such mean as may seem fit to raise moneys for that purpose. An it is recommended to the annual conferences to make special inquiry of their members respecting this par of their duty.

"4. Those preachers who refuse to occupy the houses which may be provided for them on the station and circuits where they are from time to time appoint ed, shall be allowed nothing for house rent, nor receive any thing more than quarterage for themselves, thei wives, and children, and their travelling expenses Nevertheless, this rule shall not apply to those preach ers whose families are either established within the bounds of their circuits, or are so situated that in the judgment of the stewards, or the above-mentioned com mittee, it is not necessary, for the benefit of the circuit to remove them.

"5. It shall be the duty of the said committee, o one appointed for that purpose, who shall be member of our church, to make an estimate of the amount necessary to furnish fuel and table expenses for the family or families of preachers stationed with them, and the stewards shall provide, by such means as they may devise, to meet such expenses, in money or otherwise : provided the stewards shall not appropriate the moneys collected for the regular quarterly allowance of the preachers to the payment of family expenses.

" 6. There shall be a meeting in every district, of one steward from each station and circuit, to be selected from among the stewards by the quarterly meeting conference, whose duty it shall be, by and with the advice of the presiding elder, (who shall preside in such meeting,) to take into consideration the general state of the district in regard to temporalities, and to furnish a house, fuel, and table expenses for the presiding elder."

1824. The following new paragraphs were added :—

" 7. The book agents and the book committee in New-York shall be a committee to estimate the amount necessary to meet the family expenses of the bishops, which shall be annually paid by the book agents out of the funds of the Book Concern.

" 8." [A paragraph relating to the appointment of a committee on missions, at each conference, for which, with the subsequent changes in it, see Section 6, On Missions.]

1828. The following added to paragraph 2, (1800) :—

" The stewards of each circuit and station shall be a standing committee, (where no trustees are constituted for that purpose,) to provide houses for the families of our married preachers, or to assist the preachers to obtain houses for themselves when they are appointed to labour among them."

1832. Paragraph 7, of 1824, struck out, and the part about missions made a separate section. (See Section 6.)

1836. The following clause added to paragraph 6 :—" and to apportion his entire claim among the different circuits and stations in the district according to their several ability."

The following provision made for estimating the allowance of a bishop, in lieu of the one struck out in 832 :—

" 7. Each annual conference, in which a bishop or bishops may reside, shall annually appoint a committee of three or more, whose duty it shall be to estimate the amount necessary to furnish a house, fuel, and table expenses for said bishop or bishops, and that they be authorized to draw on the funds of the Book Concern for said amount."

SECTION VI.

Support of Missions.

This first appears as a separate section in 1832, but provisions on the subject existed before.

1824. The following paragraph was appended to the section on " Raising annual Supplies, &c."

" 8. (1.) It shall be the duty of each annual conference, where missionaries are to be employed, to appoint a committee, whose duty it shall be, in conjunction with the president of the conference, to determine on the amount which may be necessary for the support of each missionary, (agreeably to the regulations of the Discipline,) from year to year, for which amount the president of the conference for the time shall have authority to draw on the treasurer of the society in quarterly instalments in behalf of the missions."

1828. The following paragraphs added :—

" (3.) It is recommended that within the bounds of each annual conference there be established a conference missionary society, auxiliary to the Missionary Society of the Methodist Episcopal Church, with branches, under such regulations as the conferences respectively shall prescribe. Each conference mis-

ionary society shall annually transmit to the corres
onding secretary of the parent society a copy of its
nnual report, embracing the operations of its branches,
nd shall also notify the treasurer of the amount col
ected in aid of the missionary cause, which amount
hall be subject to the order of the treasurer of the
arent society.

" (4.) The treasurer of the parent society, under the
irection of the board of managers, shall give informa-
ion to the bishops annually, or oftener, if the board
judge it expedient, of the state of the funds and the
ums which may be drawn by them for the missionary
urposes contemplated by the constitution. Agreeably
o which information the bishops shall have authority
o draw upon the treasurer for any sum within the
mount designated, which the missionary committee of
he annual conferences respectively shall judge neces-
ary for the support of the missionaries and of the mis-
ion schools under their care. Provided always, that
he sums so allowed for the support of a missionary
hall not exceed the usual allowance of other itinerant
reachers. The bishops shall always promptly notify
he treasurer of all drafts made by them, and shall
equire regular quarterly communications to be made
y each of the missionaries to the corresponding secre-
ary of the parent society, giving information of the
tate and prospects of the several missions in which
hey are employed. No one shall be acknowledged a
missionary, or receive support out of the funds of the
ociety, who has not some definite field assigned to
im, or who could not be an effective labourer on a
ircuit.

" (5.) In all cases of the appointment of a missionary,
he name of such missionary and the district in which
e is to labour, together with the probable expenses
f the mission, shall be communicated by the bishop
r the mission committee of each annual conference to
he treasurer of the parent society, that a proper record
f the same may be preserved.

"(6.) In all places where drafts are drawn in favou
of any mission if there be funds in the possession of
any auxiliary conference missionary society, where
such mission is established, the drafts for the suppor
of the mission shall be paid from said funds : if there
be no auxiliary society, and there be money belonging
to the Book Concern, the book committee or presiding
elders, or preachers, shall pay the missionary draft
from the book money which may be in their posses
sion ; which drafts, when paid, shall be transmitted to
the treasurer at New-York; and in no case, where any
such moneys are at command, shall the drafts be sen
to the treasurer in New-York to be paid."

1832. A distinct section was framed on this sub
ject, and the following alterations were made in the
previous provisions :—

Some change was made in the phraseology of para
graph 1, (1824,) but none in substance, except these
It required the mission committee to "keep a record
of its doings, and report the same to its conference.
And instead of saying that they are to estimate th
amount "necessary for the support of the missionary
agreeably to the regulations of the Discipline," it says
"necessary for the support of each mission and missio
school, in addition to the regular allowance of the Dis
cipline to preachers and their families."

The following was inserted as the second para
graph :—

"2. Whenever a mission is to be established in an
new place, or in any place beyond the bounds of a
annual conference, either among the aborigines of ou
country or elsewhere, it shall be the duty of the bishop
making such appointment immediately to notify th
treasurer of the Missionary Society of the place, th
number of missionaries to be employed, together wit
the probable amount necessary for the support of an
such mission, which information shall be laid befor
the managers of the society ; and they shall make a
appropriation according to their judgment, from year t

year, of the amount called for to sustain and prosecute the mission or missions designated ; for which amount the missionary, or the superintendent of the mission or missions, shall have authority to draw on the treasurer of the society in quarterly or half-yearly instalments."

1836. The following paragraphs were added :—

"7. The corresponding secretary shall, by virtue of his office, be a member of the New-York Conference, to which, in the interval of the General Conference, he shall be held responsible for his conduct, and the New-York Conference shall have power, by and with the advice of the managers of the Missionary Society of the Methodist Episcopal Church, and consent of the bishop presiding, to remove him from office ; and in case of removal, death, or resignation, the New-York Conference, with the concurrence of the presiding bishop, shall fill the vacancy until the next ensuing General Conference.

"8. (10.) It shall be the duty of the bishops to instruct all our foreign missionaries, that whenever they come in contact with any of the missionaries belonging to the Wesleyan Methodist Conference, they shall not interfere in their respective charges any further than to help them in their work when requested ; but shall, on all occasions, cultivate a spirit of friendship and brotherly affection, as brethren engaged in the same common cause, namely, the salvation of the world, by grace through faith in the Lord Jesus Christ."

1840. In paragraph 7, the word "resident" is left out of the secretary's title, and the following new paragraphs are inserted :—

"8. There shall also be a secretary for the south and south-west, to labour in connection with the missions to the slaves, and to attend to the interests of the Missionary Society in such way and manner as the board of managers may direct. Should his office become vacant by death or otherwise, the board may fill the place until the next sitting of the annual conference to which he belongs, who shall then fill the

vacancy until the next session of the General Confer·
ence.

"9. There shall be another secretary, to reside ii
the west, to labour in connection with the Indian mis·
sions, and to attend to the interests of the Missionary
Society in such way and manner as the board of mana·
gers may direct. Should his office become vacant by
death or otherwise, the board may fill the place unti
the next sitting of the annual conference to which he
belongs, who shall then fill the vacancy until the nex
session of the General Conference."

SECTION VII.

Of the Chartered Fund.

This section was first introduced in 1796. It wa:
as follows :—

1796. " *Quest.* 1. What further provision shal
be made for the distressed travelling preachers, for the
families of travelling preachers, and for the superannu
ated and worn-out preachers, and the widows and or
phans of preachers ?

" *Ans.* There shall be a chartered fund, to be sup
ported by the voluntary contributions of our friends . the
principal stock of which shall be funded under the di
rection of trustees, and the interest applied under the
direction of the General Conference, according to the
following regulations :"—

1. That no sum exceeding sixty-four dollars shall ii
any one year be applied to the use of an itinerant, su
perannuated, or worn-out *single* preacher.

2. That no sum exceeding one hundred and twenty
eight dollars in any one year shall be applied to th
use of any itinerant, superannuated, or worn-out *mar
ried* preacher.

3. That no sum exceeding sixty-four dollars in an·
one year shall be applied for the use of each widow o
itinerant, superannuated, or worn-out preachers.

4. That no sum exceeding sixteen dollars shall b

applied in any one year for the use of each child or orphan of itinerant, superannuated, or worn-out preachers.

5. That the elders, and those who have the oversight of circuits, shall be collectors and receivers of subscriptions, &c., for this fund.

6. The money shall, if possible, be conveyed by bills of exchange, through the means of the post, to John Dickins, our general book steward in Philadelphia, who shall pay it to the trustees of the fund : otherwise it shall be brought to the ensuing yearly conference.

7. There shall be no money drawn out of the fund till the first day of August, 1798.

8. The interest shall be divided into six* parts, and each of the yearly conferences shall have authority to draw that sixth part out of the fund, according to the regulations before prescribed : and if in one or more conferences a part less than one-sixth be drawn out of the fund in any given year, then in such case or cases the other yearly conferences, held in the same year, shall have authority, if they judge it necessary, to draw out of the fund, according to the above regulation, such surplus of the interest which has not been applied by the former conferences : and the bishops shall bring the necessary information of the state of the interest of the fund, respecting the year in question, from conference to conference.

9. The present stock of the preachers' fund shall be thrown into the chartered fund.

10. The produce of the sale of our books, after the book debts are paid, and a sufficient capital is provided for carrying on the business, shall be regularly paid into the chartered fund.

11. The money subscribed for the chartered fund may be lodged on proper securities in the states respectively in which it has been subscribed, under the

---

* The number varies, from time to time, according to the number of conferences.

direction of deputies living in such states respectively *provided* such securities and such deputies be propose as shall be approved of by the trustees in Philadelphia and the stock in which it is proposed to lodge the mc ney be sufficiently productive to give satisfaction to th trustees.

1800.   The following changes were made namely :—The first four paragraphs were struck out.

In paragraph 6 (2) it is provided that the mone may be conveyed "by bills of exchange or otherwise, and the name of the book steward is left out.   Para graph 7 was omitted, and the following new paragrapl was inserted :—

"4. All drafts on the chartered fund shall be made o the president of the said fund, by order of the annus conference, signed by the president, and countersigne by the secretary of the said conference."

In paragraph 9, (5,) for "present stock," we hav "old stock."   At the end of paragraph 10, (6,) the fol lowing clause was added :—"to be applied, with th annual interest of the funded stock, to the support o the itinerant ministry, &c., agreeably to the design an rules of the chartered fund, and the twenty-sixth sec tion of this Discipline." [Sec. 5, Part ii.]

The following new paragraph was inserted :—

"7. In case of the death, expulsion from society, o resignation of one or more of the trustees of the char tered fund, during the recess of the General Confer ence, the Philadelphia Annual Conference is authorized in such case, to elect one or more trustees to fill th place or places, so vacated, till the next General Con ference."

1804.   Paragraph 10 of 1796, and paragrapl 7 of 1800, were left out.

1812.   Paragraph 9 of 1796 struck out.

[handwritten annotation]

SECTION VIII.

Of the printing and circulating of Books, and of the Profits arising therefrom.

This subject was first introduced into the Discipline in

1787,[*] as follows :—

" As it has been frequently recommended by the preachers and people, that such books as are wanted be printed in this country, we therefore propose,

" 1. That the advice of the conference shall be desired concerning any valuable impression, and their consent be obtained before any steps be taken for the printing thereof.

" 2. That the profits of the books, after all the necessary expenses are defrayed, shall be applied, according to the discretion of the conference, toward the college, the preachers' fund, the deficiencies of the preachers, the distant missions, or the debts on our churches."

1790. The last clause was altered, so as to provide that the profits " be applied, as the bishop and Council[†] shall direct."

1792. The following was substituted as the entire section :—

" *Quest.* 1. Who is employed to manage the printing business ?

" *Ans.* John Dickins.

" *Quest.* 2. What allowances shall be paid him annually for his services ?

" *Ans.* 1. Two hundred dollars for a dwelling house and for a book room.

" 2. Eighty dollars for a boy.

" 3. Fifty-three dollars and one-third for firewood ; and,

---

[*] See Lee's Hist. of the Meth., p. 129.

[†] " The Council" was a body that had a brief existence at that time. (See Lee's History of the Methodists, pp. 149–159.)

" 4. Three hundred and thirty-three dollars to clothe and feed himself, his wife, and his children.   In all six hundred and sixty-six dollars and one-third.

" *Quest.* 3. What powers shall be granted him ?

" *Ans.* 1. To regulate the publications according to the state of the finances.

" 2. To determine, with the approbation of the book committee, on the amount of the drafts which may be drawn from time to time on the book fund.

" 3. To complain to the district conferences if any preachers shall neglect to make due payment for books.

" 4. To publish from time to time such books or treatises, as he and the other members of the book committee shall unanimously judge proper.

" *Quest.* 4. Who shall form the book committee ?

" *Ans.* John Dickins, Henry Willis, Thomas Haskins, and the preacher who is stationed in Philadelphia from time to time.   •

" *Quest.* 5. How much shall be annually allowed out of the book fund for Cokesbury College till the next General Conference ?

" *Ans.* Eight hundred dollars for the ensuing year ; and one thousand sixty-six dollars and two-thirds for each of the remaining three years.

" *Quest.* 6. What directions shall be given concerning the application of the money allowed as above for Cokesbury College ?

" *Ans.* The money shall be applied as follows :—

" 1. For the education and board of the boys that are now on the charitable part of the foundation.   But no boy shall be again placed on the charity till the next General Conference.

" 2. The surplus of the money, after the charity is supplied, shall be from time to time appropriated to the payment of the debt of the college, and to the finishing of the building, under the direction of the bishop and the committee of safety.

" N. B. The present debt of the college is about

eleven hundred dollars. The present expense of the
charity is about nine hundred and sixty-three dollars
annually; but this will probably sink into less than
one-half before the next General Conference.

" *Quest.* 7. What sum of money shall be allowed
distressed preachers out of the book fund, till the next
General Conference?

" *Ans.* Two hundred and sixty-six dollars and one-
third per annum.

" *Quest.* 8. How is the money mentioned above, for
the benefit of distressed preachers, to be drawn out of
the book fund?

" *Ans.* By the bishop, according to the united judgment of himself and the district conferences.

" *Quest.* 9. What shall be allowed the bishop out
of the book fund, for the benefit of district schools, till
the next General Conference?

" *Ans.* Sixty-four dollars per annum.

" *Quest.* 10. How shall the surplus of the book fund
be applied till the next General Conference, after the
provisions above mentioned are made?

" *Ans.* To the forming of a capital stock for the
carrying on of the concerns of the books."

1796. The following alterations were made:—
Under Question 3, Answers 2 and 4 were struck
out. Question 4 was struck out. Also all that relates
to the college, (Questions 5 and 6,) it having been destroyed by fire the preceding year.

Questions 9 and 10 struck out, and the following
added:—

" *Quest.* 6. In what manner shall the accounts of
the general book steward be examined?

" *Ans.* The Philadelphia Conference shall from year
to year appoint a committee, who shall examine quarterly his receipts and disbursements and other accounts.

" *Quest.* 7. What mode shall be struck out for the
recovery of bad or suspected book debts?

" *Ans.* 1. Let every yearly conference appoint a

committee or committees for the examination of the accounts of the travelling book stewards in their re spective districts.

" 2. Let every presiding elder, and every preache; who has the oversight of a circuit, do every thing in their power to recover all the debts in their circuit o; district, and also all books which may remain in the hands of persons who shall have resigned, or beer withdrawn from the office of a travelling book steward

" *Quest.* 8. Shall any drafts be made on the bool fund before all its debts are discharged ?

" *Ans.* There shall be none 'till the debts are dis charged, except in the case of distressed travelling preachers.

" *Quest.* 9. What directions shall be given concern ing the regulation of our press ?

" *Ans.* The general book steward shall print no books or tracts of any kind without the consent of a bishop and two-thirds of the Philadelphia Conference.'

" *Quest.* 10. Will the conference recommend and engage to promote the publication of a magazine, en titled, *The Methodist Magazine*, which shall consis of compilations from the British magazines, and of original accounts of the experience of pious persons and shall be published in monthly numbers ?

" *Ans.* The conference will recommend such a magazine, and desire that it may be printed."

---

* In accordance with the direction of the General Conference (Quest. 6,) the Philadelphia Conference, in 1797, appointed a bool committee, and the following note was entered on the Annual Minute; for that year :—

· " The above committee are to meet at Philadelphia on the 2d of January, 1798, and once a quarter afterward, or oftener if necessary to consider and determine what manuscripts, books, or pamphlet; shall be printed.

· " Four of the said committee, when met as above, shall proceed to business, provided that the chairman and one of the presiding elder be present. And the general book steward shall lay before the com mittee all manuscripts, books, and pamphlets which are designed for publication, except such as the General Conference has authorized him to publish."

1800. The form of questions and answers laid aside, and the whole section remodelled as follows:—

" 1. Ezekiel Cooper is appointed the superintendent of the Book Concern, who shall have authority to regulate the publications, and all other parts of the business, according to the state of the finances from time to time. It shall be his duty to inform the annual conferences if any of the preachers or private members of the society neglect to make due payment. He may publish any books or tracts which, at any time, may be approved of or recommended by the majority of an annual conference, provided such books or tracts be also approved of by the book committee, which shall be appointed by the Philadelphia Annual Conference. He may reprint any book or tract which has once been approved and published by us, when, in his judgment, the same ought to be reprinted. Let his accounts and books be examined by the Philadelphia Conference at the time of the sitting of the said conference.

" 2. It shall be the duty of every presiding elder, where no book steward is appointed, to see that his district be fully supplied with books. He is to order such books as are wanted, and to give direction to whose care the same are to be sent; and he is to take the oversight of all our books sent into his district, and to account with the superintendent for the same. He is to have the books distributed among the several circuits in his district, and is to keep an account with each preacher who receives or sells the books; and is to receive the money, and to forward it to the superintendent. When a presiding elder is removed, he is to make a full settlement for all the books sold or remaining in his district; and is also to make a transfer to his successor of all the books and accounts left with the preachers in the district, the amount of which shall go to his credit, and pass to the debit of his successor.

" 3. It shall be the duty of every preacher, who has the charge of a circuit, to see that his circuit be duly supplied with books, and to take charge of all the

books which are sent to him, from time to time, or
which may be in his circuit ; and he is to account with
the presiding elder for the same.   When a preacher
leaves his circuit, he must settle with the presiding
elder for all the books he has disposed of ; he is also
to make out an inventory of all that are remaining unsold, which shall be collected at one place ; the amoun
of which shall go to his credit, and be transferred to
his successor, who is to take charge of the same.   Ii
the preacher who has the charge of the circuit be
negligent in dispersing the books, the presiding elde:
shall commit the charge of the books to another.

"4. The superintendent of the book business may
from time to time, supply the preachers with books ii
those circuits which are adjacent or convenient to
Philadelphia, and settle with them for the same : ii
such cases the regulations respecting the presiding
elders are not to apply.

"5. In all cases where books are sent to distant places
the presiding elders or preachers shall be allowed to
put a small additional price on such books as will bes
bear it, in order to pay the expense of freight o
carriage : but the addition must not be more than wha
is necessary to defray such expenses.

"6. Every annual conference shall appoint a commit
tee or committees to examine the accounts of the presid
ing elders, preachers, and book stewards, in their respec
tive districts or circuits.   Every presiding elder, minister
and preacher, shall do every thing in their power to re
cover all debts due to the Concern, and also all the book
belonging to the Concern, which may remain in the
hands of any person within their districts or circuite
If any preacher or member be indebted to the Bool
Concern, and refuse to make payment, or to come to a
just settlement, let him be dealt with for a breach of
trust, and such effectual measures be adopted for the
recovery of such debts as shall be agreeable to the di
rection of the annual conferences respectively.

"7. There shall be no drafts made upon the Bool

Concern till its debts are discharged, and a sufficient capital provided for carrying on the business; after which, the profits arising from the books shall be regularly paid to the chartered fund, and be applied, with the annual income of the funded stock, to the support of the distressed travelling preachers and their families, the widows and orphans of preachers, &c.[*]

" 8. It shall be the duty of the preacher or preachers who travel with any of the bishops, if he or they be authorized by the superintendent of the Book Concern, to act as an agent in the settlement of accounts, collecting money, or in transacting any business belonging to the Book Concern.

" 9. In case of the death, dismission, or resignation of the superintendent, during the recess of the General Conference, the Philadelphia Conference shall have power to appoint another superintendent, till the next General Conference.

" 10. No travelling preacher shall print or circulate any books or pamphlets, without the consent of the annual conference to which he belongs, except as an agent of the superintendent of the Book Concern.

" 11. The Form of Discipline shall be printed by itself, and the bishops' explanatory notes by themselves; but in such a manner that the notes may be conveniently bound up with the Form of Discipline. And every presiding elder, preacher, or other person, who has the charge of the books, may send for as many copies of the Form as he pleases, with or without the notes."

1804. The following alterations were made :—

The title, " superintendent of the Book Concern," which was adopted in 1800, was now dropped, and the old title, " general book steward," restored.

Paragraph 1, begins, " The book business shall be removed to and carried on in the city of New-York. Ezekiel Cooper is reappointed general book steward,

---

[*] This " &c.," so singularly inappropriate in such a connection, has been perpetuated in every subsequent edition.

who shall have authority, &c." It is further provided
that the publications shall be regulated not only by " the
state of the finances," but also by " the demands of the
connection." For the rest of the paragraph, after the
word "payment," the following is substituted : " He
shall publish such books and tracts as are recommend
ed by the General Conference, and such as may be
approved of and recommended by an annual conference
and none other. But he may reprint any book or tract
which has once been approved of and published by us
when in his judgment, and the judgment of the book
committee, the same ought to be reprinted. The
book committee, consisting of five, shall be annually
appointed by the New-York Conference, who shall
previous to each annual sitting, examine into the ac
counts of the general book steward, and report to the
conference the state of the Concern. John Wilson i
appointed assistant editor and general book steward
and in case of the death or resignation of the editor and
general book steward, the assistant shall carry on the
Concern till the sitting of the next New-York Confer
ence."

In paragraphs 4 and 9, " Philadelphia" changed t
" New-York."

Paragraph 7 struck out, and the following substi
tuted :—

" 7. The profits arising from the Book Concern, afte
a sufficient capital to carry on the business is retained
shall be regularly applied to the support of the distress
ed travelling preachers and their families, the widow
and orphans of preachers, &c. The general bool
steward shall every year send forward to each annua
conference an account of the dividend which the seve
ral annual conferences may draw that year ; and each
conference may draw for their proportionate part, or
any person who has book money in hand, and the
drafts, with the receipt of the conference thereon, shal
be sent to the general book steward, and be placed to
the credit of the person who paid the same. But each

262   *Printing and circulating of Books.*   [Part 2.

annual conference is authorized, at all events, to draw on the general book steward for one hundred dollars."

Paragraphs 8, 10, and 11, of 1800, were struck out.

1808. The following alterations were made :—
The names of the general book steward and his assistant are omitted.

Paragraph 4 is struck out; also paragraph 5, and the following substituted for it :—

" 4. The Book Concern shall pay all the expense of the conveyance of books to presiding elders, until they are within the bounds of their districts."

The last sentence of paragraph 7, of 1804, struck out.

To paragraph 9, of 1800, (7,) the following sentence added :—" But no general book steward or editor in the Book Concern shall serve in that department for more than eight years successively."

A paragraph corresponding to No. 10, of 1800, (which was struck out in 1804,) restored as follows :—
" 8. No travelling preacher is permitted to publish any book or pamphlet, without the approbation of the annual conference to which he belongs, or of a committee chosen by them."

1812. The following sentence, transferred from Part i, Sec. 12, (p. 146,) was added at the end of the section :—
" It is recommended to the annual conferences to caution and restrict our preachers from improper publications."

1816. In paragraph 1, (1804,) after the first sentence, the following was inserted :—
" There shall be one editor and general book steward, and an assistant to act under his direction, both of whom shall be chosen from among the travelling preachers, and by virtue of their appointment shall be members of the New-York Annual Conference, to whom, in the interval of the General Conference, they shall be responsible for their conduct in the book business. And the New-York Conference, in the interval of the

General Conference, shall have power, if they deem it necessary, by and with the advice and consent of the bishops and book committee, to remove either of them; and, in case of removal, death, or resignation, to appoint a successor to act until the next ensuing General Conference."

It was now ordered (paragraph 1) that the publications should be regulated " as the state of the finances will admit, and the demands may require."

1820.   The following alterations were made :—

The general book steward, instead of being restricted from publishing any books but such "as are recommended by the General Conference," or " approved and recommended by an annual conference," was authorized to " publish any new work not before published by us, which shall be approved and recommended" by the book committee.

The following new paragraphs were inserted :—

" 2. There shall be a book agent who shall reside in Cincinnati, and manage the Concern in the western country, under the direction of the editor at New-York; and who, by virtue of his appointment, shall be a member of the Ohio Annual Conference, under the same regulations by which the agents at New-York are members of the New-York Annual Conference.   And the Ohio Conference shall appoint a committee of three, whose duty it shall be to examine the accounts of said agent and report to the said conference annually ; and in case of the death or resignation of the agent, the Ohio Conference shall have authority to appoint a successor until the sitting of the ensuing General Conference."

"4. It shall be the duty of all presiding elders having accounts open with the Concern, to pay over to the agents annually, or oftener, all the money in their hands, or which may be due from them ; rendering, at the same time, an account of all the books remaining in their districts unsold; and it shall be the duty of preachers in circuits and stations, having accounts with the presiding elder, to make settlements and render payments in a similar way."

1824. The paragraph prohibiting travelling preachers from publishing without the approbation of conference (see 1808 and 1812) was struck out, and the following substituted :—

" 9. Any travelling preacher who may publish any work or book of his own shall be responsible to his conference for any obnoxious matter or doctrine therein contained."

1828. The following alterations were made :—

It is made the duty of the general book steward " also to send a copy of the annual exhibit to each of the several annual conferences, so as that such exhibit may be laid before said conferences, if possible, at their sessions next succeeding the making thereof."

It is provided that the assistant shall carry on the Concern in case of the death or resignation of the general book steward, " or of the editor of the Christian Advocate and Journal."

The following new paragraph was inserted :—

" 2. There shall be also an editor of the Christian Advocate and Journal, (elected in the same way and for the same time as the editor and general book steward,) who shall have power, if need be, with the advice and consent of the book committee and book agents at New-York, to employ an assistant. He shall have charge of the clerks in that department, and of all business connected with it, and shall be responsible for its due and efficient management. He shall also edit and publish the Child's Magazine, Sunday school books and tracts, and be *ex officio* a member of the New-York Book Committee." It was provided that only four of the book committee should be chosen by the New-York Conference, the fifth being the editor of the Christian Advocate and Journal.

But the most important of all the alterations was the striking out of all the paragraphs relating to the old system of selling books on commission, (see 2, 3, of 1800,

4 of 1808, and 4 of 1820,) in place of which the fol
lowing were substituted :—

" 5. No books shall hereafter be issued on *commis
sion,* either from New-York or Cincinnati."

" 7. At each annual conference next ensuing th
passage of this resolution, the presiding elders shall de
liver into the hands of the book agents, (or book com
mittee of such conference,) for all the books in the seve
ral circuits and stations in their districts, the receipts o
those persons in whose care such books shall hav
been left.   After the appointments for the year ensuin
have been announced, the agents or book committe
shall give to each preacher the receipts belonging t
his circuit or station, retaining an exact account of th
amount called for by such receipts, which shall b
charged against said preacher, and accounted for b
him at the next annual conference ; provided, that th
several presiding elders shall be at equal liberty to sell an
such books on the same terms and principles with othe
preachers, and shall account therefor with the preacher
to whom they have been charged, or with the agents o
the book committees of their respective conferences.

1832.   The first part of the section was remo
delled as follows :—

" 1. The principal establishment of the book busi
ness shall be in the city of New-York ; and there shal
be such subordinate establishments in other places a
the General Conference may deem expedient.

" 2. There shall be one editor appointed to tak
charge of the Methodist Magazine and Quarterly Re
view, and all the editorial business of the Book Con
cern, not included in the department of our other peri
odical works.

" There shall be another editor, to whose superin
tendency shall be assigned the Christian Advocate an
Journal and Zion's Herald, Youth's Instructor and Sab
bath School and Bible Class Assistant, Child's Maga
zine, Sunday-school books and tracts ; and in this de
partment there shall be an assistant editor.

" 8. There shall be an agent, or general book steward, and an assistant, who shall act as chief clerk, both of whom, together with the editors and assistant editor, shall be chosen from among the travelling preachers, &c."

The other provisions in regard to the jurisdiction of the New-York Conference, the term of office, and the duties and powers of the general book steward, remained substantially the same, except that " what belongs to editorial departments" is exempted from being regulated by him, and for the republication of a work before published at the Book Room, it was sufficient that it meet the judgment of the agent and of the editors, and for the publication of a new work he must have the approbation both of the editors and of the book committee.

The annual exhibit was now required to be sent to the conferences, " as early as possible after it shall have been prepared."

The following new organization of a book committee was adopted :—

" 5. The book committee shall consist of seven members, to be chosen annually by the New-York Annual Conference, and the three editors as herein before provided for. It shall be their duty to examine annually into the state of the Book Concern, to inspect the accounts of the agents, to make a report thereof annually to the New-York Conference, and to the General Conference at its regular sessions. They shall also attend to such matters as may be referred to them by the editors or agents in reference to editing, printing, or publishing, and also to co-operate with the editor of the Christian Advocate in the selection of Sunday-school books and tracts."

In the paragraph respecting the Western Book Concern, such changes are made in the phraseology as the changes at New-York required ; and the following substantial ones, namely :—an assistant is appointed to the agent there ; the book committee was to consist of five, and it is made their duty to report also "to the General Conference at its session," "and to give advice in any matters in reference to the branch in the west."

The following new paragraph was inserted:—

"7. There shall also be a general depository for our books, Sunday-school books, and tracts, at New-Orleans, under the charge of an agent elected by the General Conference, which shall bear the same relation to the general agency in New-York as the branch establishment at Cincinnati does, and be under the same responsibilities; and the same to the Mississippi Conference, which that at Cincinnati does to the Ohio Conference."

In the sentence relating to those who refuse to make payment to the Book Concern, the word "person" is inserted before "preacher, or member," and it is directed that they shall be "dealt with in the same manner as is directed in other cases of debt and disputed accounts."

The following new paragraphs were added:—

"13. No editor, agent, or clerk, employed in the Book Concern, or in any department belonging to it, shall be allowed in any case to publish or sell books as his own private property.

"14. The editors, the general book steward, and book committee at New-York, shall be authorized to adopt such measures as they may deem expedient, and as shall be found practicable, to secure the premises on Mulberry-street for the uses and purposes for which the purchase was made, and the buildings erected."

1836. The following alterations were made:— The branches of the Book Concern are no longer spoken of as "subordinate."

The entire editorial department at New-York is committed to one editor and an assistant.

The provision that the officers of the Book Concern should not continue in office longer than eight years, struck out.

Still another organization of the book committee was adopted, as follows:—

"5. The book committee in New-York shall consist of all the preachers stationed for the time being in that city by the New-York Annual Conference, including the editors, the resident corresponding secretary of the Missionary Society, and the presiding elder of the district." Their duties remain the same.

Some changes were made in the establishment at Cincinnati. The agents in the west were to manage the Concern so "as to co-operate with the agents at New-York." The following clause, increasing the business of the establishment, was inserted :—"They shall have authority to publish any book in our catalogue, when in their judgment and that of the book committee it shall be advantageous to the interests of the church; provided, that they shall not publish type editions of such books as are stereotyped in New-York. And there shall be an editor and an assistant editor, who shall have charge of the Western Christian Advocate, and all the editorial business of this establishment; and who, together with the agent and assistant agent, shall be chosen from among the travelling preachers, &c."

The book committee was to "consist of seven members, including the editors." It was provided that "the proceeds of this establishment, with the exception of what may be necessary to conduct the business, shall be paid annually to the agents at New-York, to be added to the profits arising from that Concern, and appropriated for the same purposes."

The following provision was made for the erection of a building at Cincinnati :—

"The agents at Cincinnati shall be authorized, with the advice and consent of the book committee, to procure ground, and erect a suitable building for a printing office, book room, and bindery; and for this end they shall be allowed to appropriate such moneys in their hands as can be spared, together with any donations that may be made to the Concern in the west for purpose."

Paragraph 7 of 1832 was struck out, and the follow
ing new paragraphs were inserted :—

" 7. In addition to the Christian Advocate and Jour
nal, and the Western Christian Advocate, there shal
be a similar paper established in the following places
namely, Charleston, S. C., Richmond, Va., and Nash
ville, Tenn., to be conducted under the direction an
patronage of this conference ; provided, that before an
such paper shall be commenced, three thousand sub
scribers shall be obtained, or subscriptions amountin
to six thousand dollars. And the annual conference
within whose bounds such paper shall be established
shall appoint from their own members a publishin
committee, consisting of three, whose duties shall b
similar to those of the book committees of New-Yorl
and Cincinnati, so far as they may be applicable t
those establishments.

" 8. The editors for the papers at Charleston an
Nashville shall be elected by this conference, and th
Virginia Conference is authorized to elect an editor fo
the paper at Richmond, until the next General Confer
ence. And in case of vacancy by death, resignation
or otherwise, in either of the other establishments, th
annual conference, where it is located, shall have au
thority to fill such vacancy as above provided.

" 9. The publishing committee in each of thes
establishments shall keep an account of the receipt
and expenditures for the paper, correspond with th
agents at New-York, hold all moneys, after defrayin
current expenses, subject to their order, and shall re
port annually on the state of the establishment to thei
conference, and to the agents at New-York. An
whenever it shall be found that such papers do not full
support themselves, it shall be the duty of the annua
conferences, within whose bounds they are establishec
to discontinue them.

" 10. The annual conferences are affectionately an
earnestly requested not, to establish any more confe
ence papers ; and where such papers exist, they ma

be discontinued when it can be done consistently with existing obligations.

" 11. It is inexpedient to establish any new depositories of books at present ; but if, in the interval of the General Conference, the presiding bishop of any annual conference shall concur with said conference in opinion, that it is expedient to establish a book store within their bounds, in such case the agents, both at New-York and Cincinnati, shall have authority to sell books to such conference book store, at a discount of forty per centum, without involving any pecuniary responsibility on the part of the Book Concern.

" 12. The salaries for the support of editors and agents in all our book and periodical establishments shall be fixed by the book or publishing committees in the several places for which such editors and agents are appointed."

1840.   The following alterations were made :—
In the establishment at New-York,

A change was made in the editorial department, as follows :—

" 2. There shall be an editor of the Methodist Quarterly Review, general books, and tracts ; and an editor and an assistant editor for the Christian Advocate and Journal, the Youth's Magazine, and the sabbath-school books, who, if chosen from among the travelling preachers, shall, by virtue of their appointment, be members of the New-York Conference, to which, in the interval of the General Conference, they shall be responsible for their conduct in office."

The clause requiring the assistant agent to act as chief clerk was struck out.

The advice and consent of the book committee (see 1816) no longer required for the removal of agents and editors from office.

The agent is not required to publish books recommended by an annual conference, unless also "approved by the editors and book committee."

In the establishment at Cincinnati,
The powers and duties of the agents were thus defined :—

" 7. They shall have authority to publish any book or tract which has been previously published by the agents at New-York, when in their judgment, and in the judgment of the book committee, the demand for such publication will justify, and the interest of the church require it.   Provided they shall not reprint our large works, such as the Commentaries, quarto Bible, Wesley's and Fletcher's Works, or any other work containing more than seven hundred pages.

" 8. They shall publish such books and tracts as are recommended to them for publication by the General Conference ; and they may publish any new work which shall be approved by the editors, and recommended by the book committee at Cincinnati, or by an annual conference."

The editors there, as well as those at New-York, allowed to be other than travelling preachers.   A German department was established there, as follows :—

" 10. There shall be an editor in the German department, who shall have charge of the Christian Apologist, and perform all the editorial duties necessary in the printing of such books and tracts as may be recommended to the agents as above, for publication in the German language."

The following new paragraphs were inserted, respecting this establishment :—

" 11. The Ohio Conference shall exercise the same jurisdiction over said agents and editors that the New-York Conference does over the agents and editors at New-York."

" 13. All books or printed sheets ordered by the agents of the Concern from New-York shall be charged at cost prices.

" 14. It shall be the duty of the agents to report the state of the western division of the Book Concern to all the annual conferences yearly, and to inform the respective conferences of any within their bounds who fail to make payment, that measures may be taken to collect, or secure such debts."

The number of the book committee then was increased to nine.

The disposition of their funds was thus arranged :—

"16. The agents of this establishment shall remit to the agents at New-York during the current year as largely and frequently as their funds will allow, and to the full amount of stock furnished, if practicable. They shall also remit any surplus funds that may be in their hands after defraying the expense of conducting their business, which shall be added to the profits of the Concern at New-York, and appropriated to the same purposes."

The former paragraph respecting the erection of buildings, struck out.

In regard to *periodicals,* an additional paper was taken under the patronage of the conference, at Pittsburgh. "A periodical for females and the Christian Apologist" are to be published at Cincinnati. The editors of all the branch "Advocates" are to be elected by the General Conference.

In regard to *depositories,* the following new provisions were made :—

"21. There shall be a depository of our books at Charleston, S. C., at Pittsburgh, Pa., and at Boston, Mass., furnished by the agents at New-York with full supplies of the books of our General Catalogue, Sunday-school books and tracts, to be sold for the Concern on the same terms as at New-York. Provided, that there shall not be more than twenty-five thousand dollars' worth of books at any one time at Charleston, nor more than fifteen thousand dollars' worth at Pittsburgh, nor more than ten thousand dollars' worth at Boston.

"22. The expenses incident to the transportation, management, and sale of our books at these deposito-

ries, having been met out of the sales according to a
arrangement with the agents at New-York, the ne:
proceeds shall be forwarded to said agents as fast a
possible.

" 23. Full statements shall be made to the agents a
New-York semi-annually, at dates fixed by them, o:
the amount of sales, and of expenses; distinguishin;
cash sales from those on credit. And also, annua
statements shall be made of the amount of stock.

" 24. If it shall appear to the agents at New-Yor!
that the business at either of the depositories is not wel
managed, or that remittances are not duly made, the:
shall give notice thereof to the committee or commis
sioners acting for the annual conference, or to the an
nual conference, who shall immediately correct th
error complained of, or cause the affairs of the deposi
tory to be wound up."

SECTION IX.

*Local Preachers to have an Allowance in givei
Cases.*

For the provisions on this subject prior to 1784, se
pp. 17, 20. For the rule in 1784, see under Questior
71, p. 65. The subsequent regulations have been a:
follows :—

1789. It was provided,—" Let them be paid fo:
their time in proportion to the salary of the travellin;
preachers."

1796. The following provisions on the subjec
are found in Section 21, " Of the Local Preachers."

" *Quest.* 2. Shall any regulations be made in respec
to allowing a recompense to local preachers for thei:
work in given cases?

" *Ans.* 1. Whenever a local preacher fills the plac
of a travelling preacher, he shall be paid for his troubl
a sum proportionable to the salary of a travellin;
preacher; which sum shall be paid by the circuit a
the next quarterly meet ag, if the travelling preache:
12*

whose place he filled up was either sick or necessarily absent; or, in other cases, out of the salary of
the travelling preacher himself.

"2. If a local preacher be distressed in his temporal
circumstances, on account of his service in the circuit,
he may apply to the quarterly meeting, who may give
him what relief they judge proper, after the salaries of
the travelling preachers and of their wives, and all other
regular allowances to the travelling preachers be discharged."

1800. The word "trouble" changed to "time."

1804. This subject was transferred to its present
place.

1816. The words "by the approbation of the
presiding elder" inserted after "travelling preacher,"
where the term first occurs, (1796.)

SECTION X.

Of Slavery.*

For the provisions on this subject prior to 1784, see
pp. 14, 15, 19, 21, 22. For the rules adopted at the
Christmas Conference, see pp. 43, 44. Not more than
six months had elapsed after the adoption of these last
rules before it was thought necessary to suspend them
Accordingly, in the Annual Minutes for 1785 the following notice was inserted:—

"It is recommended to all our brethren to suspend

---

* The Methodists in America have from the first taken an active
part in promoting the welfare of the coloured people. See pp. 16,
42, 43. In the Annual Minutes for 1787 we find the following:—
"*Quest.* 17. What directions shall we give for the promotion of
the spiritual welfare of the coloured people?
"We conjure all our ministers and preachers, by the love of God,
and the salvation of souls, and do require them, by all the authority
that is invested in us, to leave nothing undone for the spiritual benefit
and salvation of them, within their respective circuits or districts; and
for this purpose to embrace every opportunity of inquiring into the
state of their souls, and to unite in society those who appear to have
a real desire of fleeing from the wrath to come; to meet such in
class, and to exercise the whole Methodist discipline among them.

the execution of the minute on slavery till the delibera-
tions of a future conference ; and that an equal space
of time be allowed all our members for consideration,
when the minute shall be put in force.

" N. B. We do hold in the deepest abhorrence the
practice of slavery ; and shall not cease to seek its
destruction by all wise and prudent means."

This note does not seem to refer to Question 43,
(1784,) as it, with the same answer, was retained in
the Discipline of 1786.   From this till 1796 no mention, it would seem, was made of the subject except in
the General Rules.   (See p. 181.)

1796.   The following section was introduced on
the subject :—

" *Quest.* What regulations shall be made for the
extirpation of the crying evil of African slavery ?

" *Ans.* 1. We declare, that we are more than ever
convinced of the great evil of the African slavery which
still exists in these United States, and do most earnestly recommend to the yearly conferences, quarterly
meetings, and to those who have the oversight of districts and circuits, to be exceedingly cautious what
persons they admit to official stations in our church ;
and in the case of future admission to official stations,
to require such security of those who hold slaves, for
the emancipation of them, immediately or gradually,
as the laws of the states respectively, and the circumstances of the case will admit ; and we do fully authorize all the yearly conferences to make whatever regulations they judge proper, in the present case, respecting
the admission of persons to official stations in our
church.

" 2. No slaveholder shall be received into society
till the preacher who has the oversight of the circuit
has spoken to him freely and faithfully on the subject
of slavery.

" 3. Every member of the society who sells a slave
shall immediately, after full proof, be excluded the
society.   And if any member of our society purchase

a slave, the ensuing quarterly meeting shall determine on the number of years in which the slave so purchased would work out the price of his purchase. And the person so purchasing shall, immediately after such determination, execute a legal instrument for the manumission of such slave, at the expiration of the term determined, by the quarterly meeting. And in default of his executing such instrument of manumission, or on his refusal to submit his case to the judgment of the quarterly meeting, such member shall be excluded the society. *Provided also,* that in the case of a female slave, it shall be inserted in the aforesaid instrument of manumission, that all her children who shall be born during the years of her servitude, shall be free at the following times, namely : every female child at the age of twenty-one, and every male child at the age of twenty-five. *Nevertheless,* if the member of our society, executing the said instrument of manumission, judge it proper, he may fix the times of manumission of the children of the female slaves before mentioned, at an earlier age than that which is prescribed above.

"4. The preachers and other members of our society are requested to consider the subject of negro slavery with deep attention till the ensuing General Conference : and that they impart to the General Conference, through the medium of the yearly conferences, or otherwise, any important thoughts upon the subject, that the conference may have full light, in order to take further steps toward the eradicating this enormous evil from that part of the church of God to which they are united."*

1800. The following new paragraphs were inserted :—

"2. When any travelling preacher becomes an owner of a slave or slaves, by any means, he shall

---

* It may be worthy of remark that this is almost the only section upon which the bishops make no notes.

forfeit his ministerial character in our church, unless he execute, if it be practicable, a legal emancipation of such slaves, conformably to the laws of the state in which he lives."

" 6. The annual conferences are directed to draw up addresses for the gradual emancipation of the slaves, to the legislatures of those states in which no general laws have been passed for that purpose. These addresses shall urge, in the most respectful, but pointed manner, the necessity of a law for the gradual emancipation of the slaves ; proper committees shall be appointed, by the annual conferences, out of the most respectable of our friends, for the conducting of the business ; and the presiding elders, elders, deacons, and travelling preachers, shall procure as many proper signatures as possible to the addresses, and give all the assistance in their power in every respect to aid the committees, and to further this blessed undertaking. Let this be continued from year to year, till the desired end be accomplished."

1804.   The following alterations were made :—

The question reads,—" What shall be done for the extirpation of the evil of slavery ?"

In paragraph 1 (1796) instead of " more than ever convinced," we have, " as much as ever convinced," and instead of " the African slavery which still exists in these United States," we have " slavery."

In paragraph 4, (3 of 1796,) respecting the selling of a slave, before the words " shall immediately," the following clause is inserted :—" except at the request of the slave, in cases of mercy and humanity, agreeably to the judgment of a committee of the male members of the society, appointed by the preacher who has the charge of the circuit."

The following new proviso was inserted in this paragraph :—" *Provided also*, that if a member of our society shall buy a slave with a certificate of future emancipation, the terms of emancipation shall, notwithstanding, be subject to the decision of the quarterly meeting conference." All after "*neverthe-less*" was struck out, and the following substituted :— "The members of our societies in the states of North Carolina, South Carolina, Georgia, and Tennessee, shall be exempted from the operation of the above rules." The paragraphs about considering the subject of slavery and petitions to legislatures, (namely, No. 4 of 1796, and No. 6 of 1800,) were struck out, and the following added :—

"5. Let our preachers, from time to time, as occasion serves, admonish and exhort all slaves to render due respect and obedience to the commands and interests of their respective masters."

1808. All that related to slaveholding among private members (see 2 and 3 of 1796) struck out, and the following substituted :—

"3. The General Conference authorizes each annual conference to form their own regulations relative to buying and selling slaves."

Paragraph 5 of 1804 was also struck out.

1812. Paragraph 3 of 1808 was altered so as to read,—

"3. Whereas the laws of some of the states do not admit of emancipating of slaves, without a special act of the legislature; the General Conference authorizes each annual conference to form their own regulations relative to buying and selling slaves."

1816. Paragraph 1 (see 1796) was altered so as to read,—

"1. We declare that we are as much as ever convinced of the great evil of slavery : therefore no slaveholder shall be eligible to any official station in our church hereafter, where the laws of the state in which he lives will admit of emancipation, and permit the liberated slave to enjoy freedom."

1820. Paragraph 3, (see 1812,) leaving it to the annual conferences "to form their own regulations about buying and selling slaves," was struck out.

1824. The following paragraphs added :—

" 3. All our preachers shall prudently enforce upo:
our members the necessity of teaching their slaves t
read the word of God ; and to allow them time t
attend upon the public worship of God on our regula
days of divine service.

" 4. Our coloured preachers and official member
shall have all the privileges which are usual to other
in the district and quarterly conferences, where th
usages of the country do not forbid it. And the pre
siding elder may hold for them a separate district con
ference, where the number of coloured local preacher
will justify it.*

" 5. The annual conferences may employ coloure
preachers to travel and preach where their service
are judged necessary ; provided that no one shall be s
employed without having been recommended accordin;
to the Form of Discipline."

---

* These provisions respecting district conferences have been r
tained ever since, although district conferences were abolishe
in 1836.

APPENDIX.

EXTRACTS FROM THE NOTES TO THE DISCIPLINE, BY DR. COKE AND BISHOP ASBURY.

THE fact has already been noticed, that Dr. Coke and Bishop Asbury appended explanatory notes to the Discipline of 1796. These consisted partly of Scripture proofs of the doctrines and rules of the church, and partly of expositions of the Discipline. The latter, constituting about two-thirds of the whole, are inserted in this Appendix, under their respective heads. The bishops themselves disclaimed having any authority " to make laws or regulations," much less can their notes be regarded in that light, now that the Discipline has been considerably modified. Bu* they are still interesting and important, as containing the views of the first bishops of the Methodist Episcopal Church respecting its discipline at that time, and also, as having been prepared at the request of the General Conference of 1796, and having received the implied sanction of the General Conference of 1800, which directed that they should be printed in such a manner that they could be conveniently bound up with the Form of Discipline.

" SECTION I.

" *Of the Origin of the Methodist Episcopal Church.*"

" It cannot be needful in this country to vindicate the right of every Christian society to possess, within itself, all the privileges necessary or expedient for the comfort, instruction, or good government of the members thereof. The two sacraments of baptism and the Lord's supper have been allowed to be essential to the formation of a Christian church, by every party and denomination in every age and country of Christendom, with the exception only of a single modern society : and ordination by the imposition of hands has been allowed to be highly expedient, and has been practised as universally as the former. And these two points as above described, might, if need were, be confirmed by the Scriptures, and by the unanimous testimony of all the primitive fathers of the church for the three first centuries ; and, indeed, by all the able divines who have written on the subject in the different languages of the world down to the present times.

" The only point which can be disputed by any sensible person, is the *episcopal* form which we have adopted ; and this can be contested by *candid* men, only from their want of acquaintance with the history of the church. The most bigoted devotees to religious establishments (the clergy of the Church of Rome excepted) are now ashamed to support the doctrine of *the apostolic, uninterrupted succession of bishops.* Dr. Hoadley, bishop of Winchester, who was, we believe, the greatest advocate for episcopacy whom the Protestant churches ever produced, has been so completely overcome by Dr. Calamy, in respect to the uninterrupted succession, that the point has been entirely given up. Nor do we recollect that any writer of the Protestant churches has since attempted to defend what all the learned world at present know to be utterly indefensible.

" And yet nothing but *an apostolic, uninterrupted succession,* can possibly confine the right of episcopacy to any particular church. The idea, that the supreme magistrate, or legislature of a country, ought to be the head of the church in that nation, is a position, which, we think, no one *here* will presume to assert. It follows, therefore, indubitably, that every church has a right to choose, if it please, the *episcopal* plan.

" The late Rev. John Wesley recommended the *episcopal* form to his societies in America ; and the General Conference, which is the chief synod of our church, unanimously accepted of it. Mr. Wesley did more. He first consecrated one for the office of a bishop, that our episcopacy might descend from himself. The General Conference unanimously accepted of the person so consecrated, as well as of Francis Asbury, who had for many years before exercised every branch of the episcopal office, excepting that of ordination. Now, the idea of an apostolic succession being exploded, it follows, that the Methodist Church has every thing which is Scriptural and essential to justify its episcopacy. Is the unanimous approbation of the chief synod of a church necessary ? This it has had. Is the ready compliance of the members of the church with its decision, in this respect, necessary ? This it has had, and continues to have. Is it highly expedient, that the fountain of the episcopacy should be respectable ? This has been the case. The most respectable divine since the primitive ages, if not since the time of the apostles, was Mr. Wesley. His knowledge of the sciences was very extensive. He was a general scholar : and for any to call his learning in question, would be to call their own. On his death the literati of England bore testimony to his great character. And where has been the individual so useful in the spread of religion ? But in this we can appeal only to the lovers of *vital* godliness. By his long and incessant labours he raised a multitude of societies, who looked up to him for direction ; and certainly his directions in things lawful, with the full approbation of the people, were sufficient to give authenicity to what was accordingly done. He was peculiarly attached to the laws and customs of the church in the primitive times of Christianity. He knew, that the primitive churches universally followed the episcopal plan: and indeed Bishop Hoadley has demonstrated that the episcopal plan was universal till the time of the Reformation. Mr. Wesley therefore preferred the *episcopal* form of church government; and God has (glory be to his name!) wonderfully blessed it among us."

" But in all we have observed on this subject, we by no means intend to speak disrespectfully of the Presbyterian Church, or of any other: we only desire to defend our own from the unjust calumnies of its opponents."

" SECTION III.
" *Of the General and Yearly Conferences.*"

" Our societies are scattered over a vast country, extending about fourteen hundred miles from north to south, and from five to eight hundred from east to west. We could not, therefore, in justice to the work of God, nor from the state of our finances, hold our General Conferences oftener than once in four years. If they were more frequent, the long absence of so many ministers from their respective circuits and districts would be an irreparable loss to the societies and congregations. Nor do we think, that the nature of a religious constitution renders it necessary to revise more frequently the regulations by which it is governed. But there are various particulars, which do not come under the name of laws, which require more frequent assemblies or conferences for their consideration. The admission of preachers on trial and into full connection, the ordination of elders and deacons, the examination of the characters of the ministers and preachers, and the stationing of them all, as well as the management of the fund for the superannuated preachers, &c., are points of the first moment, and call for frequent meetings. On this account, the *General* Conference has appointed *yearly* conferences, divided in the best manner they were able ; to be composed, as far as possible, of at least one bishop—the president elder of each district within the control of those conferences, respectively—the elders, deacons, and the preachers in full connection. These men, who have been travelling the preceding year among all the societies in those districts and circuits, respectively, can give the fullest, the completest information on all the subjects which come under the cognizance of the yearly conferences.

" But it may be asked, Why are not *delegates* sent to these conferences from each of the circuits ? We answer, It would utterly destroy our *itinerant plan. They* would be concerned chiefly, if not only, for the interests of their own constituents.

They could not be expected, from *the nature of things*, to make the necessary sacrifices, and to enter impartially into *the good of the whole.* They would necessarily endeavour to obtain the most able and lively preachers for their respective circuits, without entering, perhaps at all, into that enlarged, apostolic spirit, which would endeavour, whatever might be the sacrifice, to make all things *tally.* The difference of gifts in the ministers, and the opposing interests of the delegates, would produce conflicts of a pernicious tendency; and, in many instances, improper means would be used for obtaining the desired point. Frequently the delegates, if unsuccessful in their application for their favourite preacher, would probably make him secret offers to settle among them; and if unsuccessful in every point, and the preacher, appointed for them and their constituents, was not agreeable to their wishes, they might grow indignant, and, through resentment, and by their unfavourable reports, on their return, might cause a separation from the general body. And those who imagine this to be a mere chimera, show, we think, but little knowledge of human nature: they do not consider how easily and powerfully the heated passions would plead in favour of a settled ministry—how easily disappointment and jealousy would present the purest and most disinterested conduct in the most unfavourable light: to say nothing of the labour and expense of such a plan. While, on the other hand, the present members who compose our conferences, who know not, when they meet, what may be their next sphere of action, and are willing to run anywhere on the errands of their Lord, are not nearly as much exposed to the temptations mentioned above.*

"The following portions of the word of God are pointed in support of the itinerant plan for the propagation of the gospel; which plan renders most of the regulations contained in this section essential to the existence of our united society: Matt. x, 5–11, ' These twelve [apostles] Jesus sent forth, and commanded them, saying, Go—to the lost sheep of the house of Israel. And *as ye go, preach*, saying, The kingdom of heaven is at hand. And into *whatsoever city or town* ye shall enter, inquire,' &c.

"* We are very far from making these remarks out of any disrespect to our *located* brethren. On the contrary, we are very conscious that many of them equal any of us, and perhaps much exceed us in grace and wisdom. We have made these observations *only* on account of their *located* situation, well knowing that our people would on no occasion choose any for their delegates who were not wise and good men. But such is the *nature* of man, and perhaps such is the *duty* of man, that he will always prefer the people for whom he acts, and to whom he is responsible, before all others. *We* should, probably, act in the same manner ourselves, if we were delegates for a single circuit or district."

Matt. xxii, 8–10, 'Then saith he to his servants, The wedding is ready, but they which were bidden were not worthy. Go ye, therefore, into *the highways, and as many as ye shall find*, bid to the marriage. So those servants went out into *the highways*,' &c. Matt. xxviii, 19, 'Go ye, therefore, and *teach all nations*,' be as extensively useful as possible. Mark vi, 7–12, 'And he calleth unto him the twelve, and began to send them forth by two and two,—and commanded them that they should take nothing for their journey, *save a staff only*.—And he said unto them, *In what place soever* ye enter into a house, there abide, till ye *depart* from that place.—And *they went out*, and preached that men should repent.' Luke x, 1–9, 'After these things, the Lord appointed other seventy also, and sent them two and two before his face *into every city and place*, whither he himself would come.—And into *whatsoever house* ye enter,' says our Lord to them, 'first say, Peace be to this house.—And into *whatsoever city* ye enter, and they receive you,—say unto them, The kingdom of God is come nigh unto you.' Luke xiv, 23, 'And the Lord said unto the servant, *Go out into the highways and hedges*, and compel them to come in, that my house may be filled.' Acts viii, 4, 'They that were scattered abroad *went everywhere* preaching the word.' Acts viii, 40, 'Philip—preached *in all the cities*, till he came to Cesarea.' Acts xvi, 36, 'Paul said unto Barnabas, Let us go *again* and visit our brethren *in every city* where we have preached the word of the Lord,' &c.

"We have already shown, that *Timothy* and *Titus* were *travelling bishops*. In short, every candid person, who is thoroughly acquainted with the New Testament, must allow, that whatever excellences other plans may have, *this* is the primitive and *apostolic plan*. But we would by no means speak with disrespect of the faithful *located* ministers of any church. We doubt not, but, from the nature and circumstances of things, there must have been many located ministers in the primitive churches : and we must acknowledge, with gratitude to God, that the *located* brethren in our church are truly useful and of considerable consequence, in their respective stations. But, on the other hand, we are so conscious of the vast importance of the *travelling plan*, that we are determined, through the grace of God, to support it to the utmost of our power ; nor will any plea which can possibly be urged, however plausible it may appear, or under whatever name proposed, induce us to make the least sacrifice in this respect, or, by the introduction of any novelty, to run the least hazard of wounding *that plan*, which God has so wonderfully owned, and which is so perfectly consistent with the apostolic and primitive practice.

"We will now humbly beg leave to drop a few *hints* (for laws or regulations we have no authority to make) *as explanatory* of those words in the introduction to this section, 'It is desired that every person speak freely whatever is in his heart :' and we propose them the more readily, as they are extracted from the Minutes drawn up by our elder brethren, the members of the British Conference :—

" 1. Be tender of the character of every brother ; but keep at the utmost distance from countenancing sin.

" 2. Say nothing in the conference but what is strictly necessary, and to the point.

" 3. If accused by any one, remember recrimination is no acquittance ; therefore avoid it.

" 4. Beware of impatience of contradiction ; be firm ; but be open to conviction. The cause is God's, and he needs not the hands of an Uzzah to support his ark. The being too tenacious of a point, because you brought it forward, may be only feeding self. Be quite easy, if a majority decide against you.

" 5. Use no craft or guile to gain any point. Genuine simplicity will always support itself. But there is no need always to say all you know or think.

" 6. Beware of too much confidence in your own abilities ; and never despise an opponent.

" 7. Avoid all lightness of spirit, even what would be innocent anywhere else.—Thou, God, seest me.

" The appointment of *the times* for holding the *yearly* conferences must necessarily be invested in the bishops, otherwise they cannot possibly form their plans for travelling through the continent, so that they may be enabled to attend each of the conferences. But the right of fixing *the places* rests with the conferences.

" We cannot omit noticing, before we conclude this section, the strict examination which the characters of the preachers pass through, in the yearly conferences. When that eminent saint of God, and great writer, John Fletcher, was once present, in the British Conference, at the examination of the characters, he seemed astonished, and expressed his surprise and approbation in very strong terms. The examination is equally strict in all the conferences throughout the connection. And we know of no church where the purity of the morals, the orthodoxy of the doctrines, and the usefulness of the lives and labours of the ministers, (for all these are included in the examination,) are more strictly attended to than in ours.

" In respect to the division of the continent, for the purpose of holding the yearly conferences, we may observe, that for several years the annual conferences were very small, consisting only of the preachers of a single district, or of two or three very small ones. This was attended with many inconveniences :—1. There were but few of the senior preachers, whose years and experience had matured their judgments, who could be present at any one conference. 2. The conferences wanted that dignity which every religious synod should possess, and which always accompanies a large assembly of gospel ministers.   3. The itinerant plan was exceedingly cramped, from the difficulty of removing preachers from one district to another.   All these inconveniences will, we trust, be removed on the present plan ; and at the same time the conferences are so arranged, that all the members, respectively may attend with little difficulty.

" To all which may be added, that the active, zealous, unmar ried preachers, may move on a larger scale, and preach the ever blessed gospel far more extensively through the sixteen states and other parts of the continent ; while the married preachers whose circumstances require them, in many instances, to be more located than the single men, will have a considerable field of action opened to them ; and also the bishops will be able to attend the conferences with greater ease, and without injury to their health.

" The regulation concerning those who are to attend the con ferences is made, that our societies and congregations may be supplied with preaching during the conferences.   We would therefore, wish to have a few of the travelling preachers among our dear flocks at those times.   But as we desire to make the conferences as respectable and weighty as possible, we can spare none at those important seasons, except the preachers upon trial They, also, will be absent from the yearly conferences only for one year, as they must be present on the second to be admitted into full connection."

"SECTION IV.

" *Of the Election and Consecration of Bishops, and of their Duty.*"

" In considering the present subject, we must observe, that no thing has been introduced into Methodism by the present episco pal form of government, which was not before fully exercised by Mr. Wesley.   He presided in the conferences ; fixed the appointments of the preachers for their several circuits ; changed received, or suspended preachers wherever he judged that necessity required it ; travelled through the European connection at large ; superintended the spiritual and temporal business : and consecrated two bishops, Thomas Coke and Alexander Mather one before the present episcopal plan took place in America, and the other afterward, besides ordaining elders and deacons.   But the authority of Mr. Wesley and that of the bishops in America differ in the following important points :—

" 1. Mr. Wesley was the patron of all the Methodist pulpits in Great Britain and Ireland *for life*, the sole right of nomination being invested in him by all the deeds of settlement, which gave him exceeding great power. But the bishops in America possess to such power. The property of the preaching-houses is invested in the trustees; and the right of nomination to the pulpits, in the General Conference—and in such as the General Conference shall, from time to time, appoint. This division of power in favour of the General Conference was absolutely necessary. Without it the itinerant plan could not exist for any long continuance. The trustees would probably, in many instances, from their *located* situation, insist upon having their favourite preachers stationed in their circuits, or endeavour to prevail on the preachers themselves to *locate* among them, or choose some other settled minister for their chapels. In other cases, the trustees of preaching-houses *in different circuits* would probably insist upon having the *same* popular or favourite preachers.* Here, then, lies the grand difference between Mr. Wesley's authority, in the present instance, and that of our American bishops. The former, as (under God) the father of the connection, was allowed to have the *sole, legal, independent* nomination of preachers to all the chapels : the latter are *entirely dependent* on the General Conference.

" But why, may it be asked, does the General Conference lodge the power of stationing the preachers in the episcopacy ? We answer, On account of their entire confidence in it. If ever, through improper conduct, it loses that confidence in any considerable degree, the General Conference will, upon evidence given, in a proportionable degree, take from it this branch of its authority. But if ever it evidently betrays a spirit of tyranny or partiality, and *this* can be proved before the General Conference, the whole will be taken from it : and we pray God, that in such case the power may be invested in other hands ! And alas ! who would envy any one the power ? There is no situation in which a bishop can be placed, no branch of duty he can possibly exercise, so delicate, or which so exposes him to the jealousies

---

" * We must repeat nearly the same observations concerning *trustees,* which we have in our notes on the last section, concerning the sending of *delegates* to our conferences. We have a great respect for our *trustees.* We consider them as men to whom the connection is greatly obliged. They fill up an important province in our church, and have a claim to a high rank among us. Humanly speaking, the work could not be carried on without them to any extent in the cities and towns. Their responsibility for the debts of our buildings, and the disinterestedness which must necessarily influence them when they make themselves responsible, lay our societies under very great obligations. We both love and honour them. But still they are *located* men. They cannot be expected to act impartially for the whole. They will think it their duty, and perhaps it is their duty, to prefer the interests of their own congregations to any other. We should probably act in the same manner in their situation."

not only of false but of true brethren, as this.   The removal of preachers from district to district, and from circuit to circuit, very nearly concerns them, and touches their tenderest feelings : and it requires no small portion of grace for a preacher to be *perfectly* contented with his appointment, when he is stationed in a circuit where the societies are small, the rides long, and the fare coarse.   Any one, therefore, may easily see, from the nature of man, that though the bishop has to deal with some of the best of men, he will sometimes raise himself opposers, who, by rather overrating their own abilities, may judge him to be partial in respect to their appointments : and these circumstances would weigh down his mind to such a degree, as those who are not well acquainted with the difficulties which necessarily accompany public and important stations among mankind, can hardly conceive.

"May we not add a few observations concerning the high expediency, if not necessity, of the present plan.   How could an itinerant ministry be preserved through this extensive continent, if the yearly conferences were to station the preachers ?   They would, of course, be taken up with the *sole* consideration of the spiritual and temporal interests of *that part* of the connection, the direction of which was intrusted to them.   The necessary consequence of this mode of proceeding would probably, in less than an age, be *the division of the body* and *the independence* of each yearly conference.   The conferences would be more and more estranged from each other for want of a mutual exchange of preachers ; and *that grand spring, the union of the body at large*, by which, under divine grace, the work is more and more extended through this vast country, would be gradually weakened, till at last it might be entirely destroyed.   The connection would no more be enabled to send missionaries to the western states and territories, in proportion to their rapid population.   The grand circulation of ministers would be at an end, and a mortal stab given to the itinerant plan.   The surplus of preachers in one conference could not be drawn out to supply the deficiencies of others, through declensions, locations, deaths, &c., and the revivals in one part of the continent could not be rendered beneficial to the others.   *Our grand plan*, in all its parts, leads to an *itinerant* ministry.   Our bishops are *travelling* bishops.   All the different orders which compose our conferences are employed in the *travelling line* ; and our local preachers are, *in some degree*, travelling preachers.   Every thing is kept moving as far as possible ; and we will be bold to say, that, next to the grace of God, there is nothing *like this* for keeping the whole body alive from the centre to the circumference, and for the continual extension of that circumference on every hand.   And we verily believe, that if our episcopacy should, at any time, through tyrannical or immoral conduct, come under the severe censure of

13

the General Conference, the members thereof would see it highly for the glory of God to preserve the present form, and *only to* change the men.

"2. Mr. Wesley, as the venerable founder (under God) of the whole Methodist society, governed without any responsibility whatever ; and the universal respect and veneration of both the preachers and people for him made them cheerfully submit to this : nor was there ever, perhaps, a mere human being who used so much power better, or with a purer eye to the Redeemer's glory, than that blessed man of God. But the American bishops are as responsible as any of the preachers. They are *perfectly subject* to the General Conference They are indeed conscious that the conference would neither degrade nor censure them, unless they deserved it. They have, on the one hand, the fullest confidence in their brethren ; and, on the other, esteem the confidence which their brethren place in them, as the highest earthly honour they can receive.

" But this is not all. They are subject to be tried by seven elders and two deacons, as prescribed above, for any immorality, or supposed immorality ; and may be suspended by two-thirds of these, not only from all public offices, but even from being private members of the society, till the ensuing General Conference. This mode subjects the bishops to a trial before a court of judicature, considerably inferior to that of a yearly conference. For there is not one of the yearly conferences which will not, probably, be attended by more presiding elders, elders and deacons, than the conference which is authorized to try a bishop, the yearly conferences consisting of from thirty to sixty members. And we can, without scruple, assert, that there are no bishops of any other episcopal church upon earth who are subject to so strict a trial as the bishops of the Methodist Episcopal Church in America. We trust, they will never *need* to be influenced by motives drawn from the fear of temporal or ecclesiastical punishments, in order to keep *from vice :* but if they do, may the rod which hangs over them have its due effect : or may they be expelled the church, as ' salt which hath lost its savour, and is thenceforth good for nothing but to be cast out, and trodden under foot of men.'

" 3. Mr. Wesley had the entire management of all the conference funds and the produce of the books. It is true, he expended all upon the work of God, and for charitable purposes ; and rather than appropriate the least of it to his own use, refused, even when he was about seventy years of age, to travel in a carriage, till his friends in London and Bristol entered into a private subscription for the extraordinary expense. That great man of God might have heaped up thousands upon thousands, if he had been so inclined ; and yet he died worth nothing but a little pocket money, 'he horses and the carriage in which he travelled, and the clothes he wore. But our American bishops have no probability of being rich. For not a cent of the public money is at their disposal : the conferences have the entire direction of the whole. Their salary is sixty-four dollars a year ; and their travelling expenses are also defrayed. And with this salary they are to travel about six thousand miles a year, ' in much patience,' and sometimes ' in afflictions, in necessities, in distresses, in labours, in watchings, in fastings,' through ' honour and dishonour, evil report and good report : as deceivers, and yet true ; as unknown, and yet well known ; as dying, and, behold,' they ' live ; as chastened, and not killed ; as sorrowful, yet alway rejoicing ; as poor, yet making many rich ; as having nothing, and yet possessing all things ;' and, we trust, they can each of them through grace say, in their small measure, with the great apostle, that ' they are determined not to know any thing, save Jesus Christ, and him crucified ; yea, doubtless, and count all things but loss for the excellency of the knowledge of Christ Jesus their Lord : for whom they have suffered the loss of all things, and do count them but dung that they may win Christ.'

" We have drawn this comparison between our venerable father and the American bishops, to show to the world that they possess not, and, we may add, they aim not to possess that power which he exercised and had a right to exercise, as the father of the connection ; that, on the contrary, they are perfectly dependent ; that their power, their usefulness, themselves, are entirely at the mercy of the General Conference, and, on the charge of immorality, at the mercy of two-thirds of the little conference of nine.

" To these observations we may add, 1. That a branch of the episcopal office, which, in every episcopal church upon earth, since the first introduction of Christianity, has been considered as essential to it, namely, *the power of ordination*, is *singularly* limited in our bishops. For they not only have no power to ordain *a person for the episcopal office* till he be first elected by the *General* Conference, but they possess no authority to ordain *an elder or a travelling deacon* till he be first elected by a *yearly* conference ; or a local deacon, till he obtain a testimonial, signifying the approbation of the society to which he belongs, countersigned by the general stewards of the circuit, three elders, three deacons, and three travelling preachers. They are, therefore, not under the temptation of ordaining through interest, affection, or any other improper motive ; because it is not in their power so to do. They have, indeed, authority to suspend the ordination of an elected person, because they are answerable *to God* for the abuse of their office, and the command of the apostle, ' Lay hands suddenly on no man,' is absolute : and we trust, where conscience was really concerned, and they had *sufficient reason* to exercise their power of suspension, they would do it

iven to the loss of the esteem of their brethren, which is more
dear to them than life; yea, even to the loss of their usefulness
in the church, which is more precious to them than all things
here below. But every one must be immediately sensible, how
cautious they will necessarily be, as men of wisdom, in the exercise of this suspending power. For unless they had such
weighty reasons for the exercise of it, as would give some degree of satisfaction to the conference which had made the election, they would throw themselves into difficulties, out of which
they would not be able to extricate themselves, but by the meek-
est and wisest conduct, and by reparation to the injured person.

" 2. The bishops are obliged to travel till the General Conference pronounces them worn out or superannuated : for that certainly is the meaning of the answer to the sixth question of this
section. What a restriction ? Where is the like in any other episcopal church ? It would be a disgrace to our episcopacy to have
bishops settled on their plantations here and there, evidencing to
all the world, that instead of breathing the spirit of their office,
they could, without remorse, *lay down their crown*, and bury the
most important talents God has given to men ! We would
rather choose that our episcopacy should be blotted out from the
face of the earth, than be spotted with such disgraceful conduct !
All the episcopal churches in the world are conscious of the
dignity of the episcopal office. The greatest part of them endeavour to preserve this dignity by large salaries, splendid dresses,
and other appendages of pomp and splendour. But if an episcopacy has neither the dignity which arises from these worldly trap-
pings, nor that infinitely superior dignity which is the attendant
of labour, of suffering and enduring hardship for the cause of
Christ, and of a venerable old age, the concluding scene of a
life devoted to the service of God, it instantly becomes the
disgrace of a church and the just ridicule of the world !

" Some may think, that the mode of travelling which the
bishops are obliged to pursue, is attended with little difficulty,
and much pleasure. Much pleasure they certainly do experience,
because they know that they move in the will of God, and that
the Lord is pleased to own their feeble labours. But if to travel
through the heat and the cold, the rain and the snow, the swamps
and the rivers, over the mountains and through the wilderness,
lying for nights together on the bare ground and in log-houses,
open to the wind on every side, fulfilling their appointments, as
far as possible, whatever be the hinderance,—if these be little difficulties, then our bishops have but little to endure.

" We have already quoted so many texts of Scripture in defence of episcopacy and the itinerant plan, that we need only
refer our reader to the notes on the first and third sections. The
whole tenor of St. Paul's epistles to Timothy and Titus clearly
evidences, that *they* were invested, on the whole, with abundantly

more power than our bishops ; nor does it appear that *they* were responsible to any but God and the apostle.   The texts quoted in the notes on the third section, in defence of the itinerant plan, we would particularly recommend to the reader's attention ; as we must insist upon it, that *the general itinerancy* would not probably exist for any length of time on this extensive continent, if the bishops were not invested with that authority which they now possess.   They alone travel through the whole connection, and therefore have such a view of the whole, as no yearly conference can possibly have.

"One bishop, with the elders present, may consecrate a bishop who has been previously elected by the General Conference This is agreeable to the Scriptures.   We read, 2 Tim. i, 6, ' put thee in remembrance, that thou stir up *the gift* of God which *is in thee*, by the putting on of *my* hands :' here we have the imposition of the hands of the apostle.   Again, we read, 1 Tim iv, 14, ' Neglect not *the gift that is in thee*, which was given thee by prophecy, with the laying on of the hands of *the presbytery :*' here we have the laying on of the hands of *the elders* And by comparing both passages, it is evident that the imposition of hands was, both in respect to the apostle and the elders, for *the same gift*.   Nor is the idea, that three bishops are necessary to consecrate a bishop, grounded on any authority whatever drawn from the Scriptures, or the practice of the apostolic age.

" The authority given to, or rather declared to exist in, the General Conference, that in case there shall be no bishop remaining in the church, they shall elect a bishop, and authorize the elders to consecrate him, will not admit of an objection, except on the supposition that the fable of an uninterrupted apostolic succession be allowed to be true.   St. Jerome, who was as strong an advocate for episcopacy as perhaps any in the primitive church, informs us, that in the church of Alexandria, (which was, in ancient times, one of the most respectable of the churches,) the college of presbyters not only elected a bishop on the decease of the former, but consecrated him by the imposition of their own hands *solely*, from the time of St. Mark, their first bishop, to the time of Dionysius, which was a space of about two hundred years : and the college of presbyters in ancient times answered to our General Conference."

"SECTION V.

" *Of the Presiding Elders, and of their Duty.*"

After citing sundry scriptures in favour of having " presiding, superintending, or ruling elders," the bishops proceed,—

" On the principles or data above mentioned, all the episcopal churches in the world have, in some measure, formed their church government. And we believe we can venture to assert, that there never has been an episcopal church of any great extent which has not had *ruling* or *presiding* elders, either expressly *by name,* as in the apostolic churches, or otherwise in effect. On this account it is, that all the modern episcopal churches have had their *presiding* or *ruling* elders under the names of grand vicars, archdeacons, rural deans, &c. The Moravians have presiding elders, who are invested with very considerable authority, though we believe they are simply termed elders. And we beg leave to repeat, that we are confident, we could, if need were, show that all the episcopal churches, ancient and modern, *of any great extent,* have had an order or set of ministers corresponding, more or less, to our presiding or ruling elders, all of whom were, more or less, invested with the superintendence of other ministers.

"Mr. Wesley informs us in his Works, that the whole plan of Methodism was introduced, step by step, by the interference and openings of divine Providence. This was the case in the present instance. When Mr. Wesley drew up a plan of government for our church in America, he desired that no more elders should be ordained in the first instance than were absolutely necessary, and that the work on the continent should be divided between them, in respect to the duties of their office. The General Conference accordingly elected twelve elders for the above purposes. Bishop Asbury and the district conferences afterward found that this order of men was so necessary that they agreed to enlarge the number, and give them *the name* by which they are at present called, and which is perfectly Scriptural, though not *the word* used in our translation : and this proceeding afterward received the approbation of Mr. Wesley.

"In 1792 the General Conference, equally conscious of the necessity of having such an office among us, not only confirmed every thing that Bishop Asbury and the district conferences had done, but also drew up or agreed to the present section for the explanation of the nature and duties of the office. The conference clearly saw that the bishops wanted assistants ; that it was impossible for one or two bishops so to superintend the vast work on this continent as to keep every thing in order in the intervals of the conference, without other official men to act under them and assist them : and as these would be only the agents of the bishops in every respect, the authority of appointing them, and of changing them, ought, from the nature of things, to be in the episcopacy. If the presiding or ruling elders were not men in whom the bishops could fully confide, or on the loss of confidence, could exchange for others, the utmost confusion would ensue. This also renders the authority invested in the bishops of fixing the extent of each district, highly expedient. They must be supposed to be the best judges of the abilities of the presiding elders whom they themselves choose : and it is a grand part of their duty to make the districts and the talents of the presiding elders who act for them, suit and agree with each other, as far as possible : for it cannot be expected, that a sufficient number of them can at any time be found, *of equal talents*, and, therefore, the extent of their field of action must be proportioned to their gifts.

" From all that has been advanced, and from those other ideas which will present themselves to the reader's mind on this subject, it will appear that the presiding elders must, of course, be appointed, directed, and changed by the episcopacy. And yet their power is so considerable that it would by no means be sufficient for them to be responsible to the bishops *only* for their conduct in their office. They are as responsible in this respect, and in every other, to the *yearly* conference to which they belong, as any other preacher ; and may be censured, suspended, or expelled from the connection, if the conference see it proper : nor have the bishops any authority to overrule, suspend, or meliorate in any degree the censures, suspensions, or expulsions of the conference.

" Many and great are the advantages arising from this institution. 1. It is a great help and blessing to the quarterly meetings respectively, through the connection, to have a man at their head, who is experienced not only in the ways of God, but in men and manners, and in all things appertaining to the order of our church. Appeals may be brought before the quarterly meeting from the judgment of the preacher who has the oversight of the circuit, who certainly would not be, in such cases, so proper to preside as the ruling elder. Nor would any local preacher, leader, or steward be a suitable president of the meeting, as his parent, his child, his brother, sister, or friend, might be more or less interested in the appeals which came before him : besides, his *local* situation would lead him almost unavoidably to *prejudge* the case, and, perhaps, to enter warmly into the interests of one or other of the parties, previously to the appeal. It is, therefore, indisputably evident, that the *ruling elder* is most likely to be impartial, and, consequently, the most proper person to *preside*.

" 2. Another advantage of this office arises from the necessity of changing preachers from circuit to circuit in the intervals of the yearly conferences. Many of the preachers are young in years and gifts ; and this must always be the case, more or less, or a fresh supply of travelling preachers in proportion to the necessities of the work could not be procured. These young men, in general, are exceedingly zealous. Their grand *forte* is to awaken souls ; and in this view they are highly necessary for the spreading of the gospel. But for some time their gifts cannot be expected to be *various ;* and, therefore half a year at a time, or sometimes even a quarter, may be sufficient for them to labour in one circuit : to change them, therefore, from circuit to circuit, in the intervals of the yearly conferences, is highly necessary in many instances. Again, the preachers themselves, for family reasons, or on other accounts, may desire, and have reason to expect, a change But who can make it in the absence of the bishops, unless there be a presiding elder appointed for the district? A recent instance proves the justice of this remark. A large district was lately without a presiding elder for a year. Many of the preachers, sensible of the necessity of a change in the course of the year, met together, and settled every preliminary for the purpose. Accordingly, when the time fixed upon for the change arrived, several of them came to their new appointments according to agreement, but, behold, the others had changed their minds, and the former were obliged to return to their old circuits, feeling not a little disgrace on account of their treatment. And this would be continually the case, and all would be confusion, *if there were no persons invested with the powers of ruling elders, by whatever name they might be called;* as it would be impossible for the bishops to be present everywhere, and enter *into the details* of all the circuits.

"3. Who is able properly to supply the vacancies in circuits *on the deaths* of preachers, or on *their withdrawing* from the travelling connection? Who can have a thorough knowledge of the state of the district, and of its resources for the filling up such vacancies, except the presiding elder who travels through the whole district? And shall circuits be often neglected for months together, and the flocks, during those times, be, more or less, without shepherds, and many of them, perhaps, perish for want of food, merely that one of the most Scriptural and useful offices among us may be abolished? Shall we not rather support it, notwithstanding every thing which may be subtilly urged by our enemies under the cry of tyranny, which is the common cry of restless spirits, even against the best governments, in order that they may throw every thing into confusion, and then ride in the whirlwind and direct the storm?

"4. When a bishop visits a district, he ought to have one to accompany him, in whom he can fully confide; one who can inform him of the whole work in a complete and comprehensive view; and, therefore, one who has travelled *through the whole,* and, by being present at all the quarterly meetings, can give all the information concerning every circuit in particular, and the district in general, which the bishop can desire. Nor is the advantage small that the bishops, when at the greatest distance, may receive from the presiding elders a full account of their respective districts, and may thereby be continually in possession of a more comprehensive knowledge of the whole work than they could possibly procure by any other means.

" 5. The only branch of the presiding elder's office, the importance and usefulness of which is not so obvious to some persons, but which is, at the same time, perhaps the most expedient of all, is *the suspending power*, for the preservation of *the purity* of our ministry, and that our people may never be burdened with preachers of *insufficient* gifts. Here we must not forget that the presiding elder acts as agent to the bishops ; and that the bishops are, the greatest part of their time, at a vast distance from him : he must, therefore, exercise episcopal authority, (ordination excepted,) or he cannot act as their agent. All power may be abused. The only way which can be devised to prevent the abuse of it, if we will have a good and effective government, is to make the executive governors completely responsible, and their responsibility within the reach of the aggrieved. And, in the present instance, not only the General Conference may expel the presiding elder—not only the episcopacy may suspend him from the exercise of his office—but the yearly conference may also impeach him, try him, and expel him : and such a threefold guard must be allowed, by every candid mind, to be as full a check to the abuse of his power, as, perhaps, human wisdom can devise.

" But is it not strange that any of *the people* should complain either of *this* or of the *episcopal* office ? *These offices* in the church are peculiarly designed to meliorate the severity of Christian discipline, as far as they respect *the people*. In them the people have a refuge, an asylum to which they may fly upon all occasions. To them they may appeal, and before them they may lay all their complaints and grievances. The persons who bear these offices are their fathers in the gospel, ever open of access, ever ready to relieve them under every oppression. And we believe we can venture to assert, that the people have never had even a *plausible* pretence to complain of the authority either of the bishops or the presiding elders.

" 6. We may add, as was just hinted above, that the bishops ought not to enter into *small details*. It is not their calling. To select the proper men who are to act as their agents—to preserve in order and in motion the wheels of the vast machine —to keep a constant and watchful eye upon the whole—and to *think deeply* for the general good—form their peculiar and important avocation. All of which shows the necessity of the office now under consideration.

" The objection brought by some that many of the most useful preachers are taken out of the circuits for this purpose, whose preaching talents are thereby lost to the connection, will by no means bear examination. Even if this was the case, the vast

13*

dvantage arising from a complete and effective superintendence
f the work would, we believe, far over-balance this considera-
on. But the objection is destitute of weight. Their preaching
bilities are, we believe, abundantly more useful. Though all
ıe preachers of matured talents and experience cannot be em-
loyed as presiding elders, yet those who are employed as such
enerally answer this character. They are qualified to build
p believers on their most holy faith, and to remove scruples,
nd answer cases of conscience, more than the younger preachers
ı general. In many circuits some parts of the society might
uffer much in respect to the divine life, for want of those gifts
eculiarly necessary for *them*, were it not for this additional
elp ; while the junction of the talents of the presiding elder
/ith those of the circuit preachers, will, in general, make the
/hole complete. And as the presiding elder is, or ought to be,
lways present at the quarterly meetings, he will have oppor-
nnities of delivering his whole mind to a very considerable part
f the people : nor is there any reasonable ground to fear that
ıe will ever wear out his talents, if we consider the extent of a
ıistrict, and the obligation the episcopacy is under to remove
ıim, at furthest, on the expiration of four years.

" To these observations we may add, that the calling of dis-
rict conferences, on the immorality of travelling preachers, on
heir deaths, the necessity of removals, &c., would be attended
vith the most pernicious consequences to the circuits on this
'ast continent, where the districts are so large, and the absence
ıf the preachers would be necessarily so long upon every such
ıccasion. And we will venture to assert, that if any effective
povernment ought to exist at all in the connection, during the
ntervals of the yearly and general conferences, there is *no
ılternative* between the authority of the bishops and their agents,
he presiding elders, on the one hand, and the holding of district
ıonferences on the other hand.

" We will conclude our notes on this section with observing,
hat there is no ground to believe that the work of God has been
njured, or the numbers of the society diminished, by the insti-
ution of this order, but just the contrary. In the year 1784,
vhen the presiding eldership did, *in fact*, though not in *name*,
ıommence, there were about fourteen thousand in society on
his continent ; and *now* the numbers amount to upward of fifty-
ix thousand : so that the society is, at present, four times as
arge as it was twelve or thirteen years ago. We do not be-
ieve that the office now under consideration was *the principal
ause* of this great revival, but the Spirit and grace of God,
nd the consequent zeal of the preachers in general. Yet
ve have no doubt but the full organization of our body, and
;iving to the whole a complete and effective executive govern-
ıent, of which the presiding eldership makes a very capital

branch, has, under God, been a grand means of preserving the peace and union of our connection, and the purity of our ministry, and, therefore, *in its consequences*, has been *a chief instrument*, under the grace of God, of this great revival."

"SECTION VI.

" *Of the Election and Ordination of Travelling Elders, and of their Duty.*"

" We need not enlarge upon the necessity of an office, which every organized Christian church in the world, in all ages, has adopted.   We would only remark, that the restriction respecting the elders withdrawing themselves from the travelling line without the consent of the yearly conference, shows the confirmed regard our church has for *the itinerant plan*, and its determination to support it by every method in its power, consistent with justice and truth.   And no elder has a right to complain as he cannot but be previously acquainted with the conditions on which he accepts of ordination."

"SECTION VII.

" *Of the Election and Ordination of Travelling Deacons, and of their Duty.*"

" As we find from the first-quoted text (Acts vi, 1—6,) that the deacons were set apart for their office by the imposition of hands, but not by the imposition of the hands of the elders, as in other cases ; so we endeavour to come as near to the Scripture mode as we can, by confining the ceremony of the imposition of hands to the episcopacy only, in the present instance, without daring to compare ourselves, as some of our enemies would most maliciously assert, to the holy apostles ; but simply, and in the fear of God, coming up to the written word as nearly as in our power.

" This office serves as an excellent probation for that of an elder.   No preacher can be eligible to the office of an elder till he has exercised the office of a deacon for two years, except in the case of missions.   For we would wish to show the utmost attention to the order of elders, and to have the fullest proof of the abilities, grace, and usefulness of those, who shall be, from time to time, proposed for so important an office as that of a presbyter in the church of God.   And we judge, that the man who has proved himself a worthy member of our society, and a useful class-leader, exhorter, and local preacher, who has been approved of for two years as a travelling preacher on trial, and has faithfully served in the office of a travelling deacon for at least two years more—has offered such proofs of fidelity and piety, as must satisfy every reasonable mind.   But as this continent is exceedingly large, and will continually open to our conferences new missions for the spread of the gospel (perhaps for ages to come) we have, in the case of missions, given a discretionary power to the yearly conferences.   We have thus been able, through the grace and providence of God, to constitute such a regular gradation in our ministry as, we trust, will contribute highly to its purity, to the dignity of the ministerial office, and to the advantage of our people.

" We have here also made the same restriction for the preservation of our important itinerant plan, in respect to the deacons withdrawing themselves from the general work, without the consent of the yearly conference, which was made before in the case of the elders, and which has been spoken to in the notes on the former section."

" SECTION VIII.

" *Of the Method of receiving Preachers, and of their Duty.*"

" To preach almost every day, and to meet societies or classes several times in the week, and to visit the sick, not only in the towns, but as far as practicable on the plantations, is a work which requires no small degree of diligence and zeal : and no person is fit to be a travelling preacher who cannot fill up these duties incessantly all the year round, except occasional indispositions incapacitate him for a season ; or some reasonable and urgent necessity call him away for a little time."

" *Punctuality* is of vast importance in every circumstance of life.   Without it, no confidence can exist : and the want of it is productive of innumerable evils to society.   But how much stronger are these observations, when applied to our situation ! The itinerant plan, which we so much and so justly venerate, would be the most pernicious in the world, without *punctuality.* It would be almost sufficient to make mankind hate religion. The man who will disappoint a congregation through any worldly motive is highly criminal, and answerable for all the evil which his negligence has caused—answerable for all the souls which through disgust do afterward despise or neglect the ordinances of God.   When an appointment is fixed, and cannot be revoked in time, it should be considered as an engagement made to God. 'Lord,' says the psalmist, ' who shall abide in thy tabernacle, and who shall dwell in thy holy hill?—He that sweareth to his own hurt and changeth not.'   See Psalm xv. And the word of a preacher of the gospel, indeed of every Christian, should be the same as his oath, or he is not even an honest man.   Alas ! the good which the best of us do is but little, and, therefore, should not suffer any subtraction. *But when the itine-*

rant preacher frequently proves himself destitute of punctuality, his life and labours become more hurtful than profitable.   He not only prevents a faithful man from filling up the office which he himself abuses, but gives continual offence, and imperceptibly drives numbers from the ordinances of God, and thereby out of the way of salvation."

"The command given by the apostle, Heb. xiii, 17, 'Obey them that have the rule over you, and submit yourselves,' is as binding on ministers as on the people.   Among us there is no exception.   Our bishops are bound to obey and submit to the General Conference ; and the preachers are bound to obey and submit to the General Conference, and also to the yearly confer- ences, in every thing except the stationing of them for their re- spective districts and circuits ; and in this respect they are bound to obey and submit to the episcopacy.   This is the order of our church : and as the New Testament is silent as to the constitu- tions of states, so is it, in a great measure, in respect to the constitutions of churches.   It only requires obedience or submis- sion to the powers that are, without which no order could possi- bly exist.   This does not, in any degree, prevent the due reformation of the constitutions of churches, any more than of those of states.   We may add to these considerations the command of St. Peter, 1st Epis. v, 5, 'Ye younger, submit yourselves unto the elder.'

"The due examination of candidates for the ministry is of the utmost importance.   The questions proposed for this purpose, in the present section, may be drawn out and enlarged upon by the bishops, as they judge necessary ; and, if duly considered, will be found to contain in them the whole of Christian and ministerial experience and practice.   In respect to doctrines, experience, and practice, the preachers will have passed already through various examinations, before they are received into the travelling con- nection.   Let us take a view of the whole, remembering that our societies form our grand nurseries or universities for minis- ters of the gospel.

"1. On application for admission into the society, they must be duly recommended to the preacher who has the oversight of the circuit, by one in whom he can place sufficient confidence, or must have met three or four times in a class, and must be truly awakened to a sense of their fallen condition.   Then the preacher who has the oversight of the circuit gives them notes of admis- sion, and they remain on trial for six months.   2. When the six months are expired, they receive tickets, if recommended by their leader, and become full members of the society.   And to prevent any future complaint on the ground of ignorance, the rules of the society must be read to them the first time they meet in class.   3. Out of these are chosen, from time to time, *the lead- ers of classes,* who should not only be deeply experienced in divine things, but have a measure of the gift of preaching, so as to feed the flock of Christ under their care, in due season. 4. Out of these, when they discover in public prayer meetings an extraordinary gift of prayer and some gift for exhortation, are chosen *the exhorters.* 5. Out of the exhorters, who are employed in the places of least consequence, or to fill up the place of a preacher, in cases of necessity, are chosen *the local preachers.* These are first to receive a license signed by the presiding elder, and by the quarterly meeting,* which is composed of the local preachers, stewards, and leaders of the circuit. Without the consent of the presiding elder, and of the majority of this meeting, which is the most proper and respectable representation of the circuit that perhaps can possibly be devised, no one can be admitted as a local preacher. And the license above mentioned must be annually renewed, till the local preacher be admitted into the deacon's office. 6. Out of the local preachers are chosen *the travelling preachers,* of whom those in full connection form the members of our conferences. These must be on trial for two years before they can be received into full connection with the conference, their characters being examined at each conference (whether they be present or absent) in respect to morals, grace, gifts, and fruit. Nor can they be received upon trial as *travelling preachers,* till they have obtained a recommendation from the quarterly meetings of their respective circuits. The bishops indeed, and the presiding elders, have authority to call them to travel, in the intervals of the conferences, when they have received the above recommendation, otherwise the circuits would be frequently destitute of preachers. But their call to travel must afterward be confirmed by the yearly conference.

"From all that has been observed, it must be clear to every candid reader, that it is not the yearly conference *only*, or the bishops or presiding elders *only*, in the intervals of the conferences, who choose the local or travelling preachers. On the contrary, *they* have no authority to choose at all, till the people, through their leaders, stewards, &c., recommend. And those who will not be satisfied with this whole process of probation, considered in all its parts, must be rigid indeed. But we bless God for the whole of this economy, and do attribute to it, under his grace and providence, the purity of our ministry. When we consider the importance of *the gospel ministry*, this severe process is by no means excessive."

" * See the twenty-first section of this chapter."

" SECTION IX.

" *Of the Salaries of the Ministers and Preachers.*"

" Those who read this section attentively will see the impossibility of our ministers becoming rich by the gospel, except in grace. And here there is no difference between bishops, elders, deacons, or preachers, except in their travelling expenses, and consequently in the greater labours of one than the other. The gifts they have to impart are not silver and gold, but, through the divine blessing on their labours, and the operations of the Holy Spirit accompanying their word, 'love, joy, peace, long-suffering, gentleness, goodness, faith, meekness, and temperance.' And we may add, that the impossibility of our enriching ourselves by *our ministry*, is another great preservation of *its* purity. The lovers of this world will not long continue travelling preachers. Indeed, we may add, that a great many of the preachers do not receive the whole of their annual pittance ; generally, we believe, through the poverty, but sometimes perhaps through the inattention of our friends.

" The clause concerning the allowance for a preacher's wife may need some explanation. The wife is to have *the same claim* in respect to salary as the travelling preacher : so that if there be a married and a single preacher in the same circuit, and the money for the support of the ministry be not sufficient to make up all the salaries, the whole is to be divided into three parts, one part of which belongs to the wife."

" SECTION X.

" *Of the Duties of those who have the Charge of Circuits.*"

" When we consider the duties of the office described in this section, we shall feel no difficulty in allowing that it is an office of no small importance.

" 1. The person who holds it, is to watch over the other travelling preachers in his circuit, not with the eye of a severe judge but with that of a tender elder brother. He should indeed be faithful to his colleagues, and tell them all their faults : but he has no power to correct them. He is to bear an equal share with them in the toils of a travelling preacher, besides having upon him the care of all the churches in his circuit. But if his colleagues will not observe his reasonable directions, or behave grossly amiss, he must inform his presiding elder, whose duty it is, as soon as possible, to judge of and rectify every thing. He is also to use his influence with the people, that his fellow-labourers may stand in need of nothing for the simple convenience, or at least necessities of this transitory life. They want but little, and that little they ought to have.   This also implies, that if his colleague be married, he should take care that neither he nor his family stand in need of any of the necessaries of life.   For his performance of this duty, as well as all the rest, he is bounden to God, as well as to the church of which he is a member."

"2. He is to deliver tickets quarterly to each member of the society, with a portion of the word of God printed on them.   This is of no small moment for the preservation of our discipline and the purity of our church.   To admit frequently unawakened persons to our society meetings and love-feasts, would be to throw a damp on those profitable assemblies, and cramp, if not entirely destroy, *that liberty of speech*, which is always made a peculiar blessing to earnest believers and sincere seekers of salvation. Besides, this regulation affords the preacher who holds the office now under consideration an opportunity of speaking closely to every person under his care on the state of their souls."

"3. He is to watch over the stewards and leaders of his circuit. He should meet them weekly, when in the towns, and as often as may be in the country.   He is to recommend to the stewards the poor of their societies, to lay before them, if necessary, the wants of his colleagues, and to stir them up to fidelity and activity in their office : but above all, he is to exhort the leaders, to instruct them in the best mode of addressing their classes, and to set before them the inestimable value of the precious souls respectively intrusted to their care."

"4. As he is the least likely to be influenced by the various circumstances arising from neighbourhood, long acquaintance, affection, consanguinity, or any other motives distinct from official talents, he is to appoint the stewards.   And as he is, or should be the best judge of the gifts and experience of the members of society, he also is to select the men, from time to time, who are to fill up the weighty office of leader.   And again, as he is the only person in the circuit who is responsible to the yearly conference for the decline of the work of God in his circuit, and the only one the conference *can make* responsible, he has the authority invested in him of changing leaders, when they have lost the life of God, or are incapacitated for or negligent of their duty. But if he ever use this power in a capricious or tyrannical manner, the people may lay their grievances before the bishops or presiding elders, who have authority to suspend him for ill conduct ; or, before the yearly conference, which may proceed even to his expulsion, if he grossly offend against that wisdom which is from above, ' and which is first pure, then peaceable, gentle, and easy to be entreated, full of mercy and good fruits, *without partiality, and without hypocrisy*,' James iii. 17.

"5. He is also to receive members upon trial, and into society, according to the Form of Discipline.   If this authority were invested in the society, or any part of it, the great work of revival would soon be at an end.   A very remarkable proof of this was given several years ago by a society in Europe.   Many of the leading members of that society were exceedingly importunate to have the whole government of their society invested in a meeting composed of the principal preacher, and a number of lay elders and *lay deacons,* as they termed them.   At last, the preacher who had the oversight of the circuit was prevailed upon, through their incessant importunity, to comply with their request.   He accordingly nominated all the *leaders* and *stewards* as lay elders and lay deacons, with the desired powers.   But alas! what was the consequence?   The great revival which was then in that society and congregation was soon extinguished.   Poor sinners newly awakened, were flocking into the church of God as doves to their windows.   But now, the wisdom and prudence of *the new court* kept them at a distance, till they had given full proof of their repentance : ' If their convictions be sincere,' said they, ' they will not withdraw themselves from the preaching of the word on account of our caution ; they themselves will see the propriety of our conduct.'   Thus, while the fervent preacher was one hour declaring the willingness of Christ immediately to receive the returning sinners, the wisdom of the lay elders and lay deacons would the next hour reject them even from being received upon trial, unless they had been before *painted sepulchres, inwardly full of dead men's bones and rottenness.*   The preacher who had the charge of the circuit nearly broke his heart, to see the precious souls which God had given him kept at a distance from him, and thrown back again upon the wide world by *the prudent lay elders and deacons.*   However, at his earnest entreaty, he was removed into another circuit by the conference, under whose control he acted, to enjoy the blessings *of the Methodist economy.* The revival of the work of God was soon extinguished ; and the society, from being one of the most lively, became one of the most languid in Europe.

" Glory be to God, *all* our societies throughout the world, now amounting to upward of one hundred and sixty thousand, have been raised, under grace, *by our ministers and preachers.   They* and they *only,* are their spiritual fathers under God ; and none others can feel for them as *they* do.   It is true, that on great revivals, the spiritually halt, and blind, and lame, will press in crowds into the church of God ; and they are welcome to all that we can do for their invaluable souls, till they prove unfaithful to convincing or converting grace.   And we will not throw back their souls on the wicked world, while groaning under the burden of sin, because many on the trial quench their convictions or perhaps were hypocritical from the beginning.   We would sooner go again into the highways and hedges, and form new societies, as at first, than we would give up a privilege so essential to the ministerial office and to the revival of the work of God

" The master of the house [God] said to his servant, Go out quickly into the streets and lanes of the city, and *bring in hither* the poor, and the maimed, and the halt, and the blind. And the servant said, ' Lord, it is done as thou hast commanded, and yet there is room.'   He obeys his God without asking permission of any society, whether he should obey him or not.   ' And the Lord said unto the servant, Go out into the highways and hedges, and *compel them to come in,* that *my house* may be filled,' *Luke* xiv, 21–23.   The servant answers not to his God, ' I will comply with thy command as far as my society, or my leaders and stewards, will permit me.'   Again, the Lord says to Ezekiel, chap. xxxiv, 1–10, ' Son of man, prophesy against the shepherds of Israel, prophesy, and say unto them, Thus saith the Lord God unto the shepherds, Wo be to the shepherds of Israel—the diseased have ye not strengthened, neither have ye healed that which was sick, neither have ye bound up that which was broken, *neither have ye brought again that which was driven away, neither have ye sought that which was lost.*   And they were scattered, because there is no shepherd : and they became meat to all the beasts of the field, when they were scattered. Therefore, ye shepherds, hear the word of the Lord : As I live, saith the Lord God, surely because my flock became a prey, and my flock became meat to every beast of the field, because there was no shepherd, neither did my shepherd search for my flock—therefore, O ye shepherds, hear the word of the Lord, Thus saith the Lord God, Behold, I am against the shepherds, and I WILL RE-QUIRE MY FLOCK AT THEIR HAND, and cause them to cease from feeding the flock,' &c.   Now, what pastors, called and owned of God, would take upon themselves this awful responsibility, if others could refuse to their spiritual children the grand external privilege of the gospel, or admit among them the most improper persons to mix with and corrupt them ?   Truly, whatever the pastors of other churches may do, we trust that ours will never put themselves under so dreadful a bondage.   It is in vain to say, that others may be as tender and cautious as *the pastors :* for *the pastors* are the persons responsible to God, and, therefore, should by no means be thus fettered in their pastoral care. And those who are desirous to wrest out of the hands of ministers this important part of their duty, should rather go out themselves to the highways and hedges, and preach the everlasting gospel, or be contented with their present providenial situation.

" Besides, the command of our Lord, Matt. xxviii, 19, ' Go ye —and teach all nations, *baptizing* them,' &c., is addressed to *pastors only*—to his disciples, and through them to all his ministering servants to the end of the world.   But if ministers are to be the judges of the proper subjects of *baptism,* which is the grand initiatory ordinance into the visible church, how much more should they have a right to determine whom they will take under *their own* care, or whom God has given them out of the world by the preaching of his word! For ministers to spend their strength, their tears, their prayers, their lives for the salvation of souls, and to have both themselves and THEIRS under the control of those who never travailed in birth for them, and, therefore, can never feel for them as their spiritual parents do, is a burden we cannot bear. .Thus it is evident that both reason and Scripture do, in the clearest manner, make the privilege or power now under consideration essential to the gospel ministry."

" 7. Though the presiding elder is far more proper to preside at the quarterly meetings than any other who regularly attends, yet the preacher who has the oversight of the circuit is, next to him, the most likely to be impartial.* It is on this principle, that the twelve judges of England make it a rule, that no one of them shall take that circuit which includes the place where he was born. Besides, every thing is finally determined by a majority of votes. On those extraordinary occasions, therefore, when, through sickness, or any other unavoidable hinderance, the presiding elder is absent, the next to him in office must be the moderator of the meeting. See the notes on the fifth section of this chapter. Let us all be willing to submit to that due subjection which is necessary to the good order of the whole, ' yea, all of you be subject one to another,' 1 Pet. v, 5.

" 8. Next to the preaching of the gospel, the spreading of religious knowledge by the press is of the greatest moment to the people. The soul, while united to the body, must be daily fed with pious ideas, otherwise it will lose ground in the divine life. Though the Lord is wonderfully kind to those of his children who are so unfortunate as not to be able to read, yet we are to use all the means in our power. And though the Bible be infinitely preferable to all other books, yet we are, even on that very account, to study the writings of those spiritual and great divines. who have by their comments, essays, sermons, or other labours. explained the Bible : otherwise, we ought not to attend the preaching of the gospel ; for what is *that* but an explanation and application of the great truths contained in the Bible. He, therefore, who has the charge of the circuit, is to be diligent in the sale of those books, which, according to the judgment of our conferences and bishops, are deemed profitable for the souls of our people. St. Paul had need of books, otherwise he would no

---

" * We do not mean that he is likely to have more grace or more integrity than the other members of the quarterly meeting, but only that he is not so much exposed to the temptations of *prejudging* a cause through consanguinity, affection, or a variety of other interests, as the other members are. We have a high esteem for all our official members, and would not intentionally offend them on any account."

have carried them with him in his extensive travels. 'The cloak that I left at Troas with Carpus, when thou comest, bring with thee, *and the books,* but especially *the parchments,*'* 2 Tim. iv, 13. And to minds which are influenced by the love of God and man, the consideration that the profit of these books is wholly applied to the work of God, will be a further inducement to them to purchase our books.

" 9. It is necessary that the yearly conference should have an exact account of the numbers in society, and of every thing material relating to each circuit under its control, otherwise it could not possibly judge of the progress of the work, and the fidelity of the preachers; nor could the episcopacy have otherwise such complete knowledge of every thing for the stationing of the preachers. 'Let all things be done,' says St. Paul, ' decently, and in order.'

" 10. It is also necessary, that the presiding elder should receive regular details of the proceedings of those who have the oversight of circuits, that he himself may have such a clear knowledge of the state of the district, as may enable him to fill up his important trust, and to give such information of his district to the bishops, as may afford them a complete view of the whole. Thus are many eyes opened upon the great work, and the wisdom of many united for the good of the whole. ' In the multitude of counsellors,' says the wise man, ' there is safety.'

" 11. The people of our special charge want all the advice we can give them: and their stations and circumstances are so different, that the rule of meeting the men and women apart, and, when the society is large, and the time will admit of it, the married and single men apart, and the married and single women apart, has been attended with many blessings. Mr. Wesley, from happy experience, considered this as a very profitable means of grace. Ministers of the gospel should think no labour lost, or means in vain, by which they may be enabled to give their whole flock their due spiritual portion. ' The Lord said, Who then is that faithful and wise steward, whom his Lord shall make ruler over his household, to give them their portion of meat in due season? Blessed is that servant, whom his lord, when he cometh, shall find so doing. Of a truth I say unto you, that he will make him ruler over all that he hath.' Luke xii, 42—44.

" 12. As the public money should be applied with the greatest fidelity, the accounts should be examined with the strictest scrutiny: and, therefore, the preacher who has the charge of the circuit is to examine the stewards' accounts, as a preparative to their being laid before the quarterly meeting; and this not out of disrespect to the stewards, whom we highly esteem for their dis-

---

" * That is, the books written on parchment, the art of printing not being known in those days."

interested labours of love, but to prevent, as far as possible, evei any plausible pretence for suspicion. ' It is required in stewards, says the apostle, 'that a man be found faithful.' No per son of integrity (and such we have reason to believe all ou stewards are, without exception) will object to this rule."

" 7. We are but one body of people, one grand society, whethe in Europe or America ; united in the closest spiritual bonds, an in external bonds as far as the circumstances of things will admit And as our numbers have increased exceedingly both in Europ and America, it is necessary we should be particularly cautiou in receiving strangers into our society, under the pretext of thei having been members in other places ; as the one end of ou whole plan is *to raise a holy people.* On this account, all ou conferences throughout the world mutually require that ever member of our society who changes his place of abode, shal previously obtain a certificate from the preacher who has th charge of his circuit, who is most likely to be acquainted witl his character, his own relations excepted : and that without sucl certificate he shall not be received into any other society."

" 11. The authority of appointing prayer meetings will not, w think, be disputed by any. Many of our greatest revivals hav been begun and chiefly carried on in our prayer meetings. W wish that the utmost zeal might be manifested by those who hav the charge of circuits in the execution of this direction. Th sacred writer, describing the effects of the day of Pentecost, ob serves, ' Then they that gladly received his word were baptized and the same day there were added unto them about *three thou sand souls.* And *they* continued steadfastly in the apotles' doc trine and fellowship, and in breaking of bread, and *in prayers.* Acts ii, 41, 42. There is no doubt but those words refer to *so cial* worship. O that every family in our connection had occa sionally a prayer meeting at stated times for the benefit of thei neighbours! There would be no danger of wanting persons t pray : God would pour forth the spirit of grace and supplication and soon the flame of divine love would glow through ever civilized part of this vast continent. The Lord hasten the day

" 12. Public fasts are to be appointed by him at the regula times, and he is of course to take care, that himself and hi helpers not only set the example, but also render those day peculiarly profitable by public meetings for the service of God.'

" 13. The whole organization of our church depends on an exac attention to all its distinctions and orders.——It has been, we doub not, the close order and organization of our church, under th grace and providence of God, which has enabled us to resist al the shocks we have lately felt from the fanatical spirit of division and to remain firm as a rock.

" We may just add, that it is customary for the presiding elders or in their absence the preachers who have the charge of circuits o hold quarterly, or half-yearly conferences with the local preachers and exhorters respectively under their care, to examine into their grace, gifts, and usefulness, and into the state of he work of God—a custom of exceeding great utility, and therefore, such as we trust will never be neglected."

" SECTION XI.

'Of the Trial of those who think they are moved by the Holy Ghost to preach."

"We have enlarged on the present subject in our notes on he eighth section of this chapter. Every reader may from hence perceive the care we take in receiving our preachers and ministers. As the presiding elders, or those who have the charge of circuits, are attentive to the examination of the local preachers and exhorters, so the yearly conferences are attentive to the gifts, grace, and usefulness of all the travelling preachers and ministers. Nothing will do for us without *the life of God.* Brilliant parts, fine address, &c., are to us but tinkling cymbals, when destitute of the power of the Holy Ghost.

"At the same time we are far from despising *talents* which may be rendered useful to the church of Christ. We know the worth of improved abilities : and nothing can equal our itinerant plan, in the opportunity it affords of suiting our various societies with men of God who are endued with gifts agreeable to their respective wants."

" SECTION XII.

" *Of the Matter and Manner of Preaching, and of other public Exercises.*"

"The preaching of the gospel is of the first importance to the welfare of mankind ; and, consequently, *the mode* of preaching must be of considerable moment. It is not the fine metaphysical reasoning ; it is not the philosophical disquisitions of the works of nature under the pretext of raising up our minds to the great Creator, which regenerate the heart, and stamp the image of God upon the soul. No. The preacher must,

"1. Convince the sinner of his dangerous condition. He must 'break up the fallow ground,' Jer. iv, 3 ; Hos. x, 12 'Cry aloud, spare not,' says the Lord to his prophet, 'lift up thy voice like a trumpet, and show my people their transgression, and the house of Jacob their sins,' Isa. lviii, 1. He must set forth the depth of original sin, and show the sinner how far he is gone from original righteousness ; he must describe the ...es of the world in their just and most striking colours, and ...r into all the sinner's pleas and excuses for sin, and drive

him from all his subterfuges and strong-holds.   He must labou
to convince the formalist of the impossibility of being justifie
before God by his ceremonial or moral righteousness.   Myriad
are continually perishing, yea, thousands of those who acknow
ledge in speculation the great truths of the gospel, through thei
dependence upon ordinances or upon an outwardly moral life
'In Christ Jesus neither circumcision availeth any thing, no
uncircumcision, but *a new creature*,' Gal. vi, 15.

"2. He must set forth the virtue of the *atoning blood*.   H
must bring the mourner to a *present* Saviour ; he must shov
the willingness of Christ *this moment* to bless him, and bring
present salvation *home* to his soul.   Here he must be indeed
son of consolation.   He must say nothing which can keep th
trembling mourner at a distance ; he must not provide for him
rich feast, and hand it up to him in dishes too hot to be touched
There must be nothing now held forth to the view of the peni
tent but the everlasting arms, and the mercy which is ready t
embrace him on every side.   'Come unto me,' says our Lord
'all ye that labour and are heavy laden, and I will give yo
rest,' Matt. xi, 28.   'Him that cometh to me, I will in n
wise cast out,' John vi, 37.   'Having, therefore, brethren
boldness to enter into the holiest by the blood of Jesus,—let u
draw near with a true heart, in full assurance of faith,' &c.
Heb. x, 19–22.

"3. He must, like a true shepherd, feed the lambs and shee
of Christ.   He must point out to the newly justified the wile
of Satan, and strengthen them if they stagger through unbelief
He must set before them the glorious privileges offered to then
in the gospel.   He must nourish them with the pure milk of th
word.   Those who are more adult in grace, he must feed wit
strong meat.   He must show them the necessity of being cruci
fied to the world, and of dying daily ; that 'if they mortify no
the deeds of the flesh, they shall die.'   He must not spare th
remaining man of sin ; he must anatomize the human heart
and follow self-will and self-love through all their windings
And all this being addressed to the children of God, he mus
do it with great tenderness.   'I protest by your rejoicin
which I have in Christ Jesus our Lord, *I die daily*,' says th
apostle. 1 Cor. xv, 31.   'If ye live after the flesh ye shal
die : but if ye, through the Spirit, do mortify the deeds o
the body, ye shall live,' Rom. viii, 13.   '*Grow in grace*, an
in the knowledge of our Lord and Saviour Jesus Christ,
2 Pet. iii, 18.

"And now he must again turn the son of consolation.   H
must hold forth Christ as an all-sufficient Saviour, as 'able t
save them to the uttermost that come unto God by him, seein
he ever liveth to make intercession for them,' Heb. vii, 25
He must describe to them, in all its richest views, the blessin

of perfect love.   He must now declare how our great Zerubbabel is *this moment* able and willing to reduce the mountain into a plain.   And all the above he must endeavour more or less to introduce into every sermon which he delivers to a mixed congregation.   'The very God of peace sanctify you wholly, and I pray God your whole spirit, soul, and body be preserved blameless unto the coming of our Lord Jesus Christ. Faithful is he that calleth you, who also *will do it*,' 1 Thess. v, 23.   'This is the will of God, even your sanctification,' 1 Thess. iv, 3.

"He must preach the law as well as the gospel.   He must hold forth our adorable Redeemer as a Prophet to teach, a Priest to atone, and a King to reign in us and over us.   He must break the *stony* heart, as well as bind up the *broken.*   But still *holiness*, inward and outward, must be his end : *holiness* must be his aim : and Antinomianism, and every doctrine which opposes *holiness*, he must contend with, till he gain the victory, or render his hearers utterly inexcusable.   Who is fit for these things ?   O Lord God, help us all !   Let us do our utmost, and leave the blessing to the Lord.

"Acts iii, 22, 'A *Prophet* shall the Lord your God raise up unto you of your brethren.'   Heb. v, 6, 'Thou art *a Priest* for ever.'   Isa. xxxii, 1, 'Behold *a King* shall reign in righteousness.'   O let us never be wearied of exalting Christ, as *living in us*, as well as *dying for us.*

"Some useful smaller advices are now given :

"1.   Never break an engagement.   This we have enlarged upon under the eighth section of this chapter.

"2.   The second advice belongs only to town congregations, where they have clocks and watches to direct them.   In such cases, if they attend not exactly at the appointed time, they will be equally tardy, if the preacher *habitually* wait for them ever so long.   But everywhere let *him* be always at the time.   It is inexcusable *in one* to make a thousand, or even a hundred, wait *for him.*   Let 'no man put a stumbling block, or an occasion to fall, in his brother's way,' Rom. xiv, 13.

"3.   The deepest seriousness at all times becomes the minister of the gospel : but in the pulpit there should not be even *the appearance* of a deviation from it.   An ambassador of an earthly government, when immediately engaged in the duties of his embassy, would be far from trifling : how much more should an ambassador of God ?   'Do the work,' therefore, 'of an *evangelist*, make *full proof* of thy ministry,' 2 Tim. iv, 5.

"4.   A preacher who seeks the honour which comes from God, and not that which comes from man, will consider the spiritual wants of his audience, and choose his text and subject accordingly.   He will not preach to show his own abilities, but merely *to do good.*   And, indeed, if he preach not from *this pure motive alone*, he has no right to expect the blessing of God upon his labours.   See Luke xii, 42–44.

"5. Be cautious of allegorizing.   It seldom informs the judgment, and still seldomer warms the heart.   It may be called a *pretty way* of talking.   The preacher may be admired but the hearer will be little edified.   And what is applause, or any thing but the salvation of souls, to the faithful minister of Christ?   The genuine language of his heart is, ' I ask not riches, honours, or pleasures, gain or applause ; I ask only for the salvation of souls !'   ' And I, brethren, when I came to you, came not with excellency of speech, or of wisdom, declaring unto you the testimony of God.   For I determined not to know any thing among you, save Jesus Christ and him crucified.' 1 Cor. ii, 1, 2.

"6. When the preacher has fixed upon the subject which he judges most suitable to the states of the souls he is going to address, he must keep to his point.   He must labour to arrange his ideas, and to speak to the understanding as well as the heart.   He must first endeavour fully to explain, and then to apply, to ' show' himself ' a workman that needeth not to be ashamed, rightly dividing the word of truth,' 2 Tim. ii, 15.

"7. He must take care that his good be not evil spoken of, or laughed at, if possible, through any awkward or unmeaning gestures in the pulpit.   When the instruction of immortal spirits is his employment, he should mind every thing, little and great, which can assist him in this glorious work, in which angels would envy him, if it were possible for them to indulge so base a passion.   ' These things speak and exhort, and rebuke with all authority.   Let no man despise thee.' Tit. ii, 15.

"8. Be not too forward in writing for the press.   Nothing disgraces a cause so much as to attempt to defend it in a feeble manner.   Let not a few friends who are attached to you, and are not in the least degree judges of composition, prevail upon you to become an author.   To write well requires a life devoted in a great measure to close and severe study.   Preaching the everlasting gospel and spiritual instruction, in season and out of season, are your grand objects.   There are so many excellent publications already in the world, which by the means of the press may be put into every hand, that there are fewer necessary to be written than many imagine.   A few good writers in one church are quite sufficient, especially in ours, which has already been honoured with a Wesley and a Fletcher. But particularly comply with our express rules on this subject. ' Of making many books there is no end,' says the wise man. Eccles. xii, 12.

"9. Scarcely any thing tends to damp divine service more than to be praying too long, and in a languid manner.   Few

14

things more tend to bring a congregation into a *formal* spirit. Sometimes, indeed, the minister is led within the veil in an unusual way, and may then justly give full vent to the holy flame. But on other occasions let the prayer be very fervent, and of a moderate length. 'When ye pray,' says our Lord, 'use not vain repetitions, as the heathen do: for they think that they shall be heard for their much speaking. Be not ye therefore like unto them.' Matt. vi, 7, 8.

"10. A comment on a portion of Scripture is sometimes very profitable to the congregation, especially when a warm application is adjoined. And it is exceedingly useful for young preachers to habituate themselves to the giving of warm exhortations, otherwise they may get into a formal way of preaching without a due application of the subject. *A fervent exhortation* is preferable to *a sermon without application.* 'Till I come,' says St. Paul to Timothy, 'give attendance to reading, *to exhortation*, to doctrine,' 1 Tim. iv, 13.

"11. Souls are of so much value that we should improve every opportunity for their good. Shall the men of the world have carnal festivals on their birth-days, and shall we not commemorate the birth-day of our Lord? The primitive fathers of the church observed *the day*, which is *now* kept sacred by most of the churches of Christendom. Irenæus, who was one of the fathers, was a disciple of St. John; and the mother of Jesus lived with *that apostle* from the crucifixion of our Lord. There cannot, therefore, be a doubt but St. John knew, and, of course, his disciples, Irenæus, Ignatius, and Polycarp, the day of our Lord's nativity; and *from them* all the fathers of the church. Again, shall states and nations celebrate the day of liberation from slavery or oppression, or some other glorious event, from year to year? And shall *we* not celebrate by a holy festival the crucifixion and resurrection of our Lord, and the mission of the Holy Spirit, to which we are indebted for blessings infinitely more valuable than any which the revolution of states can possibly afford?"

"SECTION XIII.

"Of the Duty of Preachers to God, themselves, and one another."

"1. A minister of the gospel, who has consecrated all he is and has, and all he can do and suffer, to the service of his God, should consider himself as eminently called *to walk with God.* His peculiar calling is of the most public nature. It is a public profession, that he is a reformer of mankind: it says more ~~dly~~ than any words, 'I am, or ought to be, one of the best men; follow me as I follow Christ.' It is the very depth of ~~ocrisy~~ to preach and not live the gospel. Of all hypocrites such a one is the greatest. Nay, it is in vain to preach, it is in vain to show forth the most shining talents, if the life of the preacher correspond not with his doctrines. He may possibly have the reward he seeks for here below : but the approbation of God he never will receive. 'Many will say to me in that day,' observes our Lord, ' Lord, Lord, have we not prophesied in thy name ? and in thy name have cast out devils, and in thy name done many wonderful works ? And then will I profess unto them, I never knew you : depart from me, ye that work iniquity.' Matt. vii, 22, 23.

" The work of God must also lie near his heart : yea, his very soul must enter into it. Nor must he be contented to preach, and then leave the souls he has been blessed to at the mercy of the world. He must seek out the awakened. He must fence in the flock. He must not only love, but, according to his sphere of action, recommend and enforce Christian discipline, especially the discipline of that church of which he is a member ; without which there would be nothing but anarchy and confusion ; and the word of God would in general become like water spilt upon the ground.' ' Neither count I my life dear unto myself,' says St. Paul, ' so that I might finish my course with joy, and the ministry which I have received of the Lord Jesus, to testify the gospel of the grace of God,' Acts xx, 24.

" 2. The preachers should tell each other in the spirit of love and meekness, and, at the same time, with humble boldness, all they think and all they fear of each other, in respect to every thing of consequence, particularly in regard to the spiritual life, the practice of devotion, and spiritual conversation. Faithful are the wounds of a friend,' says Solomon. Prov. xxvii, 6.

" 3. Ministers of the gospel should be eminently attentive to all the means of grace, particularly private prayer. We do rejoice that *our* ministers are examples to the flock in this respect. When in the mountains and wildernesses they have no chamber to themselves, they will retire into the woods and other solitary places, and spend much of their time in that most useful exercise. O that we may continue to preserve this spirit and practice ! ' Thou, when thou prayest,' says Christ, ' enter into thy closet : and, when thou hast shut thy door, pray to thy Father which is in secret ; and thy Father which seeth in secret, shall reward thee openly,' Matt. vi, 6. We should also in the families, where we from time to time reside, be examples to all. The whole world is composed of families. A travelling preacher may bring as many souls to glory by his fidelity in the families which he visits as by his public preaching. See the fifteenth section of this chapter.

" 4. Preachers of the gospel should be much conversant in

e Scriptures. They should never be without a Bible. That valuable book is like the starry heavens on a clear night: ist your eyes on any given part, and some bright stars will imediately strike your sight; but the more you gaze, the more ars will appear to your view. It is an inexhaustible mine of e richest treasures. The more infidels despise and oppose , the more should we love, study, and defend it. It is reproach-l to see a minister of God *lounging away* his time, when the ord of truth and salvation is within his reach."

Rules by which we should continue, or desist from, preaching at any Place."

In the notes to this section we find the following mention of a iage no longer known :—

" The stationing of the preachers is in the episcopacy, but *ie determination of the number of preachers to be sent to a cir-uit is in the yearly conference:* with powers invested in the ›iscopacy and presiding eldership to meet the openings of grace id providence in the intervals of the conference."

Of visiting from House to House, guarding against those Sins that are so common to Professors, and enforcing prac-tical Religion."

"In the plantations, which make the chief part of these ates, and in which, of course, the chief part of our societies ›side, the preachers cannot visit many of our competent families ι a day. But they may almost daily visit many of the poor— ιany of those who most want their help. Various disagreeable ιrcumstances, arising from the inattention of *the poor* to clean-ness, &c., may attend our zealous observance of the directions iven in this section on the present subject, as far as it respects ιem. But where is our zeal for God, where our crucifixion to ιe world, where our regard for souls, if such considerations ιove us in the least? Our Lord gives it as one grand proof of ιs being the Messiah, that ' the poor have the gospel preached ι them,' Matt. xi, 5. O then, if we love Christ, if we wish to ι his ministers and disciples, let us not forget the poor! We ave but little silver or gold to offer them; but we have what is ιfinitely more precious, even grace, pardon, holiness, Christ, eaven. Let us, therefore, labour *at least* as much in the ouses of the poor as of the rich or competent: and *this we* ·ainly shall, if we be not interested by carnal or tempora! ves—if we breathe the true spirit of missionaries."

" *Of the Instruction of Children.*"

" The proper education of children is of exceeding great moment to the welfare of mankind. About one half of the human race are under the age of sixteen, and may be considered, the infants excepted, as capable of instruction. The welfare of the states and countries in which they live, and, what is infinitely more, the salvation of their souls, do, under the grace and providence of God, depend in a considerable degree upon their education. But, alas! the great difficulty lies in finding men and women of genuine piety as instructers. Let us, however, endeavour to supply these *spiritual* defects. Let us follow the directions of this section, and we shall meet many on the day of judgment, who will acknowledge before the great Judge, and an assembled universe, that their first desires after Christ and salvation were received in their younger years by our instrumentality. In towns we may, without difficulty, meet the children weekly, and in the plantations advise and pray with them every time we visit their houses : nay, in the country, if we give notice that at such a time we shall spend an hour or two in such a house with those children who shall attend, many of the neighbours will esteem it a privilege to send their children to us at the time appointed. But we must exercise much patience, as well as zeal, for the successful accomplishment of this work. And if we can with love and delight condescend to their ignorance and childishness, and yet endeavour continually to raise up their little minds to the once dying but now exalted Saviour, we shall be made a blessing to thousands of them.

" But let us labour *among the poor* in this respect, as well as among the competent. O if our people in the cities, towns, and villages were but sufficiently sensible of the magnitude of this duty, and its acceptableness to God—if they would establish sabbath schools, wherever practicable, for the benefit of the children *of the poor*, and sacrifice a few public ordinances every Lord's day to this charitable and useful exercise, God would be to them instead of all the means they lose ; yea, they would find, to their present comfort and the increase of their eternal glory, the truth and sweetness of those words, ' Mercy is better than sacrifice,' Matt. ix, 13 ; xii, 7 ; Hos. vi, 6. But there is so much of the cross in all this ! O when shall we be the true followers of a crucified Saviour !"

" SECTION XVII.

" *Of employing our Time profitably, &c.*"

" We have already enlarged so much on the public and private
duties of ministers, that on the limited plan and laconic mode we
have adopted in these annotations, it may not be necessary to
say much more on this subject. We would just recommend to
our ministers and preachers, agreeably to the directions given in
this section, *much reading and study*. We have various ranks
of men to deal with, and as far as possible should be prepared for
them all ; that as scribes instructed unto the kingdom of heaven,
we may, like unto a man that is a householder, bring forth out
of our treasures things new and old. See Matt. xiii, 52. A taste
or reading profitable books is an inestimable gift. It adds to the
comfort of life far beyond what many conceive, and qualifies us,
if properly directed, for very extensive usefulness in the church
of God. It takes off all the miserable listlessness of a sluggish
life ; and gives to the mind a strength and activity it could not
otherwise acquire. But to obtain and preserve this taste for, this
delight in, profitable reading, we must daily resist the natural
tendency of man to indolence and idleness. And when we consider the astonishing activity of the enemies of revealed truth, to
disseminate their pernicious doctrines, we must allow that it be-
hooves every minister of Jesus Christ, not only to be able to
give an answer to every man that asketh him a reason of the
hope that is in him, with meekness and fear,' (1 Pet. iii, 15,)
but to answer and silence the most subtle arguments of the pro-
fessed enemies of our adorable Lord. ' Till I come,' says St.
Paul, ' GIVE ATTENDANCE TO READING,' 1 Tim. iv, 13. Heb.
i, 11, 12, ' We desire—that ye be not slothful.' See also
Ephes. v, 16 ; Col. iv, 5 ; 2 Tim. ii, 15, and iv, 13.' "

" SECTION XIX.

Of the Method by which immoral Travelling Ministers or Preachers shall be brought to Trial, &c."

" The section now under consideration is of very great moment. Let us take a view of it under the three heads into which
it divides itself.
" 1. The answer to the first question serves to remove every
reasonable objection to the *suspending* power of the presiding elder. See section fifth of this chapter. The trial of a minister or preacher for gross immorality shall be in the presence of
at least three ministers. These ministers have, of course, full
liberty to speak their sentiments either in favour or disfavour of

the person accused. This must always serve as a strong check on the presiding elder, respecting the abuse of his power. An act of tyranny would be so opposed by the ministers present, and so represented afterward in favour of the oppressed, that the presiding elder who would venture upon an arbitrary step would find himself dreadfully embarrassed. Besides, those ministers could lay the whole affair before the General Conference, if near at hand ; or before the ensuing yearly conference ; or, as soon as possible, before a bishop : in which cases, the injured person might have complete redress, and the presiding elder censured or punished according to his deserts : and those ministers could give all possible information, having been present at the whole of the trial.

" The passage in St. Matthew, ch. xviii, 15–17, ' If thy brother shall trespass against thee, go and tell him his fault between thee and him alone,' &c., has nothing to do with the present subject. We are now speaking of *gross* immoralities committed by preachers of the gospel. This does not concern the *trespass* of a private person, but the *gross offence* of a minister against the church of God. Undoubtedly, a minister *so* offending should not be suffered to remain in his office till the next yearly conference, as *many* souls might be ruined thereby in the interval. There is certainly as much mercy due to the people as to the minister ; and in the present instance more, as he is but one, and they are many ; and he is invested with his office, not for their *destruction*, but for their *edification.* See 2 Cor. x, 8, and xiii, 10. But scarcely any thing can be more destructive to the cause of God than the immoral life of a minister. *Such* an Achan in the camp must, more or less, bring down a curse upon the cause. 1 Sam. ii, 27–59, ' There came a man of God unto Eli, and said unto him, Thus saith the Lord,—Wherefore kick ye at my sacrifice and at mine offering, which I have commanded in my habitation ; *and honourest thy sons above me,*' &c. 2 Sam. xi, 12, ' Now the sons of Eli were sons of Belial ; they knew not the Lord.' 2 Sam. iii, 11–14, ' The Lord said to Samuel, Behold I will do a thing in Israel, at which both the ears of every one that heareth it shall tingle. In that day I will perform against Eli all things which I have spoken concerning his house : when I begin, I will also make an end. For I have told him, that I will judge his house for ever, for the iniquity *which he knoweth ; because his sons made themselves vile, and he restrained them not,* &c. See that whole history. Matt. vii, 22, 23, ' Many will say to me in that day, Lord, Lord, have we not prophesied in thy name ? and in thy name have cast out devils ? and in thy name done many wonderful works ? And then will I profess unto them, I never knew you : depart from me, *ye that work iniquity.*' Rom. ii, 3, ' Thinkest thou this, O man, that judgest them which do such things, and *doest the same*, that thou shalt escape the judgment of God!' 1 Tim. v, 19, 'Against an elder receive not an accusation, but *before two or three witnesses.*'

"2. The mode of process directed in the answer to the second question, is nearly according to our Lord's directions, concerning the offences of the private members of a church, in Matt. xviii, 15–17, 'If thy brother shall trespass against thee, go and tell him his fault between thee and him alone : if he shall hear thee, thou hast gained thy brother.   But if he will not hear thee, then take with thee one or two more, that in the mouth of two or three witnesses every word may be established.   And if he shall neglect to hear them, tell it unto the church : but if he neglect to hear the church, let him be unto thee as a heathen man and a publican.'   First the preacher is to be reproved by his senior in office.   On a second offence, the minister reprehend-ing, is to take with him one, two, or three witnesses : and if still incurable, the offender is to be brought before that part of the church to which he is particularly responsible, namely, the yearly conference.   He is not to be tried by the members of his circuit or district, for *they* are the complainants—the persons sup-posed to be aggrieved—but by his elders and equals.   There is, however, a considerable difference between the persons con-cerned in the directions given by our Lord in the portion of Scripture quoted above, and those who are adverted to in the present section.   *That scripture* evidently refers to the private members of a church ; and *the minister himself*, after private re-proof and public reprehension, first before two or three witnesses, and then before the church, is to exclude the person, if impeni-tent.   But of this we shall treat largely, when we come to con-sider the eighth section of the second chapter.   *Improper tempers*, manifested in the conversation or conduct of a minister of the gospel, may be productive of more evil than all his public labours can possibly compensate.   But, at the same time, he may not be so criminal, but that he may be borne with for a time, in hope of reformation.

"N. B. The reason why the expression, *one, two, or three witnesses* is mentioned in the section under this head, is, because it may, in some instances, be impossible to have more than *one* besides the reprehending minister, without sending to a neigh-bouring circuit ; and as no public censure can pass upon the offending preacher in this case till the sitting of the yearly con-ference, it would not be proper to take a minister of the gospel from his labours in another circuit, for two or three days, to an-swer the present purpose.

"' The servant of the Lord,' says St. Paul, ' must not strive ; but be gentle unto all men, apt to teach, patient ; in meekness instructing those that oppose themselves,' 2 Tim. ii, 24, 25. ' He [Christ] turned, and rebuked them, and said, Ye know not what manner of spirit ye are of,' Luke ix, 55.

" 3. It will, we believe, be allowed by all who love the truth as it is in Jesus, that the heretical doctrines are as dangerous, at least to the hearers, as the immoral life of a preacher; and, therefore, the same process is provided for both cases.   Those mus indeed be blind, who can sit for any time under the ministry of an Arian, Socinian, Universalian, or any other heretical minister ' and if the blind lead the blind, both shall fall into the ditch, Matt. xv, 14, and Luke vi, 39.   But as we would guard agains a hasty and arbitrary measure in a matter which sometimes perhaps, it may be difficult to determine, the case alluded to a present shall lie over to the yearly conference, if the preache: be perfectly silent, in public and private, on the subjects objectec to.   But if he will go on to dishonour Christ, or to oppose th(doctrines of holiness, or to introduce novel sentiments or ' vaii jangling,' (1 Tim. i, 6,) to draw our people from *the one thin[* *needful*,—CHRIST DYING FOR AND LIVING IN US,—an immediat(stop must be put to such dangerous, such pernicious proceedings " Matt. vii, 15, 16, ' Beware of false prophets, which come t(you in sheep's clothing, but inwardly they are ravening wolves. Tit. iii, 10, 11, ' A man that is a heretic, after the first anc second admonition, reject;' (here the authority of *judging* anc *rejecting* is invested in Timothy ;) ' knowing that he that is such is subverted, and sinneth, being condemned of himself.'   2 Pet. ii, 1–3, ' But there were false prophets also among the people, even as there shall be false teachers among you, who privily shall bring in damnable heresies, even denying the Lord that bought them, and bring upon themselves swift destruction.   And many shall follow their pernicious ways ; by reason of whom the way of truth shall be evil spoken of.   And through covetousness shall they, with feigned words, make merchandise of you : whose judgment now of a long time lingereth not, and their damnation slumbereth not.'   Rev. ii, 2, ' I know thy works, and thy labour, and thy patience, and how thou canst not bear them which are evil : and *thou* hast tried them which say they are apostles, and are not, and hast found them liars.'   Rev. ii, 20, ' Notwith-standing I have a few things against thee, because *thou* [the angel of the church in Thyatira] sufferest that woman, Jezebel, which calleth herself a prophetess, to teach and to seduce my servants to commit fornication, and to eat things sacrificed unto idols.'

" Before we conclude our notes on this section, we must entreat our reader to notice, not only here, but throughout the whole of our economy, *the appeals* which are allowed upon all occasions, as far as the nature and circumstances of things will possibly allow of them, without making our economy intricate and bur-densome.''

14*

" SECTION XXI.

" *Of the Local Preachers.*"

" By this mode of trial we are desirous of showing the most tender regard toward our local brethren. We are all but men. The best of us may fall into sin, or be drawn into dangerous and pernicious errors; and it is sometimes necessary to stop the plague by an immediate stroke of discipline. But we would not have so important a character as that of one of our local brethren even touched to its disadvantage by only one preacher, who possibly might be younger than the accused. We have, therefore, provided that a small meeting of respectable persons shall be held, before a single step be taken in the business. The trial will then come before the most weighty assembly in the circuit.

" We have directed the yearly conference, upon an appeal, to determine upon the merits of the cause from the memorial of the quarterly meeting, on account of the difficulty, if not impossibility, of bringing the necessary witnesses, perhaps thirty, fifty, or a hundred miles from their home : nor have we any right or authority to lay such a burden on any of our people. In short, we have done the best we can, according to the nature of the circumstances in which we are placed."

" SECTION XXII.

" *Of Baptism.*"

We need only observe here, that we are conscious that *sprinkling, pouring,* and *immersing* have been practised by different churches, in each of which the pure gospel was preached, and the life of God, more or less, experienced ; and that all these modes are, more or less, acceptable to God, when administered with sincerity. At the same time, we know well, that as much or more may be said in favour of *sprinkling* than of immersion, from the account given us in Scripture of the baptism of *John himself :* and the primitive churches *in general,* we believe, favoured the practice of *sprinkling.* However, we would meet the tender mind, and *in matters unessential* condescend, as far as we conscientiously can, to the feelings and sentiments of all."

" As we have before observed, our aim is to save souls, and not to enrich ourselves : therefore, Mr. Wesley and our General Conference placed *our whole economy* as far distant as possible from *that* of a lucrative ministry. We are determined not to sell the ordinances of God : in this no man shall make our glorying void. Matt. x, 8, 'Freely ye have received,' says, our Lord, 'freely give.' 1 Cor. ix, 11–18, 'If we have sown unto you spiritual things, is it a great thing if we shall reap your carnal things? If others be partakers of this power over you, are not we rather? Nevertheless, *we have not used this power;* but' suffer all things lest we should hinder the gospel of Christ.—I have used *none of these things;* neither have I written these things that it should be so done unto me ; for it were better for me to die than that any man should make my glorying void.' "

" SECTION XXIII.

" *Of the Lord's Supper.*"

" As the Scripture is silent about the posture of the communicants, we prefer *the most humble,* whatever our Saviour might have permitted when he instituted the sacred ordinance. Besides, as we always receive the elements *in prayer,* we for that reason also prefer the kneeling posture. We must also observe, that our elders should be very cautious how they admit to the communion persons who are not in our society. It would be highly injurious to *our brethren,* if we suffered any to partake of the Lord's supper with them, whom we would not readily admit into our society on application made to us. Those whom we judge unfit to partake of our profitable, *prudential* means of grace, we should most certainly think improper to be partakers of an ordinance which has been expressly instituted by Christ himself."

" SECTION XXIV.

" *Of Public Worship.*"

" Our church insists on the reading of the Scriptures in the congregation, and gives directions accordingly. This is of the utmost consequence, and we trust will be most sacredly observed by all our ministers and preachers. A peculiar blessing accompanies the public reading as well as preaching the word of God to attentive, believing souls. And in these days of infidelity nothing should be omitted which may lead the people to the love of the Holy Bible.

" The meeting of the society also, wherever practicable, is of considerable moment. There are various weighty subjects, peculiarly suitable to religious societies, which cannot be so well enlarged upon to a mixed congregation. Brotherly union and fellowship, Christian discipline in all its branches, and various other particulars may be enlarged upon and enforced with great propriety and success on such occasions. At these times also we may enter more minutely into the different parts of the relative

nties, than we can to unawakened souls, whose whole life is
n, and who are at the best only ' like unto whited sepulchres,
hich indeed appear beautiful outward, but are within full of
sad men's bones, and of all uncleanness.' "

" SECTION XXV.

" *Of the Spirit and Truth of Singing.*"

" The singing of psalms, and hymns, and spiritual songs, in the
ongregation, has been allowed by all the churches of God in all
ges (one modern society excepted) to be a part of divine wor-
aip ; and, *from its very nature*, it evidently belongs to the *whole*
ongregation.   It would be unseemly for the minister *alone* to
ng : but if this be the duty of *one* member of the congregation,
must be the duty of all who have voices for singing ; and there
re very few who may not join in the *tenor* part, all the defects
f their voices being swallowed up in the general sound.   Few
iings can be more pleasing to the Lord than a congregation
ith one heart and one voice, praising his holy name.   It is in-
eed to be feared, that there is seldom a large congregation,
here *every* individual is *sincere*.   However, all who do in sin-
erity desire a blessing, should strive to join in the general cho-
is—we mean, in every part of the hymn.   If one part of it be
bove the experience of the singer, he should adjoin a silent
rayer, that the Lord may give him the grace he needs ; for the
ord listens to hear what the heart speaks, and takes all as no-
iing, if the heart be silent.   Again, when his experience rises
bove the hymn, his secret prayer should be in behalf of that
art of the congregation which it suits : but in the *proper* hymns
f praise he may throw off all reserve, for we are *all* infinitely
idebted to our good God.   From these remarks we surely must
e sensible of the necessity of confining ourselves to *simple* tunes,
s the *fugue-tunes* have an unavoidable tendency to confine *to a
ew* this part of divine worship, which belongs to the whole.
nd those, we think, have made few remarks on public worship,
ho have not observed, on the one hand, how naturally the fugue-
ines puff up with vanity those who excel in them ; and on the
ther hand, how it deadens devotion, and only at the best raises
i admiration of the singers, and not of Christ.

" When it is recommended in this section to the preacher
imetimes to stop and address the people in the course of singing,
ie *substance* only of what he should say is mentioned there.   It
not intended, that he should speak *abruptly* on such occasions,
it with softness and due respect on the necessity of singing and
performing every act of devotion from the heart."

" **SECTION XXVIII.**

" *Of the Chartered Fund.*"

" We need not be urgent on our benevolent friends to promote this great charity.   Their own feelings, we well know, will sufficiently prevail, when proper light is given to them on the subject.   Our brethren who have laboured on the mountains, on the western waters, and in the poorer circuits in general, have suffered unspeakable hardships, merely for the want of some established fund, in which the competent members of our society might safely lodge what their benevolent hearts would rejoice to give, for the spread of the gospel.   On the same account, many of our worn-out preachers, some of whom quickly consumed their strength by their great exertions for the salvation of souls, have been brought into deep distress ; and the widows and orphans of our preachers have been sometimes reduced to extreme necessity, who might have lived in comfort, if not in affluence, enjoying the sweets of domestic life, if the preachers who were the husbands on one hand, and the fathers on the other, had not loved their Redeemer better than wife or children, or life itself. And it is to be lamented, if possible, with tears of blood, that we have lost scores of our most able married ministers—men who, like good householders, could upon all occasions bring things new and old out of their treasury, but were obliged to retire from the general work, because they saw nothing before them for their wives and children, if they continued itinerants, but misery and ruin.   But the present institution will, we trust, under the blessing of God, greatly relieve us in, if not entirely deliver us from, these mighty evils.   For we have full confidence, that the hearts of our friends will be engaged, and their hands stretched forth on this important occasion ; and a provision will be made, sufficient to preserve the objects of the charity from want, which is all that is aimed at or desired."

"CHAPTER II

" **SECTION I.**

" *The Nature, Design, and General Rules of the United Societies.*"

" THE present section forms, perhaps, one of the completest systems of Christian ethics or morals, for its size, which ever was published by an uninspired writer.   We speak this the more readily, because it was the work of the first divine, we believe, since the time of the apostles, the late Mr. Wesley, after matured experience, with only a small addition, which the circumstances of these states required. The rules are so clear, and so obviously approve themselves to every candid mind, that we need only touch briefly upon them, proving them by quotations from the sacred writings.

" 1. Of class meeting we shall speak hereafter : we would here only explain a few particulars concerning the office of a leader. We have found it necessary in innumerable instances to enlarge the number of the class, from the impossibility of providing a sufficiency of class-leaders, if the number were always limited to *twelve.* The office is of vast consequence. The revival of the work of God does perhaps depend as much upon *the whole body of leaders,* as it does *upon the whole body of preachers.* We have almost constantly observed, that when a leader is dull, or careless, or inactive—when he has not abilities or zeal sufficient to reprove with courage though with gentleness, and to press a present salvation upon the hearts of the sincere—the class is, in general, languid : but, on the contrary, when the leader is much alive to God and faithful in his office, the class is also, in general, lively and spiritual. This arises from the nature of the Christian plan of salvation. It is the same, in general, with a minister and his flock ; and every leader, as we have before intimated, is, *in some degree,* a gospel minister : though we may add, that among us a spiritual body of leaders may counteract the otherwise pernicious consequences of a languid ministry.

" At the beginning of Methodism, the leader called weekly upon each of his class, in which case twelve were quite sufficient for his inspection. But very soon it was found abundantly preferable for the whole class to meet the leader *together,* not only for the sake of the leader, but for the good of the people, who by that means enjoy the unspeakable advantage of Christian fellowship. At the same time the leader is expected to visit the members of his class at their own houses, especially when they are sick or confined, as often as his circumstances will admit."

" 4. The buying and selling the souls and bodies of men (for what is the body without the soul but a dead carcass?) is a complicated crime.* It was indeed, *in some measure,* overlooked in the Jews by reason of the wonderful hardness of their hearts, as was the keeping of concubines and the divorcing of wives at pleasure, but it is totally opposite to the whole spirit of the gospel. It

---

" * Are there not many proprietors to be found on this continent, who restrain their slaves from enjoying the privileges of the gospel, and thereby invade the rights of *the souls* and *consciences* of their slaves, as well as *their bodies?* At the same time we must give the credit due to multitudes who do not thus enslave *the minds* of their servants, but allow them full liberty to attend the preaching of the gospel, wherever they think they are most profited."

as an immediate tendency to fill the mind with pride and tyranny, and is frequently productive of almost every act of lust and cruelty which can disgrace the human species. Even the moral philosopher will candidly confess, that if there be a God, every perfection he possesses must be opposed to a practice so contrary to every moral idea which can influence the human mind."

"6. We are debtors to the constitution under which we live *we, especially in these United States*) for all the blessings of law and liberty which we enjoy : and without a government to support that constitution, all would be anarchy and confusion. It is, therefore, our duty to support it by bearing, with our fellow-citizens, an equal proportion of its expenses ; and it is as great a crime to rob our country, as to rob a private individual ; and the blindness of too many to this truth, injures not in the least the veracity of it."

" SECTION II.

" *Of Class Meeting.*"

" So much has been already spoken concerning the office of a leader in the notes on the preceding section, and on the tenth of the first chapter, that we have hardly room to enlarge without tautology. But from the whole we may observe, how careful our ministers should be in their choice of leaders. For our leaders, under God, are the sinews of our society, and our revivals will ever, in a great measure, rise or fall with them. Our ministers and preachers should therefore consider no time better employed than that which they bestow on the leaders, in examining them, directing them, and stirring them up to their holy and momentous duty.

" We have made many remarks in the course of our work on the necessity of Christian fellowship : but this cannot be carried on to any considerable advantage without stated solemn times of assembling. The meetings held for this purpose must have a name to distinguish them. We call ours *class meetings*, and *band meetings ;* but of the former we are to speak at present. Here we must notice, that it is *the thing itself, Christian fellowship*, and not the name, which we contend for. The experience of about sixty years has fully convinced us of its necessity ; and we ourselves can say that in the course of an extensive acquaintance with men and things, and the church of God, for about twenty or thirty years, we have rarely met with one who has been much devoted to God, and at the same time not united in close Christian fellowship to some religious society or other. Far be it from us to suppose that no fellowship meetings, except ours, are owned of God : so illiberal a sentiment never entered our minds. But we must say, that those who entirely neglect this *divinely-instituted* ordinance (however various the names given to it, or the modes of conducting it, may be) manifest that they are either ashamed to acknowledge *as their brethren* the true children of God, or 'are enemies of the cross of Christ,' Phil. iii, 18. They wish to keep up a correspondence with the world, which Christian discipline could not long tolerate; or they cannot bear to have their wounds probed to the bottom, that the balm of Gilead, the healing wine and oil of the gospel, may be applied by the divine Physician, 'and the blood of Jesus Christ the Son of God cleanse them from all sin,' 1 John i, 7.

"We have no doubt but meetings of Christian brethren for the exposition of Scripture texts may be attended with their advantages. But the most profitable exercise of any is a free inquiry into the state of the heart. We therefore confine these meetings to *Christian experience*, only adjoining singing and prayer in the introduction and conclusion. And we praise the Lord they have been made a blessing to scores of thousands. And we must add, with gratitude to the Most High, that after an accurate attention to the point ourselves, and from the impartial account of several of our oldest and most useful ministers in different parts of the globe, we have cause to believe, that out of those who have *died members of our society,* far the greatest part have entered into glory in the triumph of faith. In short, we can truly say, that through the grace of God our classes form the pillars of our work, and, as we have before observed, are in a considerable degree our universities for the ministry."

" SECTION III.

"*Of the Band Societies.*"

" Our society may be considered as a spiritual hospital, where souls come to be cured of their spiritual diseases. The members, therefore, who compose our class meetings vary exceedingly in the state of their minds and the degrees of their experience. On this account it was thought necessary by our venerable leader, Mr. Wesley, to establish a society of evangelical believers within the society composed of the whole body of Methodists, to which he gave the name of *the band society.* This institution he borrowed from the practice of the primitive churches, as indeed he did almost every thing he established.

" The heart of man *by nature* is such a cage of unclean birds that few are to be found who will lay before their brethren all its secret movements, unless the love of God be the ruling principle of their souls. And even then they are not called upon to exercise this confidence, except toward a small confidential company of true believers like themselves. When bands can

be formed on this plan (and on no other do we form them) the
become one of the most profitable means of grace in the whol
compass of Christian discipline. There is nothing we kno
of which so much quickens the soul to a desire and expectatio
of the perfect love of God as this. It includes in it all th
spiritual benefits of social intercourse. For these little familie
of love not only mutually weep and rejoice, and in every thin
sympathize with each other, as genuine friends, but each of ther
possesses a measure of 'that unction of the Holy One,' (1 Joh
ii, 20,) which teaches all spiritual knowledge. And thus ar
they enabled to 'build up themselves [and each other] on thei
most holy faith,' (Jude 20,) and to 'consider *one another*, t
provoke unto love and good works,' Heb. x, 24.

"The regularity and order which should be observed i
every solemn meeting, requires that one of the band should b
the leader, to open and close the ordinance with singing an
prayer, though all may be here considered nearly upon a
equality. Each must be at full liberty to follow the leader i
prayer, whenever they kneel down together before God.

"In large societies all the members of those little bands ar
to meet together once a week with the preacher, and to spen
an hour in speaking their experience one after another, as i
our love-feasts : and these meetings have been rendered a grea
blessing to many.

"In very large societies there should be a quarterly love
feast for the bands, as well as for the whole society, (whicl
always includes the members of the bands.)

"Wherever also it is practicable, there should be formed
select society chosen out of the members of the bands. Thi
should be composed of believers who enjoy the perfect love of
God, or who are earnestly seeking that great blessing. I
London, Bristol, &c., in Europe, and in New-York, &c., o
this continent, these select societies have been very profitable.
They also meet once a week for an hour, and the preacher pre-
sides among them. Each member is at liberty to speak his o
her experience, the preacher giving such advice respecting the
grand point their souls are aiming at, as he sees expedient.

"Thus does our economy, by its prudential ordinances, unde
the grace of God, tend to raise the members of our society
from one degree of grace to another. And we have invariably
observed, that where these meetings of the bands have been
kept up in their life and power, the revival of the work of God
has been manifest both in the addition of members to the society
and in the deepening of the life of God in general.

"We earnestly wish that our elders, deacons, and preachers
be peculiarly attentive to these blessed ordinances in thei
respective spheres of action. They probably may find earnest
evers in almost every circuit, who will be willing to meet

in band, if properly advised and encouraged. And when many of these bands are formed, the other meetings may easily be established and regulated. And we believe hardly any thing will promote the general work more than this.

" The propriety of separating the men and women in these bands must be evident to every one who considers the account here given of this means of grace. The separating of the married and single arises from the peculiar circumstances in which they are situated, and from the closer union which is likely to subsist between those who are circumstanced alike. Widowers or widows may have their choice of meeting either with the married or the single, unless a band can be formed of them alone respectively.

" *The social principle* is one of the grand springs in the soul of man. It was not the design of Christianity to annihilate this principle, but the very contrary—to improve it, to spiritualize it, and strengthen it. O then let us exercise it in spiritual intercourse, as we well know that one part of our heavenly felicity will flow from friendship and union with our brethren, the redeemed of the Lord, to all eternity! Gal. vi, 2, ' Bear ye one another's burdens, and so fulfil the law of Christ.' 1 Cor. xii, 26, 27, ' Whether one member suffer, all the members suffer with it : or one member be honoured, all the members rejoice with it. Now ye are the body of Christ, and members in particular.' Phil. ii, 1, 2, ' If there be therefore any consolation in Christ, if any comfort of love, if any fellowship of the Spirit, if any bowels and mercies : fulfil ye my joy, that ye be likeminded, having the same love, being of one accord, of one mind.' We have perhaps one hundred thousand believers in our church throughout the world ; and if all were thus of one accord, ' walking by the same rule, minding the same thing,' (Phil. iii, 16,) what a glorious church should we make ; and God would hear our prayers, and look down upon us with the same delight, as if we were all assembled in the same room, or in the same temple.

" Observe, here is nothing of auricular confession or priestly absolution : the whole is the fruit of holy confidence and Christian love."

" SECTION IV.

" *Of the Privileges granted to serious Persons who are not of the Society.*"

" It is manifestly our duty to fence in our society, and to preserve it from intruders ; otherwise we should soon become a desolate waste. God would write *Ichabod* upon us, and the glory would be departed from Israel. At the same time we should suffer those who are apparently sincere, if they request it, to see our order and discipline twice or thrice, that they themselves may judge whether it will be for their spiritua advantage to cast in their lot among us. But we should by no means exceed the indulgence here allowed ; otherwise we should make our valuable meetings for Christian fellowshi cheap and contemptible, and bring a heavy burden on the mind of our brethren."

" SECTION V.

" Of the Qualification and Duty of the Stewards of Circuits."

" In each large society there are generally two or fou stewards of that particular society for the management of it temporal concerns. These are appointed, as well as the circui stewards, by the preacher who has the charge of the circuit. He is himself to have as little as possible to do with tempora affairs, but has the appointment of the officers of the societ invested in him, as being likely to be the best judge of th society at large, and of each member in particular. Neverthe less, he is to advise with the quarterly meeting on the appoint ment of *circuit stewards,* and with the leaders of each societ respectively on the appointment of *society stewards.*"

" SECTION VIII.

" Of bringing to Trial, finding guilty, and reproving, suspend ing, or excluding disorderly Persons from Society and Churcl Privileges.

" The present section requires a very full explication ; no because Scripture and reason do not fully discover to us th truth on the present subject, but because many have objected t our Discipline in the instance before us.

" The grand point to be determined is this : whether the fina judgment of an offender in respect to both the guilt and the cen sure should be invested in the minister or the people. We sha therefore take a view of this part of our economy, first, in th light of Scripture, and, secondly, in that of reason.

" First, in the light of Scripture. Here we must confine our selves of course to the New Testament, as living under th Christian dispensation. 1. The first scripture we shall conside is the declaration of our Saviour in Matt. xviii, 15–17, ' More over, if thy brother shall trespass against thee, go and tell hin his fault between thee and him alone : if he shall hear thee, thou hast gained thy brother. But if he will not hear thee, ther take with thee one or two more, that in the mouth of two or thre witnesses every word may be established. And if he shal neglect to hear them, tell it unto the church ; but if he neglec to hear the church, let him be unto thee as a heathen man and a publican.' These words were addressed to the apostles, and through them to all the ministers of Christ to the end of the world. This is evident from the words immediately following the quotation, and which are a continuation of the same paragraph, and could not belong to the private members of a church.

" The first step then which is to be taken, is to tell the offender of his fault in private without any witness. Here is the *secret* reproof of the minister himself. But if he will not hear and amend, the second step is, that the minister take with him two or three witnesses. Here is the reproof of the minister *before witnesses*. 'And if he shall neglect to hear them,' shall these two or three witnesses proceed to exclude him ? No : they have no such authority : but 'tell it unto the church.' This is the third step. Has the church then any authority to punish him ? No : their whole authority lies in advising and reproving him. 'But if,' after such advice and reproof, 'he neglect to hear the church, *let him be* UNTO THEE *as a heathen man and a publican.*' Can any one imagine that the minister *only* is to treat the offender thus; and that the rest of the church are to give him the right hand of fellowship ? This cannot be. The minister is undoubtedly to exclude him from the communion of the church. This is the last step. Then follow immediately those words of our Lord, 'Whatsoever ye shall bind on earth shall be bound in heaven : and whatsoever ye shall loose on earth shall be loosed in heaven :' which words, as we before observed, confine the power to ministers, whose church censures, as far as they are consistent with the word of God, (for we cannot suppose the authority goes further,) shall be confirmed and supported in heaven : and the faithful ministers of God, who have been more or less invested with the superintendency of the church, have found this promise verified. The latter words cannot be supposed to relate to an external exclusion from glory, for that would preclude the necessity of the day of judgment in respect to those so excommunicated. But we repeat, here is not a word said of the church's authority either to judge or to censure. On the contrary, the whole authority is expressly delivered into the hands of the minister.

" But we may add, that this passage speaks of offences which have not yet brought a public disgrace on the church of God. The church or society of which the offender is a member is not even supposed to be generally acquainted with the fault till after the failure of the first and second attempt for his reformation. Surely, if the offence be of a scandalous nature, and has already disgraced the cause of God by its public notoriety, the offender ought to be *immediately* removed, after clear conviction, for the honour of God and his cause : much more so still, if the offender has been found guilty of some *gross* crime. For could any one think of having communion with a murderer, adulterer, or thief,

even for a moment, though the crime was not known to any but the
offender and himself: and so we may observe of many other crimes
  " But it may be urged that the offence must be first mentione
to the church, before the offender can be scripturally excluded
' Tell it to the church,' says our Lord.   And so we do.   It i
merely for the sake of convenience, that in *large* societies we tel
it only to a committee or representation of the society, or d
abundantly more, even make them the witnesses of the whol
trial.   But if such societies were to desire it, we would tell th
whole unto the church at large.   But still we must declare, from
the plain sense of the word of God, that our Lord invests the
minister with the whole authority both of judgment and censure
  " 2. Another scripture worthy of consideration on this subjec
is 1 Cor. v, 1–5, ' It is reported commonly that there is for
nication among you, and such fornication as is not so much a
named among the Gentiles, that one should have his father's
wife.   And ye are puffed up, and have not rather mourned, tha
he that hath done this deed, might be taken away from amon;
you.   For I verily as absent in body, but *present in spirit,* HAVI
JUDGED *already,* as though I were present, concerning him tha
hath so done this deed: in the name of our Lord Jesus Christ
when ye are gathered together, and *my spirit,* with the powe
of our Lord Jesus Christ, to deliver such a one unto Satan fo
the destruction of the flesh, that the spirit may be saved in the da`
of our Lord Jesus.'   It is evident, beyond the possibility of i
doubt, that the apostle, being fully persuaded of the truth of th
fact, took upon himself the whole business of deciding on the
guilt and punishment of the incestuous Corinthian.   ' *I, as pre
sent in spirit,*' says he, ' have judged *already.*'   He here act
as their chief minister, and requires them to consider *his spiri
present with them,* as he could not be so personally.   The`
were not to meet, in order to consult whether the offender shoul
be put away or not, but merely to put him from among them
because the apostle was absent.
  " It may here be asked, Why did not the chief resident minis
ter of the church of Corinth put away the incestuous person, i
he possessed the authority ?   We answer, Because he was un
faithful.   He connived at this enormous crime, either because
he did not love the cause of holiness, which is the cause of God
or because he gave way to the evil solicitations of the people
This is evident from those words in the passage before us, ' Y
are puffed up, and have not rather mourned, that he that hatl
done this deed, *might be taken away* from among you.'   He doe
not say, Ye have not mourned *that you did not put away* thi
great offender, but ' *that he might be taken away* from among you.
But as the person who had the immediate authority *did not tak
the offender away* from among them, St. Paul, as the apostle o
he Gentiles, steps in to the minister's place, and cuts him off.

" It might also be urged, that it was *an apostle* who thus acted : and we should be ready to admit this as an exempt case, if it were not agreeable to the authority given by Christ himself to his ministers—an authority, the due exercise of which by his ministers our Lord highly approves of, and the neglect of which he strongly condemns, as we shall now proceed to show.

" 3.   Rev. ii, 1, 2, ' Unto the angel of the church of Ephesus write, These things saith he that holdeth the seven stars in his right hand, who walketh in the midst of the seven golden candlesticks ; I know thy works, and thy labour, and thy patience, and *how thou canst not bear them which are evil.*'   With what high approbation does our Lord here express himself concerning the determined opposition of the chief minister of the church of Ephesus to all immoral professors ! ' Thou canst not bear them which are evil.'   But if this minister had only a single vote against immoral practices in the church, or was only chairman in the meetings of the church, to examine into the conduct of offenders or supposed offenders, is it likely that our Lord would have given so high an encomium, so strong a commendation of the conduct of the minister in this respect ?   Would he not at least have said something in commendation of the church itself, without whom in this instance, if the power of censure lay in them, the minister would be almost a cipher ? For the minister, in such case, would have little to do in the business, unless as a complainant or informer. Besides, our Lord adds in the second verse, ' And *thou* hast tried them which say they are apostles, and are not ; and hast found them liars.'   And again, verse 6, ' But this thou hast, that thou hatest the deeds of the Nicolaitans, which I also hate.'   From the whole of which it appears, that the minister was the sole judge both of the morals and doctrines of the church which he superintended, the church not being at all mentioned by our Lord as having any authority in these matters.

" 4.   Rev. ii, 12–15, ' And to the angel of the church in Pergamos write, These things saith he which hath the sharp sword with two edges ;—I have a few things against thee, because thou hast there them that hold the doctrine of Balaam, who taught Balak to cast a stumbling block before the children of Israel, to eat things sacrificed unto idols, and to commit fornication.   So hast thou also them that hold the doctrine of the Nicolaitans, which thing I hate.'   But why should our Lord *cast all this blame* on the minister *alone*, without taking the least notice of the church, *if the power of censure rested in the church*, and not in the minister ; or no further in the minister, than as having a single vote in the church ?   Is it, we must repeat, at all probable, is it morally possible, that our Lord would have written thus to the angel of the church, if that angel, or chief minister, had not possessed authority to cleanse it from the followers of the doctrine of Balaam, and of the Nicolaitans ?

" 5. Rev. ii, 18–20, ' And unto the angel of the church in Thyatira write, These things saith the Son of God, who hath his eyes like unto a flame of *fire*, and his feet are like fine brass; —I have a few things against thee, because *thou sufferest* that woman Jezebel, which calleth herself a prophetess, to teach and to seduce my servants to commit fornication, and to eat things sacrificed unto idols.' But how could he possibly avoid *suffering* her to remain in the church, if the church possessed the power of censure and excommunication, and was determined to keep her in? Or, how could he possibly have prevented her being turned out, if the church had in it the power of expulsion, and had expelled her?

" We may here just observe that most of the churches of Asia Minor, mentioned in the second and third chapters of the Revelation, if not all of them, were founded by St. Paul.

" 6. We shall instance in only two more portions of the word of God on this subject. (1.) Heb. xiii, 7, ' Remember them *which have the rule over you, who have spoken unto you the word of God:* whose faith follow, considering the end of their conversation.' And (2.) Verse 17, ' *Obey them that have the rule over you, and submit yourselves: for they watch for your souls,* as they that must give account : that they may do it with joy, and not with grief: for that is unprofitable for you.' Observe, [1.] The persons here described as having the rule, and a right to obedience and submission, were persons *who had spoken the word of God to the people,* and *watched over their souls,* and consequently were *their preachers and pastors.* But, [2.] To suppose that *they ruled in the church,* and *had a claim to obedience and submission,* and yet had not the authority *of cleansing the church from immoral and heretical persons,* would be exceedingly absurd. These last-quoted texts are collateral and inferential proofs, the former are *expressly* so.

" 2dly. Let us consider the subject in the light of reason. 1. Is there any propriety in constituting a husband the judge of the guilt or innocence of his wife, or the wife of her husband ; the parent of his child, or the child of his parent ; the brother of his sister, or the sister of her brother, &c.? Would not natural affection almost unavoidably move them in such cases to be partial to each other? Might not resentment move a master to be partial in his judgment against his servant? Might not fear, on the contrary, influence the servant in favour of his master? A long acquaintance also, perhaps even from childhood, has a powerful effect upon the minds of men, and would strongly tempt them to cover sin, to the destruction, not intentionally but eventually, of the work of God. The intermixture of temporal interests would also be a strong motive to induce many to make large allowances for the offender. ' My income is small, and my family large : such a one is my customer, and also many of his relations; and shall I vote against him to the injury of my family? Perhaps he may repent, and be better in future. Such a one has obliged me in various respects, and shall I be so ungrateful as to condemn him wholly?' Those who are acquainted with the operations of the human mind, must be very sensible how often these reasonings would warp the minds of the judges, and produce a partiality in their decisions, which would be ruinous in the last degree to the work of God. Additionally to all this, we must recollect that different countries, and different parts of the same country, are addicted to particular vices: and those are but little acquainted with human nature who do not know that men are strongly tempted to cover those sins which they themselves are inwardly inclined to, or which it is their interest to commit. For instance, in a part of the country where the maple-tree grows abundantly, and there are various manufactures of sugar, would not the church be strongly inclined to make large allowances for those who would labour in their sugar-camps on the Lord's day? Let those answer who are acquainted with the nature of that manufacture. Again, in that part of the country where the buying the souls and bodies of men is a common practice, would not many in the church be tempted to favour those who were guilty of that practice, because they themselves might be the next to fall into the snare? Yea, we have had proofs of this—of private members of the church, who have attempted to assume the power, not only of judging or rather clearing the offender, but *of judging the law itself!*

" To give therefore the authority of judging and censuring offenders to the private members of a church, would be to form a court which in innumerable instances would have the strongest temptations to partiality. We do not mention this to show the least disrespect to the private members of our society: on the contrary, many of them may exceed us in piety and every grace. But it is contrary to all the rules of justice to appoint those to be judges who may in so many instances be strongly tempted to be partial. At the same time we must observe, that THE WORD OF GOD is that which we principally stand upon, knowing well that every passage in the New Testament which relates to the present subject is wholly on our side.

" 2. Our original design in forming our religious society renders the existence of this authority in our ministers absolutely necessary. But what was this design? *To raise a holy people.* Our plan of economy shuts us up from the influence of any other motive in respect to our ministerial labours. It is impossible for us to *enrich* ourselves by Methodist preaching. Again, we bear a constant testimony against *the pleasures* of the world, and therefore should be esteemed, even by our own people, as the greatest of hypocrites, if *we* indulged ourselves in them, and would soon be excluded the connection by the various means of trial to which *all of us are*

subject.   And *as to honour*, we are almost the only despised people in Christendom, as a religious body.   The secondary rank of
mankind and the poor are the only persons (with a few exceptions)
who receive the gospel.   The rich and great in general, even
those who have not embraced the favourite doctrines of the times,
will not submit to the way of the cross, but, on the contrary, look
down on the preachers of it as the greatest enthusiasts.   And shall
we thus sacrifice all that the world holds dear and at the same time
lose the only aim of all our public labours, by false complai-
sance ?   No.   *We will have a holy people, or none.*   In every part
of our economy, as well as doctrine, we aim at crucifixion to the
world and love to God.   *This must be the price of our labours.*
We require not riches, honours, or pleasure, *but a holy people.*
We have a right to dispose of our labours as we please, as
far as they respect our fellow-creatures : and *we will not bestow
them on any other condition.*   If we labour in any place a sufficient time for a trial, and are not able to raise a people devoted
to God, we will leave it : we have a right so to do, and none have
just ground of complaint.   Again, if we have encouragement from
any people, but they afterward deceive us, and return to the
world 'like the dog to his vomit,' (2 Pet. ii, 22,) they have broken
the condition on which we labour among them ; we have nothing
more to do with them ; and if we continue in that place, it is for
the sake of others, and not of them.   But, blessed be God, if we
meet sometimes with discouragements in this respect, they are
amply compensated by the increase of vital godliness.   We love
our people ; and they in general amply repay our labours by their
holy conversation.   They are the joy of our hearts, and will, we
trust, be our crown of rejoicing on the great day.   But still we
must observe, that our immovable support, on which we rest our
sentiments upon this subject, is THE WORD OF GOD.   And we
may add, that the present point has been seldom disputed, as far
as we know, by any, except those who have been disaffected to
us, or have openly separated from us.

  " An appeal is allowed, in all the cases mentioned in this section, to the following quarterly meeting.   For though the power
of appeal be not mentioned in the last clause, which relates to the
sewing of dissensions, yet it certainly is implied.   Our work is a
present in its infancy in comparison to what, we trust, it will be
through the blessing of God.   Our ministers who have the
charge of circuits may not be always so aged and experienced as
we might wish them to be ; the appeal to the quarterly meeting
is therefore allowed to remedy this defect.   And this no one can
object to.   No one, we think, can imagine, that the members of
a class, or the members of the largest society, would form so respectable or so impartial a court of judicature as the presiding elder,
the travelling and local preachers, and the leaders and stewards
of the whole circuit.   But the point is quite out of the reach of
15

debate in respect to those who believe the sacred writings, and sincerely reverence them. The New Testament determines, beyond a doubt, that judgment and censure in the cases before us shall be in the minister : nor could we justify our conduct in investing the quarterly meeting with the authority of receiving and determining appeals, if it were not almost entirely composed of men who are more or less engaged in the ministry of the word, the stewards being the only exceptions.

" We shall now just add some portions of sacred writ, in relation to the immoralities which are referred to in this section, that our ministers who have the oversight of circuits may have them under their eye."

" SECTION X.

" Of the Sale and Use of Spirituous Liquors."

" Far be it from us to wish or endeavour to intrude upon the proper religious or civil liberty of any of our people. But the retailing of spirituous liquors, and giving drams to customers, when they call at the stores, are such prevalent customs at present, and are productive of so many evils, that we judge it our indispensable duty to form a regulation against them. The cause of God, which we prefer to every other consideration under heaven, absolutely requires us to step forth with humble boldness in this respect."

"CHAPTER III.

" SECTION I.

" Of building Churches, and the Order to be observed therein."

" ' The sitting of men and women apart' was the universal practice in the primitive church. A general mixture of the sexes in places of divine worship is obviously improper.

" In respect to the deed of settlement, we would observe, that the union of the Methodist society, through the states, requires one general deed, for the settlement of our preaching houses and the premises belonging thereto. In the above plan of settlement we have given to the trustees an authority and security they never possessed by virtue of our former deeds, namely, the power of mortgaging or selling the premises in the cases and manner above mentioned. By which we manifest to the whole world, that the property of the preaching houses will not be invested in the General Conference. But the preservation of our union and the progress of the work of God indispensably require, that the

free and full use of the pulpits should be in the hands of the G
neral Conference, and the yearly conferences authorized by thei
Of course, the travelling preachers, who are in full connectio
assembled in their conferences, are the patrons of the pulpits ⟨
our churches.   And this was absolutely necessary to give a clea
legal specification in the deed.   If the local preachers, steward
and leaders (who have an undoubted right to preach, meet the
classes, &c., in the preaching houses at due time, according to tl
Form of Discipline) were specified, it would be necessary to a⟨
a description of their orders ; which would throw such obscuri
upon the whole, that a court of justice would either reject tl
deed, or be at a loss to determine concerning the little peculiai
ties of our Form of Discipline.   But we do hereby publicly d
clare, that we have no design of limiting, in the least degre
the privileges of any of the public officers of our society, but l
this deed solely intend to preserve the property of our churⓒ
by such a clear, simple specification, as shall be fully and easi
cognizable by the laws."

" SECTION II.

*" Of the Printing of Books, and the Application of the Profi
arising therefrom."*

" The propagation of religious knowledge, by means of tl
press, is next in importance to the preaching of the gospe
To supply the people, therefore, with the most pious and usef
books, in order that they may fill up their leisure hours in tl
most profitable ways, is an object worthy of the deepest atte:
tion of their pastors.   On this account we are determined
move in the most cautious manner in respect to our publication
We have a great esteem for our general book steward, and a:
much obliged to him for his fidelity and usefulness in his impor
ant office : but we shall in future submit our publications to tl
judgment of no single person.   The books of infidelity and pr
faneness with which the states at present abound, demand o⟨
strongest exertions to counteract their pernicious influence : ai
every step shall be taken, which is consistent with our finance
to furnish our friends, from time to time, with the most usef
treatises on every branch of religious knowledge.   And the co⟨
sideration that all the profits shall be lodged in our chartere
fund for the benefit of the distressed preachers, both travellir
and superannuated, will, we trust, prove a considerable addition
inducement to our brethren to purchase our books."

INDEX.

Alabama Conference, boundaries of, 221, 227.
Annual Conference, (see Conference.)
Antinomianism, 77.
Apostolic succession, 282.
Appeal, right of, 113.
Arbitrations, (see Members,) 141.
Arkansas Conference, boundaries of, 223, 227.
Articles of Religion, 80, 83, 84, 95–110, 112, 160.
Asbury, Francis, 13, 14, 15, 17, 19, 22, 23, 81, 83, 281.
Assistant, duties of, 11, 16, 17, 19, 20, 54, 76, 126.
   General, (see Mr. Wesley, Superintendent, Bishop,) 11, 13
    21, 119.

Baltimore Conference, boundaries of, 211, 212, 213, 216, 218, 221.
      powers of, 79.
Bands, 36, 56, 84, 140, 183, 328.
  original rules of, 184.
Baptism, 174, 200.
   mode of, 45, 174, 204, 322.
   a second, 45.
Bible classes, 150.
  Society, 189.
    agents for the American, 123.
Bishops, (see Mr. Wesley, General Assistant, Superintendent,)
  use of the title, 82, 118.
  Address of the, 83, 88.
  Notes to the Discipline by the, 85, 260, 281.
  ordination of, 38, 120, 209.
  powers of, 114, 115, 118, 212, 214, 216, 219, 256, 257, 287.
  allowance of, 119, 228, 240, 246, 248.
  election of, 120, 121.
  duties of, 38, 119, 120, 121, 122, 248, 249, 250.
  trial of, 38, 120, 121, 122, 290.
  provision in case of vacancy in the office, 39, 120.
  American, compared with Mr. Wesley, 287–292.
Black River Conference, boundaries of, 222, 225.
Books, circulation of, 138, 145, 254, 260, 307, 339.
  publication of, by travelling preachers, 262, 264, 313.
    by editors, agents, or clerks of Book Concern
    267.
Book Agents, 122, 254, 262, 266.
    allowance of, 254, 270.

Book Agents, from whom chosen, 262, 271.
        powers of, 255, 258, 261.
        term of office, 262, 267.
        at Cincinnati, 263.
    Committee, 255, 257, 258, 264, 266, 267, 270.
    Concern, 113, 243, 252, 254.
        publications of, by whom selected, 254, 255, 257, 258,
           261, 263, 266, 270, 271.
        seat of, 260, 265.
        profits of, 254, 256, 260, 261.
        annual exhibit of, 264, 266.
        commission system abolished, 264.
Bribery, 38.
Burial of the dead, order of, 207.

Call to preach, evidences of, 62, 145, 310.
Calvinism, 76.
Canada Conference, boundaries of, 217.
Catechisms, 150.
Charleston, S. C., paper at, 269.
        depository at, 272.
Chartered Fund, 85, 113, 243, 251, 254, 325.
Children, instruction of, (see Education,) 13, 34, 51, 64, 147, 317.
Christian Advocate and Journal, editor of, 264.
Christian Advocate, Western, 269.
        Southern, 269.
        Richmond, 269.
        South Western, 269.
        Pittsburgh, 272.
Church of England, condition of, 93, 94.
        connection of Methodists with, 10, 13, 14, 15, 16,
          22, 55, 57.
Churches, 11, 13, 20, 69.
    building of, 76, 139, 228.
    deed for, 70, 229, 230.
    property of, 288, 338.
    order in, 71, 72.
Cincinnati, book establishment at, 263, 266, 268, 271.
Class leaders, 29, 304, 326.
    duties of, 177.
Class meetings, 133, 150, 177, 181, 326, 327.
    neglect of, 59, 183.
Cleanliness, 56, 72, 140.
Coke, Dr., 23.
    and Bishop Asbury's Notes, 281.
Cokesbury College, plan of education in, 151.
        students of, 151.
        objects of, 151.
        officers of, 151.
        studies in, 152.
        tuition fees, 154.

Cokesbury College, rules and regulations of, 154.
     collection for, 240.
     appropriation to, 254, 255.
Collections, 240.
    conference, 21.
    class, 136, 139.
    quarterly, 136, 139.
College, (see Cokesbury.)
Coloured people, 16, 42, 274, 279.
Conferences, 110.
    mode of spending time at, 26, 286.
    origin of, 47.
    General, 111, 283.
      the first, 25.
      delegated, 111.
      members of, 111, 112.
      time of meeting, 111, 112.
      quorum in, 112.
      president of, 112.
      powers of, 112, 293.
      limitations and restrictions of, 112, 113.
      expenses of delegates to, 244.
   District (of travelling preachers) 110, 118.
      (of local preachers) 166.
   Annual, 110, 114, 283.
      members of, 114, 287.
      time of, 114, 286.
      place of, 115, 286.
      order of business in, 64, 115.
      boundaries of, 118, 211, 286.
      duties of, 230.
      powers of, 234, 243, 256, 316.
      journal of, 119.
      president of, 127.
   Quarterly, 127, 128, 149, 165, 167, 168, 234, 245.
Credentials, restoring (to travelling preachers) 163.
      (to local preachers) 173, 174.

Deacon, office of, 39, 41, 129, 130.
   constituting of, 130, 299.
   probation of, 130, 131, 299.
   form of ordination, 208.
Debts, non-payment of, how treated, 143.
Depositories of books, 267, 270, 272.
Dickins, Rev. John, participation in arranging Discipline, 81.
Discipline of the Methodist Societies prior to the organization of th
   M. E. Church, 9.
   the first, 25–79.
   mode of altering, prior to 1792, 79.
   division of, 85, 119.
   title of, 87

Discipline, modifications of, in

1738. 184.

1743. 177–180, 181.

1744. 185.

1773. 10, 115.

1774. 11, 115

1775. 11.

1777. 12.

1778. 12.

1779. 12, 115.

1780. 13, 115.

1781. 16.

1782. 18, 115.

1783. 19, 115.

1784. 20–80, 87, 95, 115, 119, 125, 129, 132, 133, 135, 137, 138, 139, 140, 141, 142, 144, 147, 158, 182, 193, 200, 202, 205, 206, 207, 208, 209, 210, 228.

1785. 80, 274.

1786. 80, 87, 109, 125, 133, 134, 174, 199, 202, 204, 206, 208.

1787. 81, 118, 148, 235, 237, 254, 274.

1788. 83.

1789. 83, 88, 93, 109, 115, 120, 125, 130, 133, 134, 135, 138, 139, 140, 141, 142, 144, 145, 146, 147, 150, 158, 159, 160, 164, 168, 174, 175, 180, 181, 182, 183, 187, 188, 189, 228, 230, 235, 236, 237, 240, 241, 273.

1790. 84, 88, 90, 95, 109.

1791. 84, 91, 95, 109.

1792. 84, 91, 94, 95, 109, 111, 114, 116, 118, 121, 126, 129, 130, 133, 134, 135, 137, 138, 139, 140, 141, 144, 145, 147, 157, 158, 159, 161, 162, 164, 169, 175, 176, 181, 183, 186, 188, 189, 191, 199, 202, 204, 206, 207, 208, 209, 210, 229, 236, 237, 240, 241, 254.

1796. 84, 91, 109, 111, 114, 118, 130, 142, 143, 148, 157, 165, 169, 171, 188, 192, 211, 230, 238, 242, 251, 256, 273, 275.

1800. 85, 111, 116, 119, 138, 143, 145, 170, 188, 191, 212, 228, 229, 238, 240, 244, 253, 258, 274, 276.

1804. 85, 109, 111, 114, 117, 119, 122, 127, 129, 130, 134, 136, 146, 169, 176, 187, 188, 191, 212, 228, 238, 243, 253, 260, 274, 277.

1808. 85, 109, 111, 142, 169, 181, 187, 192, 210, 213, 243, 262, 278.

1812. 86, 92, 109, 117, 137, 143, 146, 169, 170, 172, 213, 234, 235, 244, 253, 262, 278.

1816. 86, 110, 113, 133, 144, 161, 165, 169, 170, 172, 187, 214, 236, 239, 244, 245, 262, 274, 278.

Discipline, modifications of, in
1820. 110, 123, 137, 162, 166, 170, 172, 215, 220, 234, 236, 244, 263, 278.
1824. 110, 148, 167, 170, 171, 173, 176, 217, 239, 246, 247, 264, 278.
1828. 123, 148, 167, 175, 192, 219, 234, 236, 239, 246, 247, 264.
1832. 86, 113, 117, 123, 128, 131, 139, 140, 143, 220, 239, 244, 246, 249, 265.
1836. 113, 123, 136, 138, 149, 160, 162, 163, 167, 169, 171, 173, 182, 183, 188, 189, 204, 222, 228, 239, 247, 250, 267.
1840. 86, 92, 117, 123, 128, 131, 137, 139, 149, 160, 174, 182, 192, 225, 250, 270.
Dress, 21, 36, 140, 185, 189.

Editors, 122, 123, 265, 267, 270.
    term of office, 262, 267.
Education, (see Children,) 51, 73, 92, 123, 124, 256.
    plan of, in Cokesbury College, 151.
Elders, the first, of the M. E. C., 24.
    office of, 39, 125, 129.
    election of, 125, 129.
    form of ordination, 209.
    presiding, term of office, 122, 127.
        origin of the office, 124, 293.
        by whom chosen, 126, 127.
        duties of, 126, 127, 128, 245, 257, 258, 263, 265.
        allowance of, 127, 128, 246, 247.
        powers of, 128, 166, 235, 295, 297.
        advantages of the office, 295.
Elections, treats at, 147.
Episcopacy, 282, 292.
        itinerant general, 112.
Erie Conference, boundaries of, 222, 226.
Evil speaking, 37.
Exhorters, 12, 14, 135, 144, 310.

Fasting, 12, 15, 18, 20, 22, 51, 61, 64, 68, 144, 164, 186, 309.
Fees, 45, 175, 237.
Festivals, preaching on, 314.
Forms, 80, 85, 86, 176, 193.
Frauds, investigation of, 143.
Fugue tunes, 176, 324.
Funeral sermons, 12.

General Conference, (see Conference.)
Genesee Conference, boundaries of, 214, 215, 216, 217, 220, 222, 225.
Georgia, exception in favour of slaveholders in, 278.
        Conference, boundaries of, 221.
German publications, 271.

15*

Helpers, 12, 39, 41, 62, 133.
    following trades, 49.
    mode of receiving, 63.
Holston Conference, boundaries of, 218, 221, 224, 227.
Hymn Book, 24, 81.

Illinois Conference, boundaries of, 218, 221, 223, 226.
Indiana Conference, boundaries of, 221, 223, 226.
Insolvencies, 38, 142.
Itinerancy, 39, 42, 120, 122, 125, 126, 129, 130, 283, 289, 292, 299
    300, 310.

Kentucky Conference, boundaries of, 215, 218, 219.
King's, Lord, Primitive Church, 23.
Kingswood school, 173.

Large Minutes, 25-179.
Lay delegation, 283.
Liberia Mission Annual Conference, 225.
Liturgy, (see Sunday service,) 24, 41, 134.
Local preachers, (see Preachers.)
Locating travelling preacher without his consent, 162.
Lord's Prayer, mode of repeating, 53.
    use of, 176.
    Supper, 60, 175, 193.
        posture of communicants, 44, 175, 323.
        terms of admission to, 45, 175, 323.
Love-feast, 138, 140, 150.
        tickets, 137, 304.

Magazine, Methodist, 257.
Maine Conference, boundaries of, 217.
Marriage, 37, 187.
Matrimony, form of solemnizing, 205.
Members, probation of, 17, 35, 182, 190.
    admission of, 182, 304.
    trial of, 113, 137, 189, 331.
    appeal of, 113, 191, 337.
    disputes among, 17, 58, 141.
Membership, condition of, 178.
    certificates of, 19, 56, 140, 309.
Memphis Conference, boundaries of, 227.
Methodist Societies, origin of, 46, 177.
    Episcopal Church, organization of, 22, 27, 93, 282.
        origin of, 92, 281.
Methodists, design of, 27.
    rise of, 27, 90.
    deficiencies of, 30.
Michigan Conference, boundaries of, 223, 226.
Military posts, chaplains to, 123.
Ministers, office of, 139.

Minutes, printing of, 42, 133, 138.
       General, (see Discipline.)
Missions, 86, 136, 139, 246, 247, 254, 300.
Mission committee, 247, 249.
Missionary Societies, 247.
       treasurer, 248.
       secretaries, 250.
Missionaries, 123, 136.
Mississippi Conference, boundaries of, 214, 216, 218, 221, 224, 227.
Missouri Conference, boundaries of, 214, 215, 218, 221, 223.
Mixing of men and women in church, 72, 230, 338.

Nervous disorders, causes of, 48.
       remedy for, 48.
New-England Conference, boundaries of, 211, 212, 214, 215, 217, 220, 225.
New-Hampshire Conference, boundaries of, 220.
New-Jersey Conference, boundaries of, 225, 228.
New-Orleans, preachers in, 123.
       book depository at, 267.
New-York Conference, powers of, 250, 261, 262, 266.
       boundaries of, 212, 213, 214, 215, 217, 220, 222, 225.
North Carolina, exception in favour of slaveholders in, 278.
       Conference, boundaries of, 224.
North Ohio Conference, boundaries of, 226.
Notes to the Discipline, 85, 260, 281.
Numbers in society, 138, 308.

Obedience to superiors in office, 301.
Ohio Conference, boundaries of, 213, 214, 215, 217, 220, 223, 226.
       powers of, 263, 271.
Oneida Conference, boundaries of, 220, 222.
Ordination, forms of, 208.
       power of bishops over, 291.

Pastoral duties, 30, 50, 63, 146, 150, 316.
People, their part in making preachers, 301.
Perfection, 68, 329.
Periodicals, 140, 257, 264, 265, 272.
Pews, 229.
Philadelphia Conference, powers of, 253, 256, 257, 258, 260.
       boundaries of, 211, 212, 213, 215, 216, 222, 224.
Pittsburgh, paper at, 272.
       depository at, 272.
       Conference, boundaries of, 217, 220, 222, 226.
Prayer, 60, 148, 186.
Prayer meetings, 68, 144, 164, 309.
Preacher in charge, (see Assistant, Deacon.)
       duties of, 137, 149, 235, 257, 258, 302.

Preachers, travelling, (see Helpers.)
    slaveholding by, 14, 15, 22, 276.
    trial of, 18, 20, 59, 113, 158, 318.
      for crime, 159, 318.
      for improper tempers, words, or actions, 160, 320.
      for disseminating false doctrine, 160, 321.
    appeal of, 113, 162, 321.
    interchange of, 11.
    allowance of, 11, 12, 13, 14, 18, 19, 20, 42, 237, 246, 251, 256, 303.
    licensing of, 14, 18, 42.
    duties of, 13, 14, 146, 148, 245, 300, 314.
    probation of, 13, 16, 64, 136, 137.
    receiving on trial, 132, 135.
    receiving into full connection, 64, 136.
    examination of character, 286.
    following trades, 49.
    method of employing time, 48, 49, 60, 157.
    power of, 331.
    studies of, 50, 133, 318.
    union among, 62, 158.
    houses for, 244, 246.
  supernumerary, 122.
    who, 65, 116
    provision for, 65, (see allowance of travelling preachers.)
    neglecting their work, 117.
  superannuated, 122.
    provision for, 65, 117, 241. (See allowance of travelling preachers.)
    trial of, 160, 251.
  local, 12, 14, 18, 19, 20, 21, 65, 85, 135, 144, 164, 310.
    licensing of, 165.
    election to deacon's orders, 168.
    election to elder's orders, 169.
    to meet in class, 170.
    to be enrolled on the journal of quarterly conf., 170.
    trial of, 171, 321.
    appeal of, 113, 172, 321.
  coloured, 279.
  of other denominations, reception of, 131.
  examinations of, 301.
  how made, 301.
Preaching, places for, 27, 28, 146.
  mode of, 52, 53, 145, 310
  field, 28.
  morning, 40, 134.
  evening, 39.
Printing books, 10.
Prisons, chaplains to, 123.

Privileges of those who are not members of society, 10, 29, 187, 33
    of members of society with reference to other churches, 4
Providence Conference, boundaries of, 225.
Punctuality, 300, 312.

Quarterly Conference, (see Conference.)
    meeting (see Conference, Quarterly) 15, 138, 183.

Religion, means of promoting, 18, 28, 67, 69, 74, 164, 240.
Representation in General Conference, ratio of, 112, 113.
Rock River Conference, boundaries of, 226.
Rules, General, 113, 140, 325.
    reading of, 57.
    original form of, 177.

Sabbath breaking, 37.
Sacraments, administration of, forbidden to preachers in Americ
    prior to organization of M. E. C., 10.
Sacramental services, 193.
Scriptures, 60, 186, 316, 323.
Seamen, preachers to, 123.
Sick, communion of the, 206.
Singing, 21, 53, 176, 324.
Slavery, 15, 19, 21, 22, 43, 44, 80, 85, 170, 181, 274–278, 326.
Slaves, holding, by members, 15, 43, 275.
    by local preachers, 19, 21, 170.
    by travelling preachers, 14, 22, 276.
  buying or selling, 21, 44, 275, 277, 278.
            general rule on, 181, 326.
    duties of, 278.
Smuggling, 38.
South Carolina, exception in favour of slaveholders in, 278.
            Conference, boundaries of, 212, 213, 218, 221, 224.
Spirituous liquors, manufacture of, 15, 19, 170.
            sale of, 19, 85, 86, 170, 192, 338.
            use of, 19, 36, 37, 56, 63, 185, 192, 338.
                after preaching, 54.
            general rule respecting, 181.
Stationary power, 288.
Stewards, origin of the office, 46.
    duties of, 235, 246.
    appointment of, 137, 235, 304, 331.
    supervision of, 139, 236, 308.
Sunday service, (see Liturgy,) 24, 80.
Sunday schools, 128, 139, 148, 317.
            agents for, 123, 150.
Sunday School Union, 149.
Superannuated preachers, (see Preachers.)
Supernumerary preachers, (see Preachers.)
Superintendents, (see Bishops.)
            the first, of M. E. C., 23, 94.

Talking in church, 72, 230.
Tennessee, exception in favour of slaveholders in, 278.
        Conference, boundaries of, 213, 214, 216, 218, 219, 221, 227
Texas Conference, boundaries of, 227.
Thanksgiving, 20.
Tobacco, use of, 36, 63, 185, 186.
Tracts, doctrinal, 83, 84, 85, 86, 92.
        distribution of, 128, 139.
Travelling preachers, (see Preachers.)
Troy Conference, boundaries of, 220, 222, 225.
Trustees of churches, &c., 228, 234, 288, 338.

Vacancy on circuit, mode of supplying, 59.
Vasey, Thomas, 24.
Virginia, exception in favour of slaveholders in, 44.
        Conference, boundaries of, 211, 212, 213, 214, 219, 224.

Watch-nights, 138.
Wesley's, Mr., authority in America, 10, 16, 26.
                over his societies, 45, 287, 290.
        letter to Dr. Coke, Mr. Asbury, &c., 23, 24.
        Notes, 70.
        Sermons, 70.
Wesleyan Connection, 22, 250.
                reception of preachers from the, 34.
Western Conference, boundaries of, 212, 213.
Whatcoat, Richard, 24.
Worship, public, 175, 323.

Youth. (see Children, Sunday schools, Bible classes.)

SUPPLEMENT,

CONTAINING THE ALTERATIONS OF 1787 & 1844.

Discipline of 1787.

SINCE the publication of the first edition of this work, the author has obtained, through the kindness of the Rev. Leroy M. Lee, editor of the Richmond Christian Advocate, a copy of the edition of the Discipline for 1787. An examination of this edition confirms the conjecture previously made,* that it " was substantially the same as the first thirty-one sections of that of 1789." As the author desires to present, with perfect accuracy, the precise period of the alterations of the Discipline, he has noted below such as were made in 1787.

The following alterations, though assigned in the body of the work, for the reason stated, to 1789, were made entirely in 1787, viz.: those on pp. 110, 115, 125, 130, 134, 138, 139, 140, 141, 142, 144, 145, 146, (sec. 14,) 158, 164, 175, 187, 230, 273.

The following alterations, assigned to 1789, were made in 1787, so far as specified under each head, viz.:—

P. 93, Sec. 3. Except line 19, which then read, "the greatest impediment in the world." Section 4 was added in 1789.

P. 119. The clause, "To ordain superintendents, elders, and deacons," was omitted from among the duties of a superintendent in 1787, but was restored in 1789.

P. 120. For the alterations of 1787, to answer to

* See page 82.

Question 2, add, "and the elders present." Line 4, from bottom, for "direct in," read, "settle all."

P. 133, in Answer 2, for "by the bishop or an elder, until the sitting of the conference," read, "by the elder :" and in Answer 3, strike out "or bishop :" then the answers will stand as in 1787.

P. 135. In 1787, the recommendation of a probationer was to be by "the elder or deacon," instead of "the elders and deacons present."

P. 146, Sec. 15. The first part of the alteration, under Question 15, and the alteration under Question 52, made in 1787.

P. 147, Sec. 16. All, except the last, made in 1787.

P. 174, last line. The change of form took place in 1787.

P. 228. Those paragraphs were added in 1787, except the clause, "nor act as a steward or leader."

P. 237. All except the note belongs to 1787.

P. 240, note. All, except the last sentence of Ans. 1, belongs to 1787.

P. 241, note. The alteration in Answer 7, made in 1787.

Discipline of 1844.

THE following are the changes made in the Discipline by the General Conference of 1844. The references are to the pages of the History, to which the alterations belong.

P. 118, line 2, insert :—

1844. The seventeenth item of the order of business of the annual conferences, altered by striking out the word "Bibles," and adding at the close, "and what to aid the American Bible Society, and its auxiliaries."

P. 124. At the close of Sec. 4, add :—

1844. The following additional proviso is added respecting the appointing of preachers—"*Provided,* also, that with the exceptions above named, he shall not continue a preacher in the same appointment more than two years in six ; nor in the same city more than four years in succession ; nor return him to it, after such term of service, till he shall have been absent four years."

P. 129.   At the end of Sec. 5, add :—

1844.   To the sixth item of a presiding elder's duties, is added—"and to report to the annual conference the names of all travelling preachers, within his district, who shall neglect to observe these rules." His term of service also still further restricted, so that after the words, "For any term not exceeding four years successively," (answer to Question 4, 1792,) is added—"after which he shall not be appointed to the same district for six years."

P. 133, line 27, insert :—

1844.   Paragraph 3, of 1816, so altered, that the course of reading and study is extended to four years, and is to be prescribed by the bishops alone.

P. 150, bottom, add :—

1844.   To Paragraph 2, (1840,) add—"And it is recommended that, in all cases where it can be done, our Sunday schools contribute to the amount of at least one cent per quarter for each teacher and scholar.   One half of the amount so collected in each school shall be appropriated for the purchase of tracts, to be distributed under the direction of the preachers and superintendents, and the other half shall be forwarded to the treasurer of the Sunday-School Union of the Methodist Episcopal Church, for the purposes specified in the Constitution of said Union."

P. 228, line 9, insert :—

1844.   The boundaries were fixed as follows :—

1. New-York Conference—as before, except for "White Plains" (district) read "Long Island" (district.)

2. Providence Conference—as before.

3. New-England Conference—as before.

4. Maine Conference—as before.

5. New-Hampshire Conference—as before, **except**

"that part of the state of Vermont east of the Green Mountains," which was erected into a distinct conference.

"6. Vermont Conference shall include the state of Vermont, except that part lying west of the top of the Green Mountains, embraced in the Troy Conference."

"7. Troy Conference shall include Troy, Albany, (including Sharon and Cobleskill circuits, formerly embraced in the Oneida Conference,) Saratoga, Poultney, Burlington, and Plattsburg districts."

8. Black River Conference—as before, with the addition of "Montezuma and Port Byron," at the end.

9. Oneida Conference—as before, only "Susquehannah district" altered to "Susquehannah and Wyoming districts."

10. Genesee Conference—as before.

11. Erie Conference—as before, with the insertion of "Akron and" before "Cleaveland city."

12. Pittsburgh Conference—as before, only "Middleburn circuit and Kanawha mission" changed to "Kanawha circuit."

13. Ohio Conference—as before, striking out the words, "except Westville and M'Farland," and "Allen mission."

14. North Ohio Conference—as before.

"15. Michigan Conference shall include the state of Michigan, and the Ojibway missions on the waters of Lake Superior, formerly embraced in the Rock River Conference.

"16. Indiana Conference shall include that part of the state of Indiana south of the National Road, with Elizabethtown in Ohio, and the western charge in Indianapolis, with all the towns that are immediately on the road to the state line, except Terre Haute.

"17. North Indiana Conference shall include that part of the state of Indiana north of the National Road, the eastern charge in Indianapolis, with all the towns that are immediately on the road to the eastern line of the state, together with Terre Haute in the west.

"18. Rock River Conference shall include that par
of the state of Illinois not embraced in the Illinoi
Conference, and the Wisconsin Territory.

"19. Ioway Conference shall include all the Iowa
Territory.

"20. Illinois Conference shall include that part ol
the state of Illinois south of the following line, namely
beginning at Warsaw on the Mississippi River, an
running thence to Augusta, thence to Doddsville
thence to the mouth of Spoon River, thence to Bloom
ington, thence to Danville, thence to the Indiana stat
line, embracing Warsaw town, Havannah mission
Bloomington station, and Dansville circuit.

"21. Missouri Conference shall include the stat
of Missouri.

"22. Indian Mission Conference shall be bounde
as follows, namely: on the north by the Missoui
River, east by the states of Missouri and Arkansas
south by Red River, and west by the Rocky Moun
tains."

23. Kentucky Conference—as before.

"24. Holston Conference shall include East Ten
nessee, that part of the state of North Carolina nov
embraced in the Ashville and Wytheville districts, an
so much of the state of Virginia as is now embrace
in the Wytheville district, and the districts lying wes
of New River.

"25. Tennessee Conference shall include Middl
Tennessee, and that part of North Alabama watere
by those streams flowing into the Tennessee River."

26. Memphis Conference—as before.

"27. Arkansas Conference shall include the stat
of Arkansas.

"28. Eastern Texas Conference shall embrace al
that part of the Republic of Texas east of a line be
ginning at the east pass of the Bay of Galveston
thence through said bay to the mouth of Trinity Rivei
thence up said river to the source of the middle forl
of the same.

" 29. Western Texas Conference shall embrace all that part of the Republic of Texas lying west of the Trinity River, including Galveston Island."

30. Mississippi Conference—as before.

" 31. Alabama Conference shall include all that part of the state of Alabama not included in the Tennessee Conference, West Florida, and the counties of Jackson, Greene, Wayne, Clark, Lauderdale, Kemper, Noxubee, Lowndes, and that part of Monroe east of the Tombigbee River, in the state of Mississippi.

" 32. Georgia Conference shall include all the state of Georgia, except that part which lies south of a line commencing at Fort Gaines on the Chattahoochee River, running thence in a direct line to Albany, on Flint River, thence along the line of Ocmulgee and Flint River Rail Road to the Ocmulgee River, thence down said river to the Altamaha, thence down the Altamaha to the Atlantic Ocean, and also that part of North Carolina embraced in Murphy circuit, Lafayette district.

" 33. Florida Conference shall include all that part of the state of Georgia not included in the Georgia Conference, and East and Middle Florida.

" 34. South Carolina Conference shall include the state of South Carolina, and so much of North Carolina as is included in the Lincolnton and Wilmington districts."

35, 36, 37, 38, 39, 40. North Carolina, Virginia, Baltimore, Philadelphia, New-Jersey, and Liberia Mission Annual Conference—all as before.

In answer to the question, "How are the districts to be formed?" after the words, "According to the judgment of the bishops," is added, "provided that no district shall contain more than fifteen appointments."

P. 230, line 4, insert :—·

1844. To Paragraph 2, of 1820, is added :—

" In all cases where debts for building houses of worship have been, or may be, incurred contrary to, or in disregard of, the above recommendation, our mem-

bers and friends are requested to discountenance, b
declining pecuniary aid to all agents who shall trav
abroad beyond their own circuits or districts for th
collection of funds for the discharge of such debts
except in such peculiar cases as may be approved b
an annual conference, or such agents as may be ap
pointed by their authority."

P. 247. At the end of Sec. 5, add:—

1844. In Paragraph 7, of 1836, after the word
" for said bishop or bishops," are inserted the word
" subject to the action of the conference."

P. 251. At the end of Sec. 6, add:—

1844. The following new paragraphs were ir
serted:—

" 4. It shall be the duty of each annual conferenc
to appoint some month within the conference year, i
which missionary collections shall be taken up withi
their respective bounds, and also to make such arrange
ments concerning branch societies as may be deeme
expedient.

" 5. It shall be the duty of the presiding elders t
bring the subject of our missions before the quarterl
meeting conference of each circuit and station withi
their districts, as early in the conference year as ma
be practicable, and the quarterly meeting conferenc
shall proceed to appoint a committee of not less tha
five, nor more than *nine*, all of whom shall be mem
bers of the Methodist Episcopal Church, to be calle
the Committee on Missions, whose duty it shall be t
aid the presiding elder and preacher in charge, in rai
ing missionary societies, taking up collections, and i
any other way which the quarterly meeting conferenc
may judge necessary for the purpose of raising mi
sionary funds ; such as having sermons preached, c
lectures delivered, on the subject of missions, and th
establishing of missionary prayer meetings, for the pr
motion of the cause.

" 6. It shall be the duty of the preachers in charge c
circuits and stations to organize one or more missionar

societies in their respective charges, if it should be practicable ; to bear any name which the societies may choose ; provided always that these societies shall be auxiliary to the missionary society of the annual conference to which such charges may belong, and shall be governed by such rules and regulations as the annual conference may prescribe.　It shall also be their duty to take up, or cause to be taken up, a missionary collection in each and every congregation within their respective charges, at such time as may be fixed on by the annual conference.　It shall be their duty, further, to appoint in every class within their charges a missionary collector, who shall keep a book, in which shall be enrolled the names of all the members of the class, and shall collect from each member who shall feel disposed so to contribute, at the rate of one cent per week, or fifty cents per year, and shall pay over the sums so collected to the preacher in charge, at or before the last quarterly meeting in the conference year ; and the preacher in charge shall transmit the same to the annual conference, together with such sums as may have been collected by him from the congregations, as well as all sums received from branch societies, or otherwise, all of which shall be reported in writing.

" 7. It shall be the duty of the quarterly meeting conference, from time to time, to fill up vacancies which may occur in the missionary committee, which committee shall have the right to a seat in the quarterly meeting conference, during its action on the subject of missions, but at no other time.

" 8. In order to keep up such missionary societies as may be established, it shall be the duty of the missionary committee to use their best efforts to hold at least once a year a meeting of the missionary society within the charge to which they may belong ; in doing which they shall have the aid of the preacher in charge, and also of the quarterly meeting conference, if need be.

" 9. It will be expected that in the examination in

the annual conference a reference will be had to th
faithful performance of the duty of preachers on thi
subject, in the passage of character."

Paragraph 7, of 1836, and Paragraphs 8 and 9, o
1840, struck out, and the following substituted :—

"13. The corresponding secretary shall be a mem
ber of such annual conference as he may, with th
approbation of the bishops, select.

"14. For the purpose of more effectually adminis
tering the financial concerns of the Indian Missio
Conference, as also promoting its spiritual welfare
there shall be a superintendent appointed by the bishof
who shall be a member of said conference, and resid
within its bounds, to be continued in office for an'
time not exceeding four years. It shall be his duty t
overlook all the accounts of the missionaries and th
superintendents of schools, to attend to all the interest
of our missions and schools within the bounds of sai
conference, as those interests may be connected witl
the government of the United States, and with th
Indian school fund.

"He may visit Washington city once a year, or oftenei
if it be deemed necessary; and also, as far as his time
and circumstances will permit, and it may be judgee
necessary for the interests of the mission, visit the
interior of the Indian country with a view to the ex
tension of the work within his bounds. His salar'
shall not exceed the ordinary allowance of other itine
rant preachers; and his table and other expenses shal
be estimated by the mission committee of the conference
for which amount he shall have authority to draw oi
the treasurer of the Missionary Society, in quarterl'
instalments."

P. 273. At the end of Sec. 8, add :—

1844. The substance of this section, which ha
been considerably altered, is presented below :—

1. This paragraph remains as before.

"2. There shall be an editor of the Methodist Quar
terly Review and general books; and an editor and a'

assistant editor for the Christian Advocate and Jour
nal, who, if chosen from among the travelling preachers, shall be members of such conferences as they
may, with the approbation of the bishops, select.
There shall be an editor at New-York of Sunday-school
books and tracts, whose duty it shall be, in connection
with the book agents, to superintend all such publications issued at our Book Room, and to have charge
of the Sunday-School Advocate or other Sunday-school
periodicals, and he shall be subject to the same regulations and restrictions which govern the other editors in
New-York.

"3. There shall be an agent and an assistant agent,
both of whom shall be chosen from among the travelling preachers, and shall be members of such conferences as they may, with the approbation of the bishops,
select.

"4. The agents shall have authority to regulate the
publications and all other parts of the business of the
Concern, except what belongs to the editorial departments, as the state of the finances will admit, and the
demands may require. It shall be their duty to send
an exhibit of the state of the Book Concern at New-
York to each session of the annual conferences, and
report quadrennially to the General Conference. They
shall also inform the conferences of any within their
respective bounds who neglect to make payment, that
measures may be taken to collect or secure such debts ;
and they shall not allow any claim to run beyond one
year from the time it was due without reporting it to
the conference. They shall publish such books and
tracts as are recommended by the General Conference,
and may, if approved by the editors, publish such as
are recommended by the book committee at New-
York, or recommended by an annual conference ;
and they may reprint any book or tract which has
been once approved and published by us, when, in
their judgment, and in the judgment of the editors,
the same ought to be reprinted : or they may pub-

lish any new work which may be approved by th
editors.

"5. The book committee at New-York shall consii
of six travelling ministers and the editors.   The annui
election of two by the New-York, two by the Phila
delphia, and two by the New-Jersey Conference, sha
constitute the six members of the committee.   It sha
be the duty of the book committee to examine into th
condition of the Book Concern, to inspect the account
of the agents, and make a report thereof yearly to th
three conferences named above, and to the Genera
Conference.   They shall also attend to such matter
as may be referred to them by the editors or agents fc
their action or counsel.   And they shall have powe
to suspend an editor or agent from his official relatio
as such, if they judge it necessary for the interests o
the Church and the Concern.   And a time shall be fixec
at as early a day as practicable, for the investigatio
of the official conduct of the said editor or agent, a
which two or more of the bishops shall be requeste
to attend ; and by the concurrence of the bishops pre
sent, and of the majority of the committee, he may b
removed from office in the interval of the Genera
Conference.   And in case a vacancy occurs in any o
the agencies or editorial departments authorized by th
General Conference, it shall be the duty of the bool
committee, and two or more of the general superin
tendents, as soon as practicable, to provide for suc
vacancy until the next General Conference."

6. This paragraph, respecting the agents at Cincin
nati, remains as before, except that they are allowe
the same choice of a conference as the agents at New
York.

7, 8, same as corresponding paragraphs of 184C
only strike out the words " and recommended by th
book committee at Cincinnati, or by an annual confei
ence," and substitute, "and may publish any wor
recommended by the book committee at Cincinnat
or by an annual conference, if approved by the editors.

"9. There shall be an editor of the Ladies' Repository, general books and tracts, except those in the German language, and an editor of the Western Christian Advocate, who, if chosen from among the travelling preachers, shall be members of such conferences as they may, with the approbation of the bishops, select."

10. Same as before.

"11. Printed sheets, ordered by the agents from New-York, shall be sent at fifty per cent., and bound books of the General Catalogue at forty per cent., discount from the retail prices; and those ordered from Cincinnati to New-York to be sent on the same terms, the agency sending the books to be charged with the expense of transportation.

"12. It shall be the duty of the agents to send an exhibit of the state of the Book Concern at Cincinnati to each session of all the annual conferences, and report quadrennially to the General Conference. They shall also inform the conferences of any within their respective bounds who neglect to make payment, that measures may be taken to collect or secure such debts; and they shall not allow any claim to run beyond one year from the time it was due without reporting it to the conference.

"13. The book committee of this department of the Book Concern shall consist of six members in addition to the editors, to be chosen annually, two by the Ohio, two by the Kentucky, and two by the Indiana Conference, whose powers and duties, in reference to this establishment, shall be the same as those of the book committee at New-York in relation to the Concern there.

"14. The agents of this establishment shall remit to the agents at New-York during the current year as largely and frequently as their funds will allow, and to the full amount of stock furnished, if practicable. They shall also remit any surplus funds that may be in their hands after defraying the expense of conducting their business, which shall be added to the profits of the

Concern at New-York, and appropriated to the sam purposes.

" 15. Every annual conference shall appoint a com mittee, who, in the absence of the agent, shall atten to the collection of the accounts sent out from the Boo Concern, and return an accurate report of the sam They shall also report to the conference any claim which may have been one year due, that they may b collected or secured. Every presiding elder, ministe and preacher, shall do everything in his power to re cover all debts due to the Concern, for books or per odicals, within the bounds of his charge. If any pei son, preacher, or member, be indebted to the Boo Concern, and refuse or neglect to make payment, or t come to a just settlement, let him be dealt with in th same manner as is directed in other cases of debt an disputed accounts. See chap. i, sec. 10.

" 16. Whenever a member of an annual conferenc applies for a location, it shall be asked in all cases, I he indebted to the Book Concern ? and if it be ascer tained that he is, the conference shall require him t secure said debt, if they judge it at all necessary c proper, before they grant him a location. Wheneve any claimant on the funds of a conference shall be i debt to the Book Concern, the conference of which h is a member shall have power to appropriate the amour of such claim, or any part thereof, to the payment o said debt."

17. The weekly papers same as before, with th addition of the Northern Christian Advocate, at Au burn, N. Y. The following sentence respecting it committee takes the place of the last sentence of thi paragraph (as in 1840) respecting periodical for fe males and Christian Apologist :—" The publishin committee shall be appointed by the Oneida, Genesee and Black River Conferences, and shall consist of tw members from each of these conferences."

18–24, inclusive, as before.

" 25. The salaries for the support of editors an

agents in all our book and periodical establishments shall be fixed by the General Conference, or by committees appointed by that body."

26. As before.

27. Merged in Paragraph 15.

28, 29, 30, (now 27, 28, 29,) same as before.

31. Struck out.

THE END.

BOOKS

PUBLISHED BY G. LANE AND C. B. TIPPETT,

For the Methodist Episcopal Church,

AT THE CONFERENCE OFFICE, 200 MULBERRY-STREET
NEW-YORK.

⁎ *Most of the works in this list may be had in extra bindings at an advanced price.*

DR. ADAM CLARKE'S COMMENTARY.

Six volumes, imperial 8vo. Price Eighteen dollars, bound in sheep.
The Old Testament may be had separately, in four volumes;
and the New in two volumes: Price $3 a volume.

BENSON'S COMMENTARY.

Complete in five volumes, imp. 8vo. Price Fifteen dollars, bound in sheep
The Old Testament may be had separately in three volumes ;
and the New Testament in two volumes : Price Three dollars a volume

NOTES ON THE NEW TESTAMENT.
BY REV. JOHN WESLEY, A. M.

One volume 8vo. Pages 734. Price Two dollars, bound in sheep.
A NEW EDITION IN PEARL TYPE.
Small 12mo. $1 in pln. shp. ; $1 13 shp. ex.; $2 25 mor. tucks, gt. edge

WORKS OF REV. JOHN WESLEY.

Complete in seven volumes 8vo. Price Twelve dollars bound in sheep
The following may be had separately :
SERMONS, in two volumes : $3. JOURNALS, two volumes: $4 50.

WORKS OF REV. JOHN FLETCHER.

Complete in four volumes 8vo. Price $7 50, bound in sheep.
The CHECKS may be had separately in two volumes : Price $4.

LONGKING'S NOTES.

Notes, Illustrative and Explanatory, on the Holy Gospels : arranged
according to Townsend's Chronological New Testament.
BY JOSEPH LONGKING.

Four volumes, large 18mo. Pages 390, 395, 394, 528. Price $2 12.

HORNE'S INTRODUCTION.

A Compendious Introduction to the Study of the Bible : being an Analysis of the Author's Introduction to the Critical Study of the Scriptures.

BY THOMAS HARTWELL HORNE.

In one volume 12mo. Pages 391. Price One dollar.

TOWNLEY'S BIBLICAL LITERATURE.

Illustrations of Biblical Literature, exhibiting the History and Fate of the Scriptures from the earliest Period to the present Century: with Notices of Translators and other eminent Biblical Scholars.

BY REV. JAMES TOWNLEY, D. D.

In Two volumes 8vo. Price Four dollars.

These volumes afford a more comprehensive view of the literary history of the Holy Scriptures than is to be found in any other work.—*London Eclectic Rev.*

FULFILMENT OF SCRIPTURE PROPHECY,

As exhibited in Ancient History and Modern Travels: showing the Fulfilment of the Predictions respecting the Descendants of Ishmael, the Jews, the Holy Land, Philistia, Nineveh, Babylon, Tyre, etc.

BY STEPHEN B. WICKENS.

Large 18mo. With a Map. Pages 354. Price Fifty cents.

SCRIPTURE CHARACTERS:

Letters on the Distinguishing Excellences of Scripture Personages.

BY REV. ROBERT HUSTON.

Large 18mo. Pages 245. Price Thirty-eight cents.

HISTORICAL CONFIRMATION OF SCRIPTURE;

With Especial Reference to Jewish and Ancient Heathen Testimony.

BY WILLIAM BLATCH.

Large 18mo. Pages 144. Price Thirty-one cents.

A CONCISE DICTIONARY OF THE BIBLE.

BY REV. JAMES COVEL.

Large 18mo. With Maps and Engravings. Price One dollar.

THE MIRACLES OF CHRIST:

With Explanatory Observations, and Illustrations from Modern Travels.

INTENDED FOR THE YOUNG.

Large 18mo. With Engravings. Pages 265. Price Forty-four cents.

HARE ON JUSTIFICATION.

A Treatise on the Scripture Doctrine of Justification.

BY REV. EDWARD HARE.

18mo. Pages 253. Price Forty-four cents.

CHRISTIAN PERFECTION:

The Scripture Doctrine stated and defended; with a Critical and Historical Examination of the Controversy, both Ancient and Modern; also Practical Illustrations and Advices: in a Series of Lectures.

BY REV. GEORGE PECK, D. D.

One volume 12mo. Pages 484. Price One dollar.

PECK ON CHRISTIAN PERFECTION:

AN ABRIDGED EDITION,

In which the Critical and Historical Examination of the Controversy is omitted.

Large 18mo. Price Fifty cents.

SCRIPTURE VIEWS OF HEAVEN.

BY JONATHAN EDMONDSON, M. A.

Large 18mo. Pages 250. Price Thirty-eight cents.

M'OWAN ON THE SABBATH.

Practical Considerations on the Christian Sabbath: setting forth the Origin and General Design of the Sabbath; the Moral Obligations of the Day; its Change from the Seventh to the First Day of the Week; and the Spirit and Manner in which it ought to be sanctified.

BY REV. PETER M'OWAN.

Large 18mo. Pages 200. Price Thirty-eight cents.

ADMONITORY COUNSELS,

Addressed to a Methodist, on Subjects of Christian Experience and Practice.

BY JOHN BAKEWELL.

Large 18mo. Pages 228. Price Thirty-eight cents.

TREATISE ON SECRET AND SOCIAL PRAYER

BY RICHARD TREFFRY.

(The author of this excellent work was fifty years a traveling preacher.)

Large 18mo. Price Thirty-eight cents.

THE GREAT EFFICACY OF SIMPLE FAITH IN THE ATONEMENT OF CHRIST, EXEMPLIFIED IN A

MEMOIR OF MR. WILLIAM CARVOSSO,

SIXTY YEARS A METHODIST CLASS-LEADER.

Written by Himself, and edited by his Eldest Son.

He staggered not at the promise of God through unbelief; but was strong in the faith, giving glory to God. Rom. iv, 20.

(Near *fifty thousand copies* of this work have been circulated.)
Large 18mo. With a Portrait. Price Fifty cents.

THE LIFE OF JOHN BUNYAN,

AUTHOR OF THE PILGRIM'S PROGRESS, HOLY WAR, ETC.

BY STEPHEN B. WICKENS.

This volume embraces the substance of Bunyan's remarkable autobiography entitled, Grace Abounding to the Chief of Sinners; together with what else is known respecting his life, labors, writings, and character. It is embellished with a portrait and several wood-cuts.

Second Edition. Large 18mo. Pages 344. Price Fifty cents.

THE VILLAGE BLACKSMITH:

Or Piety and Usefulness exemplified in a Memoir of Samuel Hick, late of Micklefield, Yorkshire, Eng.

BY THE REV. JAMES EVERETT.

One volume large 18mo. Pages 352. Price Fifty cents.

To all classes of readers this Memoir will be a fund of entertainment and instruction. It stands alone. There is nothing like it in ancient or modern biography.—*Rev. G. Cookman.*

THE WALL'S-END MINER:

Or a brief Memoir of the Life of William Crister: Including an Account of the Catastrophe of June 18, 1835.

BY THE REV. JAMES EVERETT.

This work will be found to be not less interesting, and, we think, even more edifying than the story of the Village Blacksmith, by the same author.

18mo. Pages 176. Price Thirty-one cents.

MEMOIR OF JONATHAN SAVILLE,

Of Halifax, Eng. Including his Autobiography.

BY FRANCIS A. WEST.

This is the Memoir of a poor little orphan boy, who by ill usage became a cripple for life, and who afterward became a Wesleyan local preacher of extensive usefulness.

Large 18mo. Price Twenty-five cents, bound in sheep.